WHEN CHILDREN KILL CHILDREN

CLARENDON STUDIES IN CRIMINOLOGY

Published under the auspices of the Institute of Criminology,
University of Cambridge; the Mannheim Centre, London School of
Economics; and the Centre for Criminological Research,
University of Oxford.

GENERAL EDITOR: ALISON LIEBLING
(*University of Cambridge*)

EDITORS: MANUEL EISNER AND PER-OLOF
(*University of Cambridge*)

PAUL ROCK, JILL PEAY, AND TIM NEWBURN
(*London School of Economics*)

LUCIA ZEDNER, JULIAN ROBERTS, AND IAN LOADER
(*University of Oxford*)

Recent titles in this series:

When Children Kill Children

Penal Populism and Political Culture

DAVID A GREEN

OXFORD
UNIVERSITY PRESS

OXFORD
UNIVERSITY PRESS

Great Clarendon Street, Oxford OX2 6DP

Oxford University Press is a department of the University of Oxford.
It furthers the University's objective of excellence in research, scholarship,
and education by publishing worldwide in

Oxford New York

Auckland Cape Town Dar es Salaam Hong Kong Karachi
Kuala Lumpur Madrid Melbourne Mexico City Nairobi
New Delhi Shanghai Taipei Toronto

With offices in

Argentina Austria Brazil Chile Czech Republic France Greece
Guatemala Hungary Italy Japan Poland Portugal Singapore
South Korea Switzerland Thailand Turkey Ukraine Vietnam

Oxford is a registered trade mark of Oxford University Press
in the UK and in certain other countries

Published in the United States
by Oxford University Press Inc., New York

© David A Green 2008

The moral rights of the author has been asserted

Crown copyright material is reproduced under Class Licence
Number C01P0000148 with the permission of OPSI
and the Queen's Printer for Scotland

Database right Oxford University Press (maker)

First published 2008
First published in paperback 2012

British Library Cataloguing in Publication Data

Data available

Library of Congress Cataloging in Publication Data

Green, David, 1970–
    When children kill children : penal populism and political culture / David A. Green.
        p. cm. — (Clarendon studies in criminology)
    Includes bibliographical references and index.
    ISBN 978-0-19-923096-9 (hardback : alk. paper)   1. Criminal justice, Administration
of—Great Britain—Public opinion.   2. Criminal justice, Administration of—Norway— Public
opinion.   3. Violence in children—England.   4. Violence in children—Norway. 5. Bulger, James
Patrick, 1990–1993.   6. Redergard, Silje.   7. Children—Crimes against—England—Bootle
(Sefton)—Case studies.   8. Children—Crimes against—
Norway—Trondheim—Case studies.   9. Public opinion—England.   10. Public opinion—Norway.   I. Title.
HV9960.G7G74   2008
365'. 60830941—dc22   2008000393

Typeset by Newgen Imaging Systems (P) Ltd., Chennai, India
Printed in Great Britain
on acid-free paper by
CPI Group (UK) Ltd, Croydon, CR0 4YY

ISBN 978-0-19-923096-9
ISBN 978-0-19-965352-2(pbk.)

10 9 8 7 6 5 4 3 2 1

General Editor's Introduction

Clarendon Studies in Criminology aims to provide a forum for outstanding empirical and theoretical work in all aspects of criminology, criminal justice, penology, and the wider field of deviant behaviour. The Editors welcome excellent PhD work, as well as submissions from established scholars. The *Series* was inaugurated in 1994, with Roger Hood at its first General Editor, following energetic discussions between Oxford University Press and three Criminology Centres. It is edited under the auspices of these three Criminological Centres: the Cambridge Institute of Criminology, the Mannheim Centre for Criminology at the London School of Economics, and the Oxford Centre for Criminology. Each supplies members of the Editorial Board.

David Green's carefully argued book, *When Children Kill Children: Penal Populism and Political Culture*, analyses the contrasting public, media, and policy responses to two cases of killings by children of children, in Britain and in Norway, respectively. In Britain, the case of James Bulger marked a turning point in penal sensibilities. The harshening of sentencing, including drastic increases in the imprisonment of children, can be traced to this event and to the volatile public and political responses to it. In Norway, by contrast, a similar case led to virtually no policy impact. David Green shows, using his painstaking analysis of a wide range of sources, how the different responses in these two countries 'are deeply rooted in cultural constructions of childhood and the moral culpability of children'. The result of his close analysis is a highly absorbing account of the nature and effects of consensual versus highly partisan, adversarial, political cultures, of egalitarian welfare versus neo-liberal economies, and of subscription versus competitive media. In Britain, Green argues, aspects of this political culture help explain 'why the Bulger case became a vehicle for the expression of growing moral uncertainty' and fear. He describes a 'somewhat diminished appetite for imprisonment in most of the consensus democracies', a characteristic linked, he argues, to higher levels of trust among citizens, and between citizens and political structures. In Norway, the death of Silje Redergard 'served no secondary purpose as it did in England'. He ends with a well-developed set of proposals for better, more informed public deliberation.

David Green's book arises from his outstanding PhD work. It illustrates the value of careful comparative research, and continues a longstanding tradition of key criminological analyses of attitudes to punishment in contrasting jurisdictions.

The editors welcome this important addition to the Clarendon Studies.

Alison Liebling
University of Cambridge,
September 2007

For Fiore

'The instinct of vengeance is, in sum, only the instinct of conser-
vation exacerbated by peril.'

Durkheim

Foreword

This important book by David Green takes three giant steps forward. In a literature that consists mostly of case studies of penal policies and practices in individual countries, and synthetic writings generalizing from them, *When Children Kill Children* is the first genuinely comparative study. In a literature that also exists almost entirely within the narrow boundaries of academic criminology and criminal justice, *When Children Kill Children* is genuinely multidisciplinary, incorporating insights and analyses from comparative politics and communication studies that have not heretofore percolated through studies of penal policy. Most importantly though, Green's work shows that studies of the determinants of penal policies are at least as important for the light they shed on countries' national and political cultures as for what they say about the penal matters that are their *raison d 'être*.

When Children Kill Children is a sure-to-be-classic refutation of David Garland's magisterial 2001 book *The Culture of Control*. Garland argued there that a number of developments associated with 'late-modernity'—economic disruption, sensationalistic media, rapid social change, the 'criminology of the other', the ubiquity of crime, and the limited capacities of the state—combined to produce severe expressive policies, harsher practices, and rising prison populations. Garland wrote primarily about the United States and England but his analysis, if correct, ought to apply to all developed western countries which, after all, experienced all those changes. Writers less imaginative than Garland took that step, writing on the development of 'penal populism' and 'populist punitiveness' throughout the West.

Green has shown that it is just not so. Both England and Norway are rich, stable, well-educated North Atlantic democracies, equally exposed to all the ailments of late-modernity. Both benefited in recent decades from profits from North Sea oil. Both in the early 1990s experienced horrifying killings of children by children. There the similarity stops. In England, the killing of James Bulger became a decade-long national preoccupation that continues to fester, and his killers became embodiments in the media and popular culture of evil and moral decline. In Norway, the killing of Silje Redegård was a personal tragedy that received little media or political attention, and her killers became objects of concern about their future well-being.

As Green makes clear, the differences in the emotions the two cases provoked, and in how they were handled, have nothing inherently to do with late-modernity and everything to do with differences in political and national cultures. The English media are sensationalistic and irresponsible; the Norwegian media are much less so. English political culture is highly oppositional and confrontational; the Norwegian is more cooperative and consensual. English people have little trust in government (or one another) and the legitimacy of many institutions in citizens' eyes is low; Norwegians have much more trust in government and each other, and greater confidence in legal institutions.

The great strength of Green's study is that he examines the same questions in both countries, using the same kinds of sources and the same kinds of informants. He demonstrates why multidisciplinary comparative studies will be indispensable to further advances in knowledge. Using insights from comparative politics, he documents important differences in how politics and government work in the two countries, and what differences those differences make. Using discourse-analytic and other techniques from media and communications studies, he demonstrates differences in the ways English and Norwegian journalists and politicians speak and think, and what differences those differences make.

In the end what Green demonstrates is how starkly different the political and legal cultures of England and Norway are, and how those differences explain why politicians and ordinary citizens in the two countries responded as they did to the Bulger and Redegård cases. Child-on-child killings provide an especially chilling occasion for teasing out differences in how countries respond to crime and disorder, but analyses like Green's can illuminate other, even starker differences. Why did Finnish culture tolerate a 30-year decline in the use of imprisonment during a period when crime rates rose substantially and other countries used imprisonment more? Why, in the face of nearly identical trends in crime rates over four decades in Canada and the United States, did imprisonment rates in America skyrocket and those in Canada hold steady? *When Children Kill Children* cannot explain why such stark cultural differences exist, and whether it is possible for the Englands and Americas of the world to become more like the Norways and Canadas, but Green's analyses inexorably raise the fundamental questions that others so far have glossed over.

When Children Kill Children has lifted comparative studies of national differences in penal policies and practices to a new and higher level. For years to come it will be the standard by which others' work is measured.

Michael Tonry

Preface and Acknowledgements

Neatly stencilled graffiti on the pavement steps of a steep side street in Bergen, Norway suggests the reader 'Think dangerously, Live dangerously'. This seems particularly apt as I reflect upon the research experiences in Norway and England that have informed this book. There are extraordinary perils in offering a book like this to the world, even—or maybe especially—a very circumscribed academic world. These perils are of two kinds. The first will be familiar to anyone who has approached a topic from a multidisciplinary perspective. This leaves the researcher open to attack on multiple flanks simultaneously. This book approaches the responses to two cases of children who killed other children through the lenses of several established literatures. I am a criminologist by training, which I recognize as a constellation of approaches that comprise a field, rather than a discipline in its own right. The methodological, normative, and interpretive splits within criminology alone are yawning and growing, and this is terrain that is better navigated and better defended by others than by me. I also adopt approaches informed by comparative politics and media studies literatures with which I am more of a novice. This means I am likely to alienate, irritate, and exasperate some readers within criminology, as well as some who reside outside the bounded criminological world.

The second peril involves the book's comparative aspects. To calculate this, just take everything in the preceding paragraph and multiply it by two countries of which I am not a native. Natives will certainly find infuriating instances when I overlook something obvious, misstate something fundamental, or misinterpret something ignorantly. A Norwegian news story provides an example of how this can happen. An Uzbekistani man in a town in the north of the country killed his Norwegian wife and their daughter before killing himself during a visit I made to Norway in May 2007. A headline in the broadsheet newspaper *Aftenposten* in the days that followed indicated the man had grown up in a 'brutal dictatorship'. As a foreigner reading this, and aware of the politicization of immigration that has gone on in Norway for some years, I interpreted the headline to imply that the Norwegian government through its immigration laws had been somehow complicit in the murder by permitting a deranged man to enter a peaceful country to kill an innocent woman and her daughter. I mentioned this interpretation to a few Norwegian colleagues, who suggested this might be an American interpretation. I was told that a Norwegian would be likely to interpret such a headline less cynically, and accept it as nothing more than a valid explanation for why such a horrible incident had occurred. Studying the English media has apparently conditioned me to expect a newspaper to adopt such a critical, provocative line in the wake of such a horrible crime.

These perils are unavoidable, and at least now, while writing, I am happy to face them. The research has fascinated me for most of the seven years I spent as a resident in England. Perhaps I will feel differently after it is received, but I doubt it. I have consulted widely with many whom I know to be better placed than most to assess my data and my analysis and interpretations of it. Of course, however, any oversights, misstatements, or misinterpretations are mine alone and should in no way reflect on those who have been kind enough to help me over these years.

The PhD research upon which this book is based was made possible by a Gates Cambridge Scholarship. St John's College, Cambridge provided additional funding for me to travel to Norway and for Norwegian language tuition, thanks to the efforts of Ray Jobling and Maire Ní Mhaonaigh. The study was informed by approximately 40 hours of material from twenty-two tape-recorded interviews with individuals from politics, academia, psychiatry, and journalism in Norway from 2002, 2003, and 2007. The British Academy provided a Small Research Grant for the Norway visits in 2007. Many at the University of Cambridge Institute of Criminology deserve thanks, especially Tony Bottoms, Ben Crewe, Manuel Eisner, Stuart Feathers, Joanne Garner, Lorraine Gelsthorpe, Mary Gower, Sara Harrop, Adam Hart, Lila Kazemian, Anna King, Helen Krarup, Alison Liebling, Shadd Maruna, Amanda Matravers, Sue Rex, Layla Skinns, and P-O Wikström. I am grateful to many others outside Cambridge for their guidance as well, including Rob Allen, Agneta Bäcklund, Vanessa Barker, David Downes, Britta Kyvsgaard, Rod Morgan, Norval Morris, Tim Newburn, and Annika Snare. Rob Street and Lana Brooke from the Home Office helped to locate relevant press releases.

During my time in Norway I was lucky to receive the hospitality and advice of Katja Franko Aas, Sigurd Allern, Cicilie Basberg, Atle Bersvendsen, Louise Kårikstad Bjerva, Per Kristian Bjørkeng, Nils Christie, André Oktay Dahl, Atle Dyregrov, John Olav Egeland, Jan Arild Ellingsen, Sturla Falck, Svein Arne Haavik, Unni Heltne, Paul Larsson, Jan-Erik Laure, Thomas Mathiesen, Leif Petter Olaussen, Ester Pollack, Lars Arve Røssland, and Simon Wilkinson. Borghild Tenden graciously searched the *Storting* debate archives (in vain) for mentions of the relevant homicide cases. Kari Bråtveit, Jeannette Nyquist, and Marianne Saether assisted in translating the Norwegian newspaper coverage. Bent Grøver and Roger Norum provided additional translations of journal articles and government documents.

Christ Church, Oxford provided the postdoctoral Junior Research Fellowship and idyllic setting to allow me to develop the book. The faculty and staff of the University of Oxford Centre for Criminology were welcoming and supportive throughout my time there. In particular, I am grateful to Catherine Appleton, Andrew Ashworth, Cathy Byford, Martina Feilzer, Michelle Grossman, Ian Loader, Federico Varese, Cory Way, and Lucia Zedner. Julian Roberts deserves special thanks for his assistance and his kindness. My thinking was considerably influenced by a London conference on penal populism he invited me to attend as a student in 2001, and his work has consistently inspired mine.

It is probably impossible to overstate the debt of gratitude I owe to Michael Tonry for his wisdom and guidance throughout the development of this study and beyond. As my PhD supervisor, he consistently but kindly expected more from me than I believed I was capable of producing. He has been a far more generous mentor than I ever expected, and I am deeply grateful to him. Jennifer Green convinced me the pursuit of postgraduate education was a worthwhile thing to do in the first place, and her ceaseless faith and encouragement helped ensure the book's completion. The Cournoyer, Green, and Kelley families provided all kinds of support throughout our time in the UK.

I would finally like to thank the editors of the Clarendon Studies in Criminology series and the three reviewers for their suggestions, as well as my editors from Oxford University Press, Gwen Booth and Lindsey Davis, for their patience. Parts of this book were published previously in *Crime and Justice—A Review of Research* and as a chapter in *Fear of crime – Punitivity: New*

Developments in Theory and Research edited by Helmut Kury and published by Universitaetsverlag Brockmeyer. A shorter, modified version of Chapter 10 was published in *British Journal of Criminology,* and sections of Chapter 7 appeared in an article in *Crime, Media, Culture.* They are reprinted with permission.

David A Green
Oxford

Contents

List of Tables

List of Figures

1

When Children Kill Children

Introduction

The James Bulger case

Most Britons and many people from elsewhere will be familiar with much of the following story. On the afternoon of 12 February 1993 in Bootle, Merseyside, outside Liverpool, two ten-year-old boys, later named as Robert Thompson and Jon Venables, who were truanting from school, abducted two-year-old James Bulger from the Strand Shopping Centre while his mother was being served at a butcher shop. The abduction was caught on the shopping centre's security video, the now iconic and chilling images from which were widely publicized and used to track down the boys. They led James on a journey of two-and-a-half miles through town, battering him along the way, past at least thirty-eight witnesses, none of whom effectively intervened. As darkness fell they brought him finally to a railway line where they brutally kicked and beat him to death with bricks and an iron bar, leaving his partially stripped body on the tracks to be severed later by a train.

Press interest in the case was high to begin with, and the lead investigator further raised its profile and the concern associated with it by appearing on the BBC's *Crimewatch* programme. After several false accusations and arrests, the police finally identified and arrested the two young boys on 18 February. Press interest increased. Each boy was interviewed separately by police on the day of the arrests and for the two days to follow, for no longer than forty-five minutes at a time. Robert Thompson was interviewed on ten occasions during this period for a total of seven hours and six minutes, and Jon Venables was interviewed nine times (Smith, 1994). Each boy blamed the other, though Venables admitted complicity during the interviews. They were both formally charged on the evening of 20 February.

The boys' first appearance at South Sefton Magistrates' Court two days later was marked by mob violence as a crowd of hundreds turned out to condemn the accused, some pelting the window-less transport van with rocks and eggs. Six people were arrested. The boys were assessed by psychiatrists, but only to determine whether they were mature enough to be tried. After nine months awaiting trial in secure custody without psychological treatment, the two boys were tried for kidnapping[1] and murder in a specially adapted (adult) Crown Court in November 1993. The courtroom featured a raised dock so the boys could see the proceedings during the month-long trial. Both were found guilty of abduction and murder, and were sentenced to be 'detained at Her Majesty's pleasure', the mandatory equivalent of an indeterminate life sentence for those between 10 and 18 who commit murder. After the trial some of the victim's family pledged vengeance and to kill the boys if they were ever released (Morrison, 1997: 231).

A month later the trial judge, Justice Morland, set the tariff, or the minimum term to be served before parole can be considered, at eight years. Then the Lord Chief Justice, Lord Taylor, increased the tariff to ten years in December 1993. Then in July 1994, the Home Secretary, Michael Howard, raised the tariff again to fifteen years taking into account 'the judicial recommendations as well as all other relevant factors including the circumstances of the case, public concern about the case and the need to maintain public confidence in the criminal justice system' (Home Office, 1994a). Howard had received a petition with 278,300 signatures, demanding the two boys never be released under any circumstances, and 22,638 other items of correspondence, including 21,281 clip-out coupons from the tabloid *Sun* newspaper demanding a 'whole-life tariff' (*R v Secretary of State for the Home Department, ex p Venables* [1997] 3 All ER 97, HL).

In 1997 the English Court of Appeal ([1997] 2 WLR 67) and a majority in the House of Lords ([1997] 3 All ER 97) quashed the Home Secretary's decision on the grounds that a government minister should be barred from deciding sentences. The European Court of Human Rights (*T v United Kingdom*; *V v United Kingdom* (2003) 30 EHRR 121) later ruled that Thompson and Venables did not get a fair trial and that it was unlawful for government ministers to set tariffs, which is a judicial function.[2]

---

[1] Both were also charged with the attempted kidnapping of a second boy whom the prosecution claimed they tried to abduct earlier the same day.

[2] The practice was outlawed in the Criminal Justice Act 2003.

No decision about the tariff was made until 26 October 2000 when Lord Chief Justice Woolf set it to expire on 21 February 2001, reflecting the initial eight years set by the trial judge.

Upon Lord Woolf's announcement in October 2000 that Robert Thompson and Jon Venables would probably be released within the year and given new identities for their protection, the mother of James Bulger, Denise Fergus, said the children 'got away with murder in every sense'. She also said, 'I think I'm in danger because they know how hard I fought to keep them locked up...I am not going to hunt them down and I am not going to try and kill them. But I'm urging people to look out for an 18-year-old moving into the area. If it's Thompson or Venables, I'd say "do what you can to get them out because they're still dangerous". I know they'll kill again' (BBC News, 2001a).

The Bulger case sparked debate about a range of social and moral issues in Britain (Gelsthorpe, 2002; Newburn, 2001; Young, 1996a, 1996b), including single motherhood, 'home alone' children, bad parenting, and rating systems for 'video nasties' and violent video games. Some details of the murder itself appeared to be similar to some violent depictions in the movie *Child's Play 3*, believed by some to have been rented by the father of one of the killers. The trial judge suggested the link after passing sentence, a link that an investigating officer later rejected. The concern catalyzed by the Bulger case was evidenced in the general tide of condemnatory attitudes toward offenders evident in rhetoric at the October 1993 Conservative Party conference, as well as the increasingly punitive New Labour 'law and order' platform of the time. It shaped the Criminal Justice and Public Order Act 1994, which 'effectively reversed the decarcerative provisions of youth justice law and policy—in respect of children aged 12–14 years—that dated back to the Children Act 1908' (Goldson and Muncie, 2006b: 143). The 1994 Act lowered the age at which a child could receive an indeterminate sentence from 14 to 10, it doubled from one year to two the maximum sentence in a young offenders' institution for 15–17 year-olds, and it created the 'Secure Training Orders' to make it easier to lock up persistent 12–14-year-old juvenile offenders in privately run 'Secure Training Centres'. The case also played a role in the interest shown by some English politicians in American-style boot camps for young offenders. The Bulger murder appears as well to have influenced the striking increases in adult prison admissions that immediately

Figure 1.1 Prison population and public concern about crime in England and Wales, January 1992–November 1994

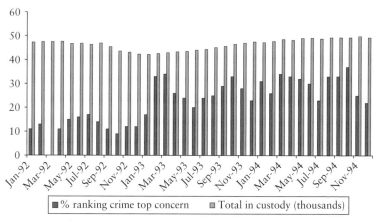

Source: Home Office (1993b, 1994b, 1995) and MORI (2002b).

followed it. Figure 1.1 shows how concern about crime spiked very sharply after James Bulger was killed and the prison population, having been in decline, began to rise once again at a time when crime was beginning to fall.

Stepping a bit farther back to include a broader time span, Figure 1.2 below shows the relationship between offending (notifiable offences),[3] the use of custody (annual numbers received into custody),[4] and levels of public concern about crime (percentage of poll respondents indicating crime as their top concern) (MORI, 2002b). It illustrates the rise in both public concern and prison admissions in the early 1990s just as recorded crime was declining.

Stepping back still further, Figure 1.3 below depicts the adult prison population from 1989 to 2000, pinpointing critical events and policies. From the early declines between 1990 and 1992, the prison population began the nearly inexorable rise that continues today. Former Chief Justice of the US Supreme Court William Rehnquist once argued, 'Judges, so long as they are relatively

[3] Notifiable offences obtained from Home Office (1993a) and Povey, Prime and Taylor (1997).

[4] Sources for annual numbers of prisoners received into custody: 1989–93 data from Home Office (1994b); 1994–96 data from White and Woodbridge (1997).

Figure 1.2 Custodial sentences, crime, and public concern in England and Wales, 1989–96

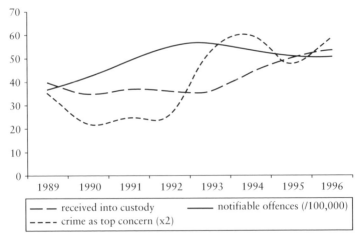

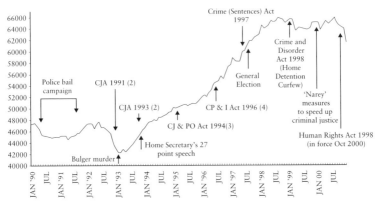

Source: Notifiable offences obtained from Home Office (1993a) and Povey, Prime and Taylor (1997). Annual numbers of prisoners received into custody: 1989–93 data from Home Office (1994b); 1994–6 data from White and Woodbridge (1997). Public concern data from MORI (MORI, 2002b).

Figure 1.3 Prison population (1) policy interventions 1990–2000 in England and Wales

1. Seasonally adjusted series
2. CJA = Criminal Justice Act
3. CJ & PO Act = Criminal Justice and Public Order Act
4. CP & I Act = Criminal Procedure and Investigations Act

Source: Home Office (2001c: 6).

normal human beings, can no more escape being influenced by public opinion in the long run than can people working at other jobs' (see also Gibson, 1980; quoted in Pritchard, 1992). It appears the Bulger case and the massive outpouring of press and public concern that followed in its wake had something to do with the rapid change in the penal climate, and things have not been the same since. Crime has since become and remained highly politicized, and neither of the two major political parties will allow the other to retain a stance on law and order that appears tougher than their own. The prison population has nearly doubled since 1993, and Rod Morgan, veteran criminologist and former head of the Youth Justice Board, believes that to understand the harshening of sentencing over this period, 'James Bulger is seminal' (Campbell, 2007).

Today the Bulger case is still frequently invoked in Parliament and referenced in news stories across the world, especially, but not only, when children hurt other children. For instance, press coverage of the disappearance of Madeleine McCann in Portugal in the summer of 2007 has repeatedly linked it to the Bulger case. Members of the Bulger family remain outspoken critics of the rehabilitative treatment the two killers received, and the press continues to report any developments in the case and any issues tangential to it. It was recently revealed, for instance, that the government has spent £13,000 to protect the anonymity of Thompson and Venables (*Sun*, 8 April 2007; *Scotsman*, 9 April 2007; *Yorkshire Post*, 9 April 2007). Tabloid stories allege that 'Evil Venables' has become a born-again Christian (*People*, 27 May 2007), and that 'Devil Dad' Robert Thompson fathered a child with his girlfriend, who it is said does not know of his past (*Sunday Mirror*, 1 January 2006). More recently, it has been more widely reported, as far away as Australia, that Venables is now engaged to be married, though he has apparently been advised not to disclose his real identity even to his fiancée, for his own protection, should someone close to them leak the information (*Brisbane Times*, 23 July 2007; *Melbourne Herald Sun*, 23 July 2007; *Daily Mail*, 22 July 2007). While this precaution might be understandable given the fury in much of the tabloid coverage of the case over the years, Eamonn Holmes, a tabloid columnist and news presenter for Rupert Murdoch's Sky News, contends, 'To conceal such a dark and ghastly secret is yet another example of how our society panders to the guilty at the expense of the innocent' (*The People*, 5 August 2007). Any press-consuming Briton would find it very difficult to avoid reminders of the Bulger case.

The Silje Redergård case

Far fewer Norwegians and only a handful of people from elsewhere will be familiar with any of the following story. On 15 October 1994, in the Heimdal borough of Norway's third largest city of Trondheim, three six-year-old boys killed five-year-old Silje Marie Redergård while they were playing together by a toboggan run, enjoying the first snow of the season. The boys first asked her to undress, and after she had partially taken off her snowsuit, they then took it in turns to hit and kick her, beat her with stones, and stomp on her. They left her unconscious in the frozen mud to die of hypothermia. As the boys were well below the age of criminal responsibility, which is 15 in Norway, none was either prosecuted or punished in any way. Though the police briefly questioned them, the case became a matter solely for the child welfare services (*barnevarnet*) once the boys' parents withdrew their consent for the police to question them further. Teams of social workers and psychologists successfully reintegrated the boys, while fostering an open environment for the community to ask questions, to seek counselling, and to grieve. Though parents in the area feared for their children's safety—especially in the early stages of the case before the perpetrators were identified and their exceptionally young ages were discovered—these teams successfully quelled or invalidated the rumours that began to spread about the boys believed to be responsible. There was no mass outpouring of anger or outrage from the family, the community, or the press, no cries for vigilante justice, and no political manoeuvring by any party's politicians to politicize the incident.

Press coverage of the case was substantial, but the bulk of it appeared during the first week of the case. The killing of Silje was constructed in the press as a tragic accident, a terrible aberration, a non-criminal act in every sense, perpetrated by innocents on the innocent. Once police identified the three children responsible, the mayor of Trondheim made a public statement asking the international journalists who had assembled to cover another Bulger-like child murder to leave the community in peace to allow its members to grieve. The press complied and, in keeping with

Norwegian law, the names of the perpetrators and their families were kept confidential.

All those involved, from the mother of the victim to the lead police investigator, believed condemnatory punishment to be the wrong way forward, and that the best course of action was to try immediately to reintegrate the children back into the community and to do everything possible to avoid stigmatizing them. The killers were offered places in kindergarten within a week to facilitate this (BBC News, 2000) under the watchful eyes of teachers and counsellors (BBC, 2000). Silje had often played with her attackers prior to the incident, and her mother, Beathe Redergård, knew two of the children well, saying in an interview that she believed in time she would be able to forgive the boys for what they did to her daughter.

References in the press to Silje's death have since been few. Those stories that have appeared focus on how her mother has indeed forgiven the killers, the efforts she has made to comfort the families of other murder victims, her refusal to accept a half a million kroner (around £45,000)— 'blood money' in her words (Sønstelie, 1995)—from a British tabloid in exchange for an exclusive on her story, and, in the British media, her support for raising the age of criminal responsibility in England and Wales to 15.

Though there was virtually no traceable policy impact from the case in Norway, some child psychologists in Trondheim at the time believed the killing was indicative of a breakdown of the community's moral health (Clifford, 1996), a view possibly echoed elsewhere, but one that was not picked up by the national press or political leaders. Others pointed to violent children's television shows, specifically the *Power Rangers* programme, as an influence on the killers after one of Silje's attackers mentioned a similarly violent children's programme (*Teenage Mutant Ninja Turtles*) in an interview with police. The Scandinavian network TV3 temporarily dropped the *Power Rangers* show from its roster. Grete Faremo, the Minister of Justice at the time of Silje's death—the counterpart of Home Secretaries Kenneth Clarke and later Michael Howard—was never mentioned or quoted in any of the Silje case press coverage. This may not be surprising, given that the case was never a criminal case, but what is perhaps surprising is the near absence of comment from other Norwegian government spokespeople about the case. There are two exceptions: a brief and comparatively reasoned set of remarks made by the Culture Minister—confirming that a bill would be brought before the *Storting*, the Norwegian Parliament, to subject video rentals to the same regulation as films shown in cinemas (Sønstelie, 1994)—and another by the Children's Minister—arguing that without the cooperation of international media firms, the government was 'powerless' to limit the flow of violent television shows broadcast in Norway (Solberg, 1994).

Why were the English[5] so vociferous in their condemnation of James Bulger's killers and so responsive in policy terms while their Norwegian counterparts remained so compassionate and restrained in their responses? This book adopts a comparative case study approach to examine the relationship between crime, politics, public opinion, and the news media in both Norway and England in an attempt to answer this question. These two cases of children killing children from the early 1990s are used as lenses through which to view this interaction. A discourse-analytic approach is used to study the meanings and effects of newspaper coverage of both homicides in order to explain the cases' dissimilar effects. These case studies are the vehicles by which the culture-specific penal sensibilities governing penal policy decision-making are assessed and compared. Drawing upon newspaper coverage about the cases and parliamentary debates invoking them, I reveal the discursive 'hidden hands' shaping public and political responses to these events, and consider why these particular forces retain the influence they do.

Explaining Difference

There are several plausible but ultimately unconvincing explanations for the contrast in response to the Bulger and Redergård cases. The first is the difference in the age of killers in the two cases. Certainly the fact that Silje's killers were only six years old made a repeat of the intense response that England witnessed to the ten-year-old killers of James less likely. Most would consider ten-year-olds to be at least somewhat more culpable for the acts they commit than six-year-olds would be, and yet three points undermine this line of argument when used to account for the disparity of responses in these two cases. First, there is a four-year

---

[5] For brevity's sake, 'English' and 'England' will be used throughout the book to refer to the legal jurisdiction of England and Wales.

difference in the ages of the killers in the two cases, but a five-year difference in the age at which a young person becomes criminally responsible in the two countries. This suggests a pre-existing cultural difference in the way that childhood is constructed. Second, Norway actually raised its age of criminal responsibility from 14 to 15 in 1990. Just eight years later, England lurched in the opposite direction by abolishing *doli incapax*, a legal presumption of innocence in England and Wales which the prosecution was charged to rebut to obtain a conviction. Again, these divergent policy changes suggest a deeper cultural divide between the two countries. Third, as the Bulger case prosecutor declared during the trial, 'Some criminal acts are more obviously seriously wrong than others. These crimes are most seriously obviously wrong, not merely to a 10-year-old but to a child of perhaps half that age or even less' (Faux, 1993). This statement hints at the reaction that might have been deemed morally appropriate in England, though legally moot, had the boys who killed James been six years old, like Silje's killers were. The differences in responses in these two countries go well beyond age and are deeply rooted in cultural constructions of childhood and the moral culpability of children.

A second red herring is the plausible contention that higher English crime rates can somehow account for the intensity of the punitive English response to the Bulger case. The next chapter shows that existing data fail to support this view. In short, if crime rates could be expected to have mechanical or hydraulic effects on public concerns and policy action, by most measures Norwegians should be just as concerned and active as the English are.

It is likely that the reactions of the families played an important role in how the cases were constructed in the press and assessed by the public and politicians. For instance, had the Bulger family quietly accepted the sentences received by the killers' of their son, as Silje's mother quietly accepted the decision of the child welfare services to reintegrate the boys who killed her daughter, it is possible that much less might have been made of the case in the press. However, the Bulger family were outspoken in their belief that Thompson and Venables were not sufficiently punished for what they did, and such views tend to be newsworthy. James's mother, Denise Fergus, began 'Justice for James', a pressure group which campaigned to keep the two in custody for life. Some involved in the campaign threatened vigilante justice upon receiving news of their release. All of these factors made the Bulger case far more newsworthy than the Silje case ever became, even more so when the protracted drama of a criminal trial is factored in. That Silje's killers were never charged or prosecuted made it far easier for the case to be handled quietly and for it to fade from the collective memory.

Though these factors are certainly components of a comprehensive explanation, they seem insufficient to account for the diametrically opposed reactions experienced in Norway and England. Much more is going on, and I would like to shine the light on two overlooked factors that go much farther toward explaining why much less was made of a Norwegian child murder than perhaps could have been under different conditions. The first of these is political culture, which will be explored more in the next chapter and discussed throughout the book. Different political cultures and the structures that sustain them create different incentives to respond to crime in particular ways. The second factor concerns differences in press markets and media cultures. These differences are also introduced in the next chapter but are discussed repeatedly in the rest of the book as well.

The argument

The general argument in brief runs as follows. The volatile public, press, and political reactions to the murder of James Bulger were strongly influenced by tabloid newspapers struggling to attract and retain consumers in a media market that is probably unprecedented in its competitiveness. A continuing tendency on the part of English politicians to defer to the media, and what is loosely conceived as public opinion, helps these strong media forces retain their powerful role in shaping political and public agendas. This would not present the problems it does if the opinions and commentary that the media circulated were accurately representative. Instead, the media that matter most in English culture and that maintain the highest readerships—the tabloids—present selectively homogenized accounts of crime and punishment issues that do not even come close to providing citizens with the knowledge required to contribute responsibly to the debates in which politicians are increasingly compelled to engage them. In addition, the hunger for knowledge of what the public wants and what the public thinks has increased, yet the quality of those assessments has not improved with that demand. Myriad public opinion assessments are insufficiently meaningful to justify the influence they now have on penal policy matters.

These factors are conditioned by a number of features of 'late-modernity'—including 'the restructuring of social and economic relations, the fluidity of social process, the speed of technological change, and the remarkable cultural heterogeneity' (Garland and Sparks, 2001: 1). This 'distinctive pattern of social, economic and cultural relations that emerged in America, Britain and elsewhere in the developed world in the last third of the twentieth century—brings with it a cluster of risks, insecurities, and control problems that have played a crucial role in shaping our changing responses to crime' (Garland, 2001: viii). These pressures, as the thinking goes, have forced governments to be seen to be doing more about the issues of crime and punishment about which their publics are so concerned.

However, as others point out (Albrecht, 2001; Tonry, 2007) and as this study confirms, Garland was perhaps careless in lumping developments in America and Britain in with those 'elsewhere'. It is likely that politicians elsewhere feel the pressure to respond to the proliferation of 24-hour, rolling news agendas and the staple that crime news has become, and that some of the rhetoric used to respond to apparent rises in public concern about crime and inse-curity may be increasingly similar across many Western nations. But the pressures for politicians and sentencers to act in consonance with that rhetoric, or with the same degree of urgency, are not experienced equally everywhere.

The subdued response to the Redergård case in Norway mirrors comparatively subdued responses to crime more generally. Official crime figures in Norway, as in most other Western nations, have followed an upward trend since the 1950s and appear to have declined overall since around the mid-1990s. In the face of this period of rising crime, the Norwegian imprisonment rate has remained remarkably flat for the same period (von Hofer, 1999). In contrast, the prison populations in England and the USA have risen sharply in response to similar overall crime trends, espe-cially since the early 1990s, continuing to do so in spite of recent declines.

It is a well-established criminological maxim that crime and punishment levels fluctuate independently of one another, in part because of the relationship between politics and punishment with which this book is concerned (Tonry, 1998). In addition, regardless of whether welfare- or penal-oriented models of crime control are embraced, international crime trends fluctuate similarly over time (Storgaard, 2004). While many criminological analysts point to the role the politicization of crime has played in the growth of public and political appetites for imprisonment in countries like England and the USA, most have neglected to consider the role of political culture—in particular the distinction Arend Lijphart (1968; 1969; 1991; 1999) makes between consensus and majoritarian democracy—in explaining the relative stability of imprisonment rates in countries like Norway.

Though this study is not chiefly concerned with imprisonment rates per se, it is concerned to understand the cultural mechanisms and discursive practices that make responding to crimes with more punishment an appropriate or inappropriate thing to do. The Norway example suggests that features of Nordic consensual political culture have allowed it to weather late-modern pressures more adaptively than its counterparts in, for instance, England, the USA, and Australia. So, just as studying only English or American experiences forces the adoption of too parochial a view of the ways advanced democracies have coped with late-modernity, there are also dangers in developing too parochial a view of political culture based on the English model of highly partisan politics.

I use Lijphart's distinction to represent two 'ideal types' (Weber, 1968) to be used as generalized, though not invariable, frameworks to compare cases. This means that any one case might not conform in every detail to the idealized category in which it is placed, but as is made clear below, the differences are so significant with the two cases of Norway and England as to make such a categorization useful. Lijphart succinctly summarizes the two ideal types of democratic systems as follows: 'the majoritarian model of democracy is exclusive, competitive, and adversarial, whereas the consensus model is characterized by inclusiveness, bargaining, and compromise' (Lijphart, 1999: 2). Structurally, consensus democracies tend to have coalition or minority governments, multi- rather than dual-party systems, strong legislatures rather than the strong executives majoritarian democracies have, proportional representation rather than winner-takes-all systems, and systems of coordinated interest groups instead of the competitive interest group systems found in England and the USA (Lijphart, 1998).

This book shows that Norway and other countries with consensual political cultures appear to retain structural and cultural
features that retard, counteract, or delay many of the adverse
effects associated with late-modernity—pressures that have
forced England and the USA into a frenzy of legislative activity,
much of it symbolic rather than instrumental, intended to express
moral condemnation for crime and to reassure an anxious public
who are increasingly invited to voice their concerns. Put another
way, the penal culture in Norway, and the discourses that indicate and support it, are constructed differently and in such a way
as to minimize the chances that an event like the death of Silje
Redergård will act as a lightning rod to attract and exorcize late-
modern fears. I argue that political cultures create incentives for
politicians and policymakers to react to crime and the perception
of insecurity in particular ways, some of them counterproductive,
and that these incentives help to account for the extremely dissimilar responses to the two child killings studied here.

Many of these issues have been addressed in the criminological
literature, some more than others. There has been considerable
theoretical interest in the interplay between politics and punishment (Barker, 2006; Beckett, 1997; Bottoms, 1995; Downes,
1988; Downes and Morgan, 1997, 2002; Garland, 2001; Roberts
et al, 2003; Savelsberg, 1994, 1999; Simon, 1997, 2007; Tonry,
2004a, 2004b), but the implications of the different ways of doing
politics in consensus and majoritarian democracies has been
largely overlooked. Comparing political cultures helps one to recognize the contingency of existing conditions, and to appreciate
and learn from different ways of doing politics.

Also neglected has been a practical approach to improve the
conditions suffered by adversarial late-modern democracies, a
strategy that might improve and render more meaningful the communication between citizens and their leaders that misrepresenta-
tive media portrayals and shallow, untrustworthy opinion polls
now inadequately accomplish. This book attempts to help redress
this by offering a reform programme based around the concept of
deliberation, or the open and informed dialogue between equals.

Decades of public opinion research suggest that the public
is consistently less punitive and repressive in their attitudes to
offenders than simple opinion polls and the news media typically suggest. What Daniel Yankelovich (1991) calls 'public judgment' is a more refined conception of informed public opinion,

achieved only after deliberators have thoughtfully considered the range of available information on a topic and chosen preferences for which they are willing to take responsibility. More nuanced public judgments about crime and punishment issues are likely to deprive political leaders of the ability to defend decisions to legislate harshly and rashly in the face of high-profile crimes by referring to a monolithically punitive public.

Until recently there was no readily available means to distinguish between public judgment and other lower quality assessments of public opinion, but a relatively new means of approximating public judgment has recently been developed. The 'Deliberative Poll' (Fishkin, 1995) was designed to assess the informed and reflective judgments of the public on particular topics in order to correct the flawed and simplistic traditional opinion poll, which tends only to reflect the unconsidered, on-the-spot, top-of-the-head responses to a pollster's questions. The Deliberative Poll combines structured and intense deliberative opportunities with a large, statistically representative participant sample. It provides the sample the incentive, opportunity, materials, expertise, and support needed to discuss and consider fully the issues presented to them. It generates the preferences the general public would choose had they been privy to the range of available views, research, and other information about a particular topic to which their participating peers were exposed.

By institutionalizing the routine utilization of Deliberative Polls on the most pressing issues of the day, as well as other tools of 'deliberative will formation' (Jacobsson, 1997), politicians and practitioners would be provided with more durable assessments of public judgment that could be more defensibly invoked to justify policy decisions. For instance, Deliberative Polls on particular issues could be conducted perennially (for example, as a part of the British Crime Survey), at key stages in the policymaking process (for example, as part of the consultations that inform government White Papers), and on an ad hoc basis (for example, in the wake of high-profile crimes that alarm the public). These steps would help to move the construct of public opinion beyond the very loosely defined, easily manipulated political commodity it is currently, and to produce an informed, more defensibly invoked, public will. The institutionalization of public deliberation also shows promise in de-escalating the tensions characteristic of penal policy debates by increasing trust in the way the state functions and increasing the state's democratic legitimacy (Jacobsson, 1997).

English crime and politics

English political culture is such that politicians of both major parties are impelled to respond loudly and swiftly in response to high-profile crimes. The highly adversarial nature of English politics demands they be seen to be as 'tough on crime' as possible and to react demonstrably to crime and insecurity. Politics is typically viewed as a zero-sum game; for one's own party to win, political opponents must lose. This means that any opportunity to exploit weakness in political opponents is unlikely to be neglected, and crime, which invokes a tangle of complex, emotive, and easily accessible concerns, is always exploitable. The result is a political 'Mexican standoff' in which representatives of one major party stand armed against each other, and if one side decides to pull the trigger, so must they both. Each side is thereby mutually assured some level of destruction. This style of politics is further maintained by an adversarial press culture that is shaped by a highly competitive press market with strong political allegiances. Virtually all players from either party thus cannot afford to embrace alternatives to the zero-sum game approach unless they all do.

The routine publication of English crime figures and the political reactions to their release reveal a familiar tendency. For instance, on the morning of 21 July 2005 the Home Office released both its recorded crime figures and the findings of the latest British Crime Survey (BCS). Recorded figures showed a 6 per cent decrease in overall crime, but a 7 per cent increase in violent incidents. The BCS also showed the same decrease overall, but it found that violent crime had actually fallen by 11 per cent. The response from the news media was predictable. Before the BBC Breakfast news programme reported Home Office minister Hazel Blear's interpretation of the findings, it aired the reaction of the shadow Home Secretary, David Davis,[6] who said the figures clearly showed that violent crime under Labour continued to 'spiral out of control'.

---

[6] He was the favourite at the time to succeed Michael Howard as the Tory party leader but lost the leadership election to David Cameron. At the time of writing, Davis remains in his post as shadow Home Secretary.

Rises in recorded crime can reflect increased police activity, and if, for instance, police are more heavily patrolling city centres and cracking down on drunken violence there, then the crime figures will show an increase in reported violent crimes. Perversely then, more police activity tends to mean more recorded crime. The BCS, which is a household victimization survey, has its flaws as well. It is criticized for failing to reach those most affected by crime, particularly young men living in cities, and for failing to record many offences that are not included in the survey. For all its flaws, the BCS is considered an important complement to the skewed view that recorded crime figures project. Experts generally regard victimization data as more reliable indices of crime trends and levels (Langan and Farrington, 1998), particularly when the rules for counting crimes frequently change at the Home Office. Yet the BCS results, as well as the recorded crime numbers that do not comport with the rising crime frame used to construct dramatic headlines and soundbites, typically fail to get much headline-level press attention.

To illustrate, though the press in the summer of 2005 could have chosen to emphasize a number of angles in their crime figure coverage, all but one of the daily newspapers focused on the most dramatic, worst-case interpretation. The *Daily Star* carried the headline 'Violent Crimes Hit One Million Mark', the same factoid that the BBC Breakfast news coverage used to introduce its story and one that means little if not considered in tandem with overall population increases. The *Daily Mail* ran the headline, 'Drunken Yobs Blamed for Record Violent Crimes', and the *Sun* went with '10 Crimes a Year Solved', failing even to mention the BCS figures that the *Star* briefly referenced in the body of its story. The *Mirror* ran a similar story under the headline, 'Reclaim Our Streets: PC Plodders—Average Cop Detects Just 10 Crimes A YEAR'. This selective focus on the worst-case readings of the figures is not just a tabloid phenomenon, as the following broadsheet headlines indicate: 'One Million Assaults as Violent Crime Rises 8%' (*Independent*), 'Violent Attacks Reach 1M' (*The Times*), 'Violent Crime at New Heights' (*Daily Telegraph*). Only the *Guardian* chose to emphasize a different angle with the headline: 'Crime Down By 44% Since 1995'.

Two years later and the release of the crime figures generated another round of similarly bleak headlines. Though recorded crime fell, gun crime dropped by 13 per cent, and homicides hit

an eight-year low, the headlines of 19 July 2007 painted a predictably gloomy picture: 'An Adult Is Attacked Every 12 Seconds'
(*Daily Mail*), 'Violent Crime Rises' and (somewhat contradictorily)
'Crime Fear Rises as Offences Remain Steady' (*Mirror*), 'Violent
Crime Up 5%' (*Guardian*, *Daily Telegraph*, *Independent*, *Sun*),
and 'Violent Crime and Robbery on the Rise, New Figures Show'
(*The Times*). The news websites followed the pattern. Sky News
reported 'Survey Shows Rise in Violent Crime', 'Street Crime
and Robberies Up', and 'Robbery and Drug Offences Increase',
while the BBC went with the more equivocal 'Crime "Stable" But
Robbery Rises'. In response, David Davis echoed himself on earlier occasions by stressing the bleakest appraisal, saying the crime
figures demonstrated Labour's 'serial failure to protect the public'
(*Guardian*).

With headlines like these it is not difficult to understand why
the English public fails to believe the government when it tries
to say crime has been falling overall for over a decade. Alarming
headlines attract attention and sell newspapers. Just as simple
public opinion survey data can be found to support practically
any assertion one might like to make, the lack of clear and consistent evidence from a variety of sources that supports the notion
of a drop in crime is unlikely to prevent opposition politicians
from exploiting selected inconsistencies in the findings. Data like
these are easily exploited if the will to do so is strong enough, and
in England, the will is very strong indeed.

The Norwegian contrast

In contrast, Norwegian political culture appears to generate
fewer incentives to politicize crime to the same extent. This culture is reflected and supported within a much less adversarial,
multi-party system built upon a tradition of consensus building
and compromise. Because fewer players are excluded from policymaking and all tend to contribute, there are fewer incentives for
members of one political party to attack their opponents. Crimes
are thus less likely to become means to gain political capital in
the way they are in countries with adversarial political cultures,
like England and the USA. The win-at-all-costs ethos at the heart
of politics in these countries almost demands the exploitation
of any exploitable political opportunity, even if the cost is bad
policy, high incarceration rates, high concern for the crimes the

lawmakers legislate to stop, and greater distrust in government officials who seem ceaselessly to bicker among themselves.

Because there are fewer incentives to politicize sensitive crime and punishment issues in consensus democracies, the political culture and the structures supporting it seem to remain in better condition and to retain public trust. The Nordic countries, for instance, all of which are consensus democracies, tend to have lower fear of crime, higher trust in government, and lower imprisonment rates. This does not mean that crime is never politicized, for it is (Larsson, 1993; Mathiesen, 2003), but the incentives to politicize it are significantly reduced. Newspapers, which in Norway are sold mostly by subscription (Lappi-Seppälä, 2005), report crime more responsibly and dispassionately, perhaps in part because there is less of a need to catch the eye of a passing commuter with a salacious or fear-inducing headline of the sort advertised daily on the placards of English newsagents. Even the Norwegian tabloid press presents a wide array of views and opinions from a range of claims-makers, including those types of experts that the English tabloids tend often to denigrate. The market is less competitive and editorial standards are more strictly enforced, which conduces to balanced reporting because the coverage is aimed at a wider audience, rather than a particularly ideologically and economically allegiant sub-audience, as in England.

Addressing Penal Populism

The politicization of penal policy debates in England has meant that policymakers now defer to assessments of public opinion to an extent unseen in earlier post-war decades. The media have simultaneously expanded their influence on public affairs, often speaking for the public, and politicians tend to court the public via the media, often conflating the two. Lost in these interactions is both a sense of an unmediated and informed public will, and a public forum where the issues are engaged on a level proportionate to their importance.

Law and order politics is predicated largely on the erroneous notion of a punitive and unforgiving public. Setting aside the fact that the public is generally highly un- and misinformed about the extent of crime and the severity of existing punishments, researchers have for decades demonstrated that when better informed the public tend to be less punitive than the average politician can publicly assert (Hough and Roberts, 1998; Roberts and Stalans, 1997; Walker and Hough, 1988), and highly ambivalent about issues of crime and punishment (Cullen, Fisher and Applegate 2000; Cullen et al, 2002)—wanting both to execute criminals *and* rehabilitate them; to blame individuals for their offending *and* blame their social circumstances; to 'let them rot in jail' *and* prevent them from reoffending. This indicates that politicians have more room to manoeuvre on these issues than their rhetoric and behaviour often suggest. Nonetheless, in May 2007, in a farewell article written for the *Economist* at the end of his premiership—a premiership which purported to herald an embrace of 'evidence-based policy'—Tony Blair declared, 'Today the public distinguishes clearly between personal lifestyle issues, where they are liberal, and crime, where they are definitely not' (Blair, 2007). Even in light of all the literature that has been generated about the public's contradictory and ambivalent attitudes about these issues, the message to be gleaned from decades of public opinion research is either not getting through to politicians, or politicians are simply ignoring it.

In an influential contribution written over a decade ago, Tony Bottoms (1995: 40, emphasis added) observed that:

> …it is clear that we cannot speak in any straightforward fashion about 'public opinion' on crime in a way that automatically equates it with a heavily punitive approach. On the other hand, it is, I believe, appropriate to speak of politicians or legislators adopting 'populist punitive' policies, for these are political stances, normally adopted in the clear belief that they will be popular with the public (and usually with an awareness that, in general and abstract opinion polls, punitive policies are favoured by a majority of the public…). Hence, the term 'populist punitiveness' is intended to convey the notion of politicians tapping into, and using for their own purposes, what *they believe to be* the public's generally punitive stance.

Though Roberts et al (2003: 64) suggest 'penal populism' is 'a term equivalent to populist punitivenes', it actually differs in one important respect. Roberts et al write that the 'combination of [the public's] concern and lack of knowledge [about crime and punishment] can present politicians with the temptation to promote policies which promote electoral advantage without doing much about crime. The more wilful that such politicians are in their disregard of the evidence about effectiveness and equity, the more we are inclined to regard them as penal populists' (Roberts et al, 2003: 65). Bottoms's definition of populist punitiveness is less accusatory than this. He does not intimate that politicians know better and yet choose cynically to exploit the public's ignorance and ambivalence. Instead he suggests that politicians are acting in accordance with what they actually believe is a reliable enough assessment of public opinion. It is not unreasonable, however, to expect that politicians *should* know better by now.

Most authors use these two terms interchangeably, but this distinction between populist punitiveness and penal populism is too important to overlook. Throughout this book I use the term penal populism, not simply because it is a little less inelegant and easier to pronounce, but also because of its implication of wilful cynicism.

Regardless of whether the myth of a monolithically punitive public is perpetuated ingenuously or cynically, it is clear that both naïve populist punitiveness and wilful penal populism could both be reduced if more durable and trustworthy assessments of informed public opinion were made more readily available. The Deliberative Poll provides the means of approximating public judgment, a more durable assessment of the informed public will which is less susceptible to populist manipulation and distortion than current, weaker assessments of public opinion. In addition, by providing more opportunities for public deliberation, countries in which the public's trust in government is eroding, like England, might also generate the kind of trust in political institutions and among citizens that characterizes those nations, like Norway, where the politicization of crime is not as pressing an issue.

Three Caveats

I offer three caveats at the outset. The first involves scale. Frank Zimring (2001) remarked that David Garland's comparison of English and American imprisonment rates and penal cultures in *The Culture of Control* was like comparing a haircut to a beheading. Scale is an important consideration. Scandinavian colleagues have cautioned against the development of too rosy a view of Nordic penal culture, and a growing literature cites an alarming rise in penal populist, tough-on-crime rhetoric throughout the Nordic countries (Balvig, 2004; Estrada, 2004; Kyvsgaard, 2001; Larsson, 1993, 2001; Mathiesen, 1996, 2003; Snare, 1995; Tham, 2001; Victor, 1995; von Hofer, 2004). Some insist that Garland's influential description of changes in late-modern penality capture developments in Scandinavia as well and point to the harshening of sentencing and public attitudes as evidence. It would be foolish to disagree entirely, but in comparative terms—and it is only through comparison that differences are perceived—the level of harshening in England since the early 1990s is on a scale that makes Norway's seem almost insignificant. Chapter 3 provides the evidence.

The second caveat concerns exceptions. The majoritarian-consensus continuum is not intended to categorize democracies monolithically, and there are examples that appear to contradict the usefulness of the distinction. For example, for Lijphart, the consensus democracies include all the Nordic countries, the Netherlands, Belgium, Luxembourg, Germany, Switzerland, Austria, Italy, and Portugal. The majoritarian countries include the USA, UK, Canada, Australia, and New Zealand. The Netherlands and Portugal currently have imprisonment rates of 129 and 120 per 100,000 of the population, respectively—considerably higher than the other European consensus democracies and higher even than Canada. Conversely, in spite of its inclusion in the majoritarian end of Liphart's continuum, Canada has withstood late-modern change without resorting to increases in imprisonment, in part by talking tough (through tough-sounding, expressive legislation, including mandatory minimum sentences and higher maximum penalties) but acting more considerately (through strictly limiting the numbers of offenders subject to them) (Doob and Webster, 2006). Just as consensus democracies may fall victim to bouts of penal populism, so too might some majoritarian countries be better able to weather those conditions that impel others to react with penal populism. The hypothesis suggesting that consensus political culture creates fewer incentives for politicians to adopt tough-on-crime postures and to legislate in kind does not suggest that such postures are unknown in consensus democracies. Instead, it only suggests that countervailing political-cultural values minimize both the need for posturing and the chances that punitive policy will result. The intention here is to draw attention to those conditions in consensus democracies that seem to work as a windbreak preventing the force of the winds of late-modernity from blowing through at full strength.

The third caveat involves forecasting the future. In his comparative study of Dutch and English penal policymaking in the 1980s, David Downes found evidence that, in the Netherlands, 'largely detached from public monitoring...a small professional elite, with a fringe of complementary groups, dominate[d] practice in the field of criminal justice. Shared training, position, norms, and values provide[d] an effective boundary maintaining system shielding the operations of criminal justice from public opinion' (Johnson and Heijder, 1983: 10, quoted in Downes 1991: 117). He believed there to be a 'relative absence' of 'authoritarian public opinion' in the Netherlands 'which plays on those who administer criminal justice policies in general, and penal policies in particular, to deliver harsher penalties and conditions' (Downes, 1991: 117). Mick Ryan (1999: 5) explains the importance of these findings: 'Dutch elites, therefore, were (and are) not required to act as a barrier against a punitive popular culture, or at least not to anything like the same extent as they do in England and Wales'. However, Downes has since argued that the politics of accommodation that characterizes Lijphart's consensus distinction has recently unravelled in the Netherlands, which has recently experienced the largest increase in the number of people under some form of detention in Western Europe (Downes and van Swaaningen, 2005). This Dutch shift to a more repressive, intolerant penal climate indicates that any characterization of such a contingent set of conditions is always in flux, and must constantly be revisited and reassessed.

So, that the public, the press, and politicians in Norway failed to react excessively or punitively to Silje's death does not mean they will necessarily remain so deliberate in their responses to reasonably similar cases indefinitely. According to many Norwegian observers (Allern, 2007; Christie, 2002, 2007; Dahl, 2007; Larsson, 1993; 1996; Mathiesen, 2002, 2007; Røssland, 2007a, 2007b), the expanding Norwegian news media sensationalize crime and capitalize on the fear of it more so than hitherto, though the level of this activity is again on a smaller scale when compared to the same tendencies in England. Features of consensus political culture appear to have some, though certainly not absolute, prophylactic effects on the kind of penal populism that is rampant in England and the USA.

Plan of the Book

By examining the responses to the Bulger and Redergård homicides, this book describes a set of interlinked problems facing professional experts and penal policymakers, most of which are more acutely experienced in England than in Norway. Culture-specific variations within a constellation of factors help to explain the variable susceptibility to penal populism in these two countries. Norway's consensual political culture and less sensationalistic news media exert less pressure upon politicians to act in ways that an ill-informed public might favour. In England, an adversarial political culture, a highly competitive and sensationalistic mass media, and poor measures of public opinion each constrain the range of choices available to policymakers, minimizing opportunities for the equal consideration of all available knowledge. The book also provides ameliorative proposals to broaden the range of choices policymakers consider to include knowledges politicians often ignore, the media often overlook, and opinion polls often fail to measure.

Conspiracy theories are inherently suspect, in part because they ascribe to individuals levels of lucidity and agency that most do not really possess. Therefore, this book begins with the premise that there is more at work shaping the English penal climate than merely the cynical wills of politicians or journalists to make political capital out of the public's worst fears. Forces conduce to provide incentives for particular kinds of behaviour, and this book represents an appreciative approach to the study of those incentives and the forces shaping them. This also suggests that incentives can be reworked to reflect more defensible and democratic practices that generate fewer costs and more gains in terms of public trust, penal expenditure, democratic legitimacy, and social capital.

Chapters 2 and 3 profile the Norwegian and English post-war penal policy contexts to help situate the discussions that follow. Chapter 2 compares the countries historically, economically, culturally, and politically. It also compares and contrasts developments in Norwegian and English press markets and media cultures. Chapter 3 focuses exclusively on the experience of crime and justice in both countries. It compares the available cross-national data on crime rates and trends, punishment rates and trends, developments in youth justice, and public attitudes to crime and punishment.

Chapter 4 more thoroughly introduces the theoretical and analytical tools used in the rest of the book, and offers two conceptual models. The first describes the reciprocal ways that knowledge, discourses, and public sensibilities interact with media culture and political culture to influence the penal climate. The second models the ways in which political culture and political structures constrain the flow of the various forms of knowledge informing policy. Chapter 5 provides a broadly framed justification for the employment of discourse analysis to study changing cultural penal sensibilities and penal culture. It draws as well upon the political science literature on knowledge utilization to show how the range of existing knowledge relevant to penal policy debates is constrained both by the language used to describe it, and the political and organizational demands in a given time and place. This chapter also lays some of the theoretical groundwork for the actual discourse analysis of the two child-on-child homicides that appears in Chapter 7.

Chapter 6 continues with the theme of constraint and justifies the examination of media discourse. I consider the evolution of media effects research over the years, and point out the benefits of 'agenda-setting' theories of the mass media (McCombs, 1981; McCombs and Shaw, 1972) and the importance of the media's 'impersonal influence' (Mutz, 1998). The media provide the cognitive tools citizens use to make sense of events and issues, telling them what to think about, how to think about it, and what others purportedly think about it. As is shown throughout the book, the range of discourses used in the news media to define the parameters of penal policy debates that citizens must evaluate appears to be narrowing. Media discourse, at least in England, appears to be becoming more homogenized, severely limiting the ability of citizens to formulate meaningful judgments about the array of complex and sensitive problems whose solutions they are increasing being called upon to influence.

Chapter 7 provides the findings of a comparative analysis of the Bulger and Redergård case newspaper coverage. It examines how the cases were contextualized, who most influenced how the events were framed in each jurisdiction, how experts in each jurisdiction were regarded in the coverage, and why the themes expressed in each jurisdiction differed so starkly. Expert discourse dominates the Norwegian coverage in both the tabloid and broadsheet newspapers, while it is much harder to come by in the English press, especially the tabloids, which tend to draw upon the views and reactions of the general public. The media discourses and the range of views presented in England were highly constrained to reflect culturally established hierarchies. While the Redergård homicide was framed by experts as a tragic accident committed by normal children, the Bulger case was framed by politicians, columnists, and members of the public as a horribly brutal criminal event perpetrated by two evil boys.

Chapter 8 considers aspects of English political culture that help explain why the Bulger case became a vehicle for the expression of growing moral uncertainty in England more generally. These factors include the rise of the public voice, the power of the tabloid press and the salience of its discourse, the highly adversarial relationship between the political parties, and the emergence of New Labour as unapologetically 'tough on crime'. All of these factors helped place the Bulger case in the centre of the political arena, and all exerted powerful pressures upon politicians and policymakers to act in the ways they did. It appears that low levels of public trust in government and a sense of declining democratic legitimacy intensify these pressures shaping English political culture. Governments in turn respond with heroic rhetoric and repressive legislation that both confirm public concerns and contribute to the perception of government ineffectualness.

Chapter 9 considers the implications for democratic legitimacy of the majoritarian and consensus models of democracy. It appears that features of the Norwegian way of doing politics decreases incentives for penal populism, makes the invocation of crisis rhetoric less likely, and retains and restores high levels of public trust. The deliberative, considered approach to penal policy matters sends fewer cues to citizens to confirm or give credence to the fears they may feel. Because trust among citizens and trust in government are both high in Norway, and because there are fewer incentives for politicians to use a one-off child-on-child homicide as a means to a political end, Silje's death served no secondary purposes as it did in England.

Chapters 10 and 11 offer suggestions to help initiate 'détente' between the political parties in majoritarian countries and to de-escalate the political standoff that crime and punishment issues tend to generate. Chapter 10 sets the stage by clarifying what we typically talk about when we talk about public opinion, and considers ways of improving the facilitation and assessment of informed public judgment. I argue that the current surrogates for informed public opinion, including opinion polls, focus groups, and media representations, are all insufficient assessments that fail to match in quality or rigour the level of interest they have in the shaping of penal policy debates. I also contend that reform proposals to improve public knowledge but that lack deliberation and dialogue are unlikely to succeed.

Chapter 11 provides a reform programme anchored in deliberation. English political culture would likely benefit from adopting the more deliberative features of consensus democracies to de-escalate penal policy debates, to depoliticize crime as much as possible, to improve the ability of politicians and policymakers to reflect on the issues with the care and consideration the issues demand, and to build citizens' trust in one another and in government by enlisting them to participate more meaningfully in democratic institutions. Increasing opportunities for public deliberation, through Deliberative Polls and other exercises, would make the concept of public opinion more meaningful than it is currently, and it would have the secondary effect of bolstering government legitimacy by building the public's confidence in democratic institutions.

2

Culture, Politics, and the Media in Norway and England

A sizeable literature exists examining developments and shifts in penal policy and public sensibilities since the 1990s in England and the USA. Unfortunately, the same cannot be said of developments in the Nordic countries, especially when it comes to material in English. This study cannot provide a comprehensive analysis of every relevant dimension one might like to include in a comparison. Instead, the principal aim of this chapter is to provide some of the data and background information necessary to begin to make some comparative distinctions between Norway and England that will help to place the responses to the Bulger and Redergård homicides in some context. The implications of these comparisons will be more fully revealed as the analysis unfolds throughout the book. In the name of brevity and to avoid excessive description and irrelevant details, these country profiles are limited in scope. I focus only on those aspects most relevant to the broader arguments in the book, those that might most plausibly contribute to an explanation for the dissimilar responses to two killings. In particular, attention is focused on the similar and dissimilar ways in which the media and political systems in both countries respond to the experience of crime and punishment. These responses impact the ways that crime and punishment are experienced, both statistically and in the public mind.

Though English data are frequently drawn on in this chapter and the next to make the comparisons in these profiles more illustrative, these profiles tend to privilege Norwegian contexts for two reasons. First, most readers are likely to be familiar with many aspects of English experience and practice. Second, because part of the aim of the book is to account for the intensity of penal populism in England relative to Norway and to propose ways to neutralize it, the rest of the book examines the English context in significant detail.

This chapter has four main sections in which different comparative dimensions are introduced. The first offers a brief overview of the post-war historical and cultural contexts, including the status of children. The second section compares the political economies and economic conditions in both countries. The third section profiles the political systems and further distinguishes between the majoritarian and consensus models of democracy. The fourth section compares English and Norwegian media markets and cultures. The next chapter compares the ways in which crime and punishment are experienced in both countries, including recorded crime and victimization data, as well as various measures of punitiveness. It also provides profiles of developments in youth justice and comparative data on public attitudes toward crime and punishment. The chapters to follow illustrate that all of these components—crime and punishment, public opinion, media, and politics—are differentially interrelated in important, context-dependent ways that condition the ways that countries respond to high-profile crimes like the Bulger and Redergård cases.

Zedner (1995) argues that our 'exposure to other possible ways of seeing and shaping the world not only excites us out of the torpor of parochialism but demands that we regard our domestic topography anew'. Comparative research has the 'capacity to render the invisible visible' (Blumler and Gurevitch, 1995: 76) and can 'sensitize us to variation...[and] to similarity' (Hallin and Mancini, 2004: 3) by increasing 'the "visibility" of one structure by contrasting it with another' (Bendix, 1963: 537). When viewed alongside a comparator, less is taken for granted because both the peculiarity and similarity of the status quo in different settings become more apparent. This means comparative research prevents us from jumping to premature generalizations by being both 'an effective antidote to unwitting parochialism [and] an essential antidote to naïve universalism' (Blumler and Gurevitch, 1995: 75–6). This chapter offers a few steps along the path toward greater self-awareness and a broader appreciation of the variability of penal cultures.

Cultural and Historical Backdrop

Hofstede and Hofstede (2005) replicated IBM values surveys from 74 countries and analysed them along four dimensions that help distinguish cultural differences: power distance, collectivism versus individualism, femininity versus masculinity, and uncertainty avoidance. The dimension that yields the most contrasts when comparing Norway and England is the femininity versus masculinity dimension:

A society is called masculine when emotional gender roles are clearly distinct: men are supposed to be assertive, tough, and focused on material success, whereas women are supposed to be more modest, tender, and concerned with the quality of life.

A society is called feminine when emotional gender roles overlap: both men and women are supposed to be modest, tender, and concerned with the quality of life. (Hofstede and Hofstede, 2005: 120)

England scored high on the masculinity index and Norway scored at the bottom, second only to Sweden. 'Feminine' countries tend to prioritize egalitarianism, modesty, conflict resolution through compromise, and 'solidarity with the weak versus reward for the strong' (Hofstede and Hofstede, 2005: 147). All of these qualities are readily apparent in Norwegian culture.

Child education and well-being

Norway is a very child-friendly and 'radically egalitarian' society (Christensen and Peters, 1999: 143). Education in Norway reflects this egalitarianism. Virtually all Norwegian children attend the same state-run public school system with a common curriculum, which includes religious education.[1] Seven per cent of schoolchildren in the UK go to private or so-called 'public' schools, while 23 per cent of sixth-formers do (Independent Schools Council, 2007). A mainstreaming policy in Norway also ensures that children are not segregated by ability and are taught together in the same classrooms. Norwegian schools are not rigidly structured and few academic demands are made of children (Van Dijk, 1997). There is a 'structure of understanding' in schools and a deep appreciation of the role the children play in the school culture (Wilkinson, 2007). Pupil representatives liaise with teachers and voice pupils' concerns. In contrast to English schooling,

[1] Religious education was reformed in 2003 and became more inclusive and less dominated by the Church of Norway. However, the European Court of Human Rights ruled in July 2007 that the mandatory religion class taught in Norwegian schools—entitled 'Christian knowledge and religious and ethical education'—was still not pluralistic enough and violates Article 2 of the European Convention on Human Rights.

the Norwegian approach strikes one Scottish ex-pat as placing an entirely different emphasis on the socialization of children and empowering them as important individuals with important views (Wilkinson, 2007). This is in contrast to the 'adult-controlled milieu' and power structure of English schools. Upon first sending her children to an English school, a Norwegian ex-pat was stunned by the mandatory uniforms and the rigidity of the regime imposed, which seemed designed to make children look and act like 'little adults' (Bråtveit, personal communication, 6 May 2003).

From 1969 to 1996, Norwegian children started school at the age of seven and received only nine years of compulsory education (Norwegian Ministry of Education and Research, 2007). This was raised to ten in 1997 when the starting age was lowered to six in order to free up spaces in the country's kindergartens, and to honour a government pledge that every child under six should have a place in kindergarten if their parents want one (Dyregrov and Heltne, 2007; Falck, 2007). English children are currently required to receive eleven years of compulsory education, between the ages of five and sixteen. This upper age will likely be extended to 18 because of the poor performance of young people in the UK, where in 2004, 10.2 per cent of males and 10.5 per cent of females between the ages of 15 and 19 were not in education or employment. The comparable figures in Norway the same year for young males and females were 4.2 and 2.8 per cent, respectively (OECD, 2007).

According to UNICEF (2000), the UK and Norway both have high levels of single parenthood, but in Norway the poverty rate of children of single parents is one-third that of England and Wales (see Figure 2.1). In a recent report by UNICEF (2007) on child well-being in 21 OECD countries, the UK ranked last, just behind the USA, and Norway ranked seventh. The Nordic countries maintain lower rates of child poverty because of the universalist nature of their benefits provision, which avoids the targeting and stigmatization of particular groups that occurs in the UK and USA (Forssén, 2000). Everyone is entitled to a good standard of living, health care and day care are free to all, and single-parent families have the same rights and responsibilities as other families do. This universalism was even expressed by the justice committee spokesman for Norway's populist Progress Party (*Fremskrittspartiet*), who has a reputation as a hardliner. He believes that in order to avoid inadvertently punishing children

Figure 2.1 Child poverty in Norway and the UK

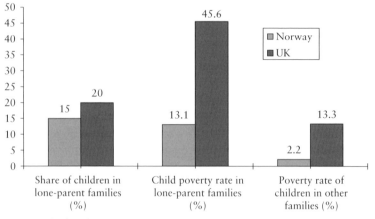

Source: UNICEF (2000).

for the crimes of their parents, mothers whose partners are in prison should be categorized as single to enable them to receive more state benefits (Ellingsen, 2007).

Social solidarity and the welfare state

When comparing any aspect of English and Norwegian culture it is important to be mindful that Norway's population is comparatively tiny. There are only about 4.6 million people in Norway, whereas the population of England and Wales is over 60.7 million. Norway also remains a relatively homogeneous place, in spite of growing concerns about immigration. The percentage of foreign-born populations in both Norway and the UK has been rising, though in Norway, it rose from 5.5 per cent in 1995 to only 7.8 per cent in 2004. The UK began in 1995 at a higher rate of 6.9 and has since risen to 9.3 per cent (OECD, 2007). Moreover, over 90 per cent of Norwegians identify themselves as Christian, while that proportion is less than 72 per cent in the UK (CIA World Factbook, 2007a, 2007b).

Due in part to this relative homogeneity, there is widespread agreement on common values in Norway, and because, unlike England, there is no history of feudalism and virtually no aristocracy (Egeland, 2007), an egalitarian concern for the common good is deeply rooted in Norway. It was also a poor country until relatively recently, and shared hardship and inter-reliance helped to forge strong social bonds (Larsson, 2007). The Nazi occupation of Norway during the Second World War did much to forge this sense of solidarity (Stjernø, 2005: 118–19). King Haakon VII and his son Crown Prince Olav fled the country when Germany invaded, and set up a government-in-exile in England. The Labour-led government's performance throughout the war conferred upon it a great deal of legitimacy on which it was able to draw to build a broad, social-democratic consensus after the war:

The battle against Nazism had brought people closer together, and the enormous work of reconstruction strengthened this cohesion. This was most clearly expressed in 1945, when all the political parties went to the polls with the same political manifesto, the Joint Programme (*Fellesprogrammet*). It had a clear social democratic bias and plainly showed that the Labour Party had gained an ideological advantage over the non-socialist parties...The war bonded people together in such a way that when it ended there was widespread agreement that the class warfare and want of the inter-war years must not return...In co-operation with private industry, the state would pave the way to a strong economic growth that would give people rising living standards and social stability. The Programme also stressed the reduction of unemployment and redistribution of wealth (Stenersen and Libæk, 2003: 133, 138)

A similar consensus also emerged in Britain, where Winston Churchill's government, a coalition of all three major parties, committed itself during the war to full employment and the building of a comprehensive welfare state based on the recommendations of the Beveridge Report. These plans were intended to heed 'the lessons of the Great Slump of the 1930s' and 'to make another Hitler impossible' (Hobsbawm, 1995: 162). The new political landscape saw a new unity of purpose emerge throughout the formerly occupied countries that united the political parties. This consensus would unravel in the years to come, but it remained more intact in Norway, with its multi-party, consensus model of democracy, than it did in England, with its divisive, partisan, majoritarian model of democracy.

The Norwegian welfare state was also built upon the ideas in the Beveridge Report (Stenersen and Libæk, 2003), which was published in Britain in 1942 to oppose the 'five giants on the road of reconstruction': Want, Disease, Ignorance, Squalor, and Idleness (Beveridge, 1942). It recommended that all workers pay national insurance which would be used to provide a minimum standard of living and ensure the care of those who could not work. Beveridge later recommended Keynesian economics and state control of the means of production to make such a state possible. Britain's welfare state, however, was never as comprehensive and universalist as Norway's, and tax rates were never as high (Cavadino and Dignan, 2006b).

Political Economy and Economic Conditions

Cavadino and Dignan (2006a; 2006b) recently developed a typology to characterize different types of political economy.[2] Appetites for punitive responses to crime tend to be highest in those countries where neo-liberalism dominates. Neo-liberalism arrived in Britain in the 1980s—though in a more diluted form than the American model–with the New Public Management movement under Margaret Thatcher, and has since continued under New Labour. It is premised on the belief that a large and interventionist public sector is inefficient and undermines individual autonomy. The remedy is the injection of private sector management principles into the public sector through privatization and more managerial, market-driven ways of thinking. With the neo-liberal project, 'The size of the public sector was to be reduced through privatization, its power delimited through deregulation, debureaucratization, and decentralization' (Olsen, 1996: 186).

The impact of neo-liberalism was much more muted in Norway. By the mid-1990s Norway had become one of the world's leading oil-producing nations. Since production began in 1971, $240 billion in oil revenues has been set aside in the Government Pension Fund (Energy Information Administration, 2007). Norway's oil wealth has buoyed its economy and has helped to stave off the kind of wholesale reconsideration of the welfare state that other countries like the UK have experienced (Olsen, 1996; Østerud, 2005). Its legitimacy has not been successfully challenged by neo-liberalism to the extent it has elsewhere. In addition, the integration of labour unions and interest groups within the institutions of government decision-making meant that neo-liberalism could be better resisted

---

[2] They distinguish between four types, only two of which are discussed here: neo-liberal (USA, England and Wales, Australia, New Zealand, South Africa), conservative corporatist (Germany, France, Italy, the Netherlands), social democratic corporatist (Sweden, Finland) and oriental corporatist (Japan).

than it could be in the UK and the USA, which lacked these corporatist institutions (Cavadino and Dignan, 2006b). Norway has also not been compelled to join the European Union. EU membership was rejected by narrow margins in referendums in 1972 and 1994, though Norway maintains associate member status and has signed up to the Schengen Agreement, which makes police coordination easier by abolishing border controls between Norway and the EU countries (Stenersen and Libæk, 2003).

In 1994, the year Silje Redergård was killed, unemployment rates in Norway reached a record high of 6.6 per cent. That year also saw UK unemployment reach a six-year high of 10.2 per cent. Between 1993 and 2005, the average was 6.5 per cent while in Norway it was 4.4 per cent. The percentage of long-term unemployed, those unemployed for more than a year, peaked in the UK in 1994 at 45.4 per cent, while Norway's rate peaked at 27.2 per cent the same year. The average between 1993 and 2005 in the UK was 32.1 per cent, a full two-and-a-half times the number in Norway where the average was 12.6 per cent over the period (OECD, 2007). The gap between the richest and the poorest is unsurprisingly smaller in Norway than in the UK,[3] and Norway spends considerably more on welfare and considerably less on law and order than the UK does (OECD, 2007).[4]

Reiner (2007) suggests neo-liberal countries like England and the other Anglo-Saxon countries 'tend to have a "dark heart" (Davies, 1998) of both serious crime and cruel punishment'. They tend to display, among other things, wide disparities between rich and poor, scaled-back welfare systems, high levels of social exclusion, right-wing political ideologies, exclusionary punishment systems, and high imprisonment rates (Cavadino and Dignan, 2006a). In contrast, Norway and the other Nordic

[3] In 2000 the poorest fifth of the Norwegian population earned 9.7 per cent of the total income while in the UK that figure was 6.1 per cent. The richest fifth in Norway earned 35.8 per cent of total income while in the UK they earned 43.2 per cent (World Resource Institute, 2003).

[4] According to comparative data compiled by the OECD, Norway spent an annual average of 3.7 per cent of GNP on law, order, and defence between 1993 and 2005, whereas the comparable figure over the same period in the UK was 5.6 per cent. Between 2001 and 2003, Norway increased its welfare expenditure (OECD's social expenditure figure) from 23.2 to 25 per cent of GDP. In the UK welfare expenditure stayed steady over the same period at around 20.1 per cent of GDP.

countries—which Cavadino and Dignan categorize as *social democratic corporatist*—have smaller cultural appetites for punishment, displaying inclusionary penal intervention, and low imprisonment rates. They also generally tend to be more egalitarian, have narrower income disparities, broad and strong welfare systems, low levels of social exclusion, and left-wing political ideologies. As Sutton (2004: 171) puts it, 'Demand for punishment seems to be higher in societies that have a strong commitment to individualistic means of social achievement and a correspondingly weak capacity for collective responses to inequality.'

Political Cultures

Consensus versus majoritarian democracy

Paraphrasing Almond and Verba (1963: 14–15), Arend Lijphart (1998: 99–100) defines political culture as 'a pattern of cognitive, affective, and evaluative orientations toward political objects among the members of a group, or, in simpler words, a group's pattern of political beliefs, feelings, and judgments'. His mentor, Gabriel Almond, discovered geographical patterns representing 'Anglo-American' and 'Continental European' systems when classifying democracies in his 1956 article 'Comparative Political Systems'. Lijphart (1998: 106) argues: 'To my mind, this geographical pattern strengthens the case for cultural explanation: I think that there is indeed . . . a major difference between the political cultures of the American and Continental European worlds, and that this cultural difference manifests itself *inter alia* in the different forms of democracy that are practiced in these two worlds'.

Lijphart has refined these distinctions through his study of Western democracies on five continents spanning a period of 150 years. He now distinguishes between two types: majoritarian democracy and consensus democracy[5] (Lijphart, 1998, 1999). Consensus and majoritarian political cultures are distinguished by the way in which political actors choose to interpret the common definition of democracy—'government by and for the people'

[5] The democratic approach now known as consensus democracy has undergone a series of name changes at the hands of Lijphart over the years. In earlier incarnations it was known as the 'politics of accommodation' (1968), 'consociational democracy' (1969), and 'power-sharing' (1985), each term generating conceptual problems that subsequent re-labellings were meant to solve.

(Lijphart, 1999). Majoritarian democracies interpret this to mean that the resolution of the conflict of citizen preferences ought to be done by majority. The interests of the majority determine the course of the policies formulated by their elected representatives. In contrast, the consensus model interprets the meaning of the same definition of democracy to mean 'as many people as possible. This is the crux of the consensus model. It does not differ from the majoritarian model in accepting that majority rule is better than minority rule, but it accepts majority rule only as a *minimum* requirement: instead of being satisfied with narrow decision-making majorities, it seeks to maximize the size of these majorities' (Lijphart, 1999: 2, emphasis in original).

Though Lijphart recognizes his distinction to be on a continuum, and is aware of the danger of blurring the smaller and important distinctions that exist between the wide range of nations included in his two categories, he nonetheless provides a useful dichotomy to apply to the study of democracies, one which has been overlooked by most criminologists who try to account for differing punishment levels in different countries. These models reflect fundamentally opposing assumptions about the ways political actors are meant to associate, both among themselves and with the people they represent. Consensus democracies like Norway tend to have coalition or minority governments, relatively strong legislatures rather than the strong executives of majoritarian democracies, multi-party systems, proportional election systems, and 'corporatist or coordinated interest group systems (instead of free-for-all competitive pluralism among interest groups)' as found in England and the USA (Lijphart, 1998: 103). Consensus democracy is a 'pattern of institutional characteristics that particular democracies have' (1998: 100), arranged in ways to produce the maximum amount of consensus between disparate stakeholders.

The implications of the ideal-typical consensus-majoritarian distinction are further explained in the chapters ahead, but at this stage it is important to note that majoritarian countries tend to demonstrate an 'exclusive, competitive, and adversarial' political culture (Lijphart, 1999: 2). They tend to have two-party systems, winner-takes-all election systems, and a zero-sum-game style of politics where one side's win is the other's loss—all the volatile ingredients that increase incentives to politicize crime and to engage in penal populism.

The consensual nature of Scandinavian political culture is particularly pronounced when comparisons are made with English or American majoritarian democracies. A Norwegian Conservative Party (*Høyre*) MP described the parliamentary atmosphere like this: 'Most of us are social democrats even though we're from the right [-leaning] party, so we're very egalitarian in our way of thinking. So it's a part of our culture that we try to agree with each other and try to find good solutions. And even though with television...you see us hating each other, but here in Parliament we are actually very good colleagues, and that is a tradition here...People from other countries are surprised by how collegial the environment is' (Dahl, 2007). Two politicians from the two most conservative parties admitted that on crime and punishment, all the parties agreed on about 95 per cent of the issues (Dahl, 2007; Ellingsen, 2007). This sharply contrasts with the attack-oriented, zero-sum-game approach to crime policy adopted so often by the opposition parties in England, even if English parliamentary arrangements retain some collegiality behind the scenes.

Tables 2.1 and 2.2 show the parties represented in Parliament in Norway and England.[6] The Liberal Democrats' influence in England has grown but it is still largely a two-horse race between Labour and the Conservatives. In Norway there are seven parties with proportional influence equal to or greater than that of the Liberal Democrats in England in recent decades.

Norway and the United Kingdom[7] are both constitutional monarchies. While the UK retains its bicameral Parliament with the House of Commons and House of Lords, Norway will soon abolish its smaller secondary parliamentary chamber (*Lagtinget*) and the *Storting* will become a unicameral legislature, creating a 'single penal bureaucracy' (Pratt, 2006). This means that Norwegian penal law should become more susceptible to influence, as only one bureaucratic barrier will stand in the way of change. But, as in Finland, which Pratt (2006) writes about, liberal influence in Norwegian penal matters still lives on, though in an admittedly more weakened state than before. This influence persists in part because trust in elites and in all institutions in Norway remains high.

---

[6] Sources for 1983–2001 data Leeke, 2003; 2005 data Mellows-Facer, 2005.

[7] The UK comprises England, Wales, Scotland, and Northern Ireland. Great Britain refers only to England, Wales, and Scotland.

Table 2.1 Parties in Parliament in Norway (% of seats)

	1981	1985	1989	1993	1997	2001	2005
Labour (*Arbeiderpartiet*)	43	45	38	41	39	26	36
Progress (*Fremskrittspartiet*)	3	1	13	6	15	16	22
Conservative (*Høyre*)	34	32	22	17	14	23	14
Christian Democrat (*Kristelig Folkepartiet*)	10	10	8	8	15	13	6.5
Centre (*Senterpartiet*)	7	8	7	19	7	14	6.5
Socialist Left (*Sosialistisk Venstrepartiet*)	3	4	10	8	5	6	9
Liberal (*Venstre*)	1	0	0	.6	4	1	6

Source: <http://electionresources.org/no/>.

Table 2.2 Parties in Parliament in England (% of seats)

	1983	1987	1992	1997	2001	2005
Labour	28	30	37	62	61	54
Conservative	69	68	61	31	31	37
Liberal Democrat	2	2	2	6	8	9

Source: 1983–2001 data Leeke (2003); 2005 data Mellows-Facer (2005).

Trust and civil society

English politicians are much more preoccupied with boosting and building public confidence in government and state institutions than are their Norwegian counterparts. In fact, one Norwegian journalist from *Aftenposten*, the country's largest broadsheet newspaper, fluent in English, who was interviewed for this study, did not understand what was meant by the salience in Norwegian politics of measures to 'build public confidence' in government. He could not understand why a government would need to do such a thing (Bjørkeng, 2003). Under Tony Blair's leadership, building public confidence often took the form of more legislation, criminalization, and penalization to signal that the government was responding to public concerns. The English government has made the year-on-year improvement of public confidence in the criminal justice system an explicit target in its Public Service Agreement (Hough and Roberts, 2004). Gordon Brown (2007) focused prominently on the need to 'renew people's trust in government' in his very first statement as prime minister. Whether he approaches this goal any differently than Blair did remains to be seen, but the evidence suggests he has reason to be concerned.

Paloheimo (2004) compiled European Social Survey data from 2002/3 on the public's participation in civil society in fifteen countries. On a range of measures of political participation—including voting, directly contacting politicians, working for a political party or other organization, signing a petition, joining a demonstration or protest, and reading a newspaper—Norway scored higher than the UK on every measure. Adding together the percentages of respondents who were politically active in various ways, Norway scored 143 and the UK scored only 93. Of Norwegian respondents rating their trust in politicians on a 10-point Likert scale, with 0 registering no trust at all and 10 registering complete trust, 31.2 per cent rated their trust between 6 and 10 on the scale. Only 21.9 per cent of UK respondents did so. 11.2 percent of UK respondents rated their trust at the 0 level whereas only 3.4 per cent of Norwegians did so.

In contrast to England, the state and its institutions retain high levels of public confidence in Norway. Though the occasional scandal may shake people's faith in particular politicians, the system itself retains legitimacy. 'People trust the state', as one Conservative MP remarked (Dahl, 2007). It is viewed as benign, well-intentioned, and reasonably efficient. Even the right-wing Progress Party—the populist party which often employs New Labour-style, tough-on-crime rhetoric[8]—remains committed to social democracy and a strong state. As a consequence, neoliberalism never took firm hold in Norway because 'institutional elites in Norway viewed an interventionist, planning state with a large public sector as a suitable means for promoting the common good' (Olsen, 1996: 186).

---

[8] The party's justice spokesman and first deputy chair of the justice committee, Jan Arild Ellingsen, spoke admiringly about the forthright manner with which Blair talked about law and order (Ellingsen, 2007).

The Norwegian combination of comparatively low immigration rates and high cultural homogeneity, low unemployment, a strong welfare state, and high levels of trust in state institutions has mitigated late-modern 'ontological insecurity' (Giddens, 1990) and the crisis of state sovereignty (Garland, 1996, 2001) that are said to have struck the neo-liberal countries so powerfully in recent decades. As the sovereignty of nations erodes with globalization—less so in Norway than in the UK, which is a member of the EU—fewer outcomes are subject to direct government control. Hardin (2006: 162) argues, 'To some extent, we are losing confidence in government precisely because we no longer think we need it in the important realm of the economy'. He believes trust in governments has eroded because many governments have accepted the triumph of neo-liberalism, and now politicians bicker instead about more trivial issues in increasingly noisy and bitter ways. This suggests that politicians focus on those aspects of political life where they can have influence, and criminal justice is one policy area where tough, symbolic rhetoric draws attention (Falck, 2002; Pollack, 2007).

This is not to say late-modern insecurity has not affected the Nordic countries. The salience of crime in the media and in political debates has increased in recent decades in Norway as in England. The Norwegian justice committee was once a political backwater but now has a high profile because of the media's interest in crime (Christie, 2004). Pollack (2002) has shown how Swedish politicians have since the 1990s become leading participants in crime debates when formerly such debates were dominated by experts.

However, it may be the case that because the Norwegian welfare state remains strong and relatively expansive relative to England's, politicians in Norway retain more control over economic matters than their English counterparts and thus retain more trust. In addition, the consensual approach to doing politics in Norway also makes the noisy and bitter sort of adversarial politics found in majoritarian counties like England and the USA less palatable to Norwegians. As the chapters ahead explore, political cultures condition the ways in which crime is featured in political debates, the reasons why it is—or is not—enlisted for political ends, and the nature of the accumulating discourse created and used to make sense of it.

Media Markets and Cultures

Press markets

England's national press differs considerably from that of the catch-all, omnibus press that normally characterizes the 'liberal media system model' typically found in majoritarian countries (Allern, 2007; Hallin and Mancini, 2004). Such a press tends to act as a 'neutral servant of the public as a whole' (Hallin and Mancini, 2004: 51), but the English press is highly partisan and class-stratified, and the market is probably the most competitive in the world (Rooney, 2000; Sparks, 1999). There are ten national daily newspapers in England—three popular-market 'tabloids',[9] two mid-market titles, and five broadsheets. Nearly half of British daily newspaper readers read either the tabloid *Sun*, *Daily Mirror*, or *Daily Star* (*Guardian*, 2007a).[10] The *Sun* alone has 3,072,392 daily readers, 28 per cent of the entire daily newspaper market. Twenty-eight per cent of English readers choose the mid-market *Daily Mail* or *Daily Express*. Thus, the tabloid and mid-market press together retain 77 per cent of the market, enjoying readerships that dwarf those of the broadsheet *Daily Telegraph*, *The Times*, *Guardian*, *Independent*, and *Financial Times*, whose combined totals retain just 23 per cent of the market. Though overall circulation figures have been dropping for years, the market shares of each segment have remained stable in relative terms.

By most measures, Norway has the highest per capita newspaper readership in the world (Østbye, 2002). Unlike in England, most newspapers in Norway—and in Scandinavia generally—are local or regional and are sold by subscription (Lappi-Seppälä, 2007; Selbyg, 1986). This may act as a brake on the kind of sensationalism that defines the English tabloid front pages at the newsstands. There are only two large-circulation national dailies

---

[9] 'Tabloid' is the term used to refer to the popular press titles, as distinguished from the mid-market and quality broadsheet newspapers. These terms have become confusing in recent years as many of the quality newspapers have moved to smaller tabloid-sized editions. I nonetheless use the traditional tabloid and broadsheet distinctions throughout the book.

[10] Circulation figures at the time James Bulger was killed in 1993: *Sun*: 3,833,539; *Daily Mirror*: 2,656,856; *Daily Mail*: 744,030, *Daily Telegraph*: 1,017,291; *Guardian*: 404,639; *The Times*: 375,495; *Independent*: 336,004; *Financial Times*: 285,203 (*Guardian*, 17 October 1994).

in Norway and both are tabloids. Though each has political sympathies, their editorial lines tend to be far more independent and objective than their English comparators. *Verdens Gang* or *VG*, with centre-right sympathies and a circulation of around 388,000, competes with the liberal-leaning *Dagbladet*, with a circulation of approximately 191,000. These two papers account for only about 20 per cent of the total newspaper circulation in Norway, and most readers who regularly read them do so along with another title (Høyer, 2000; Larsson, 2007). The newpaper with the second largest overall circulation, and the largest regional paper, is *Aftenposten*, the independent but conservative-leaning quality daily whose distribution is focused around Oslo in the southeast of the country. It has a circulation of around 263,000 for its morning edition and 168,000 for its separate evening edition, and is considered the country's dominant serious newspaper. Ninety-three per cent of *Aftenposten*'s sales are by subscription. In contrast, *VG* and *Dagbladet* rely mostly upon casual sales, like the English papers do. There are a few other daily papers distributed nationally from Oslo, but they are smaller and tend to target smaller, specialized readerships. These include *Dagens Næringsliv* (69,262), a financial paper, *Vårt Land* (26,782), the Christian newspaper, *Nationen* (16,987), the agrarian Centre Party newspaper, and *Klassekampen* (7,178), the small, socialist newspaper. While newspaper circulation figures have fallen steadily in the last few decades in England, Norway's have remained relatively stable over the same period (Høyer, 2000).

The Norwegian press is driven less by market-driven concerns and entertainment values than the highly competitive English press. The dominance of the English market by the tabloids means also that the style and tone of dominant press discourses tend to reflect sensationalism, conflict, anti-elite bias, common-sense solutions, and outrage. As shown in Chapter 7, the Norwegian press displays fewer of these traits. The great majority of newspaper readers read local or regional newspapers in Norway sold by subscription. This difference from the English press market implies several things. First, because these local papers serve relatively small audiences in smaller communities, they are more in touch with their readers and are more careful in their reporting. This is because if they are careless and too often make mistakes, readers might cancel their subscriptions, which could ruin a small newspaper. Inaccuracy and disgruntled readers can have personal costs as well. 'In all these local newspapers, journalists know that they are meeting their readers and their sources at the supermarket, at the school, and the sports club' (Allern, 2007), so they do not want to act in a way that will make living in the community uncomfortable. The few big national papers need not be so concerned about losing a few irritated readers. Second, editors are less likely to put potentially upsetting news on the front page, as the two national tabloids frequently do, in order to avoid antagonizing their readers. They are careful to consider whether 'people will still want them on the breakfast table' (Allern, 2007).

Prior to 1884 when Norway's parliamentary system was established, the press served the function of the political parties and thus the newspapers afterward remained duly aligned with the parties for nearly 100 years (Høyer, 2000; Østbye, 2002). This began to change in the 1970s, when journalism became significantly more professional and independent, as many newspapers broke their traditional links with the political parties (Røssland, 2007b). Since then, the number of monopoly newspaper markets has grown (Høst, 1999), and only ten local markets now retain two competing local newspapers (Høyer, 2000). Most papers are now omnibus papers that maintain political neutrality in an attempt to appeal to the range of readers in an area, regardless of their political affiliations. All publications are exempt from VAT in the UK. In Norway, reflecting the cultural 'assumption that media are a social institution and not simply a private business' (Hallin and Mancini, 2004: 163), only the Norwegian daily newspapers are exempted from VAT, while the more entertainment-oriented weekly newspapers are not (Høyer, 2000; Østbye, 2002).

At a Thames Valley police leadership class on policing and the media in April 2006, two tabloid journalists, one from the *Sun* and the other from the *Oxford Mail*, responded to a presentation by criminologist Martin Innes about the interrelationship between the police and journalists in the wake of serious 'signal crimes'.[11] The *Sun* reporter blamed the police and their reticence for any inaccuracies that might appear in the *Sun*'s crime stories. Both reporters spoke of the pressure to write 450 words on a particular story, whether the police will confirm facts or not. If the police will not, reporters must run with information they

---

[11] Signal crimes are high-profile crimes that are interpreted by those in an area as visible signs of high risk levels (Innes, 2003, 2004a, 2004b).

receive from other, perhaps less trustworthy sources. And if the police will not provide a photo of a murder victim, the reporter will need to go on a 'death knock', 'doorstepping' the family and neighbours for photos of and information about the victim. The Norwegian context differs in that there is less pressure to run with a story based on unconfirmed facts. Due to the high number of journalists competing with each other in a newsroom, the problem for journalists in Norway is to get a story printed, and only the best stories will be (Allern, 2007).

The Norwegian press differs in another important way from the English press. 'British society has been much more clearly marked by class divisions than Norway's. The division between *quality press* and *popular press* has likewise been much more clear-cut in Britain. Norwegian newspapers may be termed "popular" but still contain many elements that can be considered as characteristic of the "quality" press. They have been termed schizophrenic (for example Gripsrud, 1992: 85) because of this mixed profile' (Røssland, 2007b: 140). This schizophrenia is evident in *VG* and *Dagbladet* that combine some of the most trivial and sensationalist content with some of the best investigative journalism and political analysis (Allern, 2007; Egeland, 2007; Røssland, 2007a). That Norwegian tabloids differ considerably from their English comparators will be more clearly demonstrated in Chapter 7 when the analysis of the Bulger and Redergård case coverage is presented.

Until 1992, when TV2 became the country's first private, commercial, terrestrial television channel, Norway had only one terrestrial public broadcasting television station, run by the NRK, the Norwegian equivalent to the BBC. NRK only launched a second channel in 1996. TVNorge is a private station that has been on air since 1988, but it was initially available only on satellite and cable. Since the 1990s, with the proliferation of cable and satellite channels, competition in the area of crime news has escalated and even the NRK stations are covering crime more prominently. 'The last two decades have also shown a wide acceptance among Norwegian media that crime should be covered quite extensively, also by media previously unlikely to carry much crime news' (Røssland, 2007b: 140).[12]

---

[12] Two recent criminal cases provide examples of the increasing salience of crime news in Norway. The 1999 Orderud case involving a triple murder, and the Baneheia case—which involved two young men, aged 19 and 21, who raped

This proliferation of crime news has had an interesting, counterintuitive effect on the tabloids. Those at *VG* claim that crime sells fewer of their own papers than it used to (Laure and Haavik, 2002). Before the arrival of TV2 and the expansion of the news media market in Norway, *VG* and *Dagbladet* cornered the market on Norwegian crime coverage, drawing weeks of coverage from one major murder or 'good kill'. Now, because other media outlets have begun to cover crime as predominantly as the tabloids have, *VG* and *Dagbladet* have actually had to limit their own coverage of particular cases. Competition for crime stories has meant that stories no longer have the legs to be front-page fodder for as long as they used to. Now it is estimated that a crime story that would have formally produced two months of stories will now only yield two or three days of coverage (Laure and Haavik, 2002).

Of course, there are political consequences that accompany this proliferation of crime news, in Norway as elsewhere. As one observer put it, 'Of course, if *VG* and *Dagbladet* attack a problem and write a lot about it, then you will have TV2 coming on and then something from the NRK. And all of these types of web newspapers will be on the same level, will be very active, writing a lot about it. So the pressure, the media pressure, is much more. It's tougher today than just 10 years ago. You have all these different types, and you have some of the commercial radio channels going the same way' (Allern, 2007). Røssland (2007a) argues that an axis exists between TV2, *VG*, and the Progress Party on crime issues that tends to ratchet up public concern and raise the profile of crime. Though the Progress Party tends to score high in opinion polls, often edging out Labour as the most popular party, its role as an anti-government, protest party means it can play fast and loose with its rhetoric (Larsson, 2007). It is possible that because it does not have to make good on its frequent promises to get tough on crime, the Progress Party is actually more influential out of power than in, pulling the traditional parties a bit further to the right. Raising the rhetorical profile of crime has meant that other parties have had to follow rhetorical suit when the Progress Party publicly responds to the front pages of

and murdered two young girls aged 8 and 10 in Kristiansand in 2000—generated unprecedented levels of press coverage. *VG* set an all-time record by selling over 500,000 issues featuring a front-page story on the Orderud case in the summer of 1999 (Røssland, 2007a).

the tabloids or agrees with TV2's talk-show moderator's emotive demands for swift and demonstrable action against crime (Dahl, 2007; Røssland, 2007a).

Ownership

In both countries, press ownership is concentrated, though considerably more so in England. Up until the 1980s, Norwegian newspapers were mostly individually and locally owned, and while most of the small, local newspapers remain independent, this picture has since changed dramatically for the larger newspapers. Three companies—Schibsted ASA, Orkla Media, and A-Pressen—own around 60 per cent of Norwegian newspaper titles (Østbye, 2000). Schibsted is the largest and owns both the tabloid *VG* and the broadsheet *Aftenposten*. Schibsted actually wholly or partly owns nine of the ten largest circulation newspapers (Harro-Loit, 2005). In the UK, four companies own 90 per cent of newspapers (Bromley, 2001). Rupert Murdoch's News International, part of his News Corporation, alone owns *The Times*, the *Sunday Times*, the *Sun,* and the *News of the World*—a third of the UK newspaper market (Darnton, 1995; Hargreaves, 2003). All of these are most often sympathetic to a conservative agenda, though the *Sun* has supported Labour in every election since 1997 when Blair successfully lobbied for its support. The Rothermore family of Associated Newspapers owns the conservative *Daily Mail* and the *Mail on Sunday.* The Mirror Newspaper Group formerly owned by Robert Maxwell owns the left-leaning *Daily Mirror* and *Sunday Mirror* as well as the Sunday tabloid the *People.* Richard Desmond's Express Newspapers owns both the daily and Sunday editions of the conservative *Daily Express* and the *Daily Star.*

Rupert Murdoch is particularly well known for his powerful conservative political influence, and politicians tend to be very conscious of the influence of the tabloids, as elaborated further in Chapter 8. Conservative Party treasurer, Lord McAlpine, credited the tabloids with swinging the 1992 English general election toward the Conservative Party, and the *Sun* claimed a victory of its own with the headline 'It's The *Sun* Wot Won It' (*Sun,* 12 April 1992). Kinnock himself considered the tabloids to have been crucial in his defeat, a view supported by post-election MORI poll research and a Labour Party inquiry (Jones, 2001). Murdoch and the *Sun* backed Blair and New Labour in 1997, but only after Blair—with the aid of his communications director and former tabloid journalist, Alastair Campbell—launched a campaign to woo Murdoch.

Tabloid editors in England have candidly admitted their intentions to shape government crime policy. In a letter to Lord Windlesham (1996) about his editorial policy, Paul Dacre of the *Daily Mail* lamented that 'Persistent offenders under 15 years old are hardly ever taken into custody. We do want custodial sentences for persistent young offenders. We do want those who offend on bail to be suitably punished. In areas such as these, it is the aim of the *Daily Mail* to influence Government policy. Surely it is salutary for ministers in office to be made aware of the growing anger and anxiety of those who entrusted them with power. So, yes, this newspaper does seek to articulate the concern of its readers and, thereby, harden the response from this Tory administration' (quoted in Windlesham, 1996: 47). To harden government responses, the tabloids frequently run campaigns to further conservative agendas. The most notable of these are the clip-out coupons in the *Sun* urging the Home Secretary to keep the killers of James Bulger in prison for life, and the 'naming and shaming' of sex offenders in the *News of the World*, which famously spurred several vigilante incidents. This interventionist and activist agenda was in evidence more recently in the *Sun*'s name-and-shame, 'Sack the Softie' campaign in June 2006 which published the photographs of 'the top judges guilty of being soft on killers, child sex beasts, rapists and other violent criminals'. The *Sun* implored its readers to 'Force them to give us real justice' (*Sun*, 12 June 2006).

That crime is ever rising and worsening and that judges are by and large liberal 'softies' are consistent and recurrent themes in the *Sun*. Unsurprisingly, worry among English tabloid readers has consistently been twice as high as among broadsheet readers, and public knowledge is much lower among tabloid readers, with nearly twice as many believing that crime is increasing 'a lot' in spite of actual declines (Fletcher and Allen, 2003; Patterson and Thorpe, 2006). This relationship is considered more fully in the chapters ahead, but Sigurd Allern (2007), a Norwegian media scholar and former newspaper editor, could not think of one instance when a Norwegian newspaper campaigned for a cause in the way that the *Sun* and *News of the World* frequently do.

Biased agendas can be introduced slightly more subtly, too. Sky News is a rolling 24-hour television news channel in the UK owned by Murdoch's News Corporation. One if its Sunrise programme presenters is Eamonn Holmes, who, as mentioned in the previous chapter, also writes a column in the *People*. On the morning of 24 January 2007, the major morning news programmes led with a story about how the Home Secretary, John Reid, had written a letter reminding judges of the government's policy—often stated but often contradicted—that prison should be used only for serious and persistent offenders. Reid was pressed to take this action by severe prison overcrowding. The *Daily Mail* grossly exaggerated Reid's request with the front-page headline: 'Ministers Beg Judges—Don't Jail Any More Criminals!' Eamonn Holmes offered his own personal view on the controversy, saying that if anyone wanted to commit a crime, now was the time because they would 'get away with it'. This open criticism of judicial policy by a morning news presenter is remarkable in itself, but so is the assumption embedded within it that offenders are getting away with crime whenever they receive any punishment other than prison.

Accountability

The ethical codes governing the practice of journalism in both countries are similar, but how they are enforced differs significantly. Compliance with the Norwegian 'Be Careful Code' (*Vær Varsom-plakaten*) is policed by Norway's Press Complaints Commission, the *Pressens Faglige Utvalg* (PFU). The PFU is composed of four journalists and three prominent members of the public (Røssland, 2005). The UK Press Complaints Commission (PCC) has seventeen members, the majority of whom are lay people with no connections to the press, though Paul Dacre, the *Daily Mail*'s outspoken editor, is a PCC member. The PCC's Code of Practice prohibits many things, like the identification of children under sixteen, but exceptions can be made to most prohibitions in service to the nebulous concept of the 'public interest' (Press Complaints Commission, 2006). The PCC's clout has been weakened as newspaper ownership has been concentrated, and 'the *Sun* has regularly flouted its rulings' (Jones, 2001: 195). The PCC has been referred to as a 'toothless lion' (*Hansard*, col 687, 23 April 1993). Its 'rhetoric is strong, but its powers weak' (Hargreaves, 2003: 215).

Journalistic standards are higher in Norway and a sanction from the PFU is taken seriously (Allern, 2007; Egeland, 2007; Laure and Haavik, 2002). The first Norwegian Press Council that developed the ethical code was actually established in 1928 in response to 'heavy criticism of intolerable and irresponsible crime coverage' which was filled with speculation and gruesome detail (Røssland, 2007b: 141). And the success of the PFU has been due in part to a fear of the alternative to a self-governing body. Press freedom is highly valued in Norway, and should the PFU be deemed to be insufficiently robust in enforcing its own ethical guidelines, another system with a stronger state role might be implemented instead (Egeland, 2007).

Conclusion

This chapter is the first of two comparing various aspects of Norwegian and English culture and politics. Norway and England differ significantly across each of the dimensions discussed so far. Norway is a strong and egalitarian welfare state that retains high levels of public confidence. In England the welfare state has eroded and a neo-liberal political economy has emerged. Public confidence in the ability of the state to do things well has declined as political parties practise a highly partisan, adversarial style of politics. The English press tends to have overt political biases and embraces interventionist agendas on issues of crime and punishment in ways that have yet to be witnessed in Norway. All of these factors condition the ways in which crime and punishment are experienced, and more specifically, the ways in which the Redergård and Bulger homicides were interpreted—by the public, by politicians, and by the press. Attention now turns to the experience of crime and punishment in the two countries.

3

Crime and Punishment in Norway and England

This chapter continues with the last chapter's profiles that are together intended to enable the reader to situate both the Bulger and Redergård homicides in a local context. This chapter focuses exclusively on issues of crime and punishment. The first section compares aspects of the legal systems in both countries. The second examines various comparative indicators of crime rates and dispels the myth that Norway and England differ drastically in their experiences of crime and victimization. The third section compares punishment rates in various ways to reveal how much more punitive England has been when compared with Norway. The fourth section compares and contrasts recent developments in youth justice, including the extent that juveniles are incarcerated. The last section compares the available data on fear of crime and the punitiveness of public attitudes toward crime and punishment. Locating reliably comparable indicators of crime and punitiveness is a very difficult task, and deploying them in a setting like this is a dangerous but unavoidable business (Muncie and Goldson, 2006a). There are useful findings that might be defensibly used to paint portraits of Norway and England, but this requires reliance upon multiple indicators.

Legal Systems

Unlike the UK, Norway has had a written constitution since 1814. The legal systems of both countries are based a combination of common law and civil law traditions. Legal procedure in Norway reflects the adversarial system, but also retains aspects of the inquisitorial system, too. The court may clarify the evidence or order that more evidence be obtained (Strandbakken, 2001). Rules of evidence are simpler than in common law countries and all evidence is admissible (Bygrave, 1997). Unlike in England, plea bargaining is not permitted. The Norwegian Penal Code was enacted in 1902 and has been amended many times since. The Law Commission has been working on a new draft of the Penal Code for over two decades (Bygrave, 1997).

Norway has a three-tiered court system and lay participation in it is high. Criminal cases are heard in the District Courts (*Byretten* or *Herredsretten*) by a 'mixed court' of one professional judge and two lay judges, or by two professional judges and three lay judges in more serious cases (Strandbakken, 2001). Unlike lay magistrates in English magistrates' courts, who receive training and serve for extended periods, lay judges in Norway have no legal training and are recruited for single trials as jurors are. There are no juries in the District Courts. Ten-member juries do sit in the second-tier High Court or Court of Appeals (*Lagmannsretten*), but only in serious cases punishable for a term of over six years' imprisonment. Otherwise, the mixed court approach in the lower court is followed, but with three professional judges and four lay judges.

At least seven of the ten jurors must agree on guilt, though the professional judges have the right to overrule a jury's verdict in exceptional cases. Juries do not provide reasons for their verdicts, and critics have, on this basis, pushed to abolish jury trials and replace them with mixed courts. Reasons are given for the sentence. Peculiarly distinct from English practice, lay people actually outnumber judges when High Court sentences are decided. The judges consider the sentence along with the jury foreman and three other jurors chosen by lot (Strandbakken, 2001). High Court judgments can be appealed to the Supreme Court (*Høyesteretten*) where five professional judges preside. They do not reconsider the guilty verdict and 'only deal with sentencing, procedural errors or the application of the law' (Strandbakken, 2001: 232).

Crime

Recorded crime

The proposition that crime rates had something to do with both the muted response to the killing of Silje Redergård and the explosive responses to the Bulger murder does not withstand scrutiny. If we take levels of recorded crime trends as a reasonable indicator of the extent of crime—at least one that the public might occasionally encounter in press coverage or in the statements of politicians—it appears there are grounds to support the view that

Figure 3.1 Intentional homicide (completed) in Norway and England and Wales (per 100,000 population)

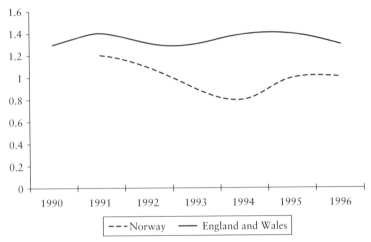

Source: WODC (1999: Table 1.B.1.2).

Norwegians should have been as or even more concerned about crime than their English counterparts.

Figure 3.1 shows the homicide rates in both countries between 1990 and 1996 (WODC, 1999). While this rate declined in the years leading up to the Redergård killing, the trend reversed itself in 1994, and other data show that between 1994 and 1998, homicide rates rose by 12 per cent in Norway to a rate of 0.86 per 100,000 population (Barclay and Tavares, 2000). Though homicide rates were then and are now higher in England and Wales, between 1994 and 1998 they remained more stable and rose by only 3 per cent in England to 1.43 per 100,000 population (Barclay and Tavares, 2000). Though rising faster in the figures, the considerably lower homicide rate in Norway might be considered predictable, considering Norway's reputation as a safe, low-crime society. However, other findings challenge these pat expectations.

Table 3.1 displays some of the little available and comparable recorded crime data from Norway and England that is reasonably contemporaneous with the two murder cases.[1] These data show

[1] The Home Office has compiled and compared cross-national recorded data for each year from 1998 to 2001 (Barclay and Tavares, 2000, 2002, 2003; Barclay, Tavares and Siddique, 2001). The earliest of these data, published in 2000, are

Table 3.1 Recorded crime in Norway and England and Wales*

	Violent crime 1994–8	Overall recorded crime** 1989–90	1998 homicide rate per 100,000 population
Norway	+25%	+33%	0.86 (+12% 1994–8)
England and Wales	+9%	+22%	1.43 (+3% 1994–8)

Source: *Barclay and Tavares (2000).
**Barclay, Tavares and Siddique (2001).

crime rates and trends in the 1990s. Between 1994 and 1998, recorded violent crime rose by 25 per cent in Norway and only 9 per cent in England. Between 1989 and 1999, the period during which James Bulger and Silje Redergård were killed, overall recorded crime rose by 33 per cent in Norway, a faster rate than in England where it rose by 22 per cent. Though the rise of overall crime in Norway was due to the targeting of greater police resources on drug offences (Larsson, 2007), any rise in the figures could nonetheless be interpreted by the public and by politicians as a cause for concern. Moreover, the most recent comparative data show that these sharper rises in Norway persisted. Between 1991 and 2001, overall recorded crime rose by 28 per cent in Norway during which time it actually fell by 11 per cent in England (Barclay and Tavares, 2003). In spite of this, average police numbers per 100,000 population between 1999 and 2001 were 178 in Norway and 241 in England and Wales (Barclay and Tavares, 2003).

Figures 3.2 and 3.3 show trends in overall recorded crime in both countries from 1988 to 1998 (Barclay and Tavares, 2000: Table 1). A consistent decline in England and Wales began at the time of the Bulger murder after peaking in 1992. The opposite occurred in Norway. After remaining relatively flat, recorded crime actually began to rise significantly just before the killing of Silje Redergård. On the basis of a range of indicators, then, overall recorded crime, violent crime, and homicide all should have appeared in the 1990s to be rising faster in Norway than

used in Table 3.1. The first edition of the *European Sourcebook of Crime and Criminal Justice Statistics* also contains some additional comparative data from 1990 to 1996.

Figure 3.2 Police recorded crime in England and Wales, 1988–98

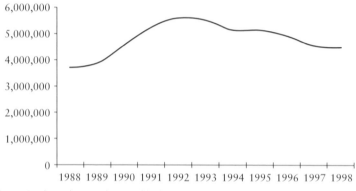

Source: Barclay and Tavares (2000: Table 1).

Figure 3.3 Police recorded crime in Norway, 1988–98

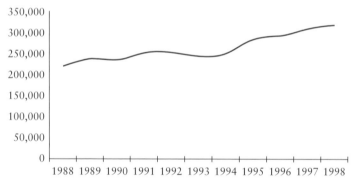

Source: Barclay and Tavares (2000: Table 1).

in England and Wales. In the wake of the killings, the recorded crime figures suggest there might have been considerable cause for concern in Norway, while concern in England ought to have declined.

Victimization

Of course, recorded crime is a highly flawed comparative measure because of differences in policing and in how and which offences are counted. For this reason, criminologists tend to favour

Table 3.2 Victimization rates in 1989 in Norway and England and Wales (% victimized one or more times in previous year)*

	Index of 10 crimes**	Robbery	Other personal theft	Pickpocketing	Assaults and threats	Assault with force	Sexual incidents among women	Sexual assaults among women
Norway	27.6	0.5	3.2	0.5	3.0	1.6	2.3	0.6
England and Wales	28.7	0.9	3.7	1.4	2.8	1.1	1.7	0.3

Source. *1989 ICVS (van Dijk and Mayhew, 1992)

**1989 ICVS (van Kesteren, Mayhew and Nieuwbeerta, 2000).

victimization survey data as a better, though certainly not ideal, comparative indicator of crime trends. These data also confound expectations and suggest remarkably similar victimization rates in both countries, according at least to the 1989 International Crime Victimization Survey (ICVS), the only such data available at the time of writing. In fact, as concerns a number of the most serious personal offences shown in Table 3.2, including assaults and sexual offences, Norwegian rates were actually higher.

By these measures it appears Norwegian victimization experience was not so different from English experience during the years preceding the two killings. If one believes that England's crime rates at the time when James Bulger was killed meant the English had plenty to be concerned about, then the same should have held true for Norwegians when Silje Redergård was killed as well. However, as the next section shows, England significantly increased its use of various punishments since the Bulger case, whereas punishment rates in Norway have remained relatively stable. So any analysis that seeks to account for Norway's comparatively benign disposition towards crime and punishment must look beyond crime and victimization rates for explanations.

Punishment

Debates persist over the suitability of various measures to compare the relative punitiveness of nations. The imprisonment rate is the most readily available barometer and the one most frequently used by scholars (Sutton, 2004; Wilkins, 1991). Some, however, like Young and Brown (1993: 8), suggest imprisonment rates are a flawed indicator in part because counting rules differ between countries, and because they 'obscure the three most important dimensions in understanding imprisonment practices: the relative influences of the remand and sentenced populations, the relative influence of the number of custodial admissions and the average length of detention, and the effect of parole and remission'. In addition, some countries have low imprisonment rates but higher rates of prison admissions than others. For instance, Norway has an imprisonment rate of 66 per 100,000 population compared to the rate in England and Wales of 149. But when considering prison admission rates, the gap between the two countries closes considerably: 239 per 100,000 population in Norway versus 249 in England and Wales (Aebi and Stadnic, 2007). In this instance, the pattern of greater Norwegian leniency survives, indicating that Norway sends fewer offenders to prison and for less time than England and Wales. However, because these two measures can contradict each other—as in Sweden where imprisonment is often used but for short periods and in Switzerland where the opposite is the case (Blumstein, Tonry, and Van Ness, 2007)—Young and Brown (1993) argue that a better measure would account for prison admissions, sentence lengths, crime rates, prosecutions, convictions, and sentences. Others consider a range of additional measures of punitiveness (Blumstein, 2007). Rather than reconcile any of these differences of opinion, I rely instead upon as many comparative measures as possible to compare English and Norwegian punitiveness, all of which consistently portray Norway as the more lenient of the two countries, sometimes dramatically so.

Imprisonment rates

According to recent Council of Europe statistics, between 2000 and 2005, prison populations increased in 20 of the 29 European countries for which data was available (Aebi and Stadnic, 2007: 20). In fact, both Norway and England and Wales experienced similar percentage increases of 14 and 15 per cent, respectively. Though these recent growth rates might be similar, there is much to distinguish Norway's prison populations and imprisonment rates from those of England and Wales (see Figure 3.4). In

Figure 3.4 Imprisonment rates per 100,000 population in Norway and England and Wales

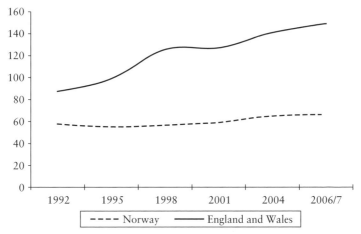

Source: World Prison Brief (International Centre for Prison Studies, 2007).

1993, the year James Bulger was killed, the imprisonment rate in England and Wales was 90 prisoners per 100,000 of the population, a rate that Norway has yet even to approach. This has risen 66 per cent since 1993 to 149 per 100,000 of the population. Though Norway's imprisonment rate has been rising year on year since 2000, it has remained stable in relative terms since 1993, hovering between 55 and 66 per 100,000 of the population (International Centre for Prison Studies, 2007). Going a bit farther back, using collected figures for both countries from 1991 (Barclay and Tavares, 2003) and the most recent available figures (International Centre for Prison Studies, 2007), England and Wales has seen a 73 per cent increase in its prison population over this period, from 46,310 to 80,316, while Norway's has increased by 20 per cent, from 2,548 to 3,048. These figures suggest that imprisonment is being utilized more in both countries, but on a scale that is hardly comparable.

Prison regimes and conditions

Both countries' prison systems are at or over capacity, and both countries have recently set new records in the numbers they incarcerate. To relieve overcrowding and to avoid the building of new prisons, English prisoners have recently been housed on wings that were formerly closed after being deemed unfit for human habitation (Chidzoy, 2007). In Norway, to accomplish the same goals, low-level offenders wait in a queue for their turn to serve their sentences. There may be as many as 4,000 offenders currently on the waiting list (Nilsen, 2006). These offenders are not counted when imprisonment rates and prison population figures are calculated, but the short sentences they serve once a place avails itself means counting them would not affect the figures very much. Most have been sentenced for drink driving or failing to pay fines, and all will serve less than six months, most less than three months, and many only twenty-one days (Falck, 2007).

Norway has twenty-nine open prisons, the smallest of which holds five prisoners, and thirty-two closed prisons, the largest of which has the capacity for 380 (Kristoffersen, 2007). There are plans to build a new prison, which would become the country's largest, to house as many as 400 prisoners (Bjerva, 2007). The three largest prisons are Oslo, Bergen, and Åna with a capacity of 354, 197, and 195 prisoners, respectively (www.straffet.com, 2007). In contrast, the three largest English prisons are Wandsworth, Birmingham, and Liverpool which hold 1,480, 1,453, and 1,349 prisoners, respectively (HM Prison Service, 2007). Of the 140 penal establishments in England and Wales, only fifteen are open prisons (BBC News, 2007).

The mission statement of the Norwegian Ministry of Justice and the Police reads as follows:

The Government will pursue an active and coherent policy of combating crime. Ensuring the security of citizens is a welfare issue and a major public responsibility. The goal is to improve prevention, solve more crimes, react more quickly and improve the rehabilitation of offenders. All this requires making determined efforts aimed at the police, the courts and the correctional services.

The Ministry of Justice and the Police shall

- reduce and prevent crime
- improve civil protection and emergency planning
- contribute to expedient legislation that is adapted to societal developments
- safeguard the due process of law and right to a fair trial
- implement punishment whose goal is to return offenders to a normal life in community
- prevent and resolve conflicts. (Norwegian Ministry of Justice and the Police, 2007)

These aims and objectives that are focused on welfare-oriented reintegration, prevention, and due process contrast rather strikingly with those of the UK's Home Office, where the protection of the public is the predominant stated aim in its mission statement:

The Home Office is the government department responsible for ensuring we live in a safe, just and tolerant society by putting public protection at the heart of all we do...To protect the public, we focus on six key objectives:

1.   protecting the UK from terrorist attack
2.   cutting crime, especially violent and drug-related crime
3.   ensuring people feel safer in their homes and daily lives, particularly through more visible, responsive and accountable local policing
4.   rebalancing the criminal justice system in favour of the law-abiding majority and the victim
5.   managing offenders to protect the public and reduce re-offending
6.   securing our borders, preventing abuse of our immigration laws and managing migration to benefit the UK. (Home Office, 2007a)

The British approach stresses public protection, public reassurance, and the protection from an apparent 'imbalance' in the criminal justice system that currently favours the rights of the accused.[2]

Unlike their English counterparts, Norwegian sentenced prisoners retain the right to vote. Weekend furloughs and home visits are common in Norway, though their legitimacy is called into question from time to time, as when, in March 2007, police found the body of a murdered restaurant owner in the trunk of a furloughed man's car on his drive back to prison. He was on furlough after serving only six years of a 21-year sentence. A prisoner is normally first eligible for a short home visit after serving one-third of his sentence, and is usually released automatically after two-thirds is served. In England and Wales, eligibility for early release is more complicated. The Criminal Justice Act 2003 stipulates that all prisoners serving determinate sentences of twelve months or more are eligible for automatic release at the halfway point, and then subject to recall and parole supervision for the remaining half. Those serving sentences under twelve months are released at the halfway point without conditions. Prisoners serving sentences of between four months and under four years who

---

[2] As Tonry (2004a) argues, the balance imagery reinforces the fallacy that criminal justice is a zero-sum game.

have not committed a violent or sexual offence are eligible for release on electronic tag between two weeks and four-and-a-half months before their halfway point under the Home Detention Curfew scheme.

Penalties and sentences

England had its last execution in 1964 and abolished the death penalty for nearly all offences in 1965, finally abolishing it entirely in 2003. Norway abolished its death penalty in 1902, though it was temporarily reinstated after the Second World War when Vidkun Quisling, Hitler's puppet during the Nazi occupation and the leader of the fascist National Unity Party (*Nasjonal Samling*), was executed by firing squad along with twenty-four other Norwegian collaborators and twelve Germans found guilty of war crimes (Stenersen and Libæk, 2003). Life sentences in Norway were abolished in 1981 (Bondeson, 2005). In England and Wales the last decade has seen a 128 per cent increase in their use (Home Office, 2007b: 40, Table 2.7). (See Figures 3.5 and 3.6).

In most cases the maximum sentence in Norway is 15 years, but 21 years is the maximum if there are aggravating circumstances. There has been, however, a rise in the number sentences to preventive detention (*forvaring*) for serious offenders at risk of

Figure 3.5 Persons under 21 sentenced to life imprisonment in England and Wales, 1995–2005

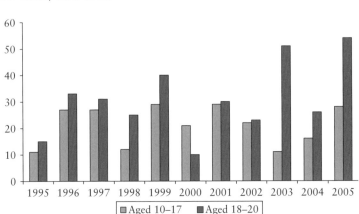

Source: Home Office (2007: 40, Table 2.7).

Figure 3.6 Persons sentenced to life imprisonment in England and Wales, 1995–2005

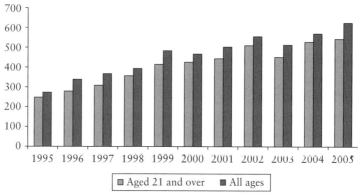

Source: Home Office (2007: 40, Table 2.7).

reoffending. *Forvaring* replaced the security order, or *sikring*,[3] in January 2002 (Kristoffersen, 2007). It allows for the indefinite detention and compulsory treatment of serious, high-risk offenders for a minimum term not exceeding ten years and a maximum term 'that should not exceed 15 years and that must not exceed 21 years' (Kriminalomsorgen [Norwegian Correctional Services], 2007). *Forvaring* can be tantamount to a life sentence, but the court periodically reviews the sentence and can only extend it in five-year intervals. Though the purpose of *forvaring* is public protection, its aim is 'to help persons sentenced to preventive detention to change their behaviour and enable them to lead a life outside prison' (Kriminalomsorgen [Norwegian Correctional Services], 2007). There are approximately 72 prisoners serving sentences of *forvaring* (Statistics Norway, 2006).

In England and Wales, the Criminal Justice Act 2003 introduced a new sentence of imprisonment for public protection (IPP), or detention for public protection (DPP) in the case of juveniles, for anyone convicted of one of 153 serious violent or sexual offences carrying a maximum sentence of ten years or more. It is essentially an indeterminate life sentence that replaced the automatic life sentence or 'two strikes and you're out' law proposed by the Conservatives and later implemented by Labour in

---

[3] The *sikring* sentence was used when the risk of reoffending was linked to an offender's mental health.

Figure 3.7 Number of life-sentence prisoners (England and Wales) and preventive-detention prisoners (Norway), 1995–2005

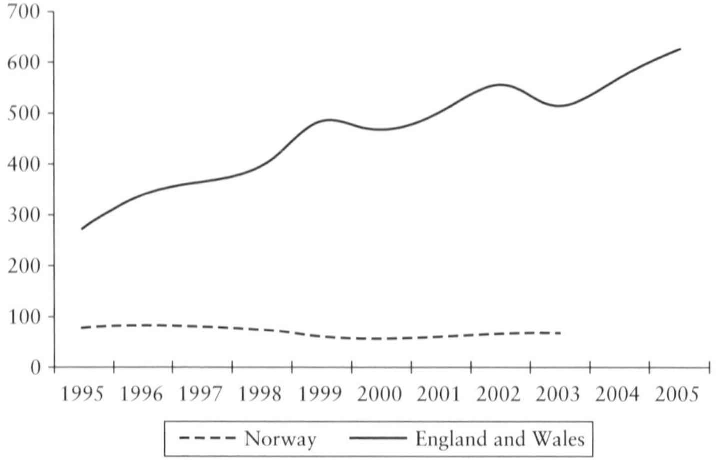

Source: Norway data: Statistics Norway (2007b); England and Wales data: Home Office (2004: 40, Table 1).

the Crime (Sentences) Act 1997. Between April 2005 when it was implemented and April 2007, there were 2,547 prisoners serving these sentences (Prison Reform Trust, 2007; Sutcliffe, 2007).[4] With the exception of *sikring* and *forvaring*, Norway abolished indeterminate sentences once the faith in treatment collapsed in the 1970s (Bondeson, 2003; Christie, 1982).

If preventive detention is taken to be the closest approximation in Norway to a life sentence in England and Wales, a divergent pattern emerges when these are compared. Figure 3.7 shows ten-year trends in the number of prisoners serving preventive detention sentences of *sikring* or *forvaring* in Norway and the number of prisoners serving life sentences in England and Wales.

Sentence lengths

Sentences have got longer in recent years in Norway as in England, but again on a significantly smaller scale. The Council of Europe

---

[4] At the time of writing, the IPP sentence was being reconsidered after Jack Straw, the former Home Secretary who is now the Justice Secretary and Lord Chancellor, ordered an urgent review of the sentence because of the impact it is having on prison places.

calculates an indicator of a country's average length of imprisonment in months.[5] By this measure, average prison sentences
in England and Wales remain at least twice as long as those in
Norway. The average length of imprisonment in Norway in 2002
was 2.8 months, rising to 3.2 months in 2003 where it held steady
in 2004. In England and Wales the average rose year on year
from 5.8 months in 2002, to 6.5 months in 2003, to 6.7 months
in 2004 (Aebi and Stadnic, 2007: Table 13.2; Council of Europe,
2006: Tables 13.1 and 13.2).

The average immediate custodial sentence length handed down
in the Crown Courts in England and Wales has increased from
20.5 months in 1995 to 25.5 months in 2005, while it held steady
at 3 months in the magistrates' courts (Home Office, 2007b: 136,
Table 5.7). In Norway in 2005, the average sentence of unconditional imprisonment for all offences was 6 months (Statistics
Norway, 2005: Table 44). Using statistics for all courts in England
and Wales, the average length of an immediate custodial sentence
for robbery was 35 months in England and Wales in 2005 (Home
Office, 2007b: 45, Table 2.11). In Norway the average comparable unconditional prison sentence length is 11 months (Statistics
Norway, 2005: Table 44). In 2005 the offence of violence against
the person brought an average immediate custodial sentence of
17.8 months in England and Wales (Home Office, 2007b: 45,
Table 2.11). In Norway, the average sentence for a similar offence
was about 8 months.

Norway's harsh sentences for drug offences reflect puritan-
ical aspects of its culture and provide the exception to the rule of
greater comparative leniency (Larsson, 2007). Norwegian official
statistics list average sentences for drug crimes separately from
'serious' drug crimes. The average unconditional prison sentence
for the former was 2.4 months in 2005, whereas the average for
the latter was 38.9 months (Statistics Norway, 2005: Table 44).
English statistics indicate that the average immediate custodial
sentence in all courts for drug offences was 35.8 months (Home
Office, 2007b: 45, Table 2.11).

Table 3.3 compares sentences in yet another way. Nearly 43 per
cent of prisoners sentenced to fixed prison terms in Norway are

---

[5] This figures is calculated by dividing the number of prisoners on a given day by
the number of entries to penal institutions and multiplying by 12.

Table 3.3 Fixed-term sentenced prisoners, 2005 (%)

	Less than 1 year	3 years or more	5 years or more
Norway	42.7	29.9	19.1
England and Wales	13.2	56.2	31.3

Source: Aebi and Stadnic (2007: Table 10).

Table 3.4 Prisoners sentenced to less than 1 year, 2005 (%)

	Less than 1 month	1 month to less than 3 months	3 months to less than 6 months	6 months to less than 1 year
Norway	10.8	36	16.5	36.7
England and Wales	2.3	12.6	41.5	43.6

Source: Aebi and Stadnic (2007: Table 11).

sentenced to less than one year. In England and Wales the comparable figure is 13 per cent. Only 7 per cent of Norwegian prisoners serve more than ten years whereas a full 17 per cent of prisoners in England and Wales are serving over ten years. In 2005, almost 10 per cent of prisoners in England and Wales were serving life sentences. This number has likely risen since the implementation of the IPP sentence. At the lower end of the scale, nearly half of sentences under one year in Norway are for less than three months. In England and Wales, 85 per cent of such sentences are for over three months or more (see Table 3.4).

Youth Justice

The Nordic diversionary consensus

The age of criminal responsibility in England and Wales is ten. In Norway, it was raised from ten to fourteen in 1902, and raised again to fifteen in 1990, in part to bring Norway in line with the other Scandinavian countries (Falck, 2002). In responding to the landmark 1997 Home Office White Paper *No More Excuses*, which among other things proposed the abolition of *doli incapax* that would later be implemented by the Crime and Disorder

Act 1998, Norwegian criminologist Sturla Falck (1998a: 597) makes the following comparative observations:

Norway has followed a path diametrically opposed to England and Wales. Norway raised the age of criminal responsibility from 14 to 15 years in 1990. The central arguments for this move were the morally unacceptable, and the negative psychological, effects on children placed in custody. Subsequent evaluation of raising the age of criminal responsibility showed no negative consequences for registered crime, or for the work of the police or social services.

In supporting this separate approach for juveniles, Falck goes on to describe the principles that still define Norwegian approaches to youth justice and that help explain why the Bulger and Redergård case responses were so different:

Penal sanctions applied to the youngest age groups serve little purpose. They simply do not know the law, and for the few that do, they do not calculate the punitive risk of their behaviour. The rationality behind their actions is very limited. Although children may know the difference between right and wrong, they have little notion of the consequences of their actions. Changes in legislation will have no preventive or other effect on their behaviour. Socialisation factors such as home and family, child-rearing practices, friends and the school will influence their behaviour far more...No matter how serious the act committed by a child, it is entitled to be treated as a child. Measures applied to the most difficult children must not only be in compliance with the UN Convention on the Rights of the Child, they must also be ethically and morally acceptable in terms of what is best for the child. (Falck, 1998a: 597)

Nordic youth justice has for decades stressed diversion from formal prosecution and mediation rather than punishment (Falck, 1998c; Paus, 2000; van Wormer, 1990). A new White Paper proposes that courts should also consider the likely rehabilitative effects of the sentences juveniles receive. Remarkably, the White Paper also proposes to abolish pre-trial custody and imprisonment for all offenders under 16, and to allow those under 18 to be imprisoned only when absolutely necessary, for public protection, and even then only for a week at a time (Norwegian Ministry of Justice and the Police, 2006). All cases involving young offenders under 15 are handled by the child services (*barnevernet*) and the county social welfare boards (*Fylkesnemnd*) they oversee (Bygrave, 1997). Most involving those between 15 and 18 are transferred from the courts to the county social welfare boards (Falck, 1998b). The UN Convention on the Rights of the Child (UNCRC) provides

that the well-being of the child is paramount, that the age of criminal responsibility should not be unduly low and should take
account of maturity levels, that custody should be used only as a
last resort, and that juveniles should be held separately from adults
when in detention (Goldson and Muncie, 2006b). Though it was
ratified by all UN member states, except the USA and Somalia,
breaches of the UNCRC are common because they are not formally sanctioned (Muncie and Goldson, 2006c). However, unlike
England and Wales, the Nordic countries tend to comply with the
Convention. One exception is the provision that juveniles shall be
held separately from adults. Norway's youth prisons were abolished
in 1975 because recidivism rates of those leaving them were as high
as 92 per cent (Falck, 2007). Now, although under-18s are housed
in adult prisons, efforts are made to separate them from 'hardcore'
offenders (Storgaard, 2004). Article 19 of the UNCRC requires that
children are protected from 'all forms of physical and mental violence... while in the care of parent(s), legal guardian(s) or any other
person who has the care of the child' (quoted in UNICEF, 2003: 3).
Of the thirty OECD countries, only the five Nordic countries,
Austria, and Germany have explicitly banned the use of physical
punishment in all settings, including at home, in schools, in penal
settings, and in other types of care settings (UNICEF, 2003).

Young people in custody

Crime has become a more urgent political issue in Norway with the
rise of private media. More coverage of crime in more media outlets has meant that those political parties who consider themselves
'tough on crime'—particularly the Conservative and Progress
Parties—must compete to be first to respond to concerns raised
in the media. But as regards responses to youth crime, no party
advocates prison as an alternative for children under 15 years old
or even older. As the member of the justice committee from the
Conservative Party explained, 'We had this debate about that a
couple of months ago. There was this discussion about how we're
going to treat youth criminals, but there was no discussion about
people under 15 going to prison. It's just common sense... It's
almost not a subject, because that will not help, and that is obvious for everybody' (Dahl, 2007). This contrasts sharply with the
call of Paul Dacre of the *Daily Mail* in England who in the name
of his readers advocated locking up juveniles under 15.

The number of juveniles aged 10–15 sentenced to custody in England and Wales has increased eightfold since 1990 (Narey, 2007). The number of juveniles aged 15–17 held in prisons in England and Wales rose from 769 to 2,089 between 1993 and 2002 (Muncie and Goldson, 2006b). By April 2007, 3 per cent of the prison population, or 2,402 offenders, were juveniles under 18. This number does not include the 256 in Secure Training Centres, and an additional 229 in Local Authority Secure Children's Homes (International Centre for Prison Studies, 2007). Only 0.3 per cent of Norway's prison population consists of juveniles under 18 (see Figure 3.8). Only 5.5 per cent of the Norwegian prison population is comprised of prisoners between 18 to 20, while that percentage is 11.4 per cent in England and Wales. Generally there have been between two and ten under-18s in Norwegian prisons in recent years, and in 2004 the average time they spent in prison was about sixty days (Norwegian Ministry of Justice and the Police, 2006). A White Paper published in 2006 suggests that imprisonment is severely damaging to juveniles and ought to be used even less often than it currently is (Norwegian Ministry of Justice and the Police, 2006).

The number of juveniles in custody in England has grown because of harsher treatment, not because of higher youth offending rates. Fewer young people than previously who offend avoid

Figure 3.8 Young people in prison in Norway and England and Wales

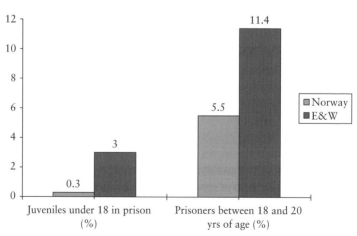

Source: International Centre for Prison Studies (2007).

formal prosecution. In 1992, 73.5 per cent of cases were diverted through the use of cautions and warnings, and by 2003, only 55.9 of case were diverted in this way (Bateman, 2006). Forty per cent of anti-social behaviour orders (ASBOs), which are civil orders issued for non-criminal behaviour but whose breach is a criminal offence,[6] are issued to juveniles under 17, and unlike in criminal cases, these juveniles are often identified on leaflets posted in their communities (*Observer*, 2007).

Though use of custody has risen and more and more young people are subject to a range of punitive orders, the story of English youth justice is not only about repression and custody. For instance, the same 1998 Act which abolished *doli incapax* also introduced multi-agency Youth Offending Teams (YOTs) (Gelsthorpe and Morris, 2002; Newburn, 2002). Youth courts now refer less serious first-time juvenile offenders to Youth Offending Panels, overseen by YOTs, who agree a plan with the offender that stresses restoration, responsibility, and reintegration (Haines and O'Mahony, 2006). Though the Crime and Disorder Act 1998 'systematically and institutionally distanced' youth justice services 'from mainstream child welfare services' (Goldson and Muncie, 2006a: 215), the restorative and interventionist aspects of these approaches tend to view young offenders 'as deprived, rather than depraved', in need of welfare-oriented support (Fionda, 2005). The English youth justice system is bifurcated (Bottoms, 1977) and schizoid, but it is the harshest approaches that get the most press attention and the most resources. For example, in spite of the efforts of the former head of the Youth Justice Board, Rod Morgan, to cut the number of youth in custody by 10 per cent during his tenure—a goal he was unable to achieve before he resigned in January 2007—the Board spent seven times more on custody for the 4 per cent of young offenders who go into custody than it did on proven early-prevention efforts (Fayle, 2007; Morgan, 2007). Morgan believes that more children are being criminalized because—in order to meet a government-imposed target to increase the number of offences brought to justice—police are compelled to go after the 'low-hanging fruit' of low-level juvenile offending which is easily cleared up (Morgan, 2007).

---

[6] However, though half of ASBOs are breached, in practice very few breaches on their own bring a custodial sentence (Taylor and Jerrom, 2005; Youth Justice Board, 2006).

Public Attitudes toward Crime and Punishment

Public punitiveness

The International Crime Victimization Survey (ICVS) asks respondents to identify their preferred sanction for a recidivist burglar from a list a several choices, including a fine, a prison sentence, or a community service order. This question has become an imperfect but commonly used indicator of punitive public attitudes in different countries. It is imperfect for several reasons. First, there are methodological faults. The ICVS excludes those under 16 years old and relies on computer-aided telephone interviews, meaning it 'undercounts households lacking telephones and undercounts young, mobile, disadvantaged groups with high offending and victimization rates' (Tonry and Farrington, 2005: 14, fn 16). Second, and importantly from a comparative standpoint, the salience of burglary in a particular jurisdiction could affect the choice of penalty respondents deem appropriate in the survey questions. For instance, in England and Wales, 9 per cent of those surveyed in 1989 believed they were 'very likely' to be burgled in the coming year, while only 2 per cent of Norwegians believed the same.[7] In England, 2.5 per cent of those surveyed had been burgled in the previous year while the comparable figure for Norway was 0.8 per cent (van Dijk and Mayhew, 1992). The higher perception of burglary risk and the higher rates of actual burglaries in England might account for some of the harsher public attitudes revealed in the survey.

The second reason the ICVS indicator is imperfect is that Norway participated in only the first and the most recent of the five ICVS sweeps. Though Olaussen (2006) has published some of the most recent data collected in 2004, no Norwegian ICVS data are available for the 14-year span between the first and last sweeps. These deficits aside, this ICVS measure is probably the best standardized comparative measure of public punitiveness available.

Figure 3.9 shows how public attitudes in Norway appear to have harshened considerably since 1989, while the picture in the rest of the Nordic countries is mixed. The Norway data show a doubling of those believing prison to be an appropriate sentence

---

[7] Unfortunately, at the time of writing only some of the 2004 ICVS data are available for Norway. This is the analysis by Olaussen who does not provide data on Norwegian concern for burglary. So the 1989 data offer the only comparable data yet available.

Figure 3.9 Percentage preferring prison sentence for recidivist burglar in Nordic countries (ICVS)

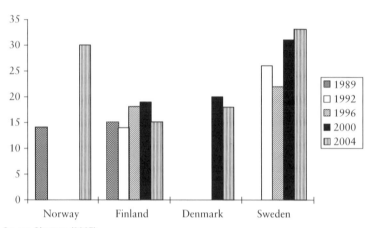

Source: Olaussen (2007).

for a recidivist burglar, from 14 per cent in 1989 to 30 per cent in 2004. Sweden has seen a continual rise in public punitiveness by this measure since the 1996 sweep, and in 2004 it has peaked at 33 per cent, just above Norway's numbers. Finland's levels, however, have hovered rather consistently around 15 per cent over the period. Denmark's remain a bit higher than Finland's but appear to be holding steady.

Most of this support for imprisonment in Norway appears to have come from draining enthusiasm for the fine as the most appropriate sanction. This number was halved from around 23 to around 12 per cent between 1989 and 2004. This apparent decline in the legitimacy of the fine might be tied to deeper cultural and economic changes in Norway since the 1980s. Olaussen (2007) suggests that because the wealth of many in Norway has increased dramatically since the discovery of oil, many Norwegians might now regard financial penalties as less morally meaningful than they once did when times were tougher economically. Those Norwegians surveyed favouring community service remained relatively stable, though dropped slightly from 47 to 45 per cent.

Though on one level the rise in support for imprisonment indicates an alarming punitive shift in public attitudes, as with much of the Nordic picture, when considered in a comparative perspective alongside English or UK data, the shift is much less alarming. As Figure 3.10 shows, in 1989, 38 per cent of those surveyed in the UK favoured imprisonment on the recidivist burglar question—significantly higher at that time than even the most

Figure 3.10 Percentage preferring prison sentence for recidivist burglar in Norway and the UK (ICVS)

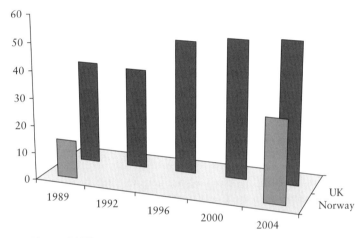

Source: Olaussen (2007).

Figure 3.11 Percentage preferring community service for recidivist burglar in Norway and the UK (ICVS)

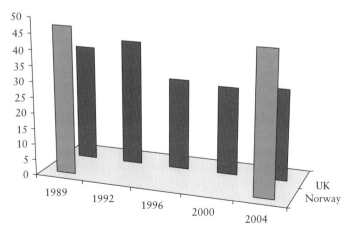

Source: Olaussen (2007).

recent Norwegian numbers—and the UK numbers have climbed continuously over the years to 52 per cent in 2004. In addition, Figure 3.11 suggests that nearly half of Norwegian respondents still prefer community service while apparent faith in that particular sanction has further declined in the UK since 1989.

So these data can be viewed through a number of lenses. Some Nordic criminologists have used this recent rise in apparent public punitiveness to suggest that those late-modern changes in penality that authors like Garland have documented in England and the USA are indeed apparent in the Nordic countries, too. However, though there appears to be some truth in this, comparisons show the scale of the differences between the Nordic countries and the Anglo-Saxon countries are drastic. The punitive shift in Norway that the latest ICVS data suggest is somewhat dramatic when viewed parochially, but much less so when compared with the UK findings.

Table 3.5 Fear of crime in Norway (%)*

	1983	1987	1991	1995	1997	2001	2004
Feared violence or threats in their home area recently	8.1	8.6	10.3	9.5	11.0	7.9	7.9
Feared thefts or criminal damage recently	—	—	—	—	21.5	14.2	14.3
Number of respondents	3898	4265	3665	3620	3359	3246	3337

Source: *Statistics Norway (2007a).

Table 3.6 Worry about crime in England and Wales (% British Crime Survey)*

	1992	1994	1996	1998	2000	2001/2	2002/3	2003/4	2004/5	2005/6
High level of worry about burglary	19	26	22	19	19	15	15	13	12	13
High level of worry about car crime	n/a	n/a	n/a	22	21	17	17	15	13	14
High level of worry about violent crime	n/a	n/a	n/a	25	24	22	21	16	16	17

Source: *Patterson and Thorpe (2006: Table 3a).

Fear of crime

Unfortunately, there are no similarly standardized measures of fear of crime in the UK and Norway to compare, but some limited data exist, and other scholars insist that fear of crime is lower throughout Scandinavia than it is in Britain (Bondeson, 2005). Statistics Norway provides some Norwegian data shown in Table 3.5 that suggest fear of violent crime has remained relatively flat and relatively low for at least twenty years. Table 3.6 shows British Crime Survey data on worry about crime, and the numbers for violent crime are twice those of Norway.

Conclusion

By nearly every available measure, and in spite of similar levels of crime victimization, Norway has been more restrained in its responses to crime than England has. Norway has fewer police, fewer adults and young people in prison and for less time, less fear of crime, greater welfare investment, greater income equality, and higher levels of child well-being. Norway's small size and relative homogeneity have certainly made restraint easier to maintain. Though many of these factors have deep cultural roots, they are also underpinned by the support structures necessary to ensure their survival. Chief among these is a consensual political culture—that eschews conflict, values compromise, and decreases incentives to engage in cynical penal populism—and a more responsible, less sensational media culture—where competition is less fierce and ethical standards are taken more seriously.

   Though pressure to respond to press-driven fears about crime and insecurity have increased in Norway since the early 1990s, in some ways dramatically, Norway has so far managed these pressures in ways that have not seen the sort of dramatic rise in punitiveness—either in terms of sentencing policy or public attitudes—that has defined the English experience since James Bulger was killed in 1993. The scale of change in Norway over the same period has been comparatively small, though still very significant when viewed more parochially. Rhetorics may indeed be getting tough all over, but the connections between tough talk and tough action are not as direct in Norway as they are in England. The next chapter offers two conceptual models to help explain why this might be.

4

The Constraints and Effects of Political Culture

This chapter more carefully defines some of the concepts used in the book to explain the differences in responses to both the Bulger and Redergård cases, and to crime and the concern about it more generally in England and Norway. It offers two descriptive models to help visualize the interrelationships between political cultures and penal climates. The first model is presented in the first section and aims to help explain why certain comparable incidents generate different cultural and political responses in different settings. In the next section, sentencing guidelines systems and the US Constitution are used as examples to illustrate the relationship between culture and structure. The third section offers a second conceptual model to explain the ways in which political culture and the assumptions embedded within it constrain the way we think about the problems we face and the ways we respond to them. The last main section examines how high-profile crimes interact with aspects of political culture in ways that, in different contexts, can both diminish and increase the discretion of politicians and policymakers to respond.

A Conceptual Model

Figure 4.1 is a model of the reciprocal interrelationships between several concepts that are used in the pages to follow. These concepts include knowledge, discourse, sensibilities, press culture, political culture, and the penal climate. *Political culture* refers to the culturally embedded assumptions influencing the flow of a range of different knowledge, from research findings to tabloid headlines. Political–cultural assumptions privilege certain relationships that link those with valued kinds of knowledge with the policymakers who make policy decisions. For instance, politicians disregarded academic and practitioner knowledge after James Bulger

Figure 4.1 Conceptual model of the relationship between political culture, press culture, and penal climate

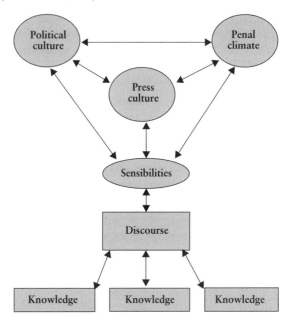

was killed, privileging instead a range of dubious indicators of public opinion, including tabloid press headlines. The Norwegian reaction to Silje Redergård's death included a heavy reliance upon expert knowledge. Exactly which kinds of knowledge are valued at a given time or in a particular place varies.

Press culture includes the ways in which the press covers crime issues, as well as the relationships that exist between the press and politicians, and the press and the public. The ability of the press to influence the public agenda varies over time and between jurisdictions. Press and political cultures have become so entangled today in English politics that it has been argued that the current political system could not exist without the press (Jones, 2001). Political culture thus implies an attendant press culture, too.

The *penal climate* refers to the degree of public, media, and political pressure exerted upon politicians and sentencers to act tough or punitively on penal policy issues. The particular composition of forces contributing to the penal climate will depend in part on both cultural factors and their structural manifestations. For instance, the 'interaction between public perception, media, politicians and sentencers' (Carter, 2003: 12) creates the 'political mood music playing in the minds of sentencers as they make their decisions' (Fayle, 2007) and policymakers as they make policy. The proportional degree to which each contributing group is allowed to impact the penal climate will differ from place to place over time depending upon how knowledge flows though the system. These channeling structures reflect cultural assumptions and priorities. 'Hot' penal climates are marked by a high degree of press, public, and political interest in penal issues—often characterized by strongly moralistic and denunciatory sentiments—and this interest tends to produce inhospitable conditions for the deliberative consideration of the range of available knowledge. 'Cool' penal climates are characterized by comparatively minimal interest in penal issues, lower levels of punitive sentiment, and more opportunities to foster policy deliberation. The Bulger case created a penal climate that was exceedingly hot, while the penal climate in the wake of the Redergård case remained cool. This was due in part to the varying effects that different models of political culture can have on penal climates.

Sensibilities refer to the normative beliefs, values, and attitudes collectively held by groups of actors in a society at a given time. They include the moral foundations that govern normative decision-making, and they are informed by the range of knowledges to which publics are exposed. Sensibilities are implicated in answers to questions asking what ought to be done, and they are made observable by analysing discourse. As discussed more fully in Chapter 5, *discourse* is the textual evidence that makes cultural sensibilities observable. Discourses define the limitations of conventional thinking, the priorities of the individuals deploying them, and the range of allowable actions that can result. In terms of penal policymaking, discourses constrain the thinking of policy actors and delimit the range of available policy action.

In the wake of tragic incidents like the Bulger and Redergård cases, political culture and press culture interact to influence and regulate the extremes in temperature of each society's penal climate. Political and press practices have observable cultural roots and infrastructures that influence the flow of various forms of knowledge (research, public opinion polls, tabloid editorials, folk wisdom, practitioner experience, etc). Some are favoured and others are rejected. The resulting penal climates are made evident in the attitudes and sensibilities of the various actors engaged in the process of responding to the incident (the public, criminologists, editors and journalists, civil servants, ministers, MPs, practitioners, etc). These cultural sensibilities are constituted through discourses. Certain discourses find favour and are reiterated, for instance, in newspaper editorials, party rhetoric, and research studies. In studying the responses to the Bulger and Redergård killings, discourse then provides the means to describe, assess, and compare cultural sensibilities and the nature of the two penal climates. As the diagram indicates, all the components in the model interact in a series of feedback loops, taking cues from one another over time.

Structure and Culture

Christensen and Peters argue that 'not much else . . . can explain the performance of political-administrative systems other than structure and culture' (1999: 1). Individual actors' room to manoeuvre in these systems is constrained by structural and cultural contingencies. Criminal justice practitioners, like judges for instance, are bounded by the law, within which some are allowed considerable discretion. Even those whose discretion is structurally unhindered are nonetheless constrained by cultural considerations. For instance, will the public construe a particular judge's sentence to be fair? The very salience of this question to a judge, if not bound in statute, is culturally dependent. The judge is most likely to consider this factor important in jurisdictions like England where the judiciary retains low levels of public confidence, where there is frequent antagonism between politicians and the judiciary, and where it is politically advantageous for politicians to invoke populist, anti-elite rhetoric that increases the public's scrutiny of judges. There are certainly other examples, but importantly, behaviour is subject to both structural and cultural constraints, and these constraints impact both individuals and the institutions in which they work. Law is a structural constraint rooted in culture, but there are also cultural constraints beyond the law. The very perception of the need for laws is in part culturally dependent, as some cultures tend to be more preoccupied by activities perceived to be threatening.

Sentencing guidelines

Two examples, sentencing guidelines systems and the US Constitution, help to illustrate the interactive relationship between structure and culture. Sentencing guidelines are meant to constrict the range of judicial discretion. Whether a jurisdiction's guidelines are non-binding (like those generated by the Sentencing Advisory Panel in England and Wales), presumptive (like those in Minnesota that allow judges to depart from them in individual cases for justifiable and transparent reasons), or rigidly fixed with little option for departure (like the US Federal guidelines), all guideline systems are structural constraints on judicial behaviour. They are structural manifestations of cultural concerns. The questions of whether guidelines are considered necessary at all in a particular jurisdiction and, if they are, what types of guideline systems ought to be considered for implementation, are questions that are culturally rooted. The degree to which judicial discretion is constrained is in part dependent on the amount of trust that the public and their elected representatives in government retain in them. Sentencing guidelines tend to be most rigidly constraining where trust in judicial discretion has waned the most.

There is, nonetheless, an important caveat which demonstrates the confusing fusion of the structural and the cultural. To continue with the example, an appreciation of a need for sentencing guidelines to correct the ills of unfettered judicial discretion can also have structural antecedents that interact with culture. For instance, some have argued the merits of guidelines as a way of essentially keeping judges honest. In jurisdictions where judges are elected, it is not difficult to imagine the pressures exerted upon a judge facing re-election who must adjudicate a high-profile case. Others who advocate guidelines do so to eliminate unfair sentencing disparities that tend disproportionately to impact minority groups. The purchase of such arguments will depend on their resonance in the specific cultural context. Reformers cannot take reforms beyond what the culture will allow. Neither can they reform what is yet to be seen as in need of reform. Racial disparities in sentencing must be first recognized as problems before structural changes can be implemented to help rectify them.

Again, however, one could go even further to argue, for instance, that the structural rules for the election of judges are culturally rooted in a distrust of the unchecked authority of powerful people.

Whether culture or structure is judged to be the most responsible force in political change seems to depend upon at what moment in time one chooses to cut the genealogy. Perhaps one of the clearest examples of the relationship between culture and political structures can be found in the American Constitution.

The US Constitution

The Founding Fathers, products of their age and emerging as they were from a war to achieve independence from the overbearing rule of the English monarchy, held deep suspicions of unchecked political power (Christensen and Peters, 1999: 23). They created an elaborate system of checks and balances to allay their fears of tyranny and domination. The Constitution represents the culturally entrenched preoccupations of its founders, while simultaneously and continuously inculcating in its citizens what is believed to be a healthy suspicion of unbridled political power. The Constitution both reflects and reconstitutes the suspicions that preoccupied its framers 220 years ago. With the relatively recent birth of a new nation like the USA, it is relatively easy to trace the role that culture played on the structures that followed. However, the reciprocal and reflexive relationship between culture and structure makes it harder to determine which factors— cultural or structural—are the most instrumental in the social and political changes experienced today, especially when viewed without a full historical appreciation of the past.

'Morphogenesis'

Social theorist Margaret Archer (1995) has developed the 'morphogenetic approach' to the study of structure and agency. Morphogenesis is another inelegant term, this time borrowed from the lexicon of embryonic development. It refers to the process whereby identical cells become differentiated under the influences of genetic codes and environmental factors. Archer uses it to describe the ways that social structures are similarly subjected to internal and external influences that induce structural adaptation and change. Though she makes a case for the primacy of structure to which a culture adapts, it seems most important to appreciate that the reciprocal interaction between the two preclude, at least for the purposes of this book, the need to solve the chicken-and-egg quandary of which came first. It is sufficient to say, as

Christensen and Peters (1999: 133) do, that 'structures tend to embody values that their members, in turn, utilize to make decisions about public policy and delivery of services to clients'.

Another example of this reciprocity comes from a story that is told more fully in Chapter 8. The decline in deference to traditional elite experts in the area of English penal policymaking since the 1980s was brought about by the interaction of social changes (i.e. economic sluggishness, late-modern insecurities) with cultural elements (i.e. growing distrust of elites, decline in penal optimism) which opened up penal policymaking structures to greater press and public scrutiny than had occurred before. The rise in importance of the public voice in turn fitted well with the adversarial political culture of English parliamentary democracy, thus creating incentives for politicians to court the public to gain power against the opposition.

The Constraints of Political Culture

Political culture and its supporting structures shape and constrain the scope of policymaking. Elkins and Simeon (1979: 131) illustrate, describing political culture in functional terms:

Political culture defines the range of acceptable possible alternatives from which groups or individuals may, other circumstances permitting, choose a course of action...Its explanatory power is primarily restricted to 'setting the agenda' over which political contests occur. Other factors must explain the choice of a particular element of the subset identified in that culture. These supplementary factors include personality, role, self-interest, and so on, at the individual level, or simply the relative power of organized groups at the societal or collective level of analysis.

Political culture is thus composed of the shared assumptions that actors in a political system hold about the best way to achieve goals, about authority, about trust.

Following from this, one way to conceive the broad process of policy development is as existing within a funnel, with a wide macro-level filter at the opening at the top and a narrower micro-level filter at the bottom (see Figure 4.2). Political culture operates at the mouth of the funnel, at the macro-level. It determines the range of policy alternatives available in a given jurisdiction. This initial selection process is often obscure because it occurs on a 'pre-rational' level predetermined by cultural assumptions.

Figure 4.2 Conceptual model of micro- and macro-level policy option 'funnelling'

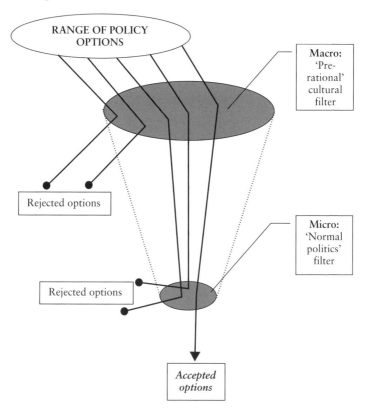

'Choice' is probably too imprecise a term to use to describe this process, as it connotes rational decision-making. If culture is understood as a 'set of cognitive constraints' (Stokes and Hewitt, 1976: 837), cultural sensibilities help align action in ways that are cognitively congenial. 'Pre-rational selection' is a more apt description because it indicates that the available range of choices is constrained even before any rational choice considerations arise. It is a cultural, and thus unconscious, process governed by norms, assumptions, and sensibilities that, while not readily made apparent by those who subscribe to them, nonetheless shape perceptions and behaviour. Often it is only by comparing existing filters with those that differ that the contingency of cultural distinctiveness can be appreciated. One means of uncovering these cultural filters is through the analysis of discourses and the sensibilities signified by them, which is more fully considered in the next chapter. The basic assumptions underpinning cultural concerns establish the repertoire of policy options, as they reflect policy actors' shared understandings of the problem they face at a specific time and place. Culture in a way then sets the agenda by pre-selecting the range of available policy options from which policymakers choose.

'Political culture' is typically used as a rather poorly operationalized, catch-all concept in the criminological literature to account for all manner of political action and procedure. Elkins and Simeon (1979: 142) note the problem and justify the utility of the concept:

Political culture has been less attractive to students of policy analysis and policymaking than to other political scientists. But our stress on culture as setting the agenda and as reducing the range of alternatives to be considered suggests that cultural explanations of policy should be explored more fully, especially in comparative settings…Culture is unlikely to be of much help in explaining why alternative A was chosen over alternative B—but it may be of great help in understanding why A and B were considered, while no thought was given to C, D, or E.

The assumptions that constitute political culture are dispositions that interact with structural factors and individual agency. Elkins and Simeon would argue that an explanation is cultural if internation differences in similar institutions can be accounted for by referring to divergent assumptions.[1] The ways in which tabloid journalists report similar crime events in different jurisdictions, or the way police respond to those events, are two examples explored in more detail in Chapter 7.

Elkins and Simeon further circumscribe the explanatory power of political culture by limiting its deployment to comparative analyses. It can only account for differences in behaviour when

---

[1] They argue that culture can only explain behavioural differences when structural variables are first eliminated as explanations, and behaviour cannot be predicted based on knowledge of cultural assumptions alone. Therefore, political culture is a ' "second-order" explanation' that cannot be used, on its own, to explain political behaviour: 'The cultural assumptions provide the lens through which these more proximate political forces are assessed; they influence what kind of interpretation will be placed on political forces, but alone they cannot account for the result' (Elkins and Simeon, 1979: 140).

individuals in similar structural or organizational positions share a different set of assumptions than either their counterparts in another country—a 'horizontal' comparison (Christensen and Peters, 1999: 10)—or their counterparts in another time. Political culture is, therefore, a construct that can only be studied through comparative analysis, either of different jurisdictions in time, or of one jurisdiction over time. These distinctions help to hone the definition and utility of the concept. Elkins and Simeon summarize their view:

> ...the most significant feature of our approach is its sharp distinction between political culture as a descriptive category and as an explanation. Political culture as descriptive of a collectivity entails only that the group exhibits a given range and distribution of (largely unconscious) assumptions about its political life. Cultural *explanations*, on the other hand, utilize this formation in conjunction with structural features to account for the differences between collectivities on certain dependent variables. The use of culture for explanation, therefore, must always be comparative. (1979: 131, emphasis in original)

Constraining choice

The study of policymaking, and of the forces that conduce to influence it, is essentially the study of constraint and choice. At the bottom of the funnel, at the micro-level, is where the processes that concern most policy analysts occur. It is here that the particular ideologies, interests, and information (Weiss, 1983) that guide policy choice decision-making come into play. It is at this micro-level that the electoral consequences of particular policy decisions must be considered, where political self-interest influences action, where the already bounded array of policy options is narrowed down and choices are made. Therefore, the use of rational choice theories to explain political decision-making on the micro-level are not incompatible with theories of political culture because, as Figure 4.2 above indicates, the latter works as an unconscious filter to accumulate *culturally appropriate* policy alternatives and to reject others that are not. For instance, unlike the British and Americans, Scandinavians no longer consider imprisonment to be a legitimate means of dealing effectively with youth offending, nor do they consider, unlike the Americans, the death penalty a humane or legitimate punishment. At a pre-rational stage, then, certain policy options are pre-selected for consideration at later stages and others never pass the test of cultural appropriateness and are discarded out of hand. The concept of political culture is meant to convey this process of pre-rational filtration. The primary interest is at this level, where cultural forces determine the range and array of considerable policies.

'The causal status of any assumption is permissive rather than deterministic' (Elkins and Simeon, 1979: 133). Political culture thus permits or constrains the agency of actors but cannot on its own dictate decisions. This is why I locate the influence of political culture further up the funnel in Figure 4.2, removed from much of the swirling pressures within the funnel itself that constrain day-to-day decision-making.

So conceived, 'political culture, then, is a shorthand expression for a "mind set" which has the effect of limiting attention to less than the full range of alternative behaviors, problems, and solutions which are logically possible. Since it represents a "disposition" in favor of a range of alternatives, by corollary another range of alternatives receives little or no attention within a particular culture' (Elkins and Simeon, 1979: 128). These dispositions solidify over time in a jurisdiction, they serve to guide subsequent political action, but they are also constantly in flux, shifting and reacting to changes in economic and social forces.

Along with Street (1994), Elkins and Simeon expand the definition of political culture to include a range of superficially nonpolitical assumptions. Some of the assumptions that they identify as important to the shaping of political culture include:

1. Assumptions about the orderliness of the universe...
2. Presumptions about the nature of causality. Is the world random? Are events foredestined? Inevitable? Are human agents more or less important than impersonal material causes?
3. What are the principal goals of political life?
4. Should one try to maximize gains, or to minimize losses? In other words, what assumptions are made about the relative payoffs of optimistic or pessimistic strategies?
5. Who belongs to one's political community? Is it a vaguely bounded community, or is it one marked by sharp 'we-they' distinctions? Do the boundaries vary with types of situations, or are they more or less unchanging? To whom or to what does one owe any obligation?
6. What types of events, actions, or institutions are deemed political (as opposed to economic, social, etc.), or is a sharp line drawn at all? Is 'the political' a positively or negatively valued domain?
7. Assumptions about others—their trustworthiness, public spiritedness, etc.—and about how one should relate to them. (Elkins and Simeon, 1979: 132)

Several of these are particularly important in a comparison of the dissimilar responses to the Bulger and Redergård cases. First, presumptions about causality will likely impact on the ways in which blame and responsibility are apportioned in each case. Whether or not events have 'systematic causes or whether they are largely fortuitous or accidental' (Elkins and Simeon, 1979: 132) will have implications for the sort of response deemed appropriate. Second, strong 'we–they' distinctions between political parties, as are made in England, are likely to create incentives both for inter-party conflict and for politicizing crime events as tools to undermine the power and credibility of the sitting government. In contrast, Norwegian political culture is less divided and political behaviour less divisive so as to minimize the need to politicize such events. Third, assumptions about the trustworthiness of individuals, and about whether humans are basically good or evil, are also important as they imply the appropriateness of compassion, forgiveness, and reintegration as well as denunciation, punishment, and expulsion.

These cultural assumptions will 'affect the ways policy makers interact and their style of behavior; what forms of behavior are legitimate; what criteria (scientific, religious, etc.) should be applied to policies; how the policy field is perceived (as consensual or conflictual, zero- or variable-sum); [and] who is permitted to participate' (Elkins and Simeon, 1979: 142). Other unmentioned assumptions that are important to this study concern the usefulness of social scientific research, the expertise of its practitioners, the deference deserved by elites, and idealized notions of justice, as in the appropriateness of vengeance versus forgiveness. These questions provide the blueprint for a discourse-focused investigation of comparative political cultures in Norway and England.

The making of culture

Street shifts the focus beyond political culture as an explanation:

If we are to take seriously attempts to link popular culture, political culture and political practice, then more attention needs to be paid to the process by which the culture itself is created and sustained. If culture provides a set of resources or collective representations, and if these help to shape action, then surely we need to know how people get access to this culture and why one set of symbols rather than another is available. Only then can we use culture to account for action. Instead of talking of the explanatory power of political culture [as Elkins and Simeon do, though

Street does not mention them], we need first to *explain political culture*. This means shifting the focus away from political action or the content of political culture, and looking instead at the ways by which that culture is sustained and disseminated. (Street, 1994: 110, emphasis in original)

This book attempts to provide one such explanation in the chapters to come. Culture is disseminated on the wings of discourse, mostly via the media, and these accumulating discourses are affirmed, or not, by a range of legitimate claims-makers embedded within prominent institutions.

Definitions of political culture have expanded since Almond and Verba (1963) examined its explanatory usefulness with *The Civic Culture*. The centrality of political culture to explanations of international differences in political behaviour requires a better understanding of how culture forms and how it recreates itself (Street, 1994). The central question of this study can be borrowed from Elkins and Simeon (1979: 136): 'What accounts for the existence of particular policies, attitudes, or behaviors in one collectivity rather than another?' Disentangling the structural from the institutional 'carriers' of culture requires a process that for the purposes of this book is not of particular importance. Suffice to say that culture also resides within institutions. For instance, in describing a relatively homogeneous nation like Norway, institutional variables like ethnicity, social economic status, relative deprivation, and religion could all be important carriers of culture. The relatively uncontested dominance of particular institutions and the cultural norms they carry can help to explain the durability and stability of Norwegian political culture. I am concerned with institutional questions too, for instance, the presence or predominance of particular groups or individuals in the debates that result (psychiatrists, social workers, academics, etc). My concern is also cultural, as I am interested in the dissimilar assumptions underpinning appropriate responses to the two cases, assumptions which interact in ways influenced by the institutional and structural variables. The concerns of this study are the dissimilar assumptions underpinning public attitudes and political action. Therefore, the question of whether these assumptions are attached to one institution's dominance over others is helpful in explaining the dominance of particular cultural norms and assumptions. Understanding the ways that culture is disseminated is also important in the process of identifying means to affect public assumptions and attitudes.

The personality of particular political actors is a less powerful force in homogeneous political cultures with a narrower range of assumptions than it is in heterogeneous jurisdictions with a wide range of assumptions (Elkins and Simeon, 1979). In more complex cultures where some assumptions might conflict, individuals are granted greater latitude to mine particular cultural seams and to ignore others. The wider political agenda and the range of policy options are still set by the political culture in these complex jurisdictions, but the room to manoeuvre—the agency of political actors—is greater than it is in more homogeneous ones. In the English context following the Bulger case, Home Secretary Michael Howard and Tony Blair, his opposition shadow in the Labour Party at the time, were able to mine with legitimacy particular seams in the culture that comported with their own political aims as competing political opponents. That there was support among the public for their competitively punitive reactions to the Bulger case is not in doubt. That they chose for political reasons to mine that seam rather than others that were in existence at the time is also not in doubt. But the adversarial nature of English political activity combined with the changes in the role played by public opinion on crime and punishment issues, explored in Chapter 8, almost demanded it.

High-Profile Cases and the 'Crisis-Reform Thesis'

Criminal justice practitioners and policymakers often work in the shadows of particular high-profile cases, finding themselves bound by the changes in discourse compelled by them. In 1959, during his tenure as Conservative Party Home Secretary, Lord R.A. Butler proposed the establishment of the Institute of Criminology at the University of Cambridge. Explaining his rationale, Butler (1974) later observed:

I was determined that there should be a long-term plan: a course of action that would lay a path for an enlightened penal policy. In particular I believed that changes should not be based on swings in emotion and opinion, prone as they are to the influence of dramatic events and bizarre cases, but upon reliable information about the phenomenon of crime, its social and personal roots and the effectiveness of the preventive and penal measures available.

Butler's statement illustrates both that concerns of this kind are not new and that many obstacles remain on the path to realizing his vision. It is clear that some jurisdictions remain more susceptible to the influence of isolated, high-profile cases than others, and that particular voices in some jurisdictions play more prominent roles in shaping dominant discourses than they do in others.

As Stan Cohen (2002: 1) first observed in 1972 when his highly influential and much talked about book first appeared:

Societies appear to be subject, every now and then, to periods of moral panic. A condition, episode, person or group of persons emerges to become defined as a threat to societal values and interests; its nature is presented in a stylized and stereotypical fashion by the mass media; the moral barricades are manned by editors, bishops, politicians and other right-thinking people...Sometimes the panic passes over and is forgotten...[A]t other times it has more serious repercussions and might produce such changes as those in legal and social policy or even in the way society conceives itself.

In the years since, the concept of moral panic has become part of the common lexicon. It was intended to refer to disproportionate responses to exaggerated threats that tend to do more harm than good. However, the concern and attention such high-profile cases can generate can be viewed in another way.

The 'crisis-reform thesis' holds that high-profile crisis events like notorious crimes tend to open 'windows of opportunity' (Moore, 1995) that create a 'situation of diminished constraints' (Resodihardjo, 2003) in the policymaking process and enhance the discretion of policy actors to get things done (Tonry, 2004b; Tonry and Green, 2003). These cases also tend to trigger normative debates, and they, like discourses, have both 'meanings and effects' (Carabine, 2001), shaping both our understanding of the world and our reactions to it. High-profile crime events tend to create shortcut paths which serve to bypass the normal obstacles, including pragmatic considerations, prudence, and rationality:

It is a fact well known to students of social policy that reforms of the system often take place not so much because of careful routine analysis by ministers and civil servants in the relevant Department of State...but because one or more individual incident(s) occurs, drawing public attention to...policy in a dramatic way which seems to demand change... [T]he reforms would not have taken place without the public attention created by the original incident. (Bottoms and Stevenson, 1992)

There are many international examples of the generative and catalyzing effects that high-profile crime events can have on policy which support the crisis-reform thesis (see Tonry and Green, 2003).

Culture and context play important roles in shaping both the definition of crises and the opportunities for reform that arise from them. Resodihardjo (2003) uses the control crisis generated by the contemporaneous escapes from two British dispersal prisons (Whitemoor in September 1994 and Parkhurst in January 1995) to illustrate the importance of context in determining the discretion available to policymakers following a crisis event. Prior to the escapes, and in contrast to Kenneth Clarke, his predecessor as Home Secretary, Michael Howard had already appeared frequently in the media espousing a 'tough on crime' approach to law and order that included a new affirmation that 'prison works'. Simultaneously, modernizers in the Labour Party, principally Tony Blair and Gordon Brown, had resolved to compete with the Conservatives as the party toughest on crime (Downes and Morgan, 1997). These two factors had already contributed to a harsh and hot penal climate, and the escapes increased the temperature.

High-profile crisis events tend to increase the temperature of the penal climate, but the severity of that increase is influenced by the political culture. Howard's reaction to the prison escapes provides an example:

> These events would have been newsworthy and controversial at any time. In the penal climate of 1993–5 they were especially so. Not only did they raise difficult questions about the division of responsibility between the Home Secretary and the Director General of the New [Prison Service] Agency, but they also followed hard on the heels of a renewed and very deliberate politicisation of penal affairs initiated by the Home Secretary himself. This prior stance—and the general tenor of retrenchment and increasing severity that went with it—seem to have conditioned the nature of the official response to the Whitemoor and Parkhurst incidents. (Sparks, Bottoms and Hay, 1996: 23)

Howard then might have actually had *less* room to manoeuvre than he might have had without the escapes crisis. The reasons for this, as Resodihardjo (2003: 8) argues, have to do with the context in which the crisis occurred:

Howard's own public image combined with the fight on law and order resulted in very little leeway for Howard. It seems, for instance, almost impossible for a Home Secretary to respond with a 'soft' approach in these circumstances. If the 'soft' approach is not an option, then this means that the Home Secretary did not have that much discretion during the crisis. In fact, it seems that Home Secretary's own actions before the crisis broke out determined what options were available to him once the crisis broke out. By portraying himself as a tough minister before the crisis broke out, Howard could do nothing but be tough once the crisis started.

What Resodihardjo describes here are the limiting manifestations of the penal climate. Most notably, this climate was created in part by the aspects of the British political culture that compelled Labour and the Conservatives to engage in a battle to outdo one another on the law and order issue. It is possible that no politician in the climate of the time, participating in that political culture, threatened by the opposition on law and order issues, could have acted much differently. That Howard's response was one-dimensionally tough and punitive may have had more to do with the penal climate and the political culture, which Howard certainly played a part in creating, than with him in particular.

Once the climate cools and the compulsion to act has diminished in intensity, constraints formerly avoided can return. For instance, the Treasury agreed to fund the implementation of the recommendations in the Woodcock report published in December 1994, investigating the circumstances behind the six Whitemoor escapes, but over time, financial support from the Treasury for the implementation of the 1995 Learmont report's[2] recommendations was never granted (Resodihardjo, 2003: 5). The money was not made available partly because of inter-agency friction between the Home Office and the Treasury. Howard applied pressure to the Treasury's Chief Secretary to commit the funds necessary to allow him to announce in the House of Commons that the government was to accept all sixty-four of the Woodcock recommendations, pressure that the Treasury would later resent (Lewis, 1997: 159). The crisis was forceful enough to generate a very public pledge to fund the recommendations, but apparently not forceful enough to carry them to fruition.

---

[2] Learmont's investigation of security in the Prison Service was initiated following the Whitemoor escapes but was expanded to include the three at Parkhurst on 3 January 1995 as well.

Similarly, as the pressure upon policymakers to act was intense in the immediate wake of the Bulger case, the Treasury initially freed up money it had previously withheld for the building of five Secure Training Centres (STCs) for the detention of 12–14-year-olds (Windlesham, 1996: 51–2). After a successful police campaign that called for Secure Training Orders (STOs) in response to what was believed by some to be an increase in the number of 'persistent young offenders', the Home Office introduced the proposal during Kenneth Clarke's tenure as Home Secretary. The Treasury had actually earlier abandoned the proposal, but resuscitated it in the wake of the Bulger case as press attention and public concern rose. The STOs were included in the Criminal Justice and Public Order Act 1994, though the Crime and Disorder Act 1998 replaced them with the Detention and Training Order (Goldson and Muncie, 2006b). Four of the five planned STCs currently exist.

These examples illustrate four points. First, the reform component of the crisis-reform thesis is subject to the conditions of the penal climate and the political culture. Second, the intensity and the duration of a crisis—or more importantly the perception of crisis—govern the degree of discretion policymakers have, in ways both more and less restricting, and the extent of reform possible. Third, there is a mutually reinforcing, reciprocal relationship between the penal climate and high-profile crisis events. Each feeds off the intensity of the other in a way and to an extent influenced by the existing political–cultural context. Fourth, this context must be central to any framework that is developed to analyse and to explain divergent policy outcomes, as this book does.

Conclusion

This chapter has explored the concept of political culture by considering the ways in which it helps to regulate the range of available policy options in the wake of a high-profile crisis event. Responses to the Bulger and Redergård killings were conditioned by jurisdictionally distinct sets of cultural assumptions about the ways in which individuals ought to interact, and about which kinds of knowledge are most valuable. The next two chapters consider the constraining effects generated by discourses and by the mass media. Chapters 8 and 9 deal in more depth with the more concrete manifestations of political–cultural constraints.

5

The Constraints of Discourse

As crime and punishment issues have become more politicized over the last quarter century in most Western countries, criminological discourse has become only one among many discursive streams competing for influence in penal policy debates. As Garland and Sparks (2001: 3) put it, 'Given the centrality, the emotiveness and the political salience of crime issues today, academic criminology can no longer aspire to monopolize "criminological" discourse or hope to claim exclusive rights over the representation and disposition of crime.' In England and the USA, assessments of public opinion on crime and punishment issues (or, more accurately, what typically stands in for it) and media representations (emphasizing the most extreme, sensational crimes, often failing to contextualize the particular offence in question and focusing on the emotional impacts of crime from victims' points of view) compete with the more rationally and systematically accumulated criminological knowledge—those concerned with questions of crime causation, prevention, and the effectiveness of penal sanctions. And most often, on the most emotive of crime and punishment issues at least, criminological knowledge has not fared well in the competition (Blumstein, 1993, 1997; Blumstein and Petersilia, 1995; Hood, 1974, 2001, 2002; Tonry and Green, 2003).

Before innovating new ways to bring criminological knowledge to bear more directly on matters of crime and punishment policy, a better understanding must be gained of the ways in which all forms of knowledge and discourse affect the public's consciousness and those of policymakers. This chapter argues the merits of more discourse-analytic approaches to criminological research that might approach this goal. The aim is to discover the dominant discourses shaping policy debates by, in a comparative perspective, tracing their outlines and the limits they impose on the breadth of considered policy options. This chapter thus provides the theoretical bedrock upon which the textual analysis of the press coverage of the Bulger and Redergård cases in Chapter 7 is built.

The focus of this research is specific, but also inevitably broad. It is comparative. It draws upon several disciplines at once and attempts to bring together strands of social theory, political theory, and theories of knowledge utilization in policymaking. By approaching the topic using comparative case studies, the aim is to tie together several theoretical threads that have yet to be joined. The study has three research goals that are useful to reiterate: first, to uncover the most likely dominant drivers of policy—the most prevalent and powerful discourses shaping the decision-making of penal policymakers in each jurisdiction at the time of the homicide; second, to attempt to describe and account for differences in the transmitted discourse—in the attitudes and behaviour exhibited by the actors involved in both the framing of issues in the newspapers subsequent to the homicide, and in shaping any political response; and third, in light of the findings, to provide a practical strategy to help inject into decision-making processes more opportunities for the rational and deliberate reflection upon research knowledge and evidence.

Specific to this study, there are three sets of questions which discourse-analytic approaches are particularly capable to address. The first concerns the *content* of the discourses and the discursive construction of child-on-child homicide. What are the similarities and differences between how the various discourses or forms of knowledge (media, public opinion, ideology, bureaucratic interests, research knowledge) are accounted for in the signification process? How prevalent in relative terms are each of these forms of 'valid knowledge' within each jurisdiction (Jäger, 2001), and which are dominant? The focus on dominant discourses is justified because the public's views and impressions of issues are most shaped by exposure to these dominant discourses (Helleiner, 1998; Van Dijk, 1997).

The questions of the second group focus on the *context* within which discourses are embedded. What are the similarities and differences between the policymaking processes of the two jurisdictions? To what extent are these explanations due to inter-jurisdictional structural differences within the agencies involved (police, media, government, public opinion) and to what extent are they due to jurisdictionally distinct legal and political cultures? How can one account for differences in the ways in which each of the two child killings was handled by the parties involved (police, media, politicians, public)?

The third set of questions concern the *quality* or diversity of the discourses flowing into the discursive stream. What discourses are missing from the dominant stream? Why are some more dominant than others? How can the discourse stream be enriched to include excluded knowledges and discourses? How can the thin public discourse informing penal policymakers be 'thickened' to include forms of expert knowledge?

This chapter provides the rationale for the discourse-analytic approach adopted in this study, and it is organized into three main sections. The first links concepts from the political science literature on knowledge utilization—including *paradigms*, *boundedness*, *congeniality*, *windows of opportunity*, *professional social inquiry*, *social learning*, and *ordinary knowledge*—and indicates how these dovetail with the concerns of discourse analysis. The second section reviews the relevant literature and summarizes the case for the discourse-analytic approach employed in this book. The fourth section sets out six reasons why discourse-analytic approaches are appropriate to this study in particular, and to comparative criminological work more generally concerned with shifts in penal trends.

Discourse and 'Knowledge Utilization'

Knowledge utilization research from the 1970s and 1980s helps illustrate the obscured and gradual ways in which social science research knowledge seeps into consciousness and influences the decision-making of policymakers. This research also provides a useful starting point to begin thinking about the ways that discourses constrain thinking and action, and how some discourses or knowledges find favour over others.

The prevailing policy culture in a society has numerous constraining boundaries with which policymakers must contend. The concept of prevailing 'shared paradigms' (Kuhn, 1996: 11) describes the existence of a dominant viewpoint or cognitive filter which tends to constrain the range of innovative options available to policymakers. To draw again on the funnel model in the previous chapter, a paradigm operates as a macro-level filter. 'Boundedness' is a term used in the knowledge utilization literature to describe the more localized pragmatic restrictions placed upon policy actors that limit their bureaucratic and organizational room for manoeuvre in a particular time and place (Weiss, 1986). Boundedness refers to the micro-level constraints at the bottom of the funnel, further filtering various kinds of information and policy options that the dominant paradigms admit for consideration. These constraints mean that research knowledge usually and eventually percolates into practice in a subtle and often frustratingly slow and indirect process, variously referred to as 'diffuse enlightenment', 'decision accretion', and 'knowledge creep' (Weiss, 1986, 1987). The soil must first be fertile if new knowledge is to take root.

The shift from an indeterminate, individualized sentencing ethos that dominated American penal thinking for most of the twentieth century to the determinate, retributive one that subsequently replaced it in many jurisdictions illustrates the relationship between dominant paradigms and the utilization of research knowledge (see Tonry and Green, 2003). In 1974 Robert Martinson famously declared that virtually 'nothing works' rehabilitatively to reduce recidivism rates among most offenders, but at the time few policymakers were listening. The shared paradigm of the time was one that embraced individualized treatment tailored to the particular needs of the offender, and significant confidence was retained in the rehabilitative treatment model in spite of the evidence challenging it.

Policymakers only absorbed Martinson's research findings, flawed and overdrawn as they might have been, once they became 'congenial' (Lempert, 1998) to the dominant paradigm, which by the late 1970s and 1980s, had shifted to a retributive, determinate sentencing model. Put another way, Martinson's findings were heeded only after a 'window of opportunity' had opened which allowed decision-makers to act upon them. Moore (1995) argues that windows of opportunity are created by the coalescence of political wills and bureaucratic utility in a particular place and time. Often this occurs cyclically, and policy issues raised and dealt with at one time come around again later. As demonstrated by the crisis-reform thesis discussed in the preceding chapter, windows are also opened by the weight of growing social problems, or by the perceptions of such problems, that have become so urgent that a policy response seems required. The size and dimensions of these windows are subject to a range of bureaucratic, structural, cultural, and political forces. These forces determine both the scale of the policy change allowed by an open window, and the duration that a window of opportunity remains open.

Jäger (2001: 48) uses the Chernobyl nuclear accident to illustrate the catalyzing, window-opening power of such a 'media discursive event'. As a result of the concerns raised by the accident and the massive media coverage it received, Germany changed its nuclear policy, a goal which the Green movement and its discourse had been unable to achieve. In other words, Chernobyl opened up a window of opportunity, facilitated by the media's interest in the story, which allowed particular activists to further their cause. To give a more pertinent example, the Bulger case became a major media discursive event in England, significantly impacting a host of subsequent discourses and opening windows of opportunity for policy change. In Norway, a similar killing did not become a media discursive event to the same extent and fewer windows of opportunity opened. The nature of the concerns generated by the killing there were such that penal policy changes were deemed inappropriate means to respond to what happened.

Lindblom and Cohen (1979: 19) explore the ways in which the learning generated by systematic research, what they call 'professional social inquiry' (PSI), influences policy. They use the concept of 'social learning' to explain how PSI, as contrasted with more fallible and commonsensical 'ordinary knowledge', is often ineffectual in altering the assumptions of ordinary knowledge. As they explain, 'until the required learning occurs, PSI may be futile…The common opinion "things will have to get worse before they get better" testifies to the possibility that a problem cannot be solved until people have had—or suffered—such experiences as will bring them to new attitudes and political dispositions'. Carol Weiss (1983) developed the 'I-I-I framework' which embodies the range of conflicting interests that constrain decision-making and helps to conceptualize the turbulent arena of micro-level policymaking. It takes account of the conflicts that arise between 'Ideology' (the values and political orientation of a group or political administration), 'Interests' (primarily the self-interest of particular bureaucrats and public officials), and 'Information' (both PSI and ordinary knowledge, gleaned from a variety of sources). Information of all kinds, much of it intuitive and experiential and in competition with the findings of research, must also compete with self-interest and ideology.

Analysing Discourse

Discourse refers in this study to the larger collection of vocabulary and concepts that define the limits placed upon crime control and penal policy debates. Only when analysed comparatively, as within two such culturally distinct jurisdictions as Norway and England, do differences in the dominant discourse become apparent. Discourse in the sense the term is used here is defined by Stuart Hall (1992: 291): 'A discourse is a group of statements which provide the language for talking about—i.e. a way of representing—a particular kind of knowledge about a topic. When statements about a topic are made within a particular discourse, the discourse makes it possible to construct the topic in a certain way. It also limits the other ways in which the topic can be constructed.' A group of statements cohere to create what Foucault (1972) calls a 'discursive formation', which represents the sociocultural 'support mechanisms' that give discourses their culturally distinct meanings (Mills, 1997: 49).

As Hall goes on to explain, 'discourse is about the production of knowledge through language. But it is itself produced by practice: "discursive practice"—the practice of producing meaning' (Hall, 1992: 291). It follows then that the various users of language produce various knowledges that can be examined. For instance, the tabloid press in England produces particular knowledges about children who kill that differ from those produced by the broadsheet press, or by criminologists, or by criminal justice practitioners. Politicians produce knowledges by debating the topic in parliaments, and these debates often yield particular laws and policies that further disseminate these knowleges. Political knowledges draw upon those produced by the other institutional players on the various tiers associated with policymaking, including the press, the public, practitioners, and the scientific community. The subsequent political discourse also reflects, in varying proportions between jurisdictions and over time, so-called ordinary knowledge and PSI. In turn these proportions can be assessed by analysing discourse to determine the justifications for the positions espoused in it.

Discourse analysis involves 'the search for patterns within language in use' (Taylor, 2001: 13). A central idea in the study of discourse is that language or discourse is 'constitutive'—that is, 'it creates what it refers to' (Taylor, 2001: 8)—but it is also referential in that it conveys information about something that actually exists. Taylor contends that a discourse analyst must struggle to determine the extent to which data is to be treated as referential, or as constitutive. According to Foucault, discourses are groups of coherent statements that are 'productive' (Carabine, 2001)—they accumulate to produce 'both meanings and effects in the real world', or in Foucauldian terms, they have 'power outcomes or effects' that define the 'truth' of what lies behind an issue (Carabine, 2001: 268). Concerning the discourse of unmarried motherhood, Carabine (2001: 269) writes:

Discourses are also fluid and often opportunistic, at one and the same time, drawing upon existing discourses about an issue whilst utilising, interacting with, and being mediated by, other dominant discourses (about, for example, family, femininity, morality, gender, race, ethnicity, sexuality, disability and class, etc.) to produce potent and new ways of conceptualising the issue or topic. This is another sense in which discourse is productive. In so doing, discourses 'hook' into normative ideas and common-sense notions, say, about sexuality (that heterosexuality is natural and normal, that homosexuality is abnormal and deviant), morality or motherhood. This produces shortcut paths into ideas which convey messages about, for example, 'good' and 'bad' (mothering, sexualities, etc.), morality and immorality (behaviours and relationships), and acceptable and inappropriate behaviours. These representations or ways of speaking not only convey meanings about the topic, they also have material effects.

Discourse is a means of simplification whereby complex and differentiated social phenomena are categorized and presented in a 'system of representation' meant to represent reality. This process of simplification is what gives discourses their constraining characteristics. Discourses construct a particular version of the issue, and are therefore said to be constitutive. These effects are particularly pronounced in news discourse.

While the intended effect of the news story is to make consumers believe that they are witnesses to reality, reality is always inferential. What appears as iconic is actually the result of a process in which journalists and sources have necessarily gone beyond the knowledge apprehended by them, reconstructing it in ways that displace the observed world. The reality is that the news is embedded in the criteria of rational acceptability of news practice, and as such it is not mind- or discourse-independent. News discourse is not about objects; it constitutes objects. News reality depends on how the comments of journalists and sources have been contextualized in the narrative, and ultimately on how this contextualization is visualized by the consumer. (Ericson, Baranek and Chan, 1991: 32)

The constitutive and productive discourses of most concern to this study are, for instance, childhood innocence and evil, and child inculpability and culpability. These are 'binary oppositions' which enable each opposing concept to 'carry meaning' or 'to signify' (Hall, 1992: 279). There has been a clear tendency for the English press and politicians to associate the killing of James Bulger with a vague concept of evil. The result has been a slow and perhaps unconscious shift enabling onlookers (newspaper readers, news consumers, voters) to envision the perpetrators of these acts as individuals essentially different from themselves. Notions of 'the Other' are explored at length elsewhere (Hall, 2001; Young, 1999), but at this point in the analysis it is enough to suggest that such notions make calls for harsh penal treatment to address the harm caused by this evil easier to hear and to accept as viable and appropriate responses. But the conception of children as evil is not fixed and permanent. It is a result of historically accumulated experience, a sign of the dominance of particular discourses over others. Edley (2001) usefully likened this accumulated knowledge to 'sedimentary rock', and Foucault called this process 'normalization' (Carabine, 2001). Discourses 'establish the norm' (Carabine, 2001: 277), answering our questions, asked and implied, about what ought to happen. Discourses vary and shift over time and between jurisdictions, changing in line with shifts in conceptions of the normative.

Knowledge and power

'Discourse' is similar to 'ideology': 'a set of statements or beliefs which produce knowledge that serves the interests of a particular group or class' (Hall, 1992: 292). However, according to Hall, Foucault favours the term discourse over ideology because:

ideology is based on a distinction between *true* statements about the world (science) and *false* statements (ideology), and the belief that the facts about the world help us to decide between true and false statements. But Foucault argues that statements about the social, political or moral world are rarely ever simply true or false; and 'the facts' do not enable us to decide definitely about their truth or falsehood, partly because 'facts' can be construed in different ways. The very language used to describe so-called facts interferes in this process of finally deciding what is true, and what is false. (Hall, 1992: 292, emphasis in original)

Perhaps nowhere else are these issues of truth and falsehood, validity and invalidity, more scrutinized than in criminology. Furthermore, even despite recent efforts in England to ground criminal justice decision-making on criminological evidence, it is still clear to many that much of the decision-making upon which criminal policy depends is strongly influenced by non-scientific, non-instrumental, normative, symbolic concerns (Garland, 2001; Hood, 2002; Tonry and Green, 2003).

Rather than analyse either the scientific or ideological evidence used to support a particular point of view or policy decision, it is more appropriate to analyse discourse, although discourse is clearly comprised—in varying degrees over time and between locations—of a mix of both kinds of evidence. Part of the justification for the use of discourse analysis is to be found in its ability to scrutinize the composition of discourse on a topic and to determine the origins of its rhetorical positions. As Hall (1992: 294–5) writes, 'the knowledge which a discourse produces constitutes a kind of power, exercised over those who are "known". When that knowledge is exercised in practice, those who are "known" in a particular way will be subject (i.e. subjected) to it. This is always a power-relation (see Foucault, 1980: 201). Those who produce the discourse also have the power to make it true—i.e. to enforce its validity, its scientific status'. For instance, after we in England come to 'know' the killers of James Bulger as 'evil' children, it is difficult to unlearn what we 'know', especially as this knowledge is reproduced and confirmed daily in the press and by legitimate claims-makers like the police and politicians.

Like Foucauldian discourse analysis, critical discourse analysis (CDA) is concerned with the relationship between knowledge and power. 'The term CDA is used nowadays to refer more specifically to the critical linguistic approach of scholars who find the larger discursive unit of text to be the basic unit of communication' (Wodak, 2001: 2). Of interest here are these larger discursive texts, specifically in order to identify the emergent consensuses implied within their assumptions, and to compare these assumptions to those implied in the discourses dominant in the other jurisdiction.

As Wodak (2001: 10) explains, 'for CDA, language is not powerful on its own—it gains power by the use powerful people make of it. This explains why ... [critical linguistics] often chooses the perspective of those who suffer, and critically analyses the language use of those in power, who are responsible for the existence of inequalities and who also have the means and opportunity to improve conditions'. This particular study is concerned with power relationships insofar as it is interested to identify the dominant discourses wielding the most influence upon policymaking in the two jurisdictions. The existence of a dominant discourse implicates dominant actors, groups, or institutions that propagate it. The study is critical in the sense that it seeks to go beyond description to discover the reasons particular discourses have dominance over others. This dominance then indicates a power relationship, requiring some consideration of the legitimacy of that relationship. Once the socially constructed nature of discourses is established and certain ones emerge as dominant or 'hegemonic' (Gramsci, 1971), an additional concern of critical discourse analysis is to determine whose interests are best served by the particular dominant discursive formations (Edley, 2001). One way to do this is to focus upon the effects of the dominant discourse and to analyse how the establishment and retention of the dominant discourse in an established hierarchy affects the control of power.

However, the intent is not critical in the sense that it is driven by ideological or normative conceptions of the right way to approach the topic, or that it adopts a particular political stance in relation to the topic.[1] The intention is to describe and to try to explain the nature and justifications for the dominance of some discourses over others in a particular jurisdiction. No more a political stand is taken than to assert that PSI and other forms of empirical knowledge deserve consideration in policy debates.[2]

As Jäger (2001: 33) explains, 'discourse analysis pertains to both everyday knowledge [ordinary knowledge] that is conveyed

---

[1] Taylor (2001: 24) points out that discourse analysis 'is not a neutral, technical form of processing but always involves theoretical backgrounding and decision making'. However, these decisions need not be highly controversial, provided the decisions are made transparently and reflexively.

[2] As to the epistemological arguments this debate over valid truth creates, I do not take the fully post-modernist position and declare that truth is entirely unknowable. I argue instead that when making policy decisions, the scientific validity of some knowledge, professional social inquiry (PSI), for instance, is preferable to that of ordinary knowledge. However, I do not discount the 'practical validity' of forms of ordinary knowledge, as it has been an extremely potent adversary to criminological PSI. Policymakers in democratic societies must consider all forms of knowledge, including, for instance, that produced by the tabloid press. However, it is defensibly preferable that PSI and the knowledge it produces should be afforded the best opportunity to inform criminal policy debates. Understanding the mechanics and content of the dominant discourses can help facilitate this.

via the media, everyday communication, school and family, and so on, and also to that particular knowledge [ie PSI] (valid at a certain place at a certain time) which is produced by the various sciences'. Part of the interest in analysing everyday knowledge and particular knowledge is to assess the degree of agreement that exists between the discourses and knowledge relied upon by journalists and editors, criminal justice practitioners, criminologists, and policymakers between and among the two jurisdictions. Of interest is the possible explanations which could account for the range of existing agreement.

For instance, at one time, before crime issues became so politicized and faith still existed that experts could solve the problem of crime, it is likely that the various lay and professional discourses, and the knowledge to which they both referred to and constituted, were more aligned than they are today. Today discourses on crime and punishment policy propagated by the tabloid press in England share little in common with the criminological discourse. One goal of this study is to gain a fuller understanding of the relationship between discourses and their construction with a view to providing some guidance about how experts can better bring the knowledges they have accumulated to bear more directly upon policy debates and the wider public discourse.

The constraints of 'interpretive repertoires'

Discourse analytic approaches are useful in illuminating the 'interpretative repertoires' (Edley, 2001) utilized to construct the discourse surrounding child innocence in Norway and child evil in England. Interpretative repertoires are defined as 'basically a lexicon or register of terms and metaphors drawn upon to characterise and evaluate actions and events' (Potter and Wetherell, 1987). Edley (2001: 198) explains that

> ...interpretative repertoires...are relatively coherent ways of talking about objects and events in the world. In discourse analytical terms, they are the 'building blocks of conversation', a range of linguistic resources that can be drawn upon and utilised in the course of everyday social interaction. Interpretative repertoires are part and parcel of any community's common sense, providing a basis for shared social understanding. They can be usefully thought of as books on the shelves of a public library, permanently available for borrowing...[W]hen people talk (or think) about things, they invariably do so in terms already provided for them by history.

Much of it is a rehearsal or recital. This is not to say, of course, that there can never be such a thing as an original or novel conversation... What it does mean, however, is that conversations are usually made up of a patchwork of 'quotations' from various interpretative repertoires. Or, in terms of a quite different metaphor, interpretative repertoires are like the pre-figured steps that can be flexibly and creatively strung together in the improvisation of dance.

The media rely upon precedent to construct news narratives, thus enhancing the recitational effect of dominant repertoires. As discussed in the later chapters, public deliberation exercises like the Deliberative Poll interrupt these recitations and ensure considered reflection on a wider range of available knowledge, including alternative interpretative repertoires.

Interpretative repertoires are located in conversations, and these conversations consist of, for the purposes here, the dialogue between and among journalists and readers, government ministers, MPs and constituents, and practitioners, as well as between and among criminologists in the journals in which they publish. Documents are conversational in the sense they are written for an audience. Newspaper coverage can be thought of as a conversation reflecting certain interpretative repertoires and indicating the relative positions of existing discourses on a hierarchy, some dominant and some secondary.

The discourse-analytic approach adopted in this study aims ultimately to account for disparate policy outcomes and public reactions which are related to the cultural distinctiveness of the two jurisdictions on the one hand, and of the various groups of claims-makers (the press, the public, government representatives and policymakers, researchers, practitioners) in each on the other. Each individual is inevitably 'located' in the dominant discourse and uses language in ways that reflect that positioning. This approach requires the analyst to move 'beyond the study of language use, that is, from the "discursive" to the "extra-discursive", probably blurring any distinction between them' (Taylor, 2001: 8). The extra-discursive implies action based upon the knowledge represented or constituted by language. The language available to people enables and constrains not only the expression of their ideas but also how they act upon them. An approach of this kind 'understands the language user not as a free agent but as one who is heavily constrained in her or his choice of language and action, even if those are not fully determined' by the dominant discourse (Taylor, 2001: 10).

Discourse and sensibilities

Various ideological and organizational limitations and restrictions conduce to particular trends in policymaking. This study is essentially a study of the limits and restrictions imposed upon particular policy debates sparked in the wake of the killing of children by children in two societies. The study of discourse can shed light on otherwise imperceptible phenomena. Michael Tonry's interest in his recent book *Thinking About Crime: Sense and Sensibility in American Penal Culture* is to account for American penal exceptionalism—to uncover the reasons why the USA's punishment levels greatly exceed those of any of its Western peers. In doing so, he writes, 'the ways people think about contentious issues change slowly but predictably. Social scientists use the word "sensibilities" to refer to prevailing social values, attitudes, and beliefs, and show how sensibilities change slowly over time and shape and reshape what people think and believe. Current American crime control policies are to a large part an outgrowth of American sensibilities of the past third of the twentieth century' (2004b: 5). Tonry's analysis of sensibilities does not specify how they are to be studied, but he implies that analysis is facilitated by historical, comparative, *ex post facto* perspectives that the passage of time and a suitably appreciative memory provide.

However, discourse-analytic methods can illuminate the grist of sensibilities as it is being churned out. By studying the language used by the various principal actors involved, these approaches can uncover the observable evidence of sensibilities as they are being shaped, and they can draw these sensibilities out into the open, trace their outlines, reveal their limitations, and possibly even discover their origins. Sensibilities are built of the knowledge produced by particular discourses, ascendant at a particular time and place, and changeable. By tracing the underlying discourses one can render observable the otherwise ethereal concept of sensibility. Discourse is the mechanism by which sensibilities actually engage with the policymaking apparatus.

Six Reasons to Study Discourse

Specific to this comparative study, there are at least six primary reasons to study discourse. First, discourse analysis can help to free the observer from preconceptions imposed by one's own localized, dominant discourses. Zedner (1995: 518) compared the salience of law and order discourses in Germany and Britain and argues that 'Awareness of the "other" (assumptions, values, languages and forms) obliges us to recognize the contingency of our own laws and legal practices, and makes it difficult to maintain uncritical adherence to the dogmas of our own legal culture.' Discourse analysis can offer us a glimpse of our own boundedness, make us aware of the shared but often overlooked paradigms within which we work, and ensure that we don't 'mistake history for nature' (Edley, 2001). To give an example, Tonry explains how, in the 1950s, the American drafters of the Model Penal Code were subject to what in hindsight is a narrowly constrained view of justice—constrained by the absence of the retributive, just deserts discourses that would later dominate penal thinking. He writes 'like [Sherlock] Holmes's non-barking dog...the absence of issues from an era offers important clues to the governing penal sensibility. And, if those times were blind to some things and acutely aware of others, in each case opposite to our own times, we're just as vulnerable to collective selective awareness' (Tonry, 2004b: 172). The discourses drawn upon to bolster and recreate penal sensibilities engender just this sort of 'collective selective awareness', because the cognitive vocabulary at our disposal at a particular time allows only for the consideration of selected evidence—the basic raw materials—of which understandings of social phenomena are constructed.

Here is another example. Mathiesen identifies three 'public spheres' in and through which knowledge flows. Though he uses these spheres to illustrate how a pro-prison ideological consensus has been successfully propagated in most countries—or as he puts it, how the 'fiasco' of prison has been 'negated'—this framework has been recognized as a useful means to trace 'the influences which shape criminal policy, including those exerted by the joint moral community' (Rutherford, 1996: 129–34). This 'joint moral community', about which Norwegian criminologists Nils Christie (2000) and Thomas Mathiesen (1996; 2000) both write in some form, constitutes the central 'kernel' or core in which the specialized knowledge of experts, including researchers, is brought to bear. The second sphere or feedback circle, which is closest to the kernel, is that occupied by criminal justice practitioners. The outer sphere consists primarily of the mass media, though others have located public opinion here (Ryan, 2003: 129).[3]

Mathiesen argues that practitioners are less able to deny or ignore the 'fiasco' of prison, and therefore must pretend to believe in its facility. This 'pretence', combined with the outer feedback circle's 'non-recognition', is met by the 'disregard' exhibited by those in the kernel who must selectively overlook certain discrepancies that, if acknowledged, might undermine the legitimacy of prison:[4] 'But it should be recognized that the information reception centres in the other spheres—journalists, in newspapers, etc, as well as police chiefs, judges and so on—actually seek confirmation rather than information, so that the message of disregard is quite *selectively* transposed on the other spheres. This makes the responsibility of those disregarding the facts of the fiasco all the greater' (Mathiesen, 2000: 145, emphasis in original).[5]

As Mathiesen describes it, this state of affairs, another case of collective selective awareness, has much in common with the ways discourse analysts view the relationship between knowledge and power. Particular cognitions or ways of understanding the world are embraced at the expense of others. The flow of information between and among the spheres then reflects a certain degree of consensus on the construction of a problem. The cognitions chosen are dependent upon structural and cultural variables like the penal climate and political culture of a jurisdiction during a period of time.

Furthermore these political cultures, and their crucial 'gate-keeping' mechanisms that allow for varying degrees of interaction between interested stakeholders in policymaking, provide a structural framework in which discourses are constructed and maintained. As discussed more fully in Chapter 8, during the post-war

---

[3] That Mathiesen does not include the public per se in his framework is telling, as it assumes that media knowledge and public knowledge are the same, or at least that they are so similar as not to require distinction. However, as shown in Chapter 10, to presume that the media merely reflect public opinion is not the full story.

[4] Mathiesen appears to believe that this state of affairs can be redressed through the persuasion of already ambivalent actors.

[5] Mathiesen does not address the possibility that he, and all others as wed to a particular ideology as he is to the abolitionist agenda, might practice the same confirmative selectivity.

period in England, penal policy debates were shaped most by a small group that Mick Ryan calls the 'penal *cognoscenti*'. Their influence generated a penal discourse limited by the particular sensibilities and expertise of its members. As Ryan (2003: 41, emphasis in original) points out:

> ...as far as those who ran the government machine were concerned everybody who needed to be consulted was being consulted during these years, and what is more, among the *cognoscenti* there was a consensus; there were no genuinely new, critical voices. This self-congratulation was deeply ingrained. Those who make penal policy could not think themselves out of it, *nor could they be expected to*. What was required was a disruption of the wider, social democratic political consensus which challenged the authority of the State and undermined our entrenched feelings of deference towards those who ran the great Leviathan from Whitehall.

The closed intellectual environment significantly circumscribed the resulting penal discourse. Innovation was stifled because dissenting voices were unlikely to come from within the '*cognoscenti*'.

A second reason to study discourse is because it provides a means to recognize the power of language to shape our understanding of the world and any subsequent policy debates. Culture is revealed to us through discourse—through the language we use. One well-worn and perhaps apocryphal example is the existence within the Inuit languages of between four and forty (depending on the source) different words for snow. The point of the example is more important than whether it is true. The arsenal of words available and the ideas they represent can alone steer the course of debate. For instance, particular irrational and violent behaviours that are now attributed to mental illness could not be so attributed until the existing concept of mental illness, and all the vocabulary which its study has created, had been developed. We now commonly take for granted that mental illness exists, when others before us were comfortable to attribute the same behaviours to demonic possession, witchcraft, or divine retribution. Discourse analysis endeavours to illuminate what has been left unsaid, appreciating both what has been taken for granted, that which is hiding in plain sight but is ignored or neglected, and the implicit subtext behind what is said.

Third, scholars studying international punishment trends tend to agree that crime and punishment issues have become much more politicized over the last quarter century. Tough-on-crime rhetoric is a cliché in penal policy debates in the USA and in England, and increasingly commonplace elsewhere, albeit in a milder form, where it once was not, as in the Scandinavian countries. Penal policymaking is thus a political enterprise. Analyses attempting to determine the reasons for criminological research's inability to have clearly demonstrable effects upon major penal policy decision-making have tended to name political interests and contingencies as major contributors to this ineffectualness. It follows that criminology as a field would benefit from a better understanding of the nature of the political pressures shaping policy decisions. Analysis of political rhetoric, and the wider discourses of which they are indicative and to which they refer, is a way of accomplishing this aim.

Fourth, discourse is the common and observable component linking all manner of otherwise ethereal social phenomena. For instance, the differences in policy outcomes and public reactions to the killings of James Bulger and Silje Redergård are due, in large part, to a combination of cultural and bureaucratic differences in the way social institutions are constructed in each country. Whatever the institution, discourse is the key to understanding the priorities of each. It is the common element that links them all together. For instance, the limitations and restrictions placed upon policy actors in a given time and place, those concepts with which knowledge utilization is concerned, can only be identified and understood by analysing the discourses that define those limitations. Discourse is the key to understanding these otherwise unobservable limitations.

Fifth, by utilizing the common links of discourse in this way, discourse analysis can demonstrate connections between previously unbridged literatures and disciplines. Connections between the policy analysis concepts of boundedness and windows of opportunity have connections with the concept of discourse. Government organizations whose windows of opportunity are limited when dealing with particular social problems face the limits and boundaries set by the dominant discourse framing the particular problem. Boundedness is tied to discourse in the same manner. The degree of boundedness experienced by a government policymaker is defined by the dominant discourses. Newspaper editors and journalists are similarly subject to their own distinct boundedness, just as they disseminate prevailing discourses. For instance, observers might pin much of the blame for English-style penal populism on those working in the tabloid press, but tabloid journalists and editors—like politicians, members of the public, and criminologists—work under the conditions and working practices imposed by their fields. Moreover, none work in a vacuum unmolested by prevailing discourses or wider cultural sensibilities. They reflect and emanate them, and not necessarily by reporting accurately or by giving voice to what the public says and feels. It is subtler than that. The dominant cultural discourses permeate the decision-making of all who are socialized within them. Simply to blame profit-driven media companies or the unscrupulous tabloid reporter for capitalizing on the public's fear of crime is not the whole story.

The sixth and perhaps most important reason to study discourse is that what governments say seems more important now than ever before. In the analysis of penal policies, some authors (for instance, Brown, 2005; Jones and Newburn, 2004) are right to caution against confusing symbol with substance, the discursive with what actually happens on the ground, as each of these spheres is often very different in character. Tough-on-crime talk can coexist with behind-the-scenes tactics and policies that run counter to the dominant punitive discursive trends of the day. Some observers seem to believe that such instances of 'doing good by stealth' (Drakeford and Vanstone, 2000: 377) should reassure anxious criminologists that punitive and authoritarian penal discourse in countries like the USA and England (Jones and Newburn, 2004) or Australia (Brown, 2005) are being quietly opposed by less discursively apparent yet practically evident commitments to progressive penal policies that go on under the radar (for example, see Webster and Doob, 2005).

But the disparity ought to be interpreted in another way. To the extent that what is *said* to be done does not comport with what *is* done, the public disclosure of such disparities can only perpetuate incentives for politicians to make more exaggerated claims that further raise public expectations and increase public disappointment. The disparity would not be such a potential problem were there not so many overtures being made to the public, with politicians wooing them amid indications of low levels of public trust. The study of discourse is increasingly important in countries where policymakers pledge transparency in policymaking, where concerns about public confidence are rife, and where penal policy action is democratized and said to be driven by public preferences and priorities. This is because under such conditions, what is said both by leaders and by those who speak for the public carries greater significance than in countries where these conditions are less noticeably apparent. When government legitimacy is questioned, trust in government is low, and politicians are eager to win trust and bolster the legitimacy of political institutions, there is a great deal at stake if they raise the public's expectations and then fail adequately to meet them. For its part, the 'will of the public' further raises the importance of the discursive because the views expressed by the public become increasingly powerful drivers of policy.

In addition, publics can only speak with the words they know. What legitimate claims-makers say matters because accumulated rhetoric contributes to the words, concepts, and narratives we routinely use that become our 'tools to think with'. When those in positions of public influence voice only tough rhetoric, we can hardly expect publics to speak and think in other ways. This does not mean that dominant discourses cannot be resisted, or that counter-discourse will be silenced entirely. It does suggest though that thinking and talking in other ways is considerably more difficult. These conditions ensure that discourse matters and call into question the wisdom of stealthy penal reform.

Conclusion

What can a discursive-analytic approach contribute to criminology in general and to the comparative study of reactions to child homicide in particular? First, as discursive data are the observable evidence of sensibilities, it can elucidate, demarcate, and render observable culturally distinct penal sensibilities. Second, it can expose the political motives that constrain the range of options available to criminal justice policymakers by unpacking the rhetoric used to justify dominant approaches. Third, using a critical approach, it can offer possible explanations for the dominance of one or more discourses over others, by asking who likely benefits from the dominance of a particular discourse and who loses. Fourth, discourse analysis allows us to untangle the dominant discourses, trace their origins, and understand why they are so well transmitted and accepted. By locating and understanding the discursive mechanisms most likely responsible for the rise of a particular point of view at a particular time, discourse analysis might help in the development of practical strategies to alter or challenge components of a dominant discourse.

Discourses and sensibilities are neither monolithic nor entirely unyielding. As Tonry (2004b: 64) puts it, 'policies do, of course, reflect beliefs and values, but those come from somewhere, and somewhen. If Americans were more self aware of why we believe what we believe, our policies about crime would be very different and we would not be fated to suffer our descendants' disapproval'. Studying the discourses we use that shape our thinking and sensibilities can facilitate this awareness and help us to recognize the contingent limitations discourses impose upon the scope of policy debates. These normative notions are not unassailable and will inevitably shift over time. As some of the moral panic literature suggests (Goode and Ben-Yehuda, 1994), such changes are not brought about by isolated incidents, but rather by a chain of similar incidents that come to be regarded as indicative of a major and impending assault on what are perceived to be traditional moral conventions. Discourse analysis can serve as a barometer indicating the level of concern that particular incidents generate and determine the ways in which that concern is shaping policy.

The distance between discourse and action is reduced, or arguably *ought to be* reduced, under conditions in which governments are struggling to retain legitimacy in the face of high public concern about crime problems. One challenge then is to find the means to incorporate all relevant discourses in ways that give each an equal hearing, and prevent the unfair domination of some discourses over others purely because current structural and cultural impediments inhibit the development of alternatives. As Surette explains:

> ...the social construction competition...is ongoing. The ultimate competition is not for the construction of crime and justice but for influence over the mass media's social construction engine. If you influence the symbol-creating and symbol-defining engine of a society, you create the social reality of that society. And *if a particular perspective of social reality gains control of a social construction engine, other constructions will never be truly competitive.* (Surette, 1998: 237, emphasis added)

The shifting changeability of discourse implies that it is susceptible to deliberate influence, provided its mechanisms are sufficiently understood. It is not inconceivable then that with such an understanding, sufficiently equipped actors could introduce additional forms of knowledge to inform the dominant discourses. The passages through which discourses pass might be made better to serve as the bridge to link the two, often divided communities of research and policy (Dunn, 1980). By exploiting open windows of opportunity and by enhancing the means for political and public deliberation, alternative counter-discourses could be usefully introduced to invoke more rational or principled criteria for the justification of particular crime control and penal policies. Before strategies of this kind can be considered, the next chapter examines how the media interact with discourses to shape public opinion and attitudes. The analysis of the press discourses generated by the Bulger and Redergård cases is presented in Chapter 7.

6

Media Constraints and the Formation of Political Opinions

American journalist Bernard Goldberg (2002: 92) writes of the first time, in the 1970s, that CBS News made money. Up until then, news was not considered profitable television network programming but simply a public service. Dick Salant, the president of the CBS News division at the time, apparently had misgivings about this development because he knew that once the news showed a profit, it would always be expected to do so, and this did not bode well for the quality of journalism.

A similar story can be told about Norway more recently, where the proliferation of mass media since the early 1990s is eroding the public service ethos that defines Norwegian journalism, though still to a significantly lesser degree than in England. The rise in importance of the media in all of its forms has, in Norway as in England, 'enabled market forces to enter the public sphere in a way unthinkable three or four decades ago, and have thus enormously accelerated the tendency for news presentations to become commodities' (Mathiesen, 2003: 5). Sensationalized media coverage is a staple in many countries, because as competition among new forms of media expands, so too does the importance of market share.

As mentioned in Chapter 2, the proliferation of media has increased the susceptibility to penal populism of both majoritarian and consensus democracies. Norwegian criminologist Thomas Mathiesen (2003: 9) explains:

With the advent of mass television and the media in general as an entertainment industry, members of the political system—the politicians rather than the slow and timid bureaucrats of earlier days—have been forced to enter the public debate on criminal policy in a way unheard of during earlier decades. Basing themselves on police values and perspectives—forceful measures and actions—they have had to satisfy their consumers in new and adamant ways. With these ingredients, series of moral panics have flared up, shaping the climate of penal policy...

This illustrates both that Norway is by no means immune to the pressures shaping harshening rhetoric and public anxieties, and that the mass media needs to be central to any strategy that aims to enrich the nature of penal policy debates to include more rigorously achieved, verifiable forms of knowledge.

This chapter focuses on the constraining roles of the media and builds on the theoretical background and research rationales provided in Chapters 4 and 5. It is presented in four primary sections. The first presents an historical overview of the research into political communication and the media, theoretically situating my own approach. Theories of 'agenda-setting' and 'impersonal influence' demonstrate the ways in which media coverage of crime issues constrains the ways in which crime problems and their solutions are assessed and addressed. The second section presents findings from an existing study of British crime-related press coverage that demonstrate the ways in which the choice of legitimate claims-makers who are sought to comment on crime events prioritize and legitimate particular discourses and silence others. These findings show how the tabloid press tends to present a particularly simplified and homogenized crime discourse that is lacking in expert views. The third section considers the way in which the media, especially the tabloid press, tend to employ simplifying frames to constrain the range of discourses that are drawn on to discuss crimes. Dichotomous, oversimplified ways of talking about problems—for instance, in terms of 'good' versus 'evil', 'tough' versus 'soft'—can have significant appeal, particularly when facing intractable, fear-inducing issues like crime. The fourth section looks at Zaller's theory of political opinion formation in light of the discursive constraints imposed by the media.

The Evolution of Political Communication Research

Political communication research has passed through three stages of development in the last century (Blumler and Gurevitch, 1982; Curran, Gurevitch and Woollacott, 1982). In the first, beginning around the turn of the twentieth century and ending with the outbreak of the Second World War, the media were believed by most observers to possess considerable power to shape the public's beliefs and opinions. These views stemmed from deep, at first European, concerns and assumptions, associated first with the Frankfurt School. These concerns were about the changing nature of late-industrial capitalist societies and the mass media's collusion with it; specifically, the cultural degradation wrought by the rise of 'mass cultures', the potential for political mass manipulation through media propaganda that had contributed to the rise of fascism, and the undermining of community ties (Hall, 1982).

The second stage, referred to as the 'pluralist' or 'liberalist' tradition, ran roughly from the 1940s to 1960s when empirical research challenged these sweeping assumptions. Research evidence suggested the media had only marginal effects on changes in the particular attitudes and beliefs of audience members. As Klapper (1960: 8) put it at the time, 'Mass communications ordinarily do not serve as a necessary and sufficient cause of audience effects'. Instead, the media were believed to exert only modest effects on individuals, as human susceptibility to influence was conceived to be variable according to individual predispositions, and media messages worked only to reinforce what was already there (Curran, Gurevitch and Woollacott, 1982: 12).

In the third and current stage, media effects once again are believed to be more pronounced than the liberal-pluralist findings held. Whereas the focus had previously been on testing for the media's influence on changes in particular attitudes and opinions, the new conception has shifted focus to the study of the media's effects on cognitions and perceptions, or on the 'categories and frameworks through which audience members perceive socio-political reality' (Blumler and Gurevitch, 1982: 262). Simultaneously, reflecting the precepts of Foucauldian discourse theory, Marxist theorists also attacked the earlier, liberalist, empirical researchers as fundamentally misguided, insisting they had missed the point by failing to appreciate the broader social-political functions served by the mass media. They failed to cast the net of inquiry wide enough and to step outside the narrow conceptions of the research problem. To rectify this failure, researchers focused on the media's 'agenda-setting function' and utilized 'social constructivist' approaches to the analysis of social problems (Curran, Gurevitch and Woollacott, 1982).

Agenda-setting

The media's agenda-setting function (McCombs, 1981, 2005; McCombs and Shaw, 1972) is most famously described by Bernard Cohen (1963: 13, emphasis in original) who wrote that the press 'may not be successful much of the time in telling people what to think, but it is stunningly successful in telling its readers what to think *about*. Moreover, the press and other media not only constrain and determine the range of terrain upon which the public casts their gaze (telling them what to think *about*), but the media also contribute to the store of cognitive tools and materials that also constrain *how* the public thinks about what they encounter on that terrain.

This extension of Cohen's characterization of agenda-setting neatly represents a joining of agenda-setting theory and discourse theory, as the concept of discourse encompasses the cognitive tools and materials individuals have at their disposal. Like political culture and discourses then, the mass media also work to constrain the thinking of publics and politicians' room to manoeuvre. The media are the means by which the public acquires most of their information about the world, the social problems they face and, importantly, the 'means to their resolution' (Negrine, 1994). The media also filter and reproduce what is commonly referred to as public opinion, in turn used in its myriad forms by politicians and policymakers to guide the course of policy. Media influence is thus not limited to the identification of the most pressing problems, but it also includes the selective presentation of the range of legitimate solutions from which government decision-makers choose. By providing the 'informational building blocks' (Blumler, 1977) to structure conceptions of social problems, causes, and solutions, the media also contribute to the store of available cognitive tools and materials that also constrain how readers and viewers think about the agendas presented. People are not only cognitively constrained by encountering the discourses they do, but they are also 'constrained by omissions from the media discourse' (Gamson, 1992: 180–1).

Impersonal influence

Diane Mutz (1998: 5, emphasis in original) usefully extends Cohen's maxim even further by arguing that the media also 'are tremendously influential in telling people what *others* are thinking about and experiencing'. She argues that we learn about the state of things with which we have little or no direct experience by looking to the media to tell us how *other people* assess them. She calls this process 'impersonal influence' and it is evident, for instance, 'when people demand that greater public resources be directed at a problem like violent crime based on their perceptions that others are increasingly victimized even though they themselves are not...This type of influence is deemed "impersonal" because it is brought about by information about the attitudes, beliefs or experiences of collectives outside of an individual's personal life space' (Mutz, 1998: 4). This is related to the concept of 'substitution' in the fear of crime literature whereby people substitute media information for other forms of direct knowledge of crime with which they lack direct experience (Surette, 1998). Impersonal influence might also be operating on the so-called 'worried well' (Farrall, Gray and Jackson, 2006) who show up prominently in fear of crime surveys—those who are significantly concerned about crime but are not themselves regularly fearful.

The constructivist approach to the study of the media is a means of analysing agenda-setting within a discourse-theory framework. As the next chapter illustrates, the approach focuses on the ways issues are 'framed' through the use of various discourses. These discourses serve to signify, for instance, 'who are virtuous and who are dangerous or inadequate, which actions will be rewarded and which penalized' (Edelman, 1988: 12). In Britain, the tabloid and mid-market press, particularly the *Sun* and the *Daily Mail*, are powerfully influential outlets: 'The rest of the media...often follows whichever newspaper has the most controversial stories...The *Mail* often starts national debates; even more often, it sets their parameters. For example, the receiving of asylum-seekers, whose hooded, dehumanized profiles have crowded the paper's pages remorselessly in recent years, now appears to most Britons as a problem and a danger, not an opportunity or a national duty' (Beckett, 2001). The thematic frames the media use to contextualize the issue draw upon discourses that imply appropriate policy reactions. These frames are culturally influenced and their resonance and reception depend on individual predispositions, of which more is said below. Important at this stage is the notion that the meanings of crime events and their effects are not fixed or absolute. They take on meaning or signification through the frames utilized in the media and the range of elite and popular discourses upon which these frames rely.

Claims-Making and the Dangers of Discourse Homogeneity

Those legitimated media claims-makers deemed worthy to comment on the issues of the day often become the 'primary definers'

(Hall et al, 1978) of social problems, setting the parameters of subsequent discussion and debate by privileging and propagating certain discourses over others. The identities of these 'authorized knowers' (Ericson, Baranek and Chan, 1991) vary between and among media outlets, and over time and space. Four graphs are configured below using data from a 1991 study of crime coverage in the British press by Schlesinger and his colleagues (see Figures 6.1–6.4). These figures indicate striking differences between the sources cited in crime-related articles in the three categories of British press, differences that are similar to those found in the analysis of the Bulger and Redergård case coverage presented in Chapter 7:

Whilst the quality dailies are focused upon Parliament and government, and offer space to the views of experts, elites and pressure groups, tabloid newspapers give far greater play to the opinions and perspectives offered by the victims of crime and their relatives and by those suspected or convicted of crimes. They are more oriented, that is, to 'common sense' thinking and discourse, and less to professionalized debate and the evaluation of policy. These variations throw light upon the complexity of the process of 'secondary definition' through the media, as they suggest that the distribution and hierarchy of discourses between different types of daily newspapers may vary significantly in relation to different readerships. (Schlesinger, Tumber and Murdock, 1991: 412–13)

Figure 6.1 Percentage of crime-related items in national dailies with comments by group—politicians

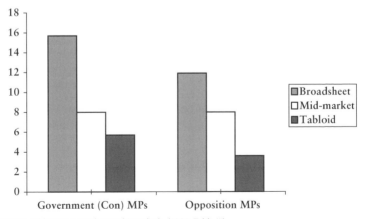

Source: Schlesinger, Tumber and Murdock, (1991: Table III).

When combined with theories of agenda-setting and impersonal influence, these findings are disquieting for at least five reasons. First, given that the media, especially the newspapers, are the primary political agenda setters in England (Garofalo, 1981; Jones, 2001; Wykes, 2001), the fact that they even further reduce the range of subsequent discourse and commentary by consistently selecting

Figure 6.2 Percentage of crime-related items in national dailies with comments by group—experts/elites/pressure groups

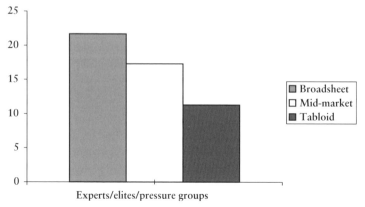

Source: Schlesinger, Tumber and Murdock, (1991: Table III).

Figure 6.3 Percentage of crime-related items in national dailies with comments by group—victims/suspect family/criminals

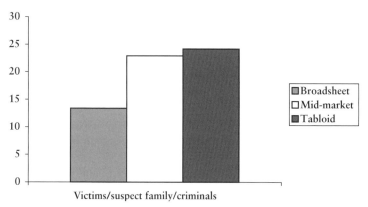

Source: Schlesinger, Tumber and Murdock, (1991: Table III).

Figure 6.4 Percentage of crime-related items in national dailies with comments by group—general public

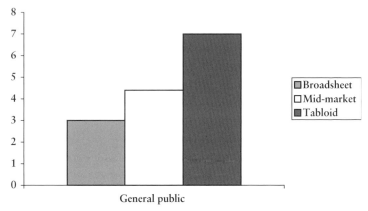

Source: Schlesinger, Tumber and Murdock, (1991: Table III).

particular groups to comment is cause for concern, as it means that readerships are not exposed equally to the range of available discourses. The views of experts and social scientists, for instance, are seldom referenced in the popular press's daily coverage of crime. Instead these papers tend to construct debates more simplistically, usually along clear moral lines (Schlesinger and Tumber, 1994: ch 8) which imply simple, morally based remedial policy action to do justice. Conversely, a critic might argue that broadsheet readers for their part are denied the rich perspective that crime victims' commentary in the tabloids provides, receiving instead more of the detached and dispassionate policy commentary delivered by experts and politicians—discourse which fails accurately to represent the damage wrought by crime victimization.

Second, and despite the hypothetical critic's last point, the array of cognitive tools offered by the tabloid and mid-market press are arguably more limited than that generated by the quality press. The textual analysis of the Bulger case in the next chapter illustrates that there is no shortage of victim-centred, emotive sentiment in the broadsheet press. The broadsheets have 'gone tabloid' in the sense that they have become more emotive in their commentary on the worst crimes, and the lines between these two press categories have blurred. As an assistant editor of *The Times* wrote during the trial of James Bulger's killers: 'The gap between tabloid and broadsheet coverage of crime, never as large as some people think, has been further closed in the past 20 years by the understanding that just because people are bank managers or bishops they are not necessarily less interested in "real life". To that extent broadsheet coverage serves the interests of the public and the public inter-est' (*The Times*, 18 November 1993). Whether the broadsheets are able to feed public debate at a level of quality that is democrati-cally satisfactory is another question, but they nonetheless retain some ability to disseminate the expert discourses ignored by the tabloids. Thus, because of the large readerships the tabloid papers enjoy, those who are intent to foster an atmosphere conducive to generate anything close to the public judgment advocated by Yankelovich, and mentioned in Chapter 1, face severe hurdles if, as is the case, most Britons get their information about issues of crime and punishment from this segment of the press.

Third, those who are most unaware or unacquainted with the wide range of social and political issues crime raises—those most in need of information in order to be brought to a level of public judgment—are precisely those who are most unlikely to receive much from their newspapers. As discussed more fully in Chapter 8, the Labour Party remade itself under Tony Blair's leadership, as, among other things, the party toughest on crime, wresting this ground from the Conservatives for the first time in the run up to their victory in the 1997 General Election (Downes and Morgan, 1997). It did this in part by fitting its rhetoric to tabloid sensibilities, and targeting its message to address the concerns voiced by focus groups (Gould, 1999). Unsurprisingly, the courting of tabloid readers and a commitment to deliberate, rational, evidence-based approaches to sensitive crime and pun-ishment issues are difficult to reconcile.

Tabloid media tend to be averse to dispassionate, evidence-based analysis, and tabloid readers tend to be more fearful of crime than broadsheet readers (Williams and Dickinson, 1993), particularly about being mugged or physically attacked (Schlesinger, Tumber and Murdock, 1991: 415). According to the British Crime Survey, 17 per cent of tabloid readers fear physical attacks, a rate nearly three times that of broadsheet readers (Fletcher and Allen, 2003: 134).[1] Tabloid readers are not

---

[1] That tabloid readers encounter more violent crime in their papers and are more fearful than broadsheet readers does not necessarily indicate a one-direc-tional causal realtionship. For instance, more fearful readers may seek out news that confirms their fears (Reiner, 2007a).

only twice as likely as broadsheet readers to believe crime has increased a lot (39 per cent versus 19 per cent), but also twice as likely to be very worried about crime (14 per cent versus 7 per cent) (Patterson and Thorpe, 2006).

These links between readership on the one hand and crime fears and knowledge on the other are not surprising. As Surette (1998: 212) puts it, 'Television and the tabloids, being more visceral and emotional in their content, would naturally tend to affect emotional attitudes such as fear of crime and concern. High-end newspapers, being factual and analytical, naturally tend to affect fact-based beliefs and preventive responses'. However paradoxically, it appears the tabloid and mid-market papers nonetheless most successfully set the current political agenda (Jones, 2001), and remain the papers whose disapproval politicians fear most. Thus, English tabloid readers have arguably become at once the most uninformed yet most politically influential segment of the population when it comes to crime policy.

Sasson (1995: 154–5) finds that social class and educational attainment appear to affect the particular frames that people conjure to explain criminal offending, further polarizing audiences along the lines of press readerships. His findings imply that participants require university education in order to utilize 'dry', factual information in support of particular frames, as opposed to the more readily digestible and 'memorable catch-phrases'. It would seem then that more sophisticatedly informative quality press discourse that relies for emphasis and legitimacy upon elite and expert opinions, and which presents a range of ideological views, is an ineffectual means of targeting comparatively less-educated consumers of the simplified discourses generated by the lower-market newspapers, those that are more reliant upon simplistic catch-phrases to persuade and entertain audiences.

Fourth, there is little in current political and media practice to suggest much corrective change is likely. The rise of the tabloid and mid-market press as the media that matter in present-day English political culture has been mirrored by a (perhaps longer term) decline in deference to traditional elites in matters of criminal justice policy (Loader, 2005; Pratt, 2006; Ryan, 1999, 2003). Understood in terms of the broader cognitive effects that media coverage has upon audiences, these media do more than set political and public agendas; they also provide the audience with the range of interpretive frameworks they use to make sense of any subsequent debate. Since the stratification of the English press falls to a large extent along class lines, with the lower and working classes consuming mostly popular and mid-market newspapers, the anti-elite bias might be further aggravated by increasing income disparities.

Fifth, the evidence suggests that the informed debate that ought to underpin democratic governance is not being adequately fostered within the current framework of institutional relationships that define British politics, especially regarding issues of penal policy. British politicians have increasingly attempted to target the readers of the popular and mid-market press without the concomitant attempt to raise the level of political debate beyond the simplistic terms the readers are used to. Expert discourses, which must rely upon the media for dissemination, do not act alone upon the consciousness of audience members, but instead interact with durable personal, cultural, and political predispositions (Zaller, 1992). But citizens must first *encounter* these discourses if they are to have any effect at all on the formation of opinions. In current English political culture, public access to the range of elite discourses is constrained in ways that are fundamentally undemocratic.

Addressing the highly competitive English press market, Colin Sparks (1999: 59) goes so far as to assert that '[p]roducing a press that sees as its main task the production of material that informs all of its readers objectively about the dangers and opportunities of their world, that presents them impartially with a range of informed opinions about desirable policy options, and that sees as one of its main functions providing them with a forum in which to articulate their own views and opinions, is an impossibility in a free market'. Often the result is the kind of press coverage that fails to provide citizens with the quality of information required for them to engage fully in civic life. 'There can be no doubt that the *Mirror* and *Sun* have abandoned the public sphere ... It is impossible to sustain an argument that the two titles are channels of rational discourse that allow private individuals to come together as a public body to form reason-based public opinion ... [or that] either newspaper is fulfilling a role as part of a mechanism by which ordinary people are able to bring their political representatives to account' (Rooney, 2000: 101, 92).

Media Frames and Discursive Constraints

The tabloids in particular typically forgo expert discourses in favour of simplified, homogenized constructions of crime problems and solutions. These representations utilize rhetorical devices that are nonetheless memorable, as they tend to conjure simple binary oppositions (for example, good versus evil; tough on crime versus soft on crime) in emotive and moralistic ways that are easily retrievable from the 'top of the head'. Thus, mass opinion is heavily influenced and shaped by overly simplistic, yet memorably emotive, discourses that present only a partial and distorted view of the problems on which they report.

Marx's structuralist approach held that things and events were granted meanings via the culturally specific processes of signification. As Hall (1982: 87) explains, 'Because meaning was not given but produced, it followed that different kinds of meaning could be ascribed to the same events. Thus, in order for one meaning to be regularly produced, it had to win a kind of credibility, legitimacy or taken-for-grantedness for itself. That involved marginalizing, down-grading or de-legitimating alternative constructions', and, by extension, alternative *constructors*. Ryan (1999, 2003) traces the history of this sort of process, as discussed in Chapter 8, as one by which the traditional liberal elites have become increasing marginalized and excluded from debates over penal policy in Britain. Hall (1982: 67–8, emphasis in original) continues:

Indeed there were certain kinds of explanations which, given the power of and credibility acquired by the preferred range of meanings were literally unthinkable or unsayable (see Hall *et al.*, 1977). Two questions followed from this. First, how did a dominant discourse warrant itself as *the* account, and sustain a limit, ban, or proscription over alternative or competing definitions? Second, how did the institutions which were responsible for describing and explaining the events of the world—in modern societies, the mass media, *par excellence*—succeed in maintaining a preferred or delimited range of meanings in the dominant systems of communication? How was this active work of privileging or giving preference practically accomplished?

Looking at the incentives to act in particular ways brings us closer to answering these questions. It seems prudent to conceive of politicians as managing incentives to act in certain ways, though this does not necessarily impart to them consciously conspiratorial motives. Political culture and its supporting structures subtly create incentives for particular kinds of political behaviour. In England, for instance, socio-political and electoral pressures exerted by deeply partisan politics have created strong incentives for politicians to engage with tabloid and mid-market press discourses on their own terms, rendering them nearly powerless to resist engaging the public with much more than simplified, moralistic rhetoric when it comes to crime and punishment. Usually, if they are expressed at all, more nuanced views on crime and punishment are left to the Liberal Democrats, a party whose chances of getting into government are only realistic if in a coalition with Labour or the Tories.

One recent and notable exception illustrates the political consequences of deviating from the usual punitive rhetoric. In July 2006 Conservative Party leader David Cameron came out against the government's support of a shopping centre's ban of the hooded tops or 'hoodies' often worn by fearsome-looking young people. He argued in a speech about the need for British society to show more love to young people, to recognize the defensive rather than aggressive function of wearing a hoodie, and to endeavour to better understand the pressures young people face. This quickly became known as Cameron's 'hug-a-hoodie speech' and it provided the press and the Labour government with a highly exploitable opportunity to ridicule Cameron's apparent 'softness'. The *Sun* claimed, 'Fury at Cam's Cuddle Scheme' (11 July 2006) and asked, 'What About the Victims, Cameron?' (7 November 2006). Cameron's attempt to shift the parameters of the debate about young people in Britain failed, and what remains in its place is a memorable catch-phrase that signals both that Cameron is soft on youth crime, and that invoking counter-discourses can have serious political consequences.

The common unwillingness of politicians to inject alternative discourses to counter dichotomous, moralistic, and oversimplified constructions of crime and justice further legitimates the existing homogenized, thin, and oversimplified discourses the media tends to disseminate. However, this politically driven unwillingness or inability to counter these discourses needs to be understood in full appreciation of the constraints and incentives with which politicians must contend every day. The reasons particular political incentives have contributed to this discourse homogenization and oversimplification are considered in more depth in Chapter 8 on English penal culture.

Loaded questions

Though the expansion of subsequent policy debates is by no means fully prohibited from moving beyond the emotive or affective, dichotomous level found today, it is difficult to make such a move. Lynch's (2002) examination of pro-death penalty discourse in the USA illustrates the point. The death penalty debate, as proponent claims-makers define it, is not about whether or not execution is defensible on ethical grounds or if it is grounded on procedurally sound policies. Instead, the existence of the death penalty is a given, and the debate is rather at a level where what is debated is for which and how many offenders it ought to be used. The debate is 'loaded'. The famous loaded question 'Have you stopped beating your wife?' has no answer that does not incriminate if answered on its own simple, yes-or-no terms. Discourses similarly load debates by setting the parameters of subsequent discussion. Again, it does not mean that another level cannot be reached, one in which debaters are able to break from the available dichotomy and assert, for example, that beating one's wife is not something one engages in. However, this requires considerable effort. This transition is made all the more difficult when the current discourse about those who commit violence and about victims is highly emotive—or to proceed with the analogy, when the one posing the wife-beating question is doing so at the top of his voice, backed up by a mob of angry supporters. Instead of beginning at a level that would allow one to avoid the implication of guilt, one instead has almost to begin guilty and try to move on from there.

The mechanics of policymaking allow serious, open, and rational consideration only when the primary definition—the frame—allows it. For example, when a penal policy debate is first primarily couched in managerialist terms, reduced to actuarial considerations of its effectiveness as evaluated on rational or instrumental terms, the wider debate of principle and the moral soundness of the policy tend to be submerged. For instance, at the time of writing, the urgent review Jack Straw has ordered of the indeterminate IPP sentence in England has been premised not upon normative or principled concerns about whether or not it is just to lock up offenders who have committed one of 153 different offences for what can be a life term (see Chapter 3). Instead, what is driving the review is the instrumental concern about the impact the sentence is having on existing prison places (Andrew Ashworth, personal communication, 8 August 2007). Conversely, when debates are first defined in moral terms, as much of the debate in the aftermath of the Bulger case was, other instrumental concerns tend to be trumped by the concerns imposed by the dominant frame or primary definition.

Simple justice

Furthermore, any frame or primary definition acts as a means to pare down and simplify problems which would otherwise be unsatisfactorily complex, especially when emotions are high and there is a demand for an affective resolution. Once problems are framed so simply, their solutions can be too. If the cause is evil, then the solution is removal of the evil. If the causes are multifaceted and cumulative, then the solutions are not so easy to prescribe and there are no simple means by which members of society can be made to feel at ease. When the debate is affectively bound, engagement with it must also begin at the emotional level. As explored more in Chapter 10, this is why expert, non-emotional, rationalized discourse has diminished purchase in penal policy debates that are affectively and morally defined. The existing moralistic frame defines the terms of engagement, and if the claim of expertise is tied to rational, evidence-led knowledges rather than moral ones, expert discourses cannot compete well on this level. It is also at least possible that the more emotive the rhetoric around a given issue, the less assailable its attendant positions become. If the emotive climate cools and the conditions conducive to rational debate return, windows open and oppositional voices and alterative discourses can be heard. Dramatic and emotional rhetoric tends to shut out much else by heating up the climate.

In his study of the construction of juvenile crime in Sweden, Estrada (2001) found that little had been written about juveniles and violence in Swedish daily newspapers between 1950 and 1985, but this shifted abruptly in 1986. Between 1980 and 1985, articles concerning juvenile violence focused on the sentences received by offenders, and the typical offender was portrayed as a 'problem child with a difficult family background' (Estrada, 2001: 648). But in the summer of 1986, following several high-profile violent crimes, including the murder of Prime Minister Olof Palme, there was a qualitative change in press coverage with the focus falling on the image of the cold and calculating juvenile 'super-predator', and the notion that juvenile violence was getting more serious and more prevalent. Explanations for offending shifted. Blame was attributed to individual choice rather than to wider socio-economic conditions. The notion that young offenders were 'compelled' to offend by their social circumstances no longer dominated the discourse, and was replaced by a conception of the offender as one who coldly and calculatedly chooses to offend. This new dominant explanation made it 'easier to profess outrage' toward the crimes committed and those who committed them (Estrada, 2001: 647). The increase in both the salience of violent juvenile crime and the shift in how it was explained were paralleled by an ideological shift in the official penal approach to such offending, from a treatment-based model to a retributive, just deserts approach.

In the case of discourses about murder and victims of murder, about the range of issues plausibly raised by the occurrence of murder, the discourses that are often constructed convey a simplified version of the issues that reduces all down to conceptions of innocent victim and evil perpetrator, often with the vengeful and severe punishment of the latter required in order to honour the memory of the former. Laws carrying the names of victims, like Megan's Law in the USA and the proposed Sarah's Law in England, are one way this is achieved. When proposed, such laws appear to honour the victim while simultaneously shaming opponents into supporting them (E. Brown, 2007). Other instrumental penological considerations tend to be relegated to positions subordinate to the primary considerations of retribution and honouring the emotionality of the crime. To attempt to expand the linear simplicity of the dichotomous conceptions that justify and perpetuate the zero-sum-game approach to penal issues—to argue that things are seldom as simple as such models presuppose—one opens oneself up to accusations of elitism, of being out of touch, and ultimately of being disrespectful of victims of violence. This seems to be tied to the belief that to understand is necessarily to excuse.

Joseph Kennedy (2000) offers one elegant interpretation of this tendency in American culture, but which seems to apply to the English context as well. He suggests that attempts to understand offending and offenders can be perceived as an intolerable weakness when it exists alongside the perception that society is in the throes of moral crisis. This response is rooted in:

a fear that knowledge of the world will disable us from protecting ourselves from it, that the more nuanced one's view of humanity and human behavior, the more likely one is to flinch from the acts necessary for one's own survival...[T]he fear is that our understanding of the roots of criminal behaviour in social inequalities or in the pathological conditions of abuse which those conditions sometimes engender will rob us of the will or the judgment to act in our collective self-defense. (Kennedy, 2000: 904–5)

The emotionalized nature of much of the discourse on offenders and their victims keeps the terms of debate simplistically conceived. To depart from it by arguing that emotions cloud rational judgment is somehow to degrade the importance and legitimacy of the emotions experienced by victims. The appeal of simplistic, dichotomous, absolutist rhetoric is understandable in these terms.[2]

Unintended consequences

Agenda-setting theory and discourse theory expand and broaden the scope of traditional Marxist conceptions of conflict and dominance. The focus of analysis need not be the legitimization of a particular political regime over its rivals. This traditional Marxist conception presumes a degree of conscious conspiratorial activity that is not only polemical, and therefore likely to be dismissed out of hand by many observers, but it also misrepresents the ways in which discourses operate. Discourses define problems and solutions in ways that develop their own momentum, and which generate unintended outcomes which can actually undermine rather than bolster the legitimacy of a political regime. This does not mean that certain discourses do not subjugate others, nor does it mean that certain powerful interests might not be served by these subjugations, as Marxists argue. It does mean, however, that the consequences of deploying certain discourses—deployment often not consciously decided upon—are not easily foreseen.

---

[2] This reasoning might also help explain the appeal of political leaders like George W. Bush (and to a lesser extent Tony Blair) whose absolutist rhetoric and embodiment of moral certainty are a heartening comfort to some in the complexities of the post-9/11 (and post-7/7) world. During the US presidential election campaign in 2004, Democratic challenger John Kerry was framed by opponents as a 'waffler' and a 'flip flopper', arguably in part because of his contention that political issues are often complex and nuanced.

For instance, since coming to power in 1997 the Labour government has intended to bolster the legitimacy of its regime in the eyes of the general public by focusing a great deal of attention on building public confidence in the criminal justice system and in government. However, this New Labour discursive preoccupation could actually be having the opposite effect on public attitudes. Persistently invoking public confidence discourse could actually undermine public confidence because it calls attention to its apparent scarcity. If public confidence needs to be restored, improved, or boosted, then it must be low to begin with. Just as Foucault argued that the so-called repression of child sexuality in Victorian times served to generate discourses which only served to confirm and reproduce its existence, so too does Labour seem to undermine its own legitimacy by trying so hard to strengthen it. Tonry (2004a: 57) draws upon BCS data to support his claim that Labour's high-profile preoccupation with anti-social behaviour has '…made a small problem larger, thereby making people more aware of it and less satisfied with their lives and their government'. Although there is some truth to the notion that 'the ideas of the ruling class are the ruling ideas of the epoch' (quoted in Blumler and Gurevitch, 1982: 261), Marxist preoccupation with class is too narrow a focus and diminishes the potency of the wider point. Public confidence discourse has acquired a momentum of its own, now possibly undermining what it was intended to sustain. Marxist conceptions may not be wrong in their description of the function and mechanics of media legitimization; it may just be that they misinterpret the means by which legitimating messages are conveyed and the intentions of those conveying them. Discourses operate more subtly than Marxist conspiracy rhetoric allows.

The political agenda is not often set consciously or deliberately. Instead the agenda is shaped in part by the media's production practices. Journalists are constrained by the 'house styles' of the papers to which they contribute—that is, the modes and styles of representation that are part of the 'tried and tested formulae of what sells best' (Berrington and Honkatukia, 2002). Their approaches to stories are also bounded by 'a vocabulary of precedents: what previous exemplars tell them should be done in the present instance' (Ericson, Baranek and Chan, 1987: 348). As Blumler and Gurevitch (1982: 262) put it, 'Read in this manner, agenda-setting research appears to converge towards the Marxist view that the ideological role of the mass media has structural roots, embedded in routines and practices of media production, which in turn may reflect interpretative frameworks dominant in society at a given time'. This book is most concerned with the analysis of mass-mediated discourses and frameworks and less with the media's production practices, though this is an important line of inquiry for comparative analysis (see Way, 2006).

The Formation of Political Opinions

In *The Nature and Origins of Mass Opinion*, Zaller (1992) explores the ways in which individuals sift through and evaluate the range of available information to formulate political preferences in ways that are influenced by their existing political predispositions and values. His theory of opinion formation is based on four ideas: First, 'citizens vary in their habitual attention to politics and hence in their exposure to political information and argumentation in the media'. Second, they can only react critically to debates if they are 'knowledgeable about political affairs'. Third, most people lack fully formed opinions and must construct opinions 'on the fly' when confronted with issues. Fourth, 'in constructing their opinion statements, people make greatest use of ideas that are, for one reason or another, most immediately salient to them—at the "top of the head"' (Zaller, 1992: 1).[3] The most important to the discussion in this chapter is the finding that '[w]hat matters for the formation of mass opinion is the relative and overall amount of media attention to contending political positions' (Zaller, 1992: 1). As illustrated above and in the next chapter, the range of knowledges to which people need to be exposed in order to deliberate and the standards of informational heterogeneity required to achieve some level of public judgment are clearly not being met through traditional mass media outlets that narrowly constrain the parameters of penal policy debates.

Figure 6.5 provides a simplified rendition of Zaller's theory of opinion formation. He defines 'political predispositions' as 'stable, individual-level traits that regulate the acceptance or non-acceptance of the political communications...Because the totality of the communications that one accepts determines one's opinions...predispositions are the critical intervening variable

[3] See also Sasson (1995).

Figure 6.5 A configuration of Zaller's model of opinion formation

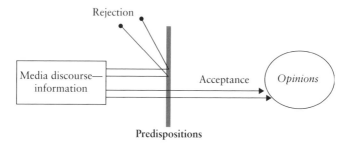

between the communications people encounter in the mass media, on one side, and their statements of political preferences on the other' (Zaller, 1992: 3). The massive effects brought upon by society-specific political culture complicates the simple model, but it nonetheless helps to visualize the roles played by each of the variables. Information from media discourse is either rejected or accepted and used to formulate opinions depending upon an individual's predispositions. Cultural forces are evident in the formulation of individual predispositions and in the generation of priorities and the hierarchies of influence within the media institutions that reproduce particular discourses for the public.

Communicated information is then filtered through political predispositions that act either to reject or accommodate it. The ideas and information carried via media discourse that are most likely to be accepted are those that are consistent with one's values, one's predispositions. It follows that when media discourse is couched in value-laden rhetoric, the assessment of whether information ought to be accepted or rejected is easier to make, as the values are explicitly made plain.

Over the long term, elite discourse can also have marked effects on public predispositions, as Zaller's example of changing racial attitudes in the USA indicates, but they are generally not subject in the shorter term to the influence of elites. Attitudes to smoking, drink driving, and even using seatbelts have shifted over recent decades, led by expert-driven public health discourses in successfully packaged media campaigns. However, all variables in the model—media discourse, individual predispositions, and the opinions that result—are shaped by the jurisdiction's political culture. This is an important point because it suggests that only so much can be done to alter opinions with media-focused discursive strategies. Zaller (1992: 163) cautiously suggests that political predispositions result from 'a distillation of a person's lifetime experiences, including childhood socialization and direct involvement with the raw ingredients of policy issues, such as earning a living, paying taxes, [and] racial discrimination', and he believes variables like personality traits and socio-economic status might also be important contributors. Most of these factors are culturally variable and culturally derived. Though this means they are constantly in flux, it also means they are relatively resilient in the short term.

Comparative research can clarify the contingency of the cultural, but any prescriptions informed by comparisons that include attempts to change mass culture are likely to be fruitless in the short term. Long-term cultural change seems possible to effect using elite discourse, but not in a timeframe that most reformers would find satisfying. As Sasson (1995: 163) puts it, '... both culture and experience—and the popular wisdom, media discourse and experiential knowledge they supply—are key factors in shaping consciousness'. This is a deceptively simple but important statement because it holds that media discourse, and the predispositions upon which political preferences are based, are subject to the wider forces exerted by culture and experience, both difficult and slow to change by discursive strategies. Culture is resistant, as are the political predispositions that culture engenders. Yet, apparently deep-seated cultural attitudes and values can shift relatively quickly. For instance, mainstream American network television programmes from the 1990s condoned homosexuality (for example, *Will and Grace*), pornography (for example, *Friends, Seinfeld*), and pre- and extra-marital sex (for example, *Will and Grace, Friends, Seinfeld*) in ways that would have been hard to predict just a decade earlier.

Conclusion

There are three sides to the problem at the heart of the interaction of English political and press culture. First, the most simplistically constructed policy debates appear in the newspapers with the widest readerships. Second, these papers tend to have the most influence in setting public and political agendas. Thus, and third, the readers whose papers and whose views are so influential are exposed less frequently, if at all, to those discourses that might generate more informed and nuanced views of social problems.

The media fundamentally affect the process of opinion formation in ways consistent with agenda-setting models of media analysis. The range of salient 'considerations' to which an individual is exposed, or 'any reason that might induce an individual to decide a political issue one way or the other' is established by media discourse (Zaller, 1992: 40, see also Sasson, 1995). The salience of particular considerations changes over time, and subsequently the considerations which are employed, usually those most easily recalled, often in the simple forms of stereotypes and catch-phrases, tend to be those most salient in media discourse (Zaller, 1992). Exposure to simplified, dichotomously defined policy debates generates similarly simplified policy preferences. Conversely, exposure to a wider range of pluralist discourses about the social problem at hand generates more nuanced policy preferences informed by a wider array of contingencies and considerations.

Zaller argues that too often public opinion research fails to distinguish values from ideologies. Some folks are deemed to be too uninformed to have ideologies, but when asked to choose they will revert to values to 'structure policy preferences'. Perhaps this helps explain the trend toward simplified political discourse which speaks more to values than to instrumental considerations, as this is the level at which most citizens, possessing low political awareness, engage the issues. It leads one to ask how long a political system can survive with such shallow exchanges between elected representatives and constituencies, especially as government officials seem to feel increasingly compelled to play to and to accommodate populist agendas and opinion.

With an appreciation of the ways in which tabloid and mid-market discourses tend toward simplified formulations of crime problems and solutions, what is most worrying of all is the power these discourses now wield. Far from rejecting such simplification and fostering the conditions necessary to achieve public judgment (Yankelovich, 1991), English political leaders have instead legitimated and assured the status of these simplified discourses in their pursuit of public approval. While democratic governments most certainly ignore public opinion at their peril, it is arguably self-defeating and counterproductive for governments to oversimplify complex policy debates with moral and emotional arguments that marginalize reasoned, deliberative approaches. Deliberation, the role it plays in democracies, and the ways it might be better facilitated by governments are discussed in Chapters 9, 10, and 11. First though, the data that will inform those discussions need to be explored. The next chapter examines in detail the nature and quality of the discourses produced about the Bulger and Redergård homicides.

7

Contextualizing Tragedy

This chapter demonstrates the ways in which the press coverage of the Bulger and Redergård cases quantitatively and qualitatively differed, both among and between press formats and jurisdictions. The first half of the chapter presents the findings from a number of mostly quantitative analyses, all of which allow an assessment to be made about the quality or diversity of the press discourses generated which inform popular sensibilities in each country.[1] The first section provides an overview of the research methods used to approach the analysis of the textual data, including the rationale and the research protocols. The second section compares the relative prominence of each homicide case as portrayed in the two newspapers chosen from each jurisdiction. The third main section contains the results of a comprehensive claims-maker analysis of the newspaper coverage of both cases. It identifies the dominant claims-makers in each newspaper in each jurisdiction, those who provide the reader with the information needed to make sense of each case, and examines the nature of the claims made. The next section compares the relative legitimacy of elite experts in each country as evidenced by the prevalence of their views in the coverage relative to those of others. In the fifth section I observe the ways in which each paper contextualizes the risk of child-on-child homicide, finding the Norwegian press to be much better at providing readers with informed assessments. The sixth section shows how the representations in the English press that the Bulger case was indicative of an overall rise in the seriousness and prevalence of juvenile crime were legitimated by the failure of English politicians to contest them.

---

[1] In order to distinguish between media and public discourse, one could do what Sasson (1995) has done and utilize focus groups to discover the crime discourses employed by members of the public, though such an approach is beyond the scope of this study.

The chapter's second half reports the findings of the qualitative discourse analysis, beginning with the seventh section, which examines the various frames, themes, and angles used to contextualize each homicide. Then the comparative saliency of the 'evil child' discourse is considered, and some reflections are offered as to why this discourse is invoked in the English press to account for the Bulger murder but is absent from the Norwegian constructions of the Redergård case. Next, the rhetorical strategies used to recruit audiences are compared, particularly the invocation of the pronoun 'we' as a means of demarcating moral boundaries in the Bulger coverage. Finally, I briefly consider the responses to another child-on-child homicide in England—the Burgess case from 1861—and consider the reasons why some high-profile incidents become imbued with greater significance and generate greater outrage than others.

The Methodology

The purpose of this comparative media analysis is to assess the 'tenor of the times', the prevailing cultural sensibilities, specifically in relation to two grave acts committed by children. Two sectors of the media 'discourse plane' are studied in each jurisdiction, representing the tabloid and broadsheet newspapers. Focusing on both sectors is intended to highlight the inter- and intra-jurisdictional similarities and differences in how the newspapers covered the two incidents—the causes the media discourses ascribe to the act, the policy implications or prescriptions offered in the text, the commentaries surrounding the acts that were committed, and the appropriate responses.

Much has been written about the Bulger case and its cultural impacts (Davis and Bourhill, 1997; Franklin and Petley, 2001; Goldson, 2001; Hay, 1995; Jenks, 1996; Rowbotham, Stevenson and Pegg, 2003; Scraton, 1997; Sereny, 1995; Smith, 1994; Valentine, 1996; Warner, 1994; Young, 1996a), and a few authors have even compared and contrasted the Bulger and Redergård cases (Clifford, 1996; Haydon and Scraton, 2000; Jewkes, 2004; Kehily and Montgomery, 2003; Morrison, 1997; Muncie, 2001). But these comparisons have been made only cursorily, and no one has yet compared the press coverage of the two cases in any systematic way. The textual analysis to follow is intended to illustrate comparatively the contextual constraints placed upon the reader of news stories about the Bulger and Redergård cases. This rather narrow methodological focus is driven by the wish to avoid, as much as possible, unnecessarily rehashing work already done in this area, though some overlap is inevitable.

Theoretical underpinnings

The particular discourse-analytic approach that most shaped the qualitative part of the analysis is that used by Widdicombe (1993), as described by Gill (2000: 180), who writes that the approach regards 'the ways in which things are said as being potential solutions to problems. The analyst's task is to identify each problem and how what is said constitutes a solution'. This highlights the inductive character of the approach, emphasizing how the texts lead the analyst toward conclusions rather than the analyst searching the text for evidence to confirm a priori theories or arguments. This inductive approach to the discursive data relies upon emergent data analysis (Altheide, 1996). Unlike quantitative content analysis where the researcher remains outside the text, applying to it a preconfigured, deductive scheme, in this qualitative approach the investigator is a central participant in the analysis, constantly refining impressions and interpretations while remaining immersed in the texts. Thus, the investigator must be reflexive about the choices made, including the corpus of texts from which samples are drawn, the particular themes chosen as exemplars, and others not chosen or disregarded.

Within the constructionist paradigm, I am also concerned with comparing the dominant thematic frames presented in the press that attempt to account for each jurisdiction's homicide. This is accomplished in part by first doing a content analysis of who the dominant claims-makers are and, second, by using a frame analytic perspective, unpacking both the 'diagnostic' and 'prognostic' components implicated by the frames. 'Frames on public problems typically feature a diagnostic component that identifies a condition as intolerable and attributes blame or causality, and a prognostic component that prescribes one or more courses of ameliorative action' (Sasson, 1995: 10).

The focus on how problems are thematically framed allows the investigator eventually to stand back and see the kinds of informational tools that readers are given to make sense of each case and to see how these frames, themes, and descriptions square with those provided in the other jurisdiction. To reiterate briefly the justification for studying discourse which was addressed in Chapter 5, Tonkiss (1998: 249) argues that:

> ...these conflicting accounts are interesting and important...because the meanings and explanations that are given to different social factors shape the practical ways that people and institutions respond to them. If a common understanding of juvenile crime rests on discourses of individual pathology (for example, crimes arise from the personal failings of the individual), it is likely that this problem will be tackled in a quite different way than if it was commonly understood in terms of a discourse of poverty (for example, crimes arise as a result of material deprivation).

My concern is the construction of discourses, and 'discourse is built or manufactured out of pre-existing linguistic resources', or as Potter and Wetherell (1990: 207) put it, 'language and linguistic practices offer a sediment of systems of terms, narrative forms, metaphors and commonplaces from which a particular account can be assembled'. This sediment metaphor also highlights the contingency of dominant discourses, as a range of accounts can be assembled from among existing discursive sediments (Gill, 2000). Choices are made to construct particular frames rather than others, and these choices are heavily influenced by social, cultural, and political contingencies that render sayable the particular discursive product those choices construct. The discourse analyst is thus 'involved *simultaneously* in analysing discourse and analysing the interpretive context' (Gill, 2000: 176, emphasis in original).

For instance, expert-generated discursive sediments, or expert knowledges, are chosen or not chosen to construct killings of children by children, and the myriad issues attendant to them, depending in part upon the levels of trust experts enjoy and the legitimacy with which they are regarded in that jurisdiction. And this trust and legitimacy is intricately intertwined with a jurisdiction's political culture. As shown below, the relative lack of expert discourse in the English tabloid reporting of the Bulger case is indicative of these factors, just as the relative lack of public voices expressed in the Norwegian press coverage of the Redergård case is indicative of the apparent lack of legitimacy such voices are deemed to have relative to those of experts when exploring the issues surrounding the case. These silences are important and comparisons make them conspicuous.

Research protocols

This is an interpretive study of the newspaper coverage aimed at raising questions and formulating hypotheses. Other analysts could glean from the same coverage themes I missed, and some might disagree with my assessment of the dominance of some themes. This is an inevitable but worthwhile risk in this sort of study. I hope that most readers nonetheless find my conclusions and assertions to be well supported and compelling.

In each country, one tabloid and one broadsheet newspaper were selected in order to facilitate comparisons between newspaper types within and between jurisdictions. Because of the vast amount of textual data generated about the Bulger case, the selection of data for both cases was limited to one year's coverage. For both cases in all four newspapers, all articles mentioning each case were included for analysis, regardless of how central to the particular news item the case might have been. This was decided upon to allow for the three main phases of the Bulger case to unfold—the pre-trial investigation, the trial itself (which occurred nine months after the murder), and the post-trial responses. This limitation was immaterial to the selection of Norwegian coverage because neither newspaper extended their coverage of either homicide beyond a year.

There are two reasons why newspapers were favoured over television and other media in this study of Norwegian and English press coverage. First, there are the practical problems of access to television news coverage from two countries divided by language. Second, and perhaps more importantly, the primary concern of this study is the agenda-setting function of the media, and the ways in which this function constrains both the conceptions of problems and the range of responses considered for their amelioration. It appears that newspapers play a more powerful role in setting the political agenda than television does (Garofalo, 1981; Jones, 2001; Wykes, 2001).

Both English papers chosen are national dailies. *The Times* (including the *Sunday Times*) is the English broadsheet and the *Daily Mirror* (including the *Sunday Mirror*) the tabloid. Practical considerations dictated the selection of the *Daily Mirror*, as a searchable archive of the newspaper is available through the British Newspaper Library.[2] Lexis-Nexis was used to obtain

---

[2] Searchable archives going back to 1993 were unfortunately not available for other English tabloids. Unsuccessful attempts were made to obtain directly from

the coverage from *The Times*. Though there is no broadsheet with national distribution in Norway, the leading broadsheet *Aftenposten* was selected because it has the second largest overall newspaper circulation and is regarded as the country's leading serious newspaper. The leading national tabloid *Verdens Gang* (*VG*) was chosen as the comparator. The Norwegian press proved far more accommodating than their English counterparts and all three newspapers that were approached (the tabloid *Dagbladet*'s coverage was collected but not analysed for this book) conducted their own archive searches and graciously provided their coverage free of charge.

Only the articles' text was analysed, as some archived coverage (*The Times, Daily Mirror, Aftenposten*) was available only in text format rather than in the illustrated, page-formatted versions readers would have encountered when the papers were purchased. Though it would have been best to include analyses of the photos and graphics accompanying the stories, this approach was impractical under the circumstances. Similarly, analysis of televised news coverage of the cases would have been ideal, yet practical issues prohibited it. All Norwegian coverage was translated prior to coding.[3]

Though any piece of social scientific research is, even obliquely, theory-driven, as many research questions develop from particular and sometimes unconscious assumptions about how the world works, the approach adopted in this analysis was inductive insofar

the *Sun* its coverage of the homicides, and their archive search service is only accessible for a prohibitive fee. Significant costs would have also been incurred to obtain photocopies of articles at the Cambridge University library, as the library does not allow readers to make copies themselves, and any such copies would have needed to be converted to an electronic text format to be analysed.

[3] Though I attempted through private tutoring in Cambridge and in Oslo to gain some knowledge of the Norwegian language in order to translate the Norwegian coverage myself, this proved an unrealistic and overly ambitious wish. Instead, the *Dagbladet* coverage of both cases (again not included for analysis here) was translated entirely by Marianne Saether, a Norwegian criminology PhD student studying in England. The *Aftenposten* coverage of both cases, as well as *VG*'s coverage of the Bulger case, was translated by Jeannette Nyquist, a Norwegian living in Oslo who tutored me during a two-week immersion language course there in September 2003. We together translated the *VG* coverage of the Bulger case during that period. My language tutor in Cambridge, Kari Brâtveit, provided additional translation support during the period when I was preparing the translated text files for coding.

as the coding protocols developed and applied to the textual data emerged over time from a series of successive textual readings or 'listenings' (Brown and Gilligan, 1992; Keating, 2003). The texts were approached as much as possible as any lay reader might read them. I tried to set aside my own criminological knowledge and training and to step into the shoes of an uninitiated reader. Coding was facilitated using HyperResearch, a Mac-compatible qualitative data analysis program. Emergent themes were inductively identified and included among a list of codes, which were later applied to the text during subsequent readings. During these later readings, the texts were deductively coded in accordance with the primary research questions and some new codes were added. The primary research questions focus on the nature and quality of the discourses to which readers of the particular newspapers were exposed:

1. What messages does a reader receive from each newspaper? Who is the intended audience?
2. Whose views are expressed most prominently?
3. Which and whose perspectives are missing?
4. How is the homicide contextualized in each article? In each newspaper?
5. To what extent are readers provided background information on similar cases and the risks of similar violence befalling others?
6. To what causes are the homicides attributed, if any, and who, if anyone, is to blame? (Diagnostic component)
7. What remedial measures are implied by what is said and unsaid? (Prognostic component)

Overview of the coverage

As might be expected, each newspaper generated more coverage of the 'domestic' homicide than the 'foreign' one, with the exception of *Aftenposten*, which included slightly more coverage of the Bulger case than the Redergård case (see Table 7.1). However, the scale of each country's press coverage of the domestic case drastically diverges. The Bulger murder drew enormous interest in the English press whereas the Redergård case comparatively paled in significance in the Norwegian press.

Figure 7.1 shows the distribution of articles dealing with the Bulger case in both *The Times* and the *Daily Mirror* for a full year

Table 7.1 Number of articles in one year per paper, per case

	The Times	Daily Mirror	Aftenposten	VG
Bulger	256	152	19	30
Redergård	2	3	16	56

Figure 7.1 Bulger case: number of articles per event in English press

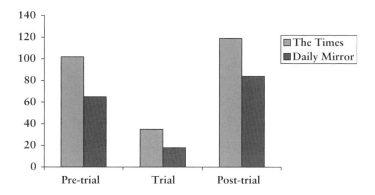

following each killing. This event-based disaggregation of articles is used to facilitate comparisons at the three key stages in the development of the Bulger murder story. As the Redergård story did not develop much past the investigation phase and was produced over a shorter duration of time, the same event-based disaggregation will not work with the Norwegian coverage. Though *The Times* offered more stories at each stage than the *Mirror*, coverage at each stage for each paper is proportionally similar. This indicates an alignment in relative prominence between tabloid and broadsheet. That the case remained an equally important story, proportionately speaking, in both papers throughout the year means that no matter which of the two papers readers chose over the course of the twelve months, the Bulger case featured just as regularly. This means the prolonged saliency of the case was not an exclusively tabloid-driven phenomenon.

The Norwegian coverage must be dealt with differently. Figure 7.2 shows the distribution of articles on both the Bulger and Redergård homicides for the year following the homicides. Again, the Redergård case did not generate any stories in either Norwegian

Figure 7.2 Number of articles in Norwegian press on each homicide

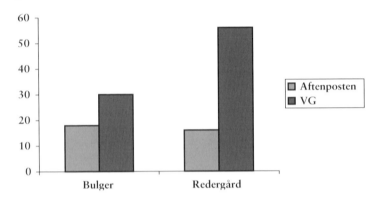

newspaper after the year limitation placed on the Bulger cover-age. The graph shows that *Aftenposten* devoted a slightly higher number of stories to the Bulger case than the Redergård case, but *VG* featured the Redergård case much more prominently. Unlike its English comparator, the Norwegian broadsheet provided less coverage of both cases than did the Norwegian tabloid. *The Times* in England conversely provided much more coverage of the Bulger case than the *Mirror*, which is perhaps due to the frequency with which columnists commented on the Bulger case in *The Times*. In contrast, *Aftenposten* presented only informational articles on both cases, while *VG* covered particular case aspects and angles in separate stand-alone articles.

Comparing Prominence

Quantitative content analysis highlights the relative prominence of similar events. The death of Silje Redergård attracted a great deal of press attention in the early days of the case as reporters from all over the world converged on the city of Trondheim. Occurring as it did only twenty months after the Bulger case, which itself attracted significant Norwegian press attention, the interest in the case was hardly surprising. However, what is interesting is that once young children were identified as Silje's attackers, and thus as the ones responsible for her death, the story became *less* of a story. In contrast, once it was learned that James Bulger's

Figure 7.3 Number of articles on the 'domestic' homicide (first fortnight)

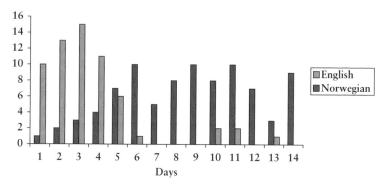

killers were ten-year-old boys—older than Silje's six-year-old attackers but still young boys—the case became *more* of a story in the English press. Figure 7.3 illustrates this drop off in overall Norwegian press interest (*Aftenposten* and *VG* combined) in the Redergård case over the course of the first fortnight after the case broke, and the rise in Bulger-case interest in the English press (*The Times* and the *Daily Mirror* combined) over a comparable time period in the unfolding of that case.

Figure 7.4 shows the distribution of front-page stories in the two English titles mentioning the Bulger murder and those in the Norwegian press mentioning the Redergård case in the first two weeks of coverage. The Silje case broke on the front pages of both Norwegian newspapers, remaining there for the first three days in both papers before it was relegated to the inside pages for the remainder of the period. The Bulger case, in contrast, made the front pages of both English newspapers for the first time on the third day, but stories mentioning aspects of the case remained there for much (6 out of 14 days in the *Mirror*)[4] or most (9 out of 14 days in *The Times*) of the fortnight. The front-page prominence

---

[4] The *Mirror*'s number would be 7 out of 14 had the front page on the twelfth day been counted. The headline reads: 'Tearaway, 13, Locked Up in Holiday Camp'. The article did not mention the Bulger case by name and was therefore not included in this analysis. However, it was nonetheless linked implicitly to the Bulger case simply though its juxtaposition to stories about it which dominated the headlines that week.

Figure 7.4 Distribution of 'domestic' homicide front pages

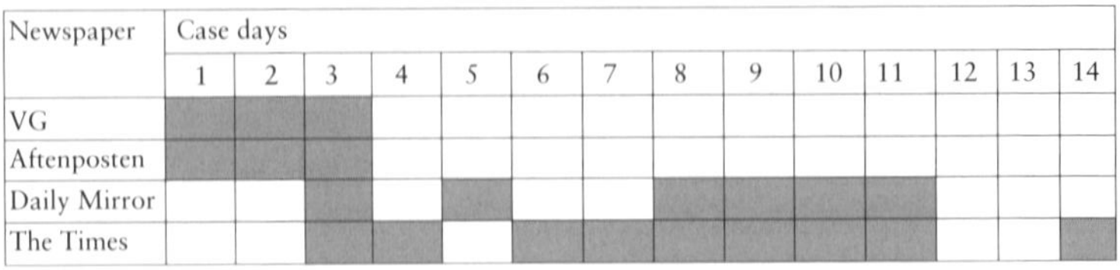

Newspaper	Case days													
	1	2	3	4	5	6	7	8	9	10	11	12	13	14
VG	█	█	█											
Aftenposten	█	█												
Daily Mirror			█					█	█	█	█			
The Times			█		█		█	█	█	█	█			█

in *The Times* may be due in part to its formerly[5] larger broadsheet size which could accommodate more headlines.[6] The patterns of prominence support the view that the Bulger case became more compelling to the English press once the assailants were identified as children, and that the opposite was true in the Norwegian press response to the Redergård case. However, the longevity of the Bulger case on the English front pages was due as much to the public reactions the case triggered than to the case itself.

Both English newspapers' minimal treatment of the Silje case consists of brief reports on the case details, both linking it to the Bulger case. Two of the three *Mirror* articles focus on the contributory role of violent children's television programmes. Beyond providing the case details in its initial report, *The Times* chose to provide legal background in its follow-up story and to quote Silje's mother, who, within the first few days after the death of her daughter, said she would be able to forgive the children responsible.

Norwegian press interest in the Bulger case was focused more on the English reaction to the case than the case itself. For instance, VG ran the headline, 'Canes and the Word of God' in the second week after the story broke. The article quotes various English

[5] The *Independent* converted to the compact, tabloid size in 2003, and *The Times* followed suit in 2004. The *Guardian* was relaunched in 2004 in a 'Berliner' format. Only the *Daily Telegraph* and *Financial Times* retain the broadsheet format.

[6] On the third day, for instance, the *Mirror* chose to lead with the front-page, fairly emotive headline 'You Bitch' in a story about a woman who left her 11-year-old daughter home alone while she went on holiday. The limited space on the front page meant that the Bulger case story ('How Can Anyone Be So Evil?') was relegated to page 2. *The Times* could have given prominence to both stories on its front page due to its larger format.

politicians who made condemnatory public responses: 'Shocked British politicians cry out about the need to end crimes of children and youths, and suggest a combination of prison, canes and the word of God' (*VG*, 23 February 1993). One of those quoted is identified erroneously, but tellingly, as a 'conservative MP' named Tony Blair.

Comparing Claims-Makers

This analysis seeks to discover dominant discourses present in the press coverage of the two homicides by comparing the characteristics of the dominant claims-makers in each newspaper in each country. This comparison reveals a great deal about the primary contributors to the discourses shaping the cultural sensibilities that drive political responses, and the cultural legitimacy enjoyed by each group relative to others. I replicated part of Schlesinger, Tumber and Murdock's (1991) analysis summarized in the last chapter by mapping the claims-makers whose views are expressed in each of the different paper's coverage of the two cases. This analysis reveals similar and considerable differences in the identities of the claims-makers that the different newspapers treated as legitimate sources, but it also makes intra- and inter-jurisdictional comparisons between the categories of newspapers in Norway and England. These claims-maker groups, which are viewed both in aggregate and disaggregated to answer particular research questions, include but are not limited to: experts,[7] members of the public,[8] the police, government politicians, main opposition party politicians, minor opposition party politicians, pressure groups, law enforcement experts, legal practitioners, prison and probation practitioners, clergy, journalists and editors, educators, victims and their families, the perpetrators and their families, and witnesses.

The first intention of this exercise was to determine the primary claims-makers in the debate and identify the discourses invoked within the frames they provide. The second intention was to

[7] Those claims-makers considered 'experts' for the sake of this analysis were coded separately by group and then aggregated. Disaggregated, these experts included psychologists and psychiatrists, medical doctors, social workers, academics, and non-academic researchers.

[8] This group includes vox pop interviews, letters to the editor from laypersons, and comments made by lay people not directly involved in the case.

determine whether and how these sources and their discourses differed within and between Norway and England. The dissemination of discourses through the press is an important focus of this study because access to a range of discourses is a prerequisite for any consideration of a full range of ameliorative policy options.

Only the articles featuring the 'domestic' coverage of the homicides in native papers were assessed in this way. This is because what is of interest is how each homicide was framed and contextualized in each jurisdiction by the two categories of press represented; that is, what cognitive resources—the knowledges that contribute to reader opinions and attitudes—were the readers of both types of newspapers in both countries offered? Figure 7.5 shows the relative distribution of selected claims-makers in the English and Norwegian newspapers. The totals represent the percentage of news stories containing claims made by each group in the coverage of the domestic homicide in each newspaper in each jurisdiction. Of most interest is the relative distribution of public views and expert views overall in each country. Clearly evident is the trend toward according the views of the public much more credence in the English press than in the Norwegian press, actually proportionally surpassing the frequency of expert views, whereas expert views are more prominent in the Norwegian press, far exceeding those of the public.

Figure 7.6 shows the frequency of articles containing claims made by experts and by members of the public in the articles

Figure 7.5 Distribution of 'domestic' case news items containing views of selected claims-makers

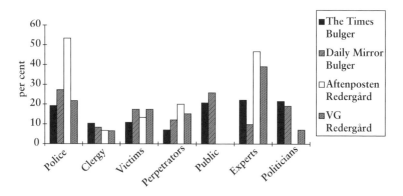

Figure 7.6 Distribution of 'domestic' case news items containing public and expert claims-makers

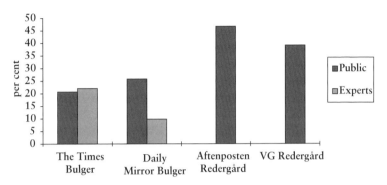

covering the domestic homicides in each country's two representative newspapers.[9] Most striking is the absence of public views and claims in the Norwegian coverage of the Redergård case in both the broadsheet *Aftenposten* and the tabloid *VG*. Expert views are expressed far more frequently in the Norwegian newspapers to contextualize the Redergård case, with the Norwegian tabloid *VG* presenting expert views at a rate nearly twice that of the English broadsheet, where expert discourse is most likely to find expression (39 per cent in *VG*, 22 per cent in *The Times*). In *The Times*' coverage of the Bulger case, the public's views are nearly as prominent as those of experts. In the *Mirror*, the public's views are expressed with a frequency two and a half times that of the experts.

Figure 7.7 shows the distribution of politicians whose claims were presented. In the Bulger case coverage in England, *The Times* presented political claims-makers slightly more often than the *Mirror* did, and both papers favoured the parties with which they are most sympathetic. *The Times* featured the views of Tory politicians more than twice as often as Labour views. The Labour-backing *Mirror* presented views of Labour politicians

---

[9] Comparing each jurisdiction and each newspaper's coverage of the domestic homicide case makes sense because of most interest are the ways the press equip their readers to deal with the homicide. In addition, comparisons on some dimensions—for instance, the frequency of claims made by experts in *VG*'s coverage of the Bulger case, or public claims made in the *Mirror* about the Redergård case—are less useful because the N is so low.

Figure 7.7 Distribution of 'domestic' case news items containing politician claims-makers

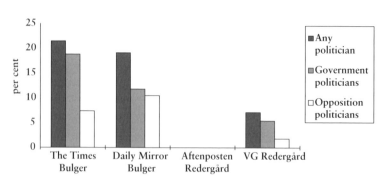

almost as frequently as those of the Conservatives, who were in government at the time. In contrast, the fact that the Silje case was never politicized is supported by the claims-maker analysis. None of *Aftenposten*'s coverage of the Silje case featured the views of politicians from any party, while *VG*'s coverage quoted politicians on only a few occasions, and never to politicize.

Comparing the Legitimacy of Elite Experts

The English tabloid coverage of the Bulger case prominently and frequently presented the views of members of the public at the expense of expert views, while the English broadsheet coverage struck more of a balance between the two. In contrast, the Norwegian coverage of the Redergård case, both tabloid and broadsheet, privileged the views of a range of experts, both to deal with the damage wrought by the homicide itself, and to contextualize the event in light of what is known about the rarity of such events, and presented none of the public views that English papers were so keen to convey. If this coverage is any guide, it appears this relative array reflects a different status hierarchy in each country; experts appear much more highly regarded in Norwegian culture than they are in English culture. In the mass-mediated debates subsequent to the homicides, the voice of the English public is ascribed a level of significance in the Bulger coverage that the Norwegian Redergård coverage only accords experts.

The apparent Norwegian faith in the ability of experts is evident in the reports about the mobilization of the 'helping services' (*hjelpeapparat*). This team of crisis psychiatrists, psychologists, and social workers play a central role in the case from the very beginning. They coordinate counselling services for the families— those of the perpetrators' and the victim both—as well as anyone else who wants it. They act as a dike to stem the inevitable flood of fearful speculation and rumours about the killers and the details of the killing itself. From the beginning there is a supportive infrastructure in place within the community that is staffed by trusted experts who appeal for calm and meet the community's needs. In the latter weeks of the case coverage, a *rykteflom* or a 'flood of rumours' had begun, centring on who the boys responsible were, but these rumours are quickly invalidated by the *hjelpeapparat*. Perhaps offering residents of the community the chance to express their fears and concerns in this way, supported by knowledgeable and trusted professionals, prevented the kind of mass outpouring of anger and vengeful emotion that characterized much of the Bulger case response.

The first example of this expert-led approach comes early in the case. On the second day of the case coverage *VG* reports what happened to one of the boys. Though it would later emerge that the boy had actually participated in the attack on Silje, at this point he has only claimed to have witnessed it: 'Yesterday afternoon and evening, both the boy and his mother were questioned by the police. After the questioning, the family was offered psychiatric help in order to work through what they had experienced' (*VG*, 16 October 1994). From the very beginning, psychiatric care is mobilized for all involved, and this approach did not change once this boy's true role in the attack was discovered. Police work and psychiatric counselling are not mutually exclusive and both are deemed equally appropriate.

The contrast with the Bulger case is striking, as Thompson and Venables were denied any psychiatric care in the nine months they spent awaiting trial in secure accommodation because of the legal impact it might have on their case. The lens through which the Bulger case was viewed focused on the criminal aspects of the case rather than any concern for the welfare of the perpetrators. The well-being of everyone involved remained the primary concern in the Redergård case. The following excerpt is from one of eight articles that appeared in *VG* on the first day. This one features the views of child psychologist Magne Raundalen who commented on the impacts Silje's death could have on other children:

> He points out . . . that children who were not witnesses but who are affected because they know the deceased or possibly the perpetrators, or because they played on the toboggan run [near where Silje was found] last evening, can also have reactions of a different sort. 'Children can react with crying and aggression, but also by withdrawing into themselves. They may show anxiety and dependence, wanting to sleep in their parents' bed or wanting to be accompanied on the way to school'. (*VG*, 16 October 1994)

It is also important to note that at this stage in the case, Silje's killers are still, by the news accounts, at large. So far, based on the information provided by the boy who 'witnessed' the attack and his father, all indications point to three assailants ranging in age from 16 to 22 years old. It should also be noted that their estimated ages far exceed those of Thompson and Venables. Before they were caught, they were judged from the Strand shopping centre security video to be as old as 12 or 13 (*Daily Mirror*, 16 February 1993). It can therefore be argued that the Norwegian residents of Heimdal had more reason to be fearful than those in Merseyside did in the wake of the Bulger case, if one accepts that older violent youths are more fearsome than younger ones. The press accounts at this early stage indicate that Silje had attempted to escape after being bullied by these three much older youths, but they had chased her and caught her again. Despite the significant unease that many in the community must have felt as a result of this frightening depiction, the emphasis in the press is nonetheless on containing the damage done to those closely and even tangentially involved, rather than focusing on and thereby stoking any fears of further attacks.

Judging from the press accounts, the Trondheim police for their part displayed none of the behaviours of the apparently more risk-averse Liverpool police. For example, before and after the boys responsible are identified, the Trondheim police did little to inflame fears by, for instance, warning parents to keep their kids indoors, though some parents did just that. This contrasts with the police response in Merseyside. In the early days after James was killed, when his killers had still not been caught, Detective Superintendent Albert Kirby told the public via the press: 'For goodness sake keep tight hold of your children. Poor James only went missing from his mother for a matter of seconds and he had gone. Until this person is caught, parents must keep hold of their children. Until we know what's happened and who is responsible, we cannot guarantee their safety' (quoted in *The Times*, 16 February 1993; *Daily Mirror*, 16 February 1993). Many readers undoubtedly found Kirby's words a chilling warning, but had another child been killed before James's killers were caught, the police could not have been accused of complacency. Again, judging from press accounts, the same might not have been said of the Trondheim police, had the same hypothetical occurred there.

Perhaps the most notable contrast when comparing the coverage of the early days of each case is how appeals for calm run through the Norwegian coverage of the Silje case, while the Bulger case's reporting is dominated by claims-makers and rhetoric that inflame concern. While the Redergård coverage is marked by child welfare discourses and by themes of compassion, forgiveness, and community, much of the Bulger case coverage invokes broader fears about life in Britain by linking the case to the perception that juvenile crime is getting somehow more prevalent and more savage, ultimately calling into question the moral health of the nation. Within six days of the Bulger murder, twenty-one children had been sought, questioned, and released by the police during their investigation (*The Times*, 18 February 1993). At least one of them—a boy of twelve who, with his family, was forced to move out of his home for fear of vigilantes[10]—was 'shopped' by his father.

One might react to these differences in tone by saying incidents like these are so rare in Norway that comparable fears there would be unjustified. After all, the father of the boy who claimed to have witnessed the attack expressed shock that something like this could happen in his neighbourhood, as he said that there had never been problems with gangs or groups of youths causing trouble there. However, it seems there had been a run of high-profile, youth-on-youth homicides in the press that did not seem to trigger much public alarm. In addition to the Bulger case, the Norwegian press compared Silje's death to those of Eric Morse in Chicago and Derrick Robie in New York, all of whom were killed within

---

[10] Neighbours were alerted to the arrest when eight police vans and three cars converged on the boy's house. The boy was met with abuse from the crowd of 80 people who had assembled outside by the time he was brought out with a blanket over his head (*The Times*, 17 February 1993).

the previous year by other children, and to another earlier and similar Norwegian case from, depending on the source, either 1989 (*Aftenposten*, 18 October 1994) or 1992 (*VG*, 19 October 1994). Silje was killed on 15 October 1994, and just over one month later, in Bjuv in Sweden, two brothers (16 and 17) stoned a 15-year-old friend to death, ultimately crushing his skull with a large stone.[11] Comparisons have also since been made with the 'Kevin case' in Arvika, Sweden, in which two brothers (5 and 7) strangled a four-year-old boy to death in 1998. Certainly the Norwegian case preceding Silje's death would have been sufficient cause for considerable alarm had there been the will to extrapolate a wider crisis from the cases. However, there is no such extrapolation in the Silje case coverage. The notion that crime narratives tend to 'carry the can' for quite different anxieties might help explain why the Norwegian press and public managed to respond so coolly to these cases and accept them as aberrations.

Attitudes to therapy

Another reason both cases differed so starkly might be found in the role played by the primary definers in each case. As the Bulger murder remained throughout its duration a criminal case, the discursive parameters, or the primary definitions of what the case was about, were set largely by the police. In the Redergård case, though the police remained instrumental claims-makers, the real primary definers were the members of the *hjelpeapparat* who channelled public requests for crisis psychiatric services through the police department. One psychologist 'stresses how important it is that the three boys to the greatest possible extent can continue to function in their habitual daily rhythm, that they get to go out and play with friends and carry on like they have done earlier. "The worst that can happen now is that peers and others in the local environment reject the boys because of what they have done"' (*VG*, 19 October 1994). Rejection of the boys is considered an indication of failure and is criticized. The message to the reader here is that this kind of response is appropriate, reflecting a more deferential culture, trusting of experts and their expertise. Again the contrast with the British response to Bulger's death is

---

[11] Silje's mother later contacted the mother of the victim in this case to offer her sympathy and support.

stark: 'A top Government expert said yesterday: "Protection of the public is more important than curing these boys. The emphasis is always on containment, not on therapy. If therapy fails, the boys face going from a secure unit to a young offenders institution, and then on to prison for the rest of their lives" ' (*Daily Mirror*, 25 November 1993).

The first of several elite-guided responses in Norway consisted of a concerted and ambitious attempt to limit the psychological and social damage caused by the incident. In both Norwegian newspapers, the reader is informed of the range of social services personnel that are present in the Trondheim community to answer questions, to offer counselling, and to defuse tensions. The *hjelpeapparat* visits two primary schools, two secondary schools, and four kindergartens in the Heimdal area of the city in the days following the homicide to help teachers help their pupils come to grips with what happened. In contrast, there is no community-centred response from the psychological professions at work in the streets of Merseyside mentioned in any of the coverage in either *The Times* or the *Mirror*. Not even the numerous witnesses in the Bulger case—those who failed to intervene on behalf of James and who had testified at the trial nine months after the murder—had been offered psychiatric help (*Daily Mirror*, 25 November 1993). Members of the jury were also not offered counselling and those who later thought they were in need of it were warned by the court not to divulge details of their deliberations during their sessions (Morrison, 1997). The scepticism of the worth of therapy is also evident in the lack of psychiatric care for Thompson and Venables while they awaited trial.

In fact, the goals of therapy seem to be undermined by the demands of the trial itself. What actually happened on the railway line where James Bulger was killed, and the role that each boy played in his death, will probably never be known. However, what is known is that each boy in his defence placed the bulk of the blame on the other, failing to take full responsibility for what he did. As Smith points out, that Venables had to mount a legal defence means there were significant pressures preventing him from admitting and facing up to what he had done. For instance, when placed in a secure unit for the first time, he was provided a cover story for his own protection. He was to say he was older than he was and that he had been caught stealing cars. His solicitor also is said to have told him, 'We're going to tell the judge you were mad when you did it' (Smith, 1994: 173) The trial placed legal demands upon the boys that hindered their ability to 'come clean'. In contrast, the aim of the reintegrative approach to the Silje case was to provide the children responsible the support and opportunity to come clean and to work past the terrible thing they did.

The status of the 'ologists'

In England, 'The crisis that ordinary people perceive in the family has rendered scholarly answers debased currency' (*Sunday Times*, 7 March 1993). In the tabloid press especially, but not exclusively, there is a suspicion and outright distrust of elites and of so-called expert opinion about crime and punishment issues. Anne Diamond in the *Mirror* writes:

Time and again, when society reaches into its soul for an explanation to violence, the so-called experts deny a link between TV, or video horror and the real thing. Well, God protect us from the 'ologists'—because their hackneyed perception is dangerous. I sometimes think that a degree in some sort of 'ology' blinds you to common sense. We all know violence begets violence. The abused become abusers. Little boys who've grown up watching daddy hit mummy end up beating their own wives. It's a cycle of despair.

This statement is interesting for two reasons. First, Diamond does a rhetorical bait-and-switch. She asserts that 'ologists' lack common sense when they deny a direct link between TV violence and real violence, and then she takes it further, implying they would dispute that early exposure to domestic violence in the household leads to violence in later life when few experts would likely challenge such a statement.

This excerpt also illustrates a second, more important point which might shed light on why expert discourse is nearly absent in English tabloid output and which helps make the case for more deliberative forums that will allow for full expression of available discourses: the caution that social scientists need to exercise for the sake of their own legitimacy has robbed them of legitimacy in the tabloids. The tabloid's discursive approach is direct, simplistic, often in denial of the complexity of the causal interplay of social factors affecting a problem, and aimed to appeal to an audience who is 'sick and tired' of claims to the contrary. Voices that stick to this sort of script are more likely to get column inches in the tabloids, while those with more qualified, cautious, and less viscerally satisfying suggestions and commentary will not, especially when this cautiousness can be interpreted as masking support for a soft or liberal response.

It would be unfair to portray tabloid coverage as entirely devoid of the kinds of cautionary qualifications that the broadsheets are better at producing. For instance, as an expert from Bath University tells the *Mirror*, 'The Bulger murder is a very extreme and exceptional case and we shouldn't be having a moral panic about it. Civilisation isn't going to end because two boys killed another child. Children who have come to crime and have lost a sense of direction in themselves, need to feel valued. They need to appreciate that they are part of the community and part of a social group in a warm family-style environment, where they can be sensitized to other people's feelings' (*Daily Mirror*, 26 November 1993). However, this kind of appeal for cool reflection is decidedly a rarity in the tabloid discourse. Experts are a regular feature in the Norwegian coverage and expert-driven discourse is mainstream, even in its tabloids. If we take the press discourse to reflect dominant strands of public sentiment, as it is often regarded in Britain, then there is a remarkable congruence between the press, expert, and public discourses in Norway. In England the press and public discourses, which are often inadvisably conflated, sharply diverge from expert discourses.

Tonry (2004b: ch 3) writes, 'what we see, think and believe depends as much upon when we stand as where'. It can also be argued that these things depend also upon with whom we stand. If the company we keep through the press we encounter includes experts, then our chances of developing an understanding of problems informed by their expertise and sensibilities are enhanced as we become subject to the discourses distinct to the cultural setting. Savelsberg (1994, 1999), like Zedner (1995, 2002), argues that Germany has experienced the same disembedding conditions of late-modernity without experiencing the concomitant rise in the kind of penal populism seen in England and the USA. He also contends that Germany's susceptibility to populism is reduced by the relatively insular nature of the knowledge production process, defining knowledge as 'cognitive and normative assumptions about the world' (Savelsberg, 1994: 912). Knowledges so conceived, and the discourses upon which they are based, again shape our understandings of the world, its problems, and solutions. Assumptions about issues are based on particular means of knowledge production, including scientific evidence, evidence from the media, experiential evidence, and evidence gleaned from political rhetoric. If we accept Savelsberg's point, then it follows that our assumptions will depend in part upon the range of knowledges to which we are exposed.

The expertise of so-called 'ologists' still survives in Norway. A broad web of therapeutic services are available to everyone in Norway, and childhood is highly 'psychologized', with a focus on psychodynamic methods of intervention with troubled children underpinned by a strong 'culture of understanding' (Wilkinson, 2007). While it is overstating things to say, as one child psychiatrist who has practised in Norway and the UK did, that 'Norwegian society understands people to death' (Wilkinson, 2007), the dominant view proliferated in the English press and political discourse would regard such a culture of understanding as an intolerably weak culture of excuse making.

Norwegian 'ologists' continue to retain relatively high status in society which affords them the opportunity to shape significantly both popular and official crime discourses in a way their English colleagues no longer can. For example, Norway's most well-known and outspoken criminologists, Nils Christie and Thomas Mathiesen, frequently engage in public debates in a way that few English criminologists would risk doing. For instance, Christie contributed to a series of articles in *Aftenposten* in early 2007. The series began with an article written by the angry father of a young man who had been killed in a fight outside a bar in Oslo. In the article he implicated the liberalism espoused by Christie and others in what the father deemed to be the unduly lenient sentence his son's killer received. Christie responded, opening an extended dialogue with the man via the *Aftenposten* series, by defending, among other things, the case for the suitability of mediation in serious crime cases. Few British criminologists would likely choose to engage in this way.

To offer another example, Mathiesen wrote a total of fifteen newspaper articles in 2001, while also participating in many television and radio interviews. Comparable figures among the English criminological community would likely paint a very different picture. A series of BBC programmes entitled 'Cracking Crime' dominated programming for nearly an entire day in September 2002. One programme called 'You Be the Judge' gathered together ex-offenders, judges, social workers, police, and victims in mock sentencing exercises. No contingent of criminologists participated, and the findings of criminological research were never mentioned during the hours of programming.

Child-on-Child Killings in Perspective

Press accounts contradictorily portrayed the Bulger murder as at once indicative of a perceived increased prevalence of violent juvenile crime and as itself an act so unique as to be beyond compare. In their reporting on the Bulger case, all four newspapers studied failed fully to put the murder they described into perspective relative to other crimes, but some were much more informative than others. To give an example, the *Mirror* declared in one headline, 'Jamie Bulger Boys Youngest Ever Charged with Murder' (*Daily Mirror*, 21 February 1993), though in the body of the article the claim was qualified with 'in living memory'. Both Norwegian newspapers made the same mistake, relying on British sources to echo the qualified point that Thompson and Venables were the youngest to be tried for murder 'this century'. Both the qualified and unqualified statements are not simply misleading but wrong.

First of all, the *Mirror*'s misleading failure to contextualize is found in the point it neglected to make: it is impossible for anyone any younger to be charged with any crime because the two boys were at the minimum age of criminal responsibility.[12] The *Mirror* was factually wrong too, as a ten-year-old was charged in 1967 with murder after stabbing another ten-year-old on the playground, according to research done by journalist David James Smith. Smith (1994), who was present in court throughout the trial of Thompson and Venables and whose book is one of two definitive accounts of it,[13] catalogued 33 comparable cases of killings committed by children under the age of 14 (25 of these killings of children by children) stretching as far back as 1748 (see Figure 7.8 for prevalence of killings by children under 14 in

---

[12] The 1963 revision of the Children and Young Person's Act established the age of criminal responsibility at ten, up from eight where it had been since 1933, when it was raised from seven, the minimum age stretching back to the Middle Ages (Smith, 1994).

[13] The other is Morrison (1997).

Figure 7.8 Prevalence of killings by children under age 14 in Britain since 1947

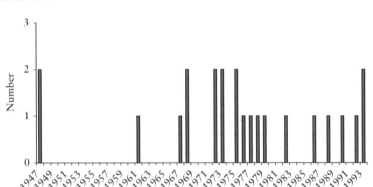

Source: Smith (1994).

Britain from 1947 to 1993). Smith's catalogue indicates that the *Mirror*'s declaration is additionally misleading because, between that particular 1967 case and the Bulger killing, there had been no less than thirteen other cases of children either under ten (and thus not chargeable) or between ten and fourteen who had faced similar allegations. Without this context, readers could be forgiven for believing, save for the notorious 1968 Mary Bell case which the *Mirror* references, that child-on-child homicide was a virtually new criminal phenomenon in 1993. Albert Kirby, the police officer who led the Bulger investigation, repeatedly called the case 'unique', apparently basing his assertion on the experiential evidence that he had personally never seen anything like it before. Though crimes like these are indeed rare, they are not unique. The Burgess murder case is another example discussed near the end of the chapter.

In its very first article on the Bulger case, the Norwegian tabloid proved to be better able to provide the perspective the English papers did not: 'Every year the last ten years, between 39 and 73 children under the age of five have been murdered in Great Britain, according to public statistics...In nearly every incident, the murders have been committed by adults who were acquainted with the children' (*VG*, 18 February 1993). In contrast with these statistics, several days later, two days after Thompson and Venables were charged with the murder, the *Mirror* ran the following 'Children's Wrist Link Offer' in its 'Mirror Woman' supplement:

KEEP 'EM AT CLOSE OF HAND

OFFER

THE tragic death of little James Bulger has focused all our minds on the subject of child safety.

You can help stop your child from straying from your side by using a wrist rein which is safe, flexible and is a lot less restrictive than the more traditional type of harness.

They're simple to put on and easy to carry with you. Many older toddlers prefer them as they allow a lot of freedom to move about.

To help you protect your kids we've joined forces with Toys R Us, the famous superstores for children. Each Toys R Us branch will give away 100 Wrist Links—and you don't have to pay a penny.

Claim

Toys R Us is famous for its huge range of children's safety items, as well as its massive choice of childcare products, from pushchairs to playpens, and carseats to cots. PLUS a vast range of nappies and babyfoods. All you have to do is visit your nearest Toys R Us store, show them a copy of today's Daily Mirror, and they'll hand over a brand new set of wrist reins, like the ones in the picture, FREE, to the first 100 people.

IT'S FIRST COME, FIRST SERVED.

And if you're not lucky enough to be among the first 100 to claim your reins, you can still buy one for only 1.99.

Toys R Us have now pledged to sell this vital safety device at a new low price—a big saving on the usual price of 3.49.

Sorry, there are no outlets in Republic of Ireland. (Daily Mirror, 24 February 1993)

The wording of this offer is striking both for its remarkably bold mix of fear legitimation and commerce, invoking and inflaming the collective fears in 'all our minds' to promote sales of a 'vital safety device', and for its failure to put the fears that mothers have in any perspective with any information about the risk of 'stranger danger', or any kind of victimization for that matter.

Legitimating Claims and the Silent Opposition

Similarly remiss, the *Mirror* never once, in all of its Bulger coverage, presented readers with the possibility that crime in Britain might actually not be rising or becoming more serious. *The Times* was more careful in its approach and presented this possibility, though very infrequently, through its columnist, Simon Jenkins, who made counterclaims to challenge the unqualified notion that violent youth crime was rising inexorably:

Brainwashed By Hysteria...There is no evidence of some new juvenile crime wave in Britain. There is merely a mass of assertion based on anecdote...The Home Office recently announced that between 1985 and 1991 the number of males under-18 cautioned or convicted of an offence in England and Wales fell from 219,000 to 149,000. 'Known offenders' under the age of 14 fell by 43 per cent. Only half of these falls were attributable to the fall in the size of the age group...'Reported crime' may have gone up but, as readers of this column know, such crime has no statistical relevance to real crime measuring only a small part of it. (*The Times*, 24 February 1993).

These counterclaims were far less frequent in *The Times* than those claims alleging that youth crime was getting both more serious and more prevalent: 'Although murder by children has been extremely rare, *we all* sense that we need to wake up to the disturbed, violent and amoral behaviour of what *seems to be* a growing number of children' (*The Times*, 27 November 1993, emphasis added). The self-referential nature of the claims about rising crime are clear, consistent with the practice of 'media looping' (Surette, 1998: 229) in which media stories and claims are removed from their contexts and used by other media for other purposes. *Sunday Times* columnist Jonathan Margolis provides another example: 'Leaving aside whether James was killed by juveniles or grown-ups, there has been a child crime wave the signs of which seem to come from all over the country. A selection from the past few months' crime stories proves little but suggests something cataclysmic' (*Sunday Times*, 21 February 1993). The *Mirror* uses similar evidence to make similar claims: 'Daily horror stories show our society has become too violent for our own good...An average day in Britain. A catalogue of horror' (*Daily Mirror*, 5 March 1993).

In two of the fourteen articles *The Times* ran on the day after the Bulger case verdict, the paper portrays rising crime as an uncontested given: 'Sir Ivan Lawrence, Queen's Counsel and Tory MP for Burton, said that a big reason for *the increase in crime* was the "constant diet of violence and depravity" that people were being fed by television, video and computer games and pornography' (*The Times*, 26 November 1993, emphasis added). Another article on the same day presents counterclaims to challenge the contention that violent media are to blame but again accepts rising juvenile crime as a fact: 'Fears that exposure to violent films may have played a key role in the Bulger case and could help to account for *rising juvenile crime* were dismissed yesterday by a leading researcher in the field' (*The Times*, 26 November 1993, emphasis added). Two days later the same is repeated: 'Gun fanciers opposed...legislation by pointing out that it is a childish delusion to believe that restricting availability of firearms will instantly end the crime problem. They are quite right just as the entertainment industry is correct in insisting that new efforts to restrict or tone down violent videos cannot overnight eliminate *the epidemic of youth crime*' (*Sunday Times*, 26 November 1993, emphasis added). Unsurprisingly, the *Mirror* presented a similar picture of 'Britain under Siege' (*Daily Mirror*, 23 February 1993) writing of 'the frightening crime statistics' (*Daily Mirror*, 23 February 1993), 'soaring crime' (*Daily Mirror*, 26 February 1993), and quoting a magistrate who is '...demanding a rethink of the [1991 Criminal Justice] Act which she—along with several judges—fears could lead to "a doubling of juvenile crime"' (*Daily Mirror*, 28 February 1993).

As Hay (1995: 206) argues, 'Within...moral panic discourses... each event is seen as symptomatic of a generalized crisis of familial authority, maternal responsibility and, hence, of the moral and social fabric of society'. In England the contest for discursive dominance was hardly a fair fight, as the claims-maker analysis above illustrates. Though Hay (1995) argues that the *Guardian*, *Independent,* and BBC2's *Newsnight* programme (and I would include *The Times* as well) all contested the notion that Britain was experiencing a juvenile crime wave at the time of the Bulger case, the contrary contention that it was was not only propagated by the tabloids and by broadsheet columnists and editorials (again including *The Times*), but it was also legitimated by those politicians who might have previously challenged such claims. As McRobbie (1994: 111) put it at the time, 'a remarkable feature of the current round of moral panics has been the lack of opposition from Labour and the silence of those close to Labour when it comes to speaking out against the scapegoating of the new folk devils'. At least part of what might explain why the Bulger case became such a lightning rod for concern—when, with an historical perspective, much of that concern seemed unwarranted—can be traced to the new political landscape that was emerging in the early 1990s. Counter-discourses challenging the dominant constructions of rampant child criminality went virtually unsupported by political leaders on the left. The reasons for this significant shift are more fully addressed in the next chapter.

Comparing Frames, Themes, and Angles

Marking off the discursive terrain

Qualitative media analysts make some useful distinctions in their terminology. *Frames*, as already mentioned, 'are the focus, a parameter or boundary, for discussing a particular event...focus[ing] on what will be discussed, how it will be discussed, and above all, how it will not be discussed...Frame refers to the particular perspective one uses to bracket or mark off something as one thing rather than another' (Altheide, 1996: 31). Like a window, news coverage frames problems in constrictive ways, and the 'characteristics of the window, its size and composition, limit what may be seen. So does its placement, that is, what aspect of the unfolding scene it makes accessible' (Tuchman, 1978: 209). *Themes* are the 'recurring typical theses that run through' the texts (Altheide, 1996: 31). By these definitions, the dominant frames used to 'mark off' the Bulger and Redergård cases are fundamentally opposed. The Bulger case is a criminal case; the Redergård case is not. The Bulger case concerns a kidnapping and a brutal and wilful murder; the Redergård case concerns the death of an innocent by innocents. The Bulger case is thus conceptualized using a 'criminal justice' frame rather than the 'child welfare' frame that came to define the Redergård case. These outer frames determine the thematic terrain that can be constructed within their boundaries and the discourses that will subsequently be invoked in descriptions and discussions of the cases.

The Redergård case coverage could be seen to reflect both sets of frames. Before the three young boys responsible for Silje's death were identified and before the child welfare frame came to dominate, the case had been defined in the criminal justice frame, as the killers in the early stages were again believed to range in age from 16 to 22 years old—well above 15, the age of criminal responsibility. This ought to provide an opportunity to glimpse how the themes and discourses that were used changed as the frames themselves changed, but it does not. It is hard to detect any real differences in the way the incident was contextualized before and after the very young ages of Silje's attackers were known. The themes constructed remain constant over the course of the case, as do the various angles used to support the themes. In the Bulger case, the dominant themes emerge within the criminal justice frame and remain there throughout the course of the case, although counter-discourses were invoked by those critical of the dominant frame.

By examining the thematic subframes and the *angles* used to prop them up, the underlying cultural sensibilities reflected in the discourse are rendered observable. For instance, within the wider criminal justice frame, the English press at times prominently portrayed the Bulger murder as an indication of a deeper moral malaise afflicting the whole of British society. The angles or evidentiary assertions used to support this thematic claim included the perceived declines in parental responsibility and discipline and the subsequent apparent rise in both the seriousness and prevalence of juvenile crime. All of these and more (see Table 7.2 below) were constructed as symptoms of this wider moral decline. In contrast, the dominant theme used to explain the Redergård homicide in the Norwegian press is the tragic accident theme, which holds to the notion that all parties in this case are victims (see Table 7.3 below).

Though the influence of violent television is a central part of the 'diagnosis' of the killing itself, Silje's death is viewed most prominently as a tragic aberration, the result of a series of unfortunate and deadly events that speaks little about the state of contemporary Norwegian society. It is not, as was the Bulger case in England, seen as somehow emblematic of societal anomie. It instead is an anomalous act committed by normal children, rather than a typical act to be expected from anomalous children. Silje's parents met those of one of the boys responsible. 'When the parent couples met later, both parties were in complete agreement that they all are victims of a great tragedy. They met in the boy's home only a few metres away from the apartment block where

Table 7.2 Dominant frames, themes, and angles in the English Bulger case coverage

| | Bulger: Criminal justice frame | |
	Diagnostic	Prognostic
THEME	Moral malaise theme	Moral reaffirmation theme
ANGLES	Rising crime	Condemn more, understand less
		Fight leniency and liberalism
		Deterrent/incapacitative penalties
		New sentencing powers
	Single- and bad parenting	Strengthen traditional family
	Violent Britain	Condemn more, understand less
		Deterrent penalties
		New sentencing powers
		Censor violent media
		Protect the children (never forget)
	Evil children	Punishment
		Condemn more, understand less (vigilantism)
		Deterrent penalties
		New sentencing powers for 'persistent young offenders'
		Teach morality
	TV/video violence	Censorship

Table 7.3 Dominant frames, themes, and angles in the Norwegian Redergård case coverage

| | Redergård: Child welfare frame | |
	Diagnostic	Prognostic
THEME	'Only victims' theme	Damage reduction theme
ANGLES	Tragic accident	Community outreach with crisis services
		Avoid stigmatization of perpetrators
		Forgiveness
		Return to normal routines
	TV violence	Censorship
	MBD Diagnosis	Treatment

Silje grew up' (*VG*, 18 October 1994). At a public meeting at the school that Silje's ten-year-old sister attended, her stepfather spoke to the pupils, describing the anger he felt when he learned of Silje's death, but also expressing sympathy for the boys who killed her whom he also considered victims. He told them, 'It is important to take care of all those who are parties in the case, and to have compassion for all the victims' (quoted in *VG*, 18 October 1994).

In the 'all victims' theme, Silje and the perpetrators are all constructed as victims using a number of angles to sustain that theme. Silje, of course, is a victim of violent mistreatment at the hands of her three playmates, but the perpetrators as well are constructed as victims of their own innocence—innocent of the knowledge of what damage their violent behaviour could bring about and innocent victims of violent television programmes. One of the three boys is constructed as a victim of child welfare services that failed properly to intervene when his mother asked for help with his aggressive behaviour in the past. The same boy also becomes a victim of Minimal Brain Dysfunction (MBD), a condition better known elsewhere as Attention Deficit Hyperactivity Disorder (ADHD) (*VG*, 19 October 1993). None of these factors to which the boys are seen to have fallen prey are at any time in the reporting portrayed as illegitimate excuses for their behaviour, as they might have been in at least some segments of the English press.

Diagnostic themes and their supporting angles are twinned with prognostic themes and angles. One set implies the other. All the prognostic or prescriptive components of the frames employed in the Redergård case are forward-looking, aligned with the Norwegian approach to child welfare and youth justice (Falck, 1998c), stressing reintegration, healing, expert-guided treatment, and inclusion. Strikingly absent are most of the themes and angles that dominate the contextualization of the Bulger case. In fact, the only angle that the native coverage of each domestic homicide shares in common is the concern about the effects of violent media and the subsequent calls for some kind of censorship. The Norwegian themes never include the contention that Silje's death is the result of moral decay, inherently evil children, or the belief that crime committed by young people is out of control—all of which represent the dominant thematic subframes in the English press, both tabloid and broadsheet alike. Also absent from the Norwegian contextualization, therefore, are the remedies advocated by the English press, including punishment, moral reaffirmation, condemnation, exclusion, and a nostalgic 'back to basics' return to decency and respect.

In short, the Bulger murder was prominently and dominantly framed as indicative of a wider moral malaise, as a symptom of something even worse. The Silje case was instead characterized as a horrible aberration, indicative of little more significant than the fact that tragic things happen.

Begotten, not made: evil and innocence

The normative notions of what ought to be done in response to children who kill and the discursive formations that construct notions of child culpability and inculpability were diametrically opposed in the two countries. A *Mirror* editorial contends that 'evil' is so attractive an explanation for brutal crimes because it absolves us from blame: 'The murder of James Bulger was so appalling that it would be foolish to pretend the evil of his two little killers could have been averted' (*Daily Mirror*, 26 November 1993). The word 'evil' is used '... seriously only on occasions such as this, perhaps to distance ourselves from what has happened; it is a way of saying that it is beyond our ambit and understanding. Ian Brady, the moors murderer, was regarded as evil, a one-off representing a dark, external force. We console ourselves that there are no general lessons to be drawn from such evil' (*Sunday Times*, 28 November 1993).

Though some in the press argued that there are 'evil acts, but there are no evil people' (*Daily Mirror*, 26 November 1993), others like the lead investigator in the case insisted that '[these] two boys were wicked beyond anyone's expectations, but not only wicked, they had a high degree of cunning and evil. They could foresee the questions to be put to them and could counter the evidence which was to be put to them. To be able to do that indicates a degree of evil on their part. All you can say is that it was evil to the extreme' (Albert Kirby quoted in *The Times*, 25 November 1993). The *Mirror* carried similar quotations in an article with the headline, 'Evil Freaks of Human Nature': 'Sgt Roberts attended several interviews with Thompson. "He had two personalities—one was evil and one was good." The evil side showed up when he was asked difficult questions: "He had that glare in his eye which is difficult to explain," said Sgt Roberts. He added that Thompson was not afraid of him. "He is not afraid of anybody as far as I can see. He has a strong character. He was quite an intelligent boy—very streetwise" ' (*Daily Mirror*, 25 November 1993).

Evil as intimated here is apparent to the observer by an unnatural ability to have wisdom beyond one's years and to lie. Though again, in the Redergård case, one of the boys responsible weaved rather elaborate lies, claiming three older youths had attacked Silje, and that he himself had hunted them down and had 'kicked one of them in the leg so he bled, just like Ninja Turtles' (*VG*, 17 October 1994). Nothing more is made of this lie in any of the Norwegian coverage. In the Bulger case, the ability to lie 'unnaturally' increases culpability and the evilness of the perpetrators. In Norway, lying when facing accusations from adults seems to be something to be expected from children caught doing wrong.

In her study of Scandinavian moral attitudes, Bondeson (2003: 157) found that most Scandinavians hold relativistic views about good and evil. Sixty-five per cent of her sample agreed with the statement: 'There can never be clear and absolute guidelines about what is good and evil. What is good and evil depends entirely upon the circumstances at the time'. Only 25 per cent agreed that: 'There are clear and absolute guidelines about what is good and evil. These always apply to everyone, whatever the circumstances'. Though, as always, comparisons are difficult, the World Values Survey uses an identical question to assess moral relativism. Combining 1981 and 1990 British data on moral relativism, 78 per cent of those 30 years old or younger endorsed the morally relativistic position, while 58 per cent of those over 30 did so (Hall, 1999: 448). These figures are not far off the mark from what Bondeson found in Scandinavia, yet indications from the comparison of the salience of evil in each nation's press discourse on these homicides paints a very different picture.

Furedi (1997) points out how the editors of *British Medical Journal* have banned the use of the word 'accident' in its pages in order to emphasize that most if not all injuries are preventable, and therefore not accidental. That most of all injuries are preventable insinuates that every injury can be blamed on someone or something. In spite of the brutality of the mistreatment Silje experienced before she died, there was a clearly apparent determination among many of those involved in the case and its aftermath, from police to tabloid journalists, to characterize what happened to Silje as an accident.

There is a distinction made between 'lived ideologies' and 'intellectual ideologies' (Edley, 2001: 202–3), echoing a similar one between public opinion and public judgment discussed more in Chapter 10. Lived ideologies and public opinion both rely on common sense and tend to be incoherent, contradictory, and experience-based. Though they are subject to change, they survive without much scrutiny. Lived ideologies present individuals with 'ideological dilemmas' (Billig et al, 1988) as they struggle to reconcile conflicting perceptions and understandings of social phenomena. Using the example of child offending and victimization, one is hard-pressed scrupulously to reconcile the dominant images of children as both morally pure victims—with the criteria for the provision of the morally pure distinction resulting purely from the victimization itself—with a contradictory image of the child perpetrator as intrinsically evil and 'born bad', simply because of the commission of a terrible act.

The 'evil child' discourse that was ascendant in England seemed to be matched by an equally firmly entrenched conception in Norway of the child as 'innocent', a characterization which in England is ascribed only to victims or potential victims. Clear distinctions between the sympathetic victim and the loathsome perpetrator are common devices employed in media discourses. Coded language is used to render subjects either more or less sympathetic depending on their role in a crime event. As victims, subjects are often described in terms that evoke sympathy ('schoolgirls', 'little', 'young', 'pals'), sometimes with a nickname. James Bulger is frequently referred to in the press as Little Jamie, which is a media creation, as the Bulger family made clear they always called him James (Morrison, 1997). Perpetrators are described in opposing terms. For instance, Anthony Walker from Liverpool was murdered in July 2005 in a shockingly vicious, racially motivated axe attack. BBC News repeatedly described the victim as an 18-year-old 'teenager' and the suspect as a 17-year-old 'man' (BBC News, 1 August 2005).

Doli incapax, which again is the legal presumption of innocence abolished by the Crime and Disorder Act 1998 introduced by the Labour government, had held that a child between the ages of ten and fourteen is so young as to be incapable of criminal intent, unless the prosecution proves otherwise. Considering the presumption in a 1990 White Paper—the same one in which it was famously declared that imprisonment 'can be an expensive way of making bad people worse'—the Conservative government argued that it did 'not intend to change these arrangements which make *proper* allowance of the *fact* that children's understanding, knowledge and ability to reason are still developing' (Home Office, 1990: para 8.4, emphasis added). *Doli incapax* was a notion born of different but once dominant childhood discourses more similar to those that still thrive today in Norway. In the wake of the Bulger case the government decided the presumption 'flies in the face of common sense' (Home Office, 1997b). Faith in child innocence cannot coexist easily alongside an opposing notion of children as 'natural born killers'. One must give to accommodate the other, and the idea that young children were incapable of criminal intent could not survive in the penal climate which had generated assertions that there should be 'no more excuses' for juvenile offending (Home Office, 1997a).

It is possible that the durability of the innocence discourse in Norway might have actually been bolstered by the occurrence of the Bulger case in England. Much of the Norwegian press's coverage of the Bulger case focused on the harshness of the English response, including the tough and condemnatory political rhetoric, the screaming tabloid headlines, and the angry mob that greeted the killers at the courthouse. It is possible that the innocence discourse in Norway may have found increasing support as efforts were mobilized to counter and condemn the discourse of evil coming at the time from England. For instance, the Norwegian Psychological Association debated whether to protest against the English decision to treat Thompson and Venables as criminals, and most Norwegians seemed to be 'appalled' by the English approach (Dyregrov and Heltne, 2007). A similar contrariness is evident in Scotland, where a nationalistic resistance to English political influence and Whitehall appears to explain in part how some of Scotland's more progressive penal policies have managed to survive the punitive turn in England (McAra, 1996). It may be that a degree of their tolerance and leniency in responding to Silje's death reflected a rejection of the nasty treatment the killers of James received, but of course it is impossible to know whether the Silje case might have been handled any differently had the Bulger case not occurred before it.

Another counterfactual is also worth considering. A reporter from *VG*, who travelled to Trondheim to cover the case in its early stages, and his editor, both claim the child status of the killers meant that their restrained approach to the case would not have differed much had the killers been ten, like James's were, or even older (Laure and Haavik, 2002). Others suggest that had the killers been as old as James's were, the content of the subsequent debate might have changed somewhat, but condemnation would still not have featured in it (Dyregrov and Heltne, 2007).

Anomalies have social functions, as James and Jenks (1996: 232) point out:

> …two kinds of 'Otherness' can be identified [in the Bulger case press coverage]: (a) the child possessed of an inherently evil nature; and (b) the composite creature, the 'adult-child'. Both are highly transgressive images, at once wilful, bizarre and demonic. In that these images instance acute fractures from the commonplace idea of 'the child' as it is understood within western society, they both constitute a powerful, and volatile, ambiguity in public accounts of childhood. Anthropological work on social classification enables us to understand such a response as one emitting from a people whose cosmologies are under threat. As Mary Douglas (1970) has shown, the identification of anomalies, whether in the form of people, plants or animals, is integral to the establishment of social order. Anomalies are, in essence, the by-products of systems of ordering. Through their remarked differences, ironically, they work to firm up the boundaries which give form and substance to the conceptual categories from which they are excluded. In this sense, by refusing children who commit acts of violence acceptance within the category of child, the public has reaffirmed to itself the essence of what children are.

These ideas have links with those of Durkheim, who envisioned the punishment of wrongdoing as, again ironically, shoring up and ensuring the moral identity of the collective: 'punishment is above all designed for upright people, for, since it serves to heal the wounds made upon collective sentiments, it can fill this role only where these sentiments exist, and commensurately with their vivacity' (Durkheim, 1893/1969: 24). It might be then that the restrained approach taken in Norway—the Norwegian lack of enthusiasm for the expulsion of children who elsewhere might be deemed anomalous deviants—could be explained by a diminished need or desire for Norwegians to rally in this way. Due to its cultural and ethnic homogeneity, the high levels of trust among citizens, and strong government legitimacy, perhaps the social order remains unthreatened by such anomalies, and expulsion to repair the damage wrought by an incident like Silje's death is inappropriate. Reintegration is chosen instead as the preferred route. It seems that the very young age of the offenders cannot alone account for the disparity.

These differences illustrate the contingency of events. 'Crises do not exist in the world. They exist in discourse. Crises are not real events, but are evaluations of the significance of what is happening' (Bruck, 1992: 108). This evaluative feature of crises means they are subjectively assessed and thus highly susceptible to manipulation. Though it is true that moral panic discourses cannot generate a crisis without considerable levels of existing concern, it is also true that the scale of those concerns can be forcibly aroused with alarmist discourses that manage to resonate with audiences who recognize the prima facie validity of the discourses:

> Moral panic discourses do not compete in terms of the sophistication of their understanding of the contexts they purport to describe. Indeed their 'success' as narratives relies not on their ability to accurately reflect the complex webs of causation that interact in complex and contingent ways to produce disparate effects (such as the abduction and murder of James Bulger), but in their ability to provide a simplified account sufficiently flexible to 'narrate' a great variety of morbid symptoms while unambiguously attributing causality and responsibility (to broken homes, irresponsible mothers, the breakdown of traditional morality, and so forth). (Hay, 1995: 217)

At the time of the Bulger murder, an economic recession was continuing in Britain, with an unemployment rate not seen since the 1930s (Hay, 1995). Highly publicized Gallup and MORI polls followed on the heels of the case, showing a sharp decline in the public's national confidence. Eighty per cent of the British public were unsatisfied under Tory leadership (*Sunday Times*, 28 February 1993), almost half of Britons were believed to want to emigrate (*The Times*, 24 February 1993), and law and order was second only to unemployment as the primary worry on British minds (*The Times*, 26 February 1993). The Bulger case only crystallized more general anxieties and broader concerns that had been accumulating, providing an opportunity for their expression. The prominence in the press of these poll results demonstrates an agenda-setting effect, providing the reading public something to think about (see Chapter 6). Whether or not commentators believe a crisis really exists, by focusing so intently on the question in the first place conveys to readers the message that such a question is a worthwhile and valid one to ask. The pessimism about Britishness that these widely talked about polls seemed to capture echoed sentiments in the 1970s that Ryan (2003) recalls when there was a broadly perceived breakdown in faith in the ability of the government to do things. Now, in 1993, it seems a similar pessimism was peaking again, topped ultimately by the Bulger case. It fit with the sentiments in *The Times* and *Mirror* columns and editorials, capturing with images and a horrible storyline a feeling that many felt already.

Both newspapers presented similarly bleak visions of a nation in the midst of a rapid and degenerative descent into moral chaos. The *Sunday Times* (21 February 1993) claims 'There is a new brutality about Britain', a view supported by a *Mirror* editorial declaring, 'There is something rotten at the heart of Britain. A creeping evil of violence and fear. The death of Jamie Bulger has focused the nation's attention on it. But it has been growing like a cancer for a long time' (*Daily Mirror*, 22 February 1993). The prognoses and prescriptions implied include a re-establishment of moral certainty, something with which 'progressive thinkers' cannot be trusted: 'The fact is there are standards and standards are slipping—we need a return to a moral consensus. Schools should teach the five R's—reading, writing, arithmetic, right and wrong. The thing that so-called progressive thinkers fail to see is that you don't punish or restrain children because you hate them, you do it because you love them and because you want to form certain moral certainties. You don't want children to think and reflect about murder being wrong—you want murder to be off the agenda completely' (*Daily Mirror*, 26 November 1993). The insinuation is that those who try to explain crime also condone it by making excuses for it, echoing Kennedy's observation noted in Chapter 6 that knowledge about threats can become associated with moral weakness.

Nostalgia for some idealized past when morals and mores were uncontested defines much of the discourse supporting the moral decay thesis. Anna King (2005) finds that of a list of both instrumental and symbolic variables contributing to punitive public attitudes, 'generational anxiety'—or the belief that the youth of today are less well behaved and more disrespectful than kids used to be—was the most highly correlated with punitive attitudes. Thus it would seem that those with punitive attitudes might find sustenance in the nostalgic media discourses that support these contentions. These beliefs that the youth are anomic, amoral, and disrespectful seem always to have defined older generations' views of the young (Pearson, 1983, 1985). This fear of youth seems linked to broader anxieties concerning moral decline more generally.

Comparing Rhetorical Strategies: Rhetoric and Resonance

Discourse analysis approaches '...social life as being character-ized by conflicts of various kinds. As such, much discourse is involved in establishing one version of the world in the face of competing versions...The emphasis on the rhetorical nature of texts directs our attention to the ways in which all discourse is organised to make itself persuasive' (Gill, 2000: 176). The dis-course analyst is thus concerned with, among other things, deter-mining what it is about the organization of particular texts that makes them persuasive.

The detached, analytic, expert-dominated discourse commonly associated with the broadsheet press is only persuasive to those readers who regard the experts whose views are expressed in it as legitimate and trustworthy authorities. The persuasive elements of expert discourses tend to rely on evidence-driven forms of per-suasion, like research findings and other forms of more rigorously tested, non-commonsensical knowledge. The prestige of the expert or the weight of his or her evidence is meant to have persuasive purchase. Other non-expert-driven discourses expressed in the press rely upon different strategies to persuade readers, reflect-ing in a Foucauldian sense their relative position in the 'hierarchy of discourses' (Jupp and Norris, 1993; Schlesinger, Tumber and Murdock, 1991). The relative prominence of views expressed in a given news medium by various claims-makers can be said to reflect the relative legitimacy those groups enjoy. For instance, the relative lack of expert views expressed in the pages of the *Daily Mirror* on issues relevant to the Bulger case suggests that expert views are not highly prized by its reporters, editors and, by exten-sion, its readers, whereas the dominance of expert views in the Redergård reporting reflects favourable attitudes toward them in Norway. A further evaluation of the status of discourses within the hierarchy might be inferred from the relative sizes of the read-erships choosing the media propagating particular discourses over others. At the very least, what can certainly be inferred from readership numbers are the relative sizes of audiences to which certain types of discourses are dispersed.

Following Althusser (1971), Hay (1995) argues that readers, through a process of 'interpellation or hailing', are called upon to 'decode' texts of crime events in two ways: first, as an isolated event, or a single crime narrative, and, second, as a component in a larger 'metanarrative'. The success of this linkage of an isolated event with the metanarrative depends in part on the degree to which the events and the texts describing them find resonance with audiences. Moral panic will not spark if the claims legitimating a panic do not have resonance, or if the claims fail to hook into consciousness.[14] The Redergård case was never amplified beyond its initial confines as a tragedy committed by children who were too young to comprehend what they were doing. The case was not recruited by the Norwegian media to take part in a crisis metanarrative, as happened in England.

Recent research on the psychological origins of punitive attitudes suggests that the identity scripts people use and narratives they draw upon to construct notions of themselves—or the ways individuals manage their own self-identities—can help explain the relative extent of punitive attitudes between groups (King, 2005). Punitive attitudes appear to be correlated with a self-identity that is communally oriented whereas non-punitive attitudes seem to correlate with more autonomous self-identities. The distinction might be illustrated by the following example: A woman standing in line at a chemist's sees a young boy attempting to pick up a prescription for a parent and turns to her companion and says disapprovingly, 'Are we sending our kids to pick up our prescriptions now?' The speaker's self-identification as part of the collective implied by her usage of 'we' and 'our' implies that her response to the scene at the chemist's would differ from someone not so communally oriented. The use of 'we' also indicates an attempt to 'hail' the listener by including him or her in the narrative. Someone else might observe and disapprove of the same scene but fail to feel in any way complicit in or culpable for it, perhaps in part because the person defines him- or herself as independent of the collective. This autonomous someone might instead react by saying, 'Are they sending their kids to pick up prescriptions now?' Both statements express disapproval, and both draw attention to an apparently new and troubling phenomenon, but the

---

[14] 'One mediated event…does not in and of itself constitute a moral panic. Through the process of discursive amplification, the "event" is translated from a particular conjuncture that must be understood on its own terms, to an event which is seem as emblematic and symptomatic of broader processes—moral decay, social malaise and the destruction of the social fabric of the family and thus society itself' (Hay, 1995: 204).

'we' used in the first reaction might indicate that the speaker's self-definition as subject to the collective, while the 'they' used in the second might denote a self-identity defined independently of the collective. This example is intended to suggest that audiences matter, that their cultural predispositions and self-identities impact on the success and resonance that certain kinds of rhetorical strategies and discourses have when they are presented.

Comparing how the pronoun 'we' is used in the reporting of the two homicides helps to identify the audience being hailed by this rhetorical strategy. James Thompson's column in *The Times* in which he invokes the Bulger case helps illustrate the point: 'Although murder by children has been extremely rare, *we all* sense that *we* need to wake up to the disturbed, violent and amoral behaviour of what seems to be a growing number of children' (*The Times*, 27 November 1993, emphasis added). Another example also comes from *The Times* in a piece written by Sally Emerson with the headline 'Beast that Hides in the Infant Breast':

... let *us* not feel too sorry for the evil in our society—evil has its own, intense pleasure as *we* have witnessed. Let *us* just say *we* have to fight it. *We* must not incite it. *We* must take care to avoid it. And *we* have to punish it as severely as *we* possibly can...What *we* need, of course, to do is bring back hell. People used to behave themselves through fear of it. If God has closed it down, let *us* open it up, although some might say *we* have already done that. It has been closed down somewhere, but opened up right here in our midst, in Liverpool, by a railway line. (*The Times*, 18 February, 1993, emphasis added)

In this collective sense, *we*, as members of the society that allowed the atrocity of the Bulger murder to occur and contributed to the moral decay that made possible the unthinkable, are thus collectively responsible for it. *We* are morally culpable. Anne Diamond employs the same strategy in her *Mirror* column in which she searches for links between the murder and the horror film *Child's Play 3*, which some erroneously claimed Jon Venables had seen before killing James: '*Our gut* tells us they must have seen your evil doll Chucky. They must have loved the film. And they must have seen it over and over again, because some of the things they did are almost exact copies of the screenplay... *We all* know violence begets violence' (*Daily Mirror*, 1 December 1993, emphasis added).

It is possible that the successful interpellation of readers and the success of their narratives to resonate with readers are more important concerns in highly competitive press markets like England's than they might be otherwise. Whatever the case may be, because there were so few Norwegian editorials and columns expressing readers' and authors' opinions about the Redergård case, most usage of 'we' in the Norwegian coverage refers to a small group of people, usually professionals, who were asked to comment on aspects of the case. 'We' is not commonly used in the Norwegian coverage as a collective term invoking society or the nation as a whole in the way it is often used in the English coverage.

The English collective approach to contextualizing and accepting responsibility for the crime sits uneasily alongside approaches appearing in the same newspapers that attempt to divorce the two perpetrators directly responsible from any collective sense of 'we' or 'us'. This othering is also more prevalent in the English coverage, both tabloid and broadsheet again, and absent in the less speculative and more informative Norwegian press. In the former case, Thompson and Venables are often discursively cast out of the community, their crimes used to re-establish moral boundaries in a Durkheimian way, their membership of the community sacrificed in order to restore social solidarity.

It would appear that the English media's coverage of the Bulger case, especially but not exclusively that of the tabloids, taps into these collective sentiments and concerns through their open editorialization and sensationally colloquial style. The reader is drawn into the speculation and hand wringing with contentions that *we*, author and reader both, are complicit in the wrong that has been done. Perhaps in so doing, this kind of reporting engenders punitive reactions by triggering guilt in the reader, guilt that is expressed in anger. The rhetorical approach of the tabloids then might be understood to facilitate these reactions because of the ways in which they appear to speak *for* the public. The excerpts from English Bulger-case coverage above that invoke collective sentiments also imply that disagreement with the author would somehow be unconscionable to 'right-thinking' people with 'common sense'. After all, it is in *our* gut that *we all* know the truth.

The tabloidization of news through these populist appeals to some vague sense of the collective appears to have significant consequences. For one thing, tabloid-style portrayals of crime tend to be correlated with higher levels of public support for harsher penalties (Doob and Roberts, 1988; Roberts and Doob, 1990). Though they do not create harsh attitudes towards offenders, the media do seem to cultivate and massage elements of readers' self-identities in those for whom this kind of coverage resonates. It is also notable that these features are not only present in the tabloid *Daily Mirror* but in *The Times* as well. This point leads to another. There appears to be a tendency for the English broadsheets to 'go tabloid' by presenting opinionated and emotive editorial content that reflects an inclination to engage the issues of public concern on this gut level. However, the tabloids appear less inclined to return the favour by 'going broadsheet' and presenting the dispassionate and antiseptic informational analysis and context that readers can still get from the broadsheets.

How the collective's state of health is perceived also matters in another important way that is picked up in the next chapter. King's (2005) findings mentioned above comport with other research (Tyler and Boeckmann, 1997) illustrating that punitive public attitudes are indicative of general concerns and anxieties about perceived changes in morality and other factors seen to threaten social solidarity. Not only are attitudes shaped by these perceptions of solidarity, but political behaviour is too. Mutz (1998) finds that people's political opinions are shaped more by 'sociotropic' concerns, or concerns about the state of the collective, than by their own personal concerns. This finding raises the stakes of impersonal influence considerably, beyond merely the influence of attitudes. It suggests as well that those outlets purporting to serve as barometers of sociotropic stability and societal health can have considerable power in shaping not just public attitudes, but subsequent political behaviour as well. It also suggests that politicians are smart to pay heed to what these barometers purport to show if they want to appear to be responsive to public concerns.

The Suitability of Vehicles

Comparison with another case of children killing a child helps to account for the different significance attached to the Bulger and Redergård killings. Rowbotham, Stevenson and Pegg (2003) compare the Bulger murder with the 1861 murder of two-year-old George Burgess in Stockport, England. The two cases share remarkable parallels: both victims were the same age, both cases involved stranger abductions in which the perpetrators in both cases led the victims on long walks of over two miles during which numerous witnesses failed to intervene satisfactorily, and both cases involved torture and the removal of some of the victim's clothing. Like the Bulger case, there was a high degree of press interest in the Burgess murder and its uniqueness, but it was only in the earlier stages that the two eight-year-old boys were demonized in the press. By the time of the trial, press opinion focused with optimism on the prospects of rehabilitating the boys and the harsh punishments advocated initially were abandoned for more reintegrative approaches. Though they faced murder charges and the death penalty, a jury found James Bradley and Peter Barratt guilty only of manslaughter, a verdict that was cheered in the court's public gallery, and they were sentenced to one month in gaol and five years in a reformatory.

It appears that public sentiments were accurately reflected in both cases. In presiding over the Burgess trial, Judge Compton said he 'believed it was mere babyish mischief' which accounted for the boy's crimes (Rowbotham, Stevenson and Pegg, 2003: 119), while Justice Morland declared the Bulger murder 'an act of unparalleled evil and barbarity' (*Sunday Times*, 28 November 1993). While some cases like the Bulger murder become suitably emblematic 'vehicles to which concerns about the overall stability of the community could be attached' (Rowbotham et al, 2003: 115), others like the Burgess and Redergård cases do not. The suitability of certain high-profile crimes as vehicles for such concerns appears to have little to do with the murder narratives themselves and more to do with questions of legitimacy and the levels of public trust in the justice system.

Lest it be assumed the climate of the time of the Burgess case to be conducive to such public acts of mercy, Rowbotham, Stevenson and Pegg point out that there was plenty on the minds of Victorian Britons in 1861 that would seem to make palatable a more vengeful Burgess case verdict: 'From its start, 1861 was characterized by a high degree of panic, with the harsh winter heightening both crime and misery levels. There was a high-profile building strike, high levels of petty crime associated with unemployment and misery, and numerous leaders in papers from *The Times* to the *News of the World* about what the *Annual Register* summed up as "the doctrine of juvenile capacity for crime" ' (Rowbotham et al, 2003:

114). Instead of accounting for the disparity between the public reactions to the Burgess and Bulger cases with reference to the social conditions of the time, the authors argue that the Victorian reaction 'was enabled because of the existing substantial popular faith in the "justness" of the system' (Rowbotham et al, 2003: 114). They point to the apparently widespread dissatisfaction with the decision to release Thompson and Venables as evidence that '... the present legal system has NOT instilled a similar popular confidence that justice is being seen to be done' (Rowbotham et al, 2003: 114). This conclusion can be taken one step further. Whether or not a particular crime event becomes a suitable vehicle for late-modern anxieties appears to be conditioned not only by the levels of confidence that the public have in their institutions and in those charged with responding to that event, but also by the incentives that particular ways of doing politics create to politicize such events and to magnify their significance. This point is explored more in the next two chapters.

From their analysis of the newspaper coverage of the Burgess and Bulger cases, Rowbotham, Stevenson and Pegg (2003: 120–1) conclude that the media:

cannot be blamed for 'creating' inconvenient feelings and actions amongst an implicitly gullible populace...Scapegoating the media provides a convenient excuse to avoid facing an uncomfortable possibility that it is modern reactions to the current management of the justice system which provide the core problem...[T]he attractiveness to consumers of the current tenor of media reporting of popular beliefs about crime should lead such authority towards a serious reassessment, not just of sentencing attitudes and expectations, but of the wider social and cultural attitudes involved, in order to arrive at a better understanding of how to achieve a working compromise between themselves and the public over the nature of justice and its delivery. Only then might it be possible for children of misfortune such as Thompson and Venables to have a genuine chance at rehabilitation and reintegration into an accepting community in a way that their Victorian [and contemporary Norwegian] counterparts achieved.

These are compelling arguments.

However, though there may be a 'worrying disjunction between popular belief in what should constitute justice and authority's attitudes to what should amount to the same thing' (Rowbotham et al, 2003: 120), it can also be said that this disjunction is at least partially due to a lack of knowledge about both the reality of existing criminal justice system practice, and the nature of informed public opinion on issues of justice, as more nuanced research into public opinion and public judgment reviewed in Chapter 10 illustrates. 'Authority' probably has as much to learn about an informed public's attitudes about justice as the public has to learn about what criminal justice elites believe constitutes justice. Exercises in public deliberation could do much both to help bridge this disjunction, and to prevent the media and politicians from exploiting it.

Conclusion

The kinds of knowledge that are deemed legitimate when a high-profile case breaks have the power to shape the thinking, understanding, and ameliorations to follow. In the wake of Silje Redergård's death, a range of expert claims-makers were prominently featured in the press to make sense of the tragedy and to ascribe meaning to it. The press coverage reflected expertise-driven, welfare-oriented discourses. Remarkably perhaps, to foreign eyes at least, no claims-makers in any of the Norwegian press coverage ever questioned the wisdom or morality of the reintegrative and non-punitive way the authorities approached the three boys who attacked Silje. These differences, and the differences in political saliency of the two cases, are due at least in part to the central role played by the array of experts who enjoyed a level of trust and deference that many Britons found hard to accept in England after James Bulger was killed. The coverage in both Norwegian newspapers is expert-dominated, measured, reserved, and practically devoid of the perspectives of the 'man on the street' or the exercised newspaper columnist. The full duration of the Redergård case coverage is characterized by deference to this expertise, and an apparent lack of deference to the views of 'the public'. There are no vox pop pieces and no letters to the editor featured in the Norwegian reporting of the Silje case. Though the discourses elites invoked differed and conflicted on some level, the dominance of elite discourses remained unchallenged by public or lay counter-discourses.

The picture in England was very different. Press-consuming Britons were exposed to press discourses that were by and large expert-phobic, opinionated, self-referential, portentous, and more homogenized than they might otherwise have been. Unlike Norwegian readers, many Britons, especially tabloid readers, were simply not exposed to the perspectives of experts and were reliant upon politicians and the press commentariat to provide context, significance, and interpretation. For this reason, one might argue that Norwegian readers consumed a different kind of homogenized press discourse, expert dominated and drained of lay perspectives. However, it can nevertheless be said that the Norwegian press accounts were better than the English accounts were at informing readers about the risk of similar kinds of victimization.

Discourse hierarchies are reproduced and influenced by aspects of each jurisdiction's political culture. The next two chapters consider in more detail the reasons why this particularly English homogenization of press discourse accumulated in the wake of the Bulger case, and examine the role political culture continues to play in maintaining the dominance of similarly narrowly constrained discourse.

8

English Penal Policy Climates and Political Culture

The flow of information between government policymakers and the range of both officially and unofficially recognized advisers on which they rely is subject to the evolutions of political and press cultures and the penal climates those cultures help to create. A remarkable merging of several discourses was apparent in the aftermath of the killing of James Bulger in England. These discourses interacted with the structural elements of 1990s English politics to create a moralistic consensus that generated—almost inevitably under the circumstances—great concern among policymakers as well as a number of legislative changes. The Bulger case generated the responses it did because of a merging of moralistic discourses and particular structural and historical contingencies, including an increasingly influential tabloid press, that made government actors more cognizant of and deferential to what was perceived to be public opinion. The complex tangle of problems that has contributed to a growth in penal populism in England has worsened since the early 1990s, and if the aim is to ameliorate some the effects of penal populism, a better understanding of what is driving it is first required.

This chapter has four main parts. The first draws upon news coverage and parliamentary debates to examine some of the political responses to the Bulger case, including the ways in which the Labour Party in general, and Tony Blair in particular, were pressed to respond. Next, I try to account for some of these responses by reviewing the four evolutionary stages of English penal policymaking, as outlined by Mick Ryan (2003), which have led to the current phase, characterized by populism and the strong influence of so-called public opinion. The third section considers changes in the interaction between the press, the public, and English political culture that has led to the routine legitimization of simplistically homogenized crime and punishment discourses by political leaders driven to be seen to be addressing the mass-mediated, filtered concerns of the public. Aspects of adversarial, majoritarian political culture narrowly constrain explanatory discourses that reinforce a narrowly constrained set of policy responses. The fourth part considers links between Labour's moralistic rhetoric, Old Testament values, and appropriation of dichotomous explanatory discourses. The chapter shows that the muscular responses to the Bulger case were not inevitable, but they were strongly influenced by powerful forces beyond the control of individuals.

The Post-Bulger Case Penal Climate

The merging of discourses

Around the time of the Bulger murder, discourses began to merge along two corridors. In the first, the Conservative and Labour Parties arrived at a consensus on issues of law and order, one that Downes and Morgan (1997; 2002; 2007) contend made it difficult to recognize any real difference between their approaches. The Labour Party 'accept[ed] and then embrac[ed]...the disciplinary agenda that the Conservatives had translated into public opinion so successfully as "common sense"' (Ryan, 2003: 122). The second occurred between New Labour rhetoric and that of the tabloids, and, like the first, was dictated largely by the political necessity to engage with, as Tony Blair's former communication director, Alastair Campbell, put it, the press that 'really matter'.

It seems clear that the Bulger case played a role in bringing Labour, Conservative, and tabloid discourse together, though Labour had already embarked on its refurbished approach to law and order before James was killed. 'Tough on crime, tough on the causes of crime' (a phrase actually credited to Gordon Brown) was first uttered by Blair, who was shadow Home Secretary at the time, in an interview on Radio 4 in January 1993, a month before James Bulger was killed (Rentoul, 2001; Resodihardjo, 2003). The statement was, in Ryan's (2003: 123) words, the 'magic hyphen' which united Labour's left and right wings. In the interview Blair was asked for his views on the rising prison population to which he replied, 'You've got to be prepared to punish...and, where necessary, that will mean custody', though adding that both aspects of the problem, crime and its causes, must be addressed (Dunbar and Langdon, 1998: 102).

In an article in the *Observer*, Nick Cohen tells an anecdote illustrating how the dramatic shift in Labour's approach to crime became apparent to him:

I was a young reporter in the early Nineties and loathed [Home Secretary Michael] Howard with the best of my liberal colleagues. He was a Tory and that was enough. My job was to get rid of Tories and, *faute de mieux*, I got to know Blair. He was a touch prissy for my tastes and his language had a formulaic ring even then. But he seemed to mean well.

In the weeks before James Bulger was killed, I got a draft of a torrid speech by David Maclean, a junior Minister in Howard's Home Office. The justice system was 'on the side of the criminal', Maclean had intended to rage, and vigilantes had a point. The police must have the power to drive offenders from the streets like 'vermin'.

We're used to such tosh today, but at the time Ministers didn't talk like that. Howard was appalled and Maclean's speech was rewritten. Instead of playing Dirty Harry, Howard required him to deliver a worthy lecture on crime prevention which, as I remember, made much of fitting good window locks.

My newspaper prepared to make mischief by comparing and contrasting the sensational original with the banal final product. I phoned Blair and invited him to join the fun. The future Prime Minister didn't want to come out and play. He listened to the 'vermin' and 'vigilantes' and fell silent.

'Come on Tony, aren't you going to condemn this?' No, actually, he wasn't. 'You see, a lot of Daily Mail readers would agree with Maclean,' he explained, and hung up. (*Observer*, 21 June 2001)

Labour's new embrace of a willingness to punish offenders, something with which Labour had not been strongly associated previously, meant that Labour could now engage in debates on ground previously controlled by the Conservatives.

In his biography of Blair, John Rentoul (1995) contends that it was Blair's political performance immediately after the Bulger abduction and murder which made him a real contender for the party's leadership. On 19 February, six days after James was killed, Blair gave a speech in Wellingborough in which he, in Rentoul's words, attempted to 'moralise politics' by speaking of moral decline and the loss of community in a way that his Labour contemporaries previously had not done:

The news bulletins of the last week have been like hammer blows struck against the sleeping conscience of the country, urging us to wake up and look unflinchingly at what we see...A solution to this disintegration doesn't simply lie in legislation. It must come from the rediscovery of a sense of direction as a country and most of all from being unafraid to start talking once again about the values and principles we believe in and what they mean for us, not just as individuals but as a community. We cannot exist in a moral vacuum. If we do not learn and then teach the value of what is right and what is wrong, then the result is simply moral chaos which engulfs us all...The importance of the notion of community is that it defines the relationship not only between us as individuals but between people and the society in which they live, one that is based on responsibilities as well as rights, on obligations as well as entitlements. Self-respect is in part derived from respect for others. (quoted in Rentoul, 2001: 200)

Rentoul writes that Blair's office was subsequently 'flooded with letters of approval and support' and that the speech helped to propel Blair to the head of the party after John Smith died unexpectedly in 1994. 'His speech was of no direct relevance to the Bulger case, but touched a national mood of anxiety over the break-up of morals and families. It was like a Conservative politician's speech, responding to a moral panic induced by an atypical case by condemning a general moral decline' (Rentoul, 2001: 200).[1]

Blair's moralism merged well with other established discourses. His moralistic response to the Bulger case, which helped outflank the Tories on law and order, was not driven entirely by political cynicism and opportunism. It was presaged by his own personal religious views. According to Rentoul, Blair joined the Christian Socialist Movement in June 1992, and wrote the foreword to a collection of Christian Socialist essays called *Reclaiming the Ground* (Bryant and Smith, 1993). In it he wrote:

[Christianity] is not utilitarian—though socialism can be explained in those terms. It is judgmental. There is right and wrong. There is good and bad. We all know this, of course, but it has become fashionable to be uncomfortable about such language. But when we look at our world today and how much needs to be done, we should not hesitate to make such judgments. And then follow them with determination. That would be Christian socialism. (Blair, 1993a: 12)

Though there were existing and growing forces pressuring politicians to be more populist, the Bulger case became what it did

---

[1] Smith apparently disapproved of Blair's strategy, believing it might alienate many on the party's left (Newburn and Jones, 2005; Seldon, 2004). While this suggests that Labour's approach to crime might have been very different had Smith survived, whether the 1997 election could have been won without New Labour's tough-on-crime makeover is another question.

partly because of Blair's decision to speak about it in the terms he did, bringing about a coalescence of discourses shaped by moralistic preoccupations and legitimated by Blair's non-utilitarian and judgmental Christianity.

The coalescence of Conservative, Labour, and tabloid rhetoric in 1993 is important because, occurring as it did at a time of great insecurity and moral panic, it represented a moralistic consensus from both major political parties and the principal agenda-setting institution. The practically united moralistic, condemnatory, punitive political response to the Bulger case and the issues it raised left little space for counter-discourses. In other words, 'there was virtually no media or political comment pointing out that murder by young children is a very rare phenomenon that occurs in all countries, and that it is hard to think of a more atypical kind of offence, or one from which it is less possible to draw general lessons' (Dunbar and Langdon, 1998: 102).

The 'contest' involved in the contestation of the juvenile crime panic was hardly that at all because the views of one side of the debate were privileged through the legitimization by political leaders who, in the New Labour mode, felt powerless to contest them without appearing soft on crime and insensitive to victims. Moral panic discourses met much less discursive opposition in the press than they might have a decade earlier. It is not difficult to see how public concerns were rapidly inflamed when there was a virtual lack of counterclaims being made by leaders. The contest instead was for the most authoritarian political response, as crime had become an issue upon which New Labour would not be made politically vulnerable. This marked the end of the 'excuse-making culture', as Labour adopted rhetoric that echoed Tory Prime Minister John Major's, who, in the wake of the Bulger murder, declared, 'Society needs to condemn a little more and understand a little less' (quoted in *Mail On Sunday*, 21 February 1993).

The pressure to get tough fast

The return of truancy officers, the introduction of warning stickers for violent video games, calls for the outright ban of 'video nasties', and the acceleration of plans to lock up persistent young offenders in Secure Training Centres were political responses with links to the Bulger case. The latter measure was precipitated through pressure from Labour. This lengthy piece from *The Times* captures well the political climate at the time:

[Home Secretary] Kenneth Clarke bowed to increasing Conservative backbench alarm over teenage crime last night by promising that he would speed up the timetable for announcing tougher measures.

After robust exchanges with anxious Tory MPs at a hurriedly convened private meeting at Westminster, the home secretary signalled that he was preparing to make a Commons statement within about a week on his plans for the reintroduction of institutions similar to approved schools.

He has decided against delaying his statement until the Home Office has completed a white paper on measures to enable courts to detain persistent young offenders in privately-run secure units.

He also appeared to hint that, with Labour support, he might be able to introduce legislation in the current session of Parliament. This looked like a *ploy to put the Opposition on the spot* after Tony Blair, the shadow home secretary, sought to steal the government's clothes by announcing proposals for curbing young delinquents...

David Shaw, MP for Dover, said: 'Our message was a tough message. We should take the opportunity Labour has given us and implement all the policies we have found difficulty in implementing before because of opposition from socialist and libertarian groups soft on crime.'

Other backbenchers said that...Mr Clarke...had been left in little doubt that his 'avuncular' manner was proving a disappointment. 'He has had some tough language from some members,' one Tory MP said. 'An avuncular approach to this is not enough. He *must be tough and seen to be tough.*'

John Townend, a member of the executive of the Conservative backbench 1922 committee who had earlier called for the return of the cane in schools, said that the *wave of national outrage* over the murder of two-year-old James Bulger had brought to the surface strong feelings that it was time the government confronted young criminals. (*The Times*, 23 February 1993, emphasis added).

Labour's tough image was not yet fully evident to everybody in early 1993. An example of the kind of rhetoric that Blair and the Labour Party faced from opponents in the immediate wake of the Bulger case is found in a Commons speech by David Evans, Conservative MP for Welwyn Hatfield, on Secure Training Centres:

I welcomed the Home Secretary's announcement this week on juvenile offenders. For the first time, those hooligans will be locked up and, as far as I am concerned, they can throw away the key. Will the Minister assure me, however, that those institutions will not be holiday camps, but prison camps where thugs can learn the meaning of right and wrong? I hope that the Minister will note that it is important that they are run not by failed social workers, who are associated with that lot on the Opposition Benches, but by sergeant-majors…What of the Labour party's law and order policy? What a joke it is. The malaise in our society that has contributed to the rise of lawlessness has largely been as a result of the ideology of the Labour party. That party has paid more attention to rehabilitating or excusing the offender than punishing him. The Labour party is pathetic…Sadly, all too often, attention is focused on the rights of the criminal. I would give the criminal rights—the right to be birched, to be flogged, to be castrated and to be given a damn good hiding. (*Hansard*, cols 601–603, 5 March 1993)

By embracing punishment and, in so doing, distancing the party from 'failed social workers' and their liberal ilk, 'the Labour Party leapt free with one bound from the shackles that had weighed it down' (Dunbar and Langdon, 1998: 102) and weakened the purchase of arguments like those of this Tory MP.

By the fall of 1993, this shift was even more apparent. An editorial from *The Times* offers a summary of Tony Blair's responses to the Bulger case that indicates just how much Labour had changed:

Tony Blair has parked his tanks on Michael Howard's lawn…[T]he [Bulger] killing inspired a moral panic across Britain. John Major announced a 'crusade against crime', and the numbers who told MORI they were worried about law and order doubled within a month. Sensing an electoral opportunity, both parties revamped their message. The public has yet to be reassured. Labour's policy switch has been the most dramatic. Soon after the Jamie Bulger killing, Tony Blair, shadow home secretary, made a speech condemning the use of social conditions as an excuse for criminality. Later he uttered words on which most of his recent predecessors would have choked: 'If we do not learn and then teach the value of what is right and what is wrong, then the result is simply moral chaos which engulfs us all.' (*The Times*, 2 October 1993)

The penal climate after the Bulger murder made some things unsayable. Just as the press legitimized dubious claims that crime was rising and worsening, politicians from all parties did the same during this period:

The government has been urged to set up a royal commission into the causes of violence in society. An all-party motion has been sponsored by David Alton, Liberal Democrat MP for Liverpool, Mossley Hill, expressing 'grave disquiet at the growth in vicious and unprovoked attacks on the most vulnerable in society, particularly on women and children.' (*The Times*, 20 February 1993)

As limited as statistics are they do show one thing that the number of youth crimes as opposed to criminals has risen by 54% in the past 10 years. And according to analysts as various as [Charles] Murray, our sample of bad boys in Birkenhead and their Labour MP, Frank Field, the vague, generalised, uneasy middle class fear that criminals are getting younger, more prevalent and massively more vicious is valid. There is evidence that our children are close in certain strata of society to being out of control. (*Sunday Times*, 21 February 1993)

Everyone from Government Ministers down has been sounding off about Britain's rising tide of juvenile crime. (*Daily Mirror*, 30 April 1993)

Timing of events is important and the scene in 1993 was thus set for a convergence of political will and public concern to get tough fast. The conspicuous lack of similar political clamouring in the wake of the Redergård case in Norway probably accounts for the failure to inflame what concerns the case generated into a moral panic. There are aspects of the Redergård case, as read via the newspaper coverage, that presented exploitable opportunities for enterprising politicians who could have made political hay. For instance, there are no stipulations in Norwegian law to deal with children as young as Silje's killers, so no one really knew how to handle the investigation into her death (*Aftenposten*, 18 October 1994). Despite this, no politicians acted to rectify this.

When raising issues for debate and weighing in on issues already under debate, MPs frequently infuse their speeches with mentions of timely, evocative events from the headlines. It is striking that the Bulger and Redergård cases generated no debate in the *Storting*, the Norwegian Parliament, while the death of James Bulger was invoked in the House of Commons in 28 separate debates between March 1993 and June 2001, and in the House of Lords in 21 debates.[2] The ways in which the case was invoked in the Commons offer insights into the pressures that MPs found themselves facing in the wake of the Bulger case.

---

[2] The Redergård case was mentioned in three of these Commons exchanges as well. However, due perhaps to the fact that most Lords are appointed for life, the Bulger case was not invoked in the second chamber until 1996, indicating perhaps diminished incentives for Lords to 'play to the gallery' to the degree that MPs in the Commons did by invoking the case.

The third invocation of the Bulger case came on 30 April 1993 in the debate about an amendment to delay implementation of the Sexual Offences Bill for a period of two months after its enactment in order to consider its likely impacts on the police, social services, and youth agencies, as well as its compatibility with other legislation. The Bill sought to abolish the presumption that 'young men', as Home Office Minister Michael Jack called them (*Hansard*, col 1265, 30 April 1993), between the ages of 10 and 14 are incapable of intercourse and therefore cannot be charged with rape. The debate referenced here is not about whether but when the Bill should become law. Conservative MP Lady Olga Maitland opposed the amendment to delay implementation with the following telling arguments:

Once the Bill is enacted, it should come into force right away. I do not believe that there is any necessity to wait two months. The public will expect us to get on with it. Why should young offenders be allowed to get away with such awful crimes? They are awful and serious crimes. Why should the perpetrators be allowed to get away with them for another two months?

There is growing public awareness of the scale of the crimes among young people. Parliament would open itself to ridicule if it were not seen to deal with the problem straight away. If it were seen to hesitate, it could make the public wonder how serious Parliament was about the issue. A difficult position could arise. What would happen if there were a horrible attack within the two months period which received saturation press coverage— such as the tragic case of little James Bulger? Would not Parliament look stupid if it were crippled by its own Act and could not take action immediately?

There is much concern about tackling the issues in the public domain. There is a feeling that young people are too precocious and believe that they can get away with their actions because society has created a climate in which all forms of violent sex are permitted. The Bill is an excellent way for the Government to be seen to take direct action and respond immediately. (*Hansard*, col 1270, 30 April 1993)

These remarkable admissions of the concerns driving the Bill's speedy implementation illustrate why high-profile cases are of interest to this study. They cast shadows over all political activity, especially when legislators let them, catalyzing reckless responses with potentially heavy impacts on notions of justice. Such cases also tend to result in expressive legislation meant to send reassuring signals to an anxious public, regardless of whether or not such action is just in principle or instrumentally justifiable. The Bill above was seen by Maitland, who was in fact a journalist for 25 years (*Hansard*, col 684, 23 April 1993), as an ideal means for the government *to be seen* to take immediate action, despite the fact that the abolition of the presumption impacts very few individual cases. The implication is that action, however flawed or inadequate, works to protect politicians from accusations of inaction and callousness. The statements also indicate a palpable fear of a hostile electorate, which is equated with the press and their saturation coverage. In short, Maitland's speech is an apt illustration of why high-profile cases are important to study, why politicians must be seen to respond to them under the conditions of English political culture, and why the interaction of the press and political machinery is so crucial.

Crises of solidarity

Arguably, part of the reason the Bulger case resonated the way it did was that Blair, along with Conservative and tabloid voices, acknowledged it as an indication of a crisis of social solidarity. Blair wrote a piece for the tabloid *Sun* (3 March 1993) in the weeks following the Bulger murder, articulating his moralistic point: 'It is not simply that horrific nature of the crimes themselves that have shocked Britons in these past weeks. It is the feeling, difficult to define but powerfully with us, that they are symbolic of a deep malaise in our country.' The Tories responded in kind. Following the trial of Thompson and Venables, Home Office minister David Maclean implicated the Church in the creeping moral chaos in Britain, declaring it 'has been strangely silent about the difference between right and wrong' (*Daily Mirror*, 26 November 1993).

Tabloid discourse thus found its message legitimated by the shadow Home Secretary as it melded with the political discourse of both the government and the opposition. In addition, the trend to echo traditionally Conservative rhetoric continued with his asser-tion: 'It is parents who bring up children, not Governments...It's a bargain—we give opportunity, we demand responsibility. There is no excuse for crime. None...The Government can't start sub-stituting its responsibility for that of the individual' (Blair, 1993b). The reasons Blair embraced this discourse were opportunistic to some extent, allowing him to use the law and order issue as a means to beat the Conservatives down in their own traditional territory. And it seemed to work. MORI polls indicated that, by early 1994, Labour had seized the law and order issue from the Conservatives for the first time since 1977, when this particular survey began (MORI, 2002a). Extraordinarily, in November 1993, just as the Bulger trial was coming to a close, Tory Home Office minister Peter Lloyd actually cited Blair in his own speech on the Government's prison expansion programme, as the following exchange in the House of Commons illustrates:

Mr. Peter Lloyd: Twenty new prisons have been built and opened since 1979. The 21st new prison, at Doncaster, is due to open in April next year. A further six new prisons are planned...

Mr. Shaw: Will my hon. Friend accept that it is a commonly held view that more prisons and more prison building will result in less crime, more fear among the criminals and less fear among our constituents? Will he also accept that Conservative Members want the Home Office to get on and build more prisons?

Mr. Lloyd: My hon. Friend is certainly right to say that prison takes the worst criminals out of circulation, while they are in prison, and it certainly serves as a deterrent for a considerable number of those contemplating crime. His view was well expressed in last Tuesday's debate by the hon. Member for Sedgefield (Mr. Blair) who said: 'Prison is necessary; those who ought to go to prison should be put there, and if that means more prisons, more prisons should be built.' [*Official Report, 23 November 1993; Vol. 233, c. 344.*] We are building them. (*Hansard*, col 574, 25 November 1993)

In February 2007, three London teenagers were shot and killed in separate incidents, and the responses from the two main party leaders at the time were interesting. Tory party leader David Cameron echoed Blair's re-moralizing response to the Bulger case in 1993 by implying the shootings were emblematic of a contemporary British society that is 'badly broken': 'That's what our society's now come to—teenagers shooting other teenagers in their homes at point blank range. It is deeply depressing' (*Guardian*, 2007b). The *Guardian* quotes an unnamed 'Cameron strategist' who said, 'It's the nearest we've got to what Tony Blair did during the James Bulger case, when he spoke for the nation'. The politicization of these tragic events might have yielded dividends, as the Tories emerged 13 points ahead of Labour in a subsequent ICM poll done for the *Guardian* on 20 February 2007. Since then Cameron has intensified his rhetoric, claiming knife crime is a sign of 'anarchy in the UK' (*Independent*, 21 August 2007). In response, former Home Secretary David Blunkett called Cameron 'puerile', and then, without irony, insisted, 'These are desperate words from the man who wants to hug a hoodie' (*Independent*, 21 August 2007). (See Chapter 6 for the origin of this phrase.)

Just as Blair's was in 1993, Cameron's invocation of crisis is the luxury of an opposition party politician, especially in adversarial democracies where blame and glory usually fall upon single parties in government. Labour had been in opposition for fourteen years when Blair made his portentous comments in 1993. The Tories have been in opposition for ten as of 2007 as Cameron makes his. It is only politically sensible to invoke crisis while in opposition, when such a crisis can be used to undermine the ruling party's credibility. This time around, as might be expected, Blair downplayed the moral significance of the string of London juvenile killings: 'What has happened in south London is horrific, shocking and for the victims and their families tragic beyond belief. However, let us be careful in our response. This tragedy is not a metaphor for the state of British society, still less for the state of British youth today, the huge majority of whom, including in this part of London, are responsible and law-abiding young people' (*Guardian*, 2007c). In 1993, Blair's success in making the Bulger case a metaphor for the state of British society is credited by many as ensuring his political success. In 2007, crisis rhetoric would only implicate his own government. That these teen homicides were not metaphors but tragedies in Blair's terms indicates just how important political culture is in shaping the way we come to interpret crime events.

The Evolution of English Penal Policy and Political Culture

To appreciate fully the contingent nature of the English penal climate and the significance of the Bulger case, it is necessary to consider English penal policymaking in a historical perspective. In his exploration of changes in the political culture in England and Wales, Ryan (1999, 2003) attempts to account for the change in the role that the public has played in the penal policymaking process since the end of the Second World War. He identifies four distinct phases through which British penal and political culture have passed. Each is defined with a particular emphasis on distinguishing those individuals and institutional representatives outside of government who most shaped penal policy decision-making, those who in his words 'sat at the top table'. He outlines the shifts that saw the decline in the influence of 'metropolitan elite' expertise and the rise in influence of public opinion (and the press—often mistaken to be one and the same).

Insulated elite dominance

The first phase in the evolution of English post-war political culture lasts until about the mid-1960s and is characterized by economic stability, trust in and public deference to government institutions and actors, and the insulation from press and public scrutiny of a small group of 'male, metropolitan elites' who were largely responsible for steering the course of penal policy. Ryan's interpretation of the penal policymaking culture in the decades immediately following the war is one in which the public, those who ran the penal system, and even Parliament, were kept at a distance. Decision-making was dominated by 'a small coterie of somewhat self-satisfied, well connected middle class, mostly male, metropolitan reformers, academics and a few sympathetic judges, sharing authority with powerful civil servants and ministers in pursuit of their own private agendas' (Ryan, 2003: 40). Ryan refers to these elites as the 'penal *cognoscenti*' (2003: 30), and describes the means of their 'backstage' influence on government as 'clubbable', as many of the informal meetings in which policy matters were discussed were held over drinks or luncheons in London clubs (2003: 21).

A cross-party consensus of sorts existed around penal issues during this period, but it was a consensus reached without deferring to public opinion in any direct way. Though politicians were concerned to remain aligned with their constituencies on matters of policy, penal policy debate and formulation was shielded from public view. The elite *cognoscenti*, including Sir Leon Radzinowicz and members of the Howard League for Penal Reform, saw themselves as an obligatory buffer between a punitive public and the sensitive workings of the penal policymaking machinery. They believed, as many of their present-day colleagues do today, that due to their potential volatility, penal issues were best dealt with carefully, away from the glare of public scrutiny. Public issues often become political issues, and an anonymously published note from the *Prison Service Journal* in 1972 warned of the dangers of such public scrutiny: 'I believe profoundly that crime and punishment must be kept out of the political arena. It is far too emotive and emotional an area to be used for political ends' (cited in Ryan, 2003: 59).

As 'government was taken to be a complex, difficult business requiring skill and judgement, and senior politicians should be allowed to get on with it' (Ryan, 2003: 35), outsider involvement in the early post-war period was at best indirect. Decisions were made virtually without any input from criminal justice practitioners, their clients, or the general public. Opinion polling was not done and the newspapers only rarely got involved in debates over penal policy. Parliament was taken to be the 'sounding board' for the public (Ryan, 2003: 35), not the newspapers, as is the case today. The eventual incorporation of outsider opinion and expertise into systems of policymaking was accomplished 'not by revolution, but by evolution' (Ryan, 2003: 37), through a process dictated by wider social, economic, and political trends.

Practitioner influence

The mid-1960s saw the beginning of a second phase in which the wisdom of the formerly insulated political mechanisms was challenged. Though Britain continued to be a prosperous nation, it lagged behind its European neighbours. Some believed that the 'closed network of consultative committees were far too insulated from scrutiny, keeping good ideas out' (Ryan, 2003: 46). In 1964 Bernard Crick called for Parliamentary Select Committees to be used as a means of making government officials more accountable to the public (Ryan, 2003: 46). Some among those working in the penal system began to question the top-down approach to government that took little account of the views of those actually providing and receiving services. In time, these practitioners and clients began to organize themselves in unions and organizations outside of traditional, established circles or power. They began to contest the credibility of the liberal elites, making their own claims as the true experts. These outsiders under the old model 'brought their knowledges from below to challenge those of the experts who had previously claimed to speak for them in the corridors of power' (Ryan, 2003: 69).

This activism from practitioners created a rift among the left in the 1960s and early 1970s, as the traditional metropolitan elites became negatively associated with the establishment. The penal lobby, formerly represented by groups like the Howard League, underwent a conversion from a corporatist 'policy community', in which lobbyists with shared values enjoy 'regular and easy' relationships with government officials, to an 'issue-oriented community', characterized by lobby groups with competing values and a relative, sometimes celebrated, lack of access to government insiders (Ryan, 2003: 69).

It is perhaps ironic that the radical left were the ones to politicize penal issues. In an effort to wrest control of penal matters from the hands of a few backstage, the radicals succeeded in bringing them to centre stage. The 'less deferential political culture' in the 1960s and 1970s helped activists to 'disturb the complacency that had surrounded the operation of the criminal justice system in Britain and to undermine the self-confidence of those who ran it' (Ryan, 2003: 71). No longer were penal issues to be debated exclusively backstage. A fundamental shift had occurred which challenged definitions of expertise, and what was once an insulated community of decision-makers found itself publicly on the defensive.

As a consequence of these events lobby groups became more diverse, more representative of the range of interests invested in all parts of the penal system, and consequently more isolated from official decision-making, all in a climate of growing politicization of penal issues and higher levels of public and media scrutiny. In addition, the association of some criminologists with the radical groups during this period may have ultimately compromised the credibility and potency of criminology as a whole, as the public and politicians began to see all criminologists as representing the more radical, 'excuse-making' members of the academy. And as Ryan (2003: 73) puts it, 'the politics of the counter culture...came to be inscribed with the iconography of moral laxness, if not decay', an ascription that would be used in the decades to come and which so survives today in debates over penal policy as to be cliché. The tabloid derision of the 'ologists' is one illustration.

Managerialism

The third phase in the evolution of British political culture began in the 1980s with the rise of the neo-liberalism of the New Right and the Conservative Party under Margaret Thatcher. At its centre was a push for the reduction of government bureaucracy by bringing market principles to bear on the provision of public services. The shift was based on the New Public Management programme, which brought managerialist, private sector management techniques into the public sector in order to ensure greater efficiency and effectiveness (Ryan, 2003: 82).

This dramatic reconfiguration had major impacts on the running of the penal system. With the focus on standards, key performance indicators, and targets, the membership of the ranks of penal policy advisers—those with the expertise considered by those in government to be important—shifted. For the first time, as Ryan puts it, 'auditors are among the new experts. They may not rule, but their "grey science", their knowledge, has become increasingly influential over and against the human sciences which once sat at the top table' (Ryan, 2003: 97–8).

However, during this period, the metropolitan elites still had considerable clout in shaping the course of debates about penal policy. As a civil servant and later as Deputy Permanent Under Secretary at the Home Office, David Faulkner gathered together an 'elite *ensemble*' comprised of academics, penal lobby groups, and civil servants to consult on issues of penal policy, and they continued to meet informally throughout the 1980s and into the early 1990s (Ryan, 2003: 78). The Criminal Justice Act 1991 was testimony to the influence of this second generation of metropolitan elites, as the retributive, just deserts model upon which many of its policies were based was first discussed in this group's meetings (Ryan, 2003: 79). However, the failure of key aspects of the Act to remain law for long is a warning that influence of the kind exercised by Faulkner's *ensemble* cannot withstand or circumvent disruption from hostile practitioners and politicians (Windlesham, 1996).

Populism and the public voice

Ryan ends his analysis of shifting British political culture with what he sees as the current phase, one dominated by populism and the rise in importance of the nebulous construct of public opinion. He sums up the changing role of public opinion in the policymaking process. First, as the debates on the abolition of capital and corporal punishment in the 1950s and 1960s demonstrated,[3] 'the broader public voice intercedes...[and] gate-crashes the penal policy making elite'. But in the early post-war period this voice was 'mostly an unwelcome guest, often mobilized by disgruntled groups within the policy making elite, and was an intruder that had to be managed rather than accommodated...[It was] not until the 1970s and 1980s that front bench politicians actively sought to go over the heads of the various pressure groups actively to mobilize broader public opinion in penal matters, to become overtly populist' (Ryan, 2003: 109).

Anderson and Mann (1997: 237) paint a dramatic picture of the fear and insecurity that gripped the country in the 1970s:

Britain in 1974 was in a state of panic; IRA terrorism, militant trade unionism, the influx of immigrants, the widely publicized antics of the revolutionary Left, the country wide expansion of youth culture, the seemingly inexorable rise of vandalism, hooliganism and violent crime—all had combined to persuade substantial sections of the middle class and the political establishment that the very foundations of the British way of life were under threat. A vocal part of the right-wing intelligentsia talked of the crisis of ungovernability, former generals set up private armies; rogue elements of the security services, believing that Soviet subversion was at the root of it all, spread black propaganda about Harold Wilson and his colleagues.

Thatcher won the leadership of the Conservative Party in 1975. Law and order became a focus of the party, the militant union activity that to many appeared anarchical was essentially equated with street crime, and the Labour Party was said not to be doing enough to combat it (Ryan, 2003: 111). In the run up to the 1979 election in which the Conservatives took power, Thatcher appealed directly to the public by encouraging ordinary people to offer their opinions on crime and punishment issues. The Conservative manifesto also promised to reopen the debate on capital punishment and to introduce tougher penalties for violent and young offenders (Ryan, 2003: 112). This 'unashamedly' populist approach was challenged by the *cognoscenti*, who believed it to be counterproductive if tougher sentencing failed perceptibly to reduce crime (Ryan, 2003: 112). However, now it was the broader public that Thatcher was claiming to represent, not the 'usual suspects' of the metropolitan elite whose liberalism was

---

[3] Several hangings that were later seen to be unjust by many thrust the issue of capital punishment onto the political agenda.

linked with notions of the 'permissive society': 'There was a distrust of metropolitan elites, of the academy, of "backstage" policy making which favoured complicated trade-offs instead of simple, uncomplicated solutions—life sentences should mean life—and a strong charismatic leader to convey these essential truths directly to the people' (Ryan, 2003: 112–13).

Douglas Hurd, who had served as Conservative Party Home Secretary from 1985–9, spoke of the disingenuous and overly influential role that interest groups, or 'sectional interests', played in policymaking in the 1980s, and that, in his view, 'masquerade[d] as the public interest' (Ryan, 2003: 124). Ryan contends that Hurd did not go so far as to advocate the exclusion of pressure groups, nor did he call for the direct involvement of public opinion. Instead, he argued only that interest groups had become too powerful in shaping the debate.

This intensified under the New Labour government, which suddenly regarded pressure groups with more hostility than the Conservatives had. When Jack Straw became Home Secretary after Labour's 1997 general election landslide victory, he too believed the degree of influence wielded by these groups was excessive, but was keener than Hurd to enlist more directly in the debate the opinion of the public and their 'lived experience'. Straw railed against the 'BMW owning Hampstead liberals' who had had such influence in policy circles (Ryan, 2003: 125). As Ryan puts it, 'he was not interested in simply using public opinion as a rhetorical backcloth, as the Conservatives had done in the 1970s and 1980s, and then expecting to be left to get on with the difficult (backstage) business of making penal policy. The traditional way of doing business, of leaving such sensitive matters to metropolitan elites, was simply not good enough' (Ryan, 2003: 124). In effect, another layer of insulation shielding those at the core of penal policymaking from the 'public temperature' and the extremes of the penal climate was removed. Straw outlined his views in an article he wrote for *The Times* (8 April 1998) in which he heralded a 'new approach to policy making' which drew upon 'the experience of local communities' instead of single-issue pressure groups, one which represented 'a victory for local communities over detached metropolitan elites' and reaffirmed the 'direct relationship between voter and their MP...[He warned] elected officials...of the dangers of becoming the agents of sectional interest and of ignoring the concerns of those who elect them'.

The Press, the Public, and Political Culture

New Labour and the 'red top' press

Before coming to power in 1997, Labour made an additional change which in earlier years would have seemed unthinkable. They began to engage seriously with the 'red top'[4] tabloid press on issues of crime and justice, with precisely those forces the *cognoscenti* had tried to avoid (Ryan, 1999: 13). Blair hired Alastair Campbell, the former political editor at the tabloids *Daily Mirror* and *Today*, as his director of communications in 1994. Unsurprisingly, the *Daily Mirror* became Labour's paper of choice.

In the immediate wake of Bulger case, Blair used the *Mirror* to equate the rarity and horror of the case with lesser offences and stoked existing fears by claiming, '…what also shocks us is knowing that minor versions of the same are happening almost every day' (*Daily Mirror*, 20 February 1993). This rhetoric was part of a strategy to tap into what Blair himself called 'gut British instincts' and reflected his belief that the public '…only listen to people who show understanding of their own plight as potential victims' (quoted in Richards, 2004: 200, 54). He shortly after chose the pages of the leading tabloid, the *Sun*, to legitimate rather than refute or qualify exaggerated tabloid claims that juvenile offending had become more prolific and more sinister. He wrote, 'We can debate the crime rate statistics until the cows come home. The Home Office says crime is falling. Others say it isn't. I say crime, like economic recovery, is something that politicians can't persuade people about one way or another. People know because they experience it. They don't need to be told. And they know crime is rising' (*Sun*, 3 March 1993).

These statements are remarkable for several reasons. First, they legitimate the commonly held belief that statistics cannot be trusted. Blair carefully indicates in the article that he understands such concerns, but makes no attempt to take sides in the debate he references. Instead he defends this failure with the remarkable admission that politicians cannot persuade the public that crime is falling if they are intent to believe otherwise. In so doing, Blair

---

[4] 'Red top' refers to the sensational red mastheads often used by tabloid newspapers. The *Mirror* began in 2002 to print its own in black as a means of distinguishing itself as more journalistically sound than its fellow tabloids.

hits on several points known to be bothersome to the public—
out-of-touch elites who insist crime is not as bad as real people
perceive it to be, statistics that gloss over that raw reality, and
liberal politicians who rely upon the advice from these two flawed
sources to make decisions. He both claims that politicians cannot persuade people, and simultaneously rubbishes any data and
evidence that could.

The public fury that erupted in the wake of the Bulger murder was sparked in part by tabloid sensationalism and just this
kind of hyperbolic amplification of an exceptional crime. Public
concern about youth crime and 'persistent young offenders' had
been on the increase since 1991, due in part to the media's
coverage of certain strains of youth offending (Newburn, 2001).
However, the House of Commons Home Affairs Committee
(HAC) inquiry, which was actually in session as the Bulger case
unfolded, was unable to show that youth crime had risen. In fact,
it appeared to have dropped 'sharply' after a peak in 1985 (HAC,
1993: 3, para 2.3). Speaking on behalf of the Home Office on
3 March 1993, John Halliday testified, 'I think we would say
with confidence that juvenile offending has decreased' (HAC,
1993: 222, para 7), basing this conclusion on the decrease in the
number of juvenile offenders known to the police. However, the
Association of Chief Police Officers (ACPO) presented evidence
to suggest an actual rise in offences since the 1980s, despite the
smaller numbers of offenders committing them. After weighing this evidence, the Committee was unable to resolve the dis-
crepancy, but did raise the possibility that a very small number
of persistent young offenders were responsible for an increased
number of offences, an assertion that itself was difficult to demonstrate with reliable evidence (see Hagell and Newburn, 1994;
Newburn, 2001). With hindsight, official figures suggest total
recorded crime began to fall around 1992 and 1993, while British
Crime Survey data suggest the decline did not begin until 1995
(Newburn, 2005). However, regardless of what the numbers
said or did not say, public concern remained high, as Committee
Chairman Sir Ivan Lawrence explained: 'What we all know, as
Members of Parliament, is that there is an immense and increasing amount of public concern [about juvenile offending]. We see
it when we do television programmes and take part in debates
or even when we meet the public at public or private meetings'
(HAC, 1993: 221, para 2).

For political leaders to endorse simplistic generalizations known to be untrue in order to appear to feel the pain of 'the people' or to outflank opponents, as Blair did, is anti-intellectual and dishonest—the hallmarks of populism (Taggart, 2000). Blair's comments implied that there is no substitute for experience, even secondhand, mass-mediated experience, and his piece in the *Sun* lent unqualified credibility to tabloid portrayals. He as much as told the public that their fear of crime, irrational or not, was more important than any unbiased assessment of the problem. For electoral reasons, it just might be, but his failure to elevate the debate beyond disparaging statistical measures of crime was irresponsible leadership.

This kind of tabloidization of New Labour discourse represented a major shift in English political culture, as it conferred upon the tabloid newspapers a degree of legitimacy in the eyes of Labour leaders and constituents that they lacked previously. It was a shift that was previously unthinkable and which would have major consequences for the penal climate. But it was also understandable.

To blame New Labour's courting[5] of the tabloid press as simply a cynical 'dumbing down' of the political debate is to ignore a number of factors that help tell the rest of the story. Blair and Campbell were so intent to get the tabloids on side in part because many believed the *Sun* had been instrumental in dashing Neil Kinnock's chances of leading the Labour Party to victory in the 1992 General Election (Gould, 1999; Jones, 2001; Seldon, 2004). Campbell regarded getting the *Sun* to back Blair in 1997 as 'his biggest achievement in politics' (Seldon, 2004: 253). As shown in Chapter 2, the tabloid and mid-market press in England also enjoy readerships that dwarf those of the broadsheets. Fully half of British daily newspaper readers read either the tabloid *Sun*, *Daily Mirror*, or *Daily Star*, and a further 28 per cent of readers choose the mid-market *Daily Mail* and *Daily Express*.

Just as Labour leaders were determined not to let the Tories retain the hold they had on the law and order issue in elections

---

[5] Testimony to the power of the tabloids is the campaign Blair launched upon becoming Labour Party leader, with the assistance of Campbell, to court Rupert Murdoch, owner of the *Sun* and *News of the World* (Oborne and Walters, 2004: 128–33).

prior to 1997, they also could not afford to ignore the importance of the tabloid press. In Alastair Campbell's words,

> ...the weight of newspapers in setting a political agenda is significant. If at the time of an election, the Tory instinct is driving news agendas, then it will affect the way the broadcasters cover it. That's why we focus on newspapers. They don't like us acknowledging that the papers that really matter are the tabloids. I think one of the reasons Tony wanted me to work for him, and why I wanted to work for Tony, was that we both acknowledge the significance to political debate of the tabloids. (*Guardian*, 17 February 1997)

Clearly with a press institution wielding such power, and with the tabloids so strongly dominating the press market over their broadsheet competitors, the reasons why Labour leaders were so intent to court them can be appreciated.

Borrowing techniques and personnel from the Democratic presidential campaign that had swept Bill Clinton to power in the USA in 1992, Labour also began rigorously to utilize opinion polling and focus groups in an attempt to reconnect with the alienated electorate (Gould, 1999). Again these changes are understandable with an appreciation of the wider social, economic, and technological forces at work in British society. This includes the rising importance of public opinion, another deeply rooted explanation for the rise in populism and the decline of deference to elite expertise in England.

The rise of the public voice

Blumler and Gurevitch (1995: 129) write about 'an upgrading of the public voice in political communication...[by which] the experience and opinions of quite ordinary people are being aired more often'. This is certainly evident in the now ubiquitous cable and satellite television news channel real-time opinion polls, text polls, and call-in lines 'measuring' viewer opinion. Inglehart (1997: 294) believes political participation is now occurring on a 'qualitatively different level' than before. 'Mass publics' are playing increasingly more direct roles in national politics, beyond merely exercising their voting rights: 'Current changes enable them to play an increasingly active role in formulating policy, and to engage in what might be called "elite-challenging", as opposed to "elite-directed" activities...The newer elite-challenging style of politics gives the public an increasingly important role in making specific *decisions*, not just a choice between two or more sets of decision makers' (Inglehart, 1997: 3, emphasis in original). When understood in this way, to argue for a return to the heyday of *cognoscenti* influence without incorporating public views in some way becomes an untenable position.

Driving this public activism is a wider trend with problematic implications for those in positions of power in society. 'One aspect in the change in values... is a decline in the legitimacy of hierarchical authority, patriotism, religion and so on, which leads to declining confidence in institutions' (Inglehart, 1997: 4). This legitimacy deficit is one of the primary factors implicated by the circumstances of late-modernity (Garland, 1996, 2001; Garland and Sparks, 2001) that for many social theorists have come to represent a shorthand discourse to explain, among other things, the rise in the salience of crime issues, the attractiveness of 'tough on crime' political agendas, and the increase in prison populations in many Western countries. To reiterate the argument, governments have become increasingly ineffectual in meeting the social needs of their citizens, especially regarding notions of security in the 'risk society' (Beck, 1992; Douglas, 2003; Lupton, 1999). Sensing the catastrophic effects this crisis of public confidence could have on the legitimacy of the government itself, manifestations of crime and disorder are targeted as a means to re-establish its power and to reassure a public made anxious by the widespread social change brought about by globalization and the erosion of traditions. A cycle is then perpetuated whereby an ineffectual government attempts to 'govern through crime' (Simon, 1997, 2007), to target crime problems as a means to reassure the public, whose anxiety is caused by social forces much greater than crime. The government's continual inability to make significant, demonstrable headway in its combat with crime tends further to inflame public anxieties.

It is a cycle that is difficult to escape because, '[w]hen faced with intractable and deeply rooted problems of deviant behaviour over which they have little direct control, legislators, and the governments they uphold, tend to fall back on the one thing they can do, which is to legislate' (Windlesham, 1996: 40). David Blunkett's introduction of an unprecedented number of crime initiatives during his tenure as Home Secretary, in the face of falling crime rates, is testimony to this (see Tonry, 2004a). The practice of raising the level of legislative action in response to the perceived failure of previous interventions keeps the issue of crime on the political and public agenda while at the same time raising expectations that the latest raft of initiatives will be successful. These expectations are unlikely to be met, especially within the short-term timescale most are allowed. 'Efforts at social control it seems, always fail, and failure is always the condition for further attempts at control' (Power, 1997: 26).

Occurring simultaneously with the declining influence of traditional social institutions is a partly technologically driven shift in the way mass publics engage with political issues and leaders. Inglehart (1997) views these changes with optimism, interpreting them as a positive re-establishment of a balance between elites and the masses. Mass publics are comparatively well educated with access to advancements in information technology that make possible the participation in the political processes and in ways that can circumvent traditional bureaucratic corridors. Increasingly, ad hoc, issue-driven organizations are using these methods to influence government decision-making. As an illustration, Ryan (2003: 133) cites the fuel strikes in 2000 in which a remarkably swift and effective mass mobilization was orchestrated using mobile phones and fax machines. In this way political action has been facilitated through non-traditional channels, without reference to or assistance from the political party arrangements.

This is reflected in recent elections in which the electorate has tended to vote on particular issues rather than along party lines (Jones, 2001). As a consequence it becomes more important for political leaders to be seen to be confronting those issues that appear most important to the public, like crime, in a forthright manner. No longer can parties rely on a bundle of party policies to obtain and retain party loyalty, especially as civic engagement and political awareness decline.

All this makes it understandable why governments must appear to be attentive to indicators of what the public appears to want. It is also likely that these tendencies have accelerated the pace at which politicians have become preoccupied with concerns to build public confidence in the government's ability to meet the public's needs. With government legitimacy flagging in the way that has been described, and faced with the potential threat from mass movements, it seems hardly surprising that British political leaders have adopted the behaviours they have.

Models of the policymaking process offered by political scientists insist on a more appreciative assessment of the pressures and factors facing political actors. Recalling Weiss (1983) from Chapter 5, policy process and outcomes must be understood with reference to policymakers' ideologies, interests, and information. With this perspective, an observer is likely better to appreciate Ryan's view of how wider social change has impacted the criminal justice system:

These wider, political and cultural changes which have upgraded the public voice have been reinforced by significant changes within the criminal justice system itself. That is to say, it seems fairly obvious to me that the repositioning of the public voice is partly a reflection of the simple fact that governments now *need* to engage with the public in a way that was not envisaged in the decades immediately after 1945. At this time the machinery of law and order...was firmly in the hands of a highly centralized State and the security of each and every one of us was entrusted to, and jealously guarded by, those who operated the formal levers of law and order. This began to change in the 1980s when it became apparent that the central State could no longer deliver on law and order from the centre and the result has been the restructuring of the delivery of these services, including penal services, to engage the public...The result is that...citizens are being invited back into the criminal justice network. (Ryan, 2003: 134, emphasis added)

Ryan notes that this more appreciative assessment has been largely ignored by the sociology of moral panics, which has employed a conceptual model that has tended to be more conspiratorial and polemical in its assessments of the motivations of the actors involved in perpetrating them (see Ryan, 2003: 135). Though there is likely to be some truth to be found in such conceptions, they do not adequately incorporate the additional factors influencing the priorities of government penal policy decision-makers. Merely to point to moral panics to account for such deep-rooted shifts in political practice fails fully to represent the daily realities generated by the changing nature of democracies, realities politicians are compelled to face. 'Something else at work, namely, that for a quite different set of reasons [that theories of moral panic ignore] our democracy is changing, and that the transmission of public preferences into the heart of government, demanding day by day that more attention be given to them, is something that all politicians increasingly have to learn to live with, and this most certainly includes home secretaries' (Ryan 2003: 135). This is also something that criminologists and other experts must also learn to live with, as painful as it might be. The final two chapters offer some strategies to facilitate this.

As the political culture in England has become more populist, the press has also become a more effective and powerful lobby than the traditional penal interest groups (Rock, 1990: 227). Echoing Douglas Hurd's concerns about the role of the penal lobby, the press has in effect become the most influential 'sectional interest' group intent to 'masquerade as the public interest'. Under these conditions, when an event such as the death of James Bulger captures such a significant level of attention from the press and subsequently from the public, political leaders—especially when pressed to do so by hostile opponents—are virtually powerless to do anything but act, to legislate, to engage in the debates into which they are drawn by the press, ostensibly in the public's name. As Stuart Hall and his colleagues discovered in their famous study of the concern over mugging in 1970s Britain:

> It is difficult to continue to consider the agencies of public signification and control, like the police, the courts and the media, as if they were passive reactors to immediate simple and clear cut crime situations. These agencies must be understood as actively and contiguously part of the whole process to which, also, they are 'reacting'. They are active in defining situations, in selecting targets, initiating 'campaigns', in structuring these campaigns, in selectively signifying their actions to the public at large... They do not simply respond to 'moral panics'. They form part of the cycle out of which more moral panics develop... [and] advertently and inadvertently, *amplify* the deviancy they seem so absolutely committed to control. (Hall et al, 1978: 52, emphasis in original)

The media provide the channels through which this signification and amplification process occurs, but politicians also play a role in these feedback loops, legitimating or contesting dominant media discourses.

New Labour, Old Testament?

The conception of deviance as indicative of moral laxity and decay can have far-reaching consequences. The empirical work on the origins of punitive public attitudes mentioned at the end of the previous chapter provides insights into the forces with which penal policymakers must contend, and which might help observers understand the reasons why politicians are now more likely than in other decades to be driven by what they perceive to be public concern and popular animus. When combined with the effects of the loss of faith in social institutions, including government, to solve social problems, concerns about moral decline in a diverse society are heightened. In their analysis of public support for California's 'three strikes and you're out' laws, Tyler and Boeckmann (1997: 237) found 'the source of people's concerns lies primarily in their evaluations of social conditions, including the decline in morality and discipline within the family and increases in the diversity of society. These concerns are about issues of moral cohesion—with people feeling that the quality and extent of social bonds and social consensus has deteriorated in American society'.

With this in mind, it becomes clear that the ways in which particular crime events are portrayed—that is, whether they are interpreted by those who frame blame and justice as threats to the existing moral order or as less serious, more instrumentally motivated offences—have consequences for determinations of appropriate penal policy responses. Moreover, offences that are interpreted as morally threatening elicit strong emotions. All crime is to some extent morally threatening, but looking to how notions of blame are attributed and to how justice is said to be done in response to a particular case can indicate when an offence qualifies as truly morally threatening. Karstedt (2002) explores how the role played by emotions in criminal justice has increased in prominence in recent decades. She cites Elster (1989: 100) who writes that 'the violation of norms triggers strong, emotional reactions, in the offender as well as in others', and she points out that the emotions resulting from norm violations tend to be 'negative emotions' like disgust, revulsion, and vengeance, as opposed to other theories of moral sentiments which stress the importance of sympathy, empathy, and 'tender-heartedness' (Karstedt, 2002: 303).

It might be the institutionalization of moralistic, judgmental, Old Testament values that sets England apart from Norway, where moral values seem more wed to a less judgmental penal discourse—what in one conversation Norwegian criminologist Paul Larsson linked to New Testament sentiments. This Old versus New Testament dichotomy might be a useful analytical tool here. The negative emotions of vengeance and disgust, those linked to the generation of punitive attitudes toward norm violations, can be linked to Old Testament notions of justice, that is, of judgment and vengeance, of an 'eye for an eye'. The 'positive' emotions identified by Karstedt, which she associates with the more enlightened moral theories of Adam Smith, Hume, and

Hutcheson, are more aligned with the New Testament values of forgiveness, rather than vengeance, of understanding, tolerance, and 'turning the other cheek', rather than judgment.

As Karstedt (2002: 306) writes,

In 1517, Martin Luther started the Reformation in Germany by hammering his 95 propositions to the door of the church in Wittenberg. In about one-third of them, Luther argued that no institution could and should interfere with individual repentance, and feelings of shame and guilt, let alone use or exploit them for institutional purposes. Interestingly, in some of his main arguments he contended that only God—not even always the offender—could know if these feelings were authentic and truthful.

Perhaps it is no coincidence that 88 per cent of Norwegians identify themselves as members of the Lutheran Church of Norway (Nilsen and Johnsen, 2000). Whatever the case, this 'judge not, lest you be judged' conception of justice, one which leaves judgment to a higher power, has diminished currency today. Whatever tolerance that might have existed in the early post-war period in England—at least among the penal *cognoscenti* and the policymakers they advised—which was reflected in shorter custodial sentences and lower prison populations, has been eroded since crime rates rose in the 1960s. What emerged instead were judgmental declarations of universal moral standards and a demand that there be 'no more excuses' for their violation. Perhaps as the perceived threats posed by moral diversity became manifest, and as faith in a higher power faded, so too did the notion of leaving questions of moral judgment to divine authorities. Instead, moral judgments became subject to human interpretation, perhaps because, with waning faith in traditional institutions, including religion, there was no alternative.

The Old versus New Testament distinction helps illustrate a change that coincided with other well-documented shifts in penality. The re-emergence of retributive rationales for punishment shadowed, and some might argue precipitated, the decline of the rehabilitative ideal and the loss of confidence in 'musclebound' modernist ideals of progress through social engineering that accompanied it (Scott, 1998). These ideals justified individualized penal interventions, and were based on an expert-dominated infrastructure and a (at least theoretically) strong foundation of expert scientific knowledge. Eventually this modernist model withered with a shift to a belief that 'nothing works'

(Martinson, 1974) and was replaced by a more cautious and less optimistic approach to penal reform. This story has been told well elsewhere (Allen, 1981; Garland, 2000, 2001), but it is important to note here because this loss of faith has direct links with particular emotional responses to crime and the penal policies to which they eventually lead. The changes Karstedt notes have followed the decline in confidence in traditional and governmental institutions and in science, especially the social sciences. Cynicism and the scaling down of expectations replaced the modernist optimism and the utopian belief in the power of human endeavour generally, and this was made evident in concerns about crime and justice. The retributive, pared-down view of penal intervention reflects a similarly pared-down conception of justice, one that is indicative of Old Testament sentiments of punishment and vengeance.

As Karstedt (2002: 303) explains,

The return of shame, restorative justice and the emotionalization of public discourse about crime and law, are responding to changes in wider emotional culture, and changing the moral imagination of these societies. The media engage their public in 'distant suffering' (Boltanski, 1999)— compassion and sympathy with victims, expressions of moral disgust towards offences and the perpetrators. An intensely emotional discourse about crime thus comes to be fuelled by the most recent and most heinous offence. Crime policies are explicitly based on the expression of collective emotions of fear and anger about crime. Politicians compete with each other in addressing the 'emotional' needs of the public, and in turn mirror these emotions back to the audience and the electorate. National and even global audiences become highly emotionalized 'moral spectators' in the spectacles of distant suffering of victims and perpetrators.

Distant suffering predisposes consumers of it to react in ways that indicate the presence of a clear moral division between perpetrator and victim. Clear-cut moral judgments become possible due to the emotional distance between the media consumer and the portrayed perpetrator. Distant suffering supports a cognitive process that is a zero-sum game, in which the interests of victims and offenders are viewed as necessarily mutually exclusive (Tonry, 2004a; Zimring, Hawkins and Kamin, 2001). In other words, 'in a public sphere constituted by distant suffering, and the emotions it arouses and the moral commitment it induces, the task of criminal justice is extremely simplified: justice for victims means making offenders suffer the harshest punishment available' (Karstedt, 2002: 303). The media serve as the mechanism for disseminating distant suffering, that which facilitates clear moral judgments and which enables harsh punishment to occur. Media representations of crime indicate the violation of moral boundaries, they place issues on the public and political agendas, and they prepare media consumers to react in particular ways toward the moral breach.

Simplified moral delineations like those widely transmitted in the wake of the Bulger case have consequences for the type of justice deemed appropriate, and for how it should be rendered. Old Testament justice is easier to mete out than notions of justice that imply tolerance and forgiveness. The retributive justice rationale is less susceptible to public criticism along utilitarian lines simply because it is non-utilitarian and not subject to evaluation. In a sense Luther's warnings are heeded. Punishment as retribution can be delivered relatively easily via deserved punishments. Though there will be debate about what is deserved, these debates are arguably less complex and problematic for policymakers and practitioners than those aroused by attempts to reform, rehabilitate, deter, incapacitate, or treat.

Conclusion

The broad social and economic shifts that have taken place in recent decades have together shaped English political culture. The same shifts have already caused publics to be sceptical of government's willingness and ability to face the issues raised by high-profile crimes like the Bulger case, so it requires a great deal of strength of leadership to cool a hot penal climate. Under the circumstances in which the Bulger case unfolded, a merging of discourses occurred, tied in part to late-modern anxieties wrought by rapid social change. These discourses attributed much of the cause for the homicide to moral decline and societal disintegration. Explanations of this kind, coupled with the sweeping changes in political culture—including the role of the tabloid press in setting policy agendas, decreasing government legitimacy, the threats posed by mass publics, and pressures to legislate on law and order to soothe an anxious public—steered government action on a particular course, one which, even in hindsight, might have been difficult to alter, especially within England's highly adversarial political environment.

Ryan shows how the rise of the public voice in English penal policymaking is linked with a concomitant decline in deference to traditional elites. Relative economic sluggishness in the 1980s led many to look internally, to rethink the structure of political institutions and to reprioritize which kinds of knowledge were most important. Declining elite influence occurred simultaneously with a rise in public influence, channelled though the press. So as the knowledge produced by elites was finding fewer channels to streams of political knowledge, public knowledge was making new inroads as the press became a more powerful influence. This chain of events and the shifts in the institutionalization of knowledge production was precipitated by a broader decline in confidence in elite expertise, part of a wider loss of faith in modernist visions of progress.

Because of the style of commentary and the emotive and visceral approach they characteristically take, the tabloid press plays a particularly pertinent role establishing the extremes of the penal climate. In contrast to the 'factual and analytical' coverage of the broadsheet press which tends to affect readers rational, 'fact-based beliefs' and assessments of possible preventative anti-crime measures, the tabloid presentational style tends to affect reader attitudes, including fear of and concern for crime (Surette, 1998: 212). Tabloid crime discourse often engages readers on an emotional level, implicating intuitive, moral judgments rather than rational reflection and factual assessment. This difference is crucial for an appreciation of the importance of the relationship between the tabloid press and the Labour Party leaders in the wake of the Bulger case. Political leaders must strike a balance between instrumental and moral concerns, and it appears the balance that results is strongly influenced by political culture.

The excessively hot post-Bulger case penal climate was created by a confluence of shared interests, when tabloid media discourses merged with those of the two major political parties. In the wake of a particular crime or type of crime, press attention can raise the public temperature even when an insulated liberal elite is advising policy decisions.[6] Temperatures can only rise when that insulation is removed.

[6] The string of high-profile cases that made many question the justness of capital punishment and which made possible its abolition in the Britain of 1965 provides one example (though the elites at the time were aligned with the abolitionist cause). Other examples include those repressive prison regimes that remained in place during even the heyday of *cognoscenti* influence in penal affairs (Ryan, 2003).

Ryan's analysis indicates that shifts in penal climates and policy cultures have irreversible historical antecedents that have made it necessary for politicians to pay heed to the public voice, however such a thing is conceived, with more urgency than before. Nostalgia is ill advised, and it is not enough simply to blame cynical political electioneering for the rise in penal populism or for the repressive English penal climate. Though the politicization of crime may be a prerequisite for penal populism, the reasons such politicization occurred in the way it did under the conditions of an adversarial English political culture need to be fully appreciated. Ryan brings us closer to that goal, and the last two chapters expand upon it. The next chapter considers how Norway's consensual political culture countered some of the same forces that affected England so dramatically.

9

Political Culture, Legitimacy, and Penal Populism

It is tempting to apply Ryan's analysis to the Norwegian context. Certainly there are parallels. Though the managerialism of the neo-liberalism had muted effects in Norway, as discussed in Chapter 2, the proliferation of mass media in Norway has led to a rise of a 'public voice' of sorts, as politicians are increasingly compelled to respond to mass-mediated cues of what is important. But the stages Ryan identifies were experienced in ways peculiar to the English political–cultural setting in which they developed, and looming large throughout all of the stages he describes is a deeply partisan politics. This divisive style of politics acted as an accelerant, and it is arguable that all of the conditions that have led to today's highly populist penal policy climate might have been weathered differently and with considerably less agitation under different political–cultural conditions. Blair's reconfiguration of New Labour and its 'tougher than you' ethos might not have been necessary had the political culture and structures not been so adversarially configured. Though it is also ill advised to engage in fantasy, it is useful to consider the consequences that particular configurations of democracy have on penal populism.

This chapter argues that the ways in which politics is done in consensus and majoritarian democracies has implications for the stability of the political system, the durability of its policies, and the trust citizens hold in government and in their fellow citizens. Put simply, in a political system in which power is shared and dispersed among many players, in which inclusiveness is the rule, and in which opportunities for open deliberation are fostered, there are fewer excluded and discontented players to mount attacks on the government's policies. Potential tensions are diffused and bridges are built between disparate parties that would often be culturally and structurally prohibited from cooperating in majoritarian democracies. The inclusive power sharing of the consensus model creates fewer incentives for opposition party members to seek power through direct conflict. As a result, the policies developed suffer less official and publicized criticism and last longer. This contributes generally to a cycle of more effective policymaking that retains greater public support.

The first section of this chapter considers the stabilizing benefits of consensual political cultures for the political system and the policies that develop. The second section explores the destructive and constructive by-products that different configurations of political culture seem to yield. The last section addresses the relationship between levels of trust, political culture, and a jurisdiction's susceptibility to populism. Nordic consensus democracies tend to retain higher levels of trust and greater legitimacy, which appear to protect them from the kind of penal populism that frequently characterizes majoritarian democracies.

Policy Deliberation and Stability

...there is a surprisingly strong and persistent tendency in political science to equate democracy solely with majoritarian democracy and to fail to recognize consensus democracy as an alternative and equally legitimate type. A particularly clear example can be found in Stephanie Lawson's (1993: 192–93) argument that a strong political opposition is 'the *sine qua non* of contemporary democracy' and that its prime purpose is 'to become the government.' This view is based on the majoritarian assumption that democracy entails a two-party system (or possibly two opposing blocs or parties) that alternate in government; it fails to take into account that governments in more consensual multiparty systems tend to be coalitions and that a change in government in these systems usually means only a partial change in the party composition of the government—instead of the opposition 'becoming' the government. (Lijphart, 1999: 6)

Lijphart (1998: 107) asserts that 'the structure of consensus democracy may either be based on a consensual culture, or that it may operate in an insufficiently consensual culture in such a way as to first produce the minimum of consensus required for a democracy and then, in the long run, make the country's political culture more consensual. That is, the structure of consensus democracy may be the product of a consensual culture or its causal agent'. Referring back to Archer's morphogenesis mentioned in Chapter 4, which stresses the dialectical interrelation of structures and cultures, structural institutions must change to keep pace with cultural change. When there are disjunctions between the cultural and the institutional, or when cultural change outpaces change within institutions, adaptation must occur to maintain the integrity of the system. The extent of this adaptation is in part dependent upon the stability of the existing system. For instance, consensual ways of doing politics in Norway tend not to subject existing structures to the same kind of frequent and rigorous challenge experienced in England. There is, as a consequence, less of a need to adjust the structures to accommodate any new thinking.

This is in part because there are simply fewer incentives to invoke crisis and to call for radical overhaul of the status quo. The legitimacy of traditional structures is not in doubt because the system is not broken, and the system is not broken because there are fewer incentives for political players to say that it is. Citizens in turn receive fewer cues that things are in crisis. In contrast, in majoritarian democracies, pledges of constant reform and floods of new proposals send cues that imply the need for change, and suggest the policy area of concern is in crisis.

Norwegian political structures and culture interact in a more 'virtuous circle'; the 'relatively well integrated' political–administrative system is 'capable of acting promptly and effectively and, for the most part, speaking with a single voice…[and] is capable of delivering a more coherent and integrated form of governance' (Christensen and Peters, 1999: 159). Policy debate involves an inclusive, corporatist approach which seeks wide consultation from stakeholders. The Norwegian system:

permits a variety of inputs from the society at the formulation and at the implementation stages, not to mention the more indirect participation through the legislative process. The cultural demands for broad and effective participation mean that policymaking usually does not proceed quickly, despite the apparent capacity to do so. This also means, however, that once government does decide to act, it can enforce its decisions rather easily, given the degree of consensus that will have been created already. (Olsen, 1996: 172)

Concerted action sends fewer mixed signals to citizens and creates fewer opportunities for opposition players to exploit inconsistencies.

In a morphogenetic sense, then, a new government administration in a consensus democracy tends to require only minor reshuffling to maintain stability. 'The Norwegian reform style has traditionally been one of compromise and incremental change. Bargaining structures among "affected parties" have been established. The technique has involved taking the time necessary to develop a new, shared understanding and to mobilize commitment and support for reforms. The policy style has been "peaceful coexistence and revolution in slow motion", based on a spirit of sharing, more than winner-takes-all' (Olsen, 1996: 187). Furthermore, careful policy deliberation is an institutionalized element in the style:

> The government of Norway has a large reservoir of legitimacy among its citizens, but in order to be able to govern effectively it must still follow carefully the 'rules of the game' in governing. These rules are not only the formal rules about how to make laws and regulations, but also include a variety of cultural understandings about how government should proceed when in the business of making decisions. In Norway, as in any parliamentary system, the government often has the formal capacity to push legislation through the Parliament, but the informal rules minimize any attempts at imposing this 'majoritarian' style of governance. (Christensen and Peters, 1999: 144)

The consensual style of governing makes such a show of political force unpalatable even to members of a majority. This determination of what is deemed unpalatable is a cultural one and contrasts sharply with the assumptions that many of us in majoritarian democracies are accustomed to. Though predisposition to something does not mean predestination, and political culture is a permissive mechanism rather than a prescriptive force, the cultural 'assumption opens the possibility of action, and it disposes the members of the group sharing it to certain actions more than others' (Elkins and Simeon, 1979: 133).

The cautious and deliberate approach to policymaking in Norway contrasts sharply with recent English examples, in which major policy changes were proposed suddenly without the sort of initial consultation that could identify criticism and seek compromise with critics. The Blair government's plans to implement a supreme court and the more successful but rashly implemented launch of the new Ministry of Justice are just two examples.[1] Policy durability is harder to achieve in England where change is swift and broad, and where high-profile public and media concerns tend to generate flurries of symbolic political posturing in

---

[1] See Tonry (2004a) for numerous others.

response, like high-profile crime 'summits' and heroic pledges for new initiatives that promise to 'tackle' crime (Tonry, 2004a). Unstable structural foundations are not conducive to deliberate policy development and policy durability. This point is important because stability appears to yield its own dividends in terms of public confidence—a construct that frequent policy action in majoritarian democracies may serve to undermine.

Political cultural arrangements have structural supports that preserve them, even in the face of international countertrends. Norwegian cultural norms and assumptions insulate policymaking from the temporary temptations or compulsions to legislate swiftly in response to high-profile issues that many politicians experience so acutely in majoritarian countries. Recall MP Lady Maitland's post-Bulger case concerns in the previous chapter. The compulsion to act in pressurized conditions, and to be seen to do so decisively and swiftly, trumped other considerations, such as whether or not the law to result was just, effective, or wise. Consensus democracies are governed by cultural norms affirming that, 'if a law is to become legitimate, it should be the product of extensive consultation in the society, with some notion that reaching a consensus among the affected parties is as important in the long run as making a decision quickly' (Olsen, 1996: 144). Though not entirely precluding 'knee-jerk' legislating, there are features of Norwegian political culture that make it less appropriate and thus less likely.

By-Products of Political Culture

Higher voter turnout and higher levels of civic engagement are positively correlated with consensus democracy (Lijphart, 1998). All Nordic democracies have proportional representation election systems (Esaiasson and Heidar, 2000), and their multi-party systems often require the formation of coalition and minority governments that must rely on cooperative rules to function effectively. In the single-member plurality, winner-takes-all system of the USA and England, even a large minority of voters whose candidates lose end up unrepresented. This sort of systematic disenfranchisement could help account for the low voter turnout in majoritarian countries and certainly runs counter to the inclusive, consensual approach which strives to bring all concerned parties together.

Figure 9.1 Imprisonment rates in consensus and majoritarian democracies 2006

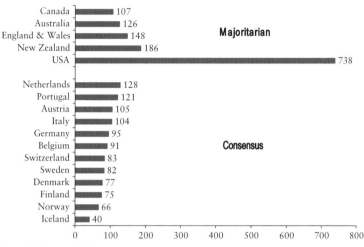

Source: Walmsley (2006).

Appetites for punishment

Lijphart contends that consensus democracies tend to be 'kinder and gentler' than their majoritarian peers, and Norway is the exemplar. Consensus democracies tend to be committed welfare states that have historically used the death penalty less than majoritarian countries. They are more protective of the environment and more generous with foreign aid. Their imprisonment rates also tend to be lower than majoritarian democracies. Figure 9.1 shows the 2006 imprisonment rate figures (Walmsley, 2006) for twelve of the thirteen consensus democracies and the five majoritarian democracies Lijphart identifies. Neither Northern Ireland nor Scotland is included in the graph because both employ proportional representation and Northern Ireland has a multi-party system. Both therefore deviate significantly from the classic majoritarianism found in England and Wales.[2] Luxembourg is also excluded from the graph because its tiny population of under half of a million people and subsequently volatile imprisonment rate make it a poor

---

[2] Since 1999 Wales has utilized a PR system in its devolved National Assembly elections. England and Wales, however, remains a single legal jurisdiction.

Figure 9.2 Changes in imprisonment rates in consensus and majoritarian democracies

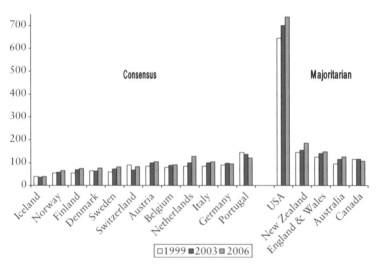

Source: Walmsley (1999, 2003, 2006).

comparator. Though there are exceptions on both sides of the consensus–majoritarian continuum, most of the consensus countries have the lower imprisonment rates that Lijphart predicts.

Imprisonment rate data from 1999, 2003, and 2006 show a similar relative pattern over time (Walmsley, 1999, 2003, 2006). The scale of the rises in recent years has been greater among most of the majoritarian countries, though with a few exceptions (see Figure 9.2).

If we use these imprisonment rates as an indicator of a country's punitiveness (see Chapter 3 for others), there appears to be an apparent, somewhat diminished appetite for imprisonment in most of the consensus democracies. This appears to be due in part to the features they retain which work to minimize incentives to penal populism, a point more fully fleshed out below.

Trust

Some suggest that the concept of social capital (Coleman, 1990) can help explain the range of benevolent, communitarian characteristics that Lijphart finds in consensus democracies. However, as Eric

Table 9.1 Confidence in selected institutions (%)

		Legal system	Press	Police	Parliament	Civil servants
Norway	1981	84	41	89	78	58
	1990	75	43	88	59	44
Britain	1981	66	29	86	40	48
	1990	54	14	77	44	44

Source: European Values Survey (1981, 1990) cited in Listhaug and Wiberg (1995).

Uslaner (2002) argues, the correlations that Robert Putnam (2000) has famously discovered between social capital and good governance cry out for an explanatory mechanism. Uslaner (2002: 1) believes he has located it in the construct of generalized trust—what he calls the 'chicken soup of social life'. Generalized trust refers to the trust people have in strangers and 'encompasses the belief that people who are different from us nevertheless are part of our "moral communities"' (Uslaner, 2004). Interpersonal trust in Norway actually rose very slightly from 65 to 65.3 per cent between 1990 and 1997, while it dropped sharply from 44 to 29.6 per cent in Britain over the same period (Grenier and Wright, 2006).

Listhaug and Wiberg (1995) examined European Values Survey (EVS) data on confidence in various public and private institutions over time in fourteen European countries. The findings for Norway and Britain appear in Table 9.1. Overall, the public's confidence in the press and in parliament is nearly twice the levels in Norway as in Britain. The Norwegian data suggest that a 'deadlock in Norwegian politics during the second half of the 1980s and 1990 produced a situation with no winners, as governments from both camps were unable to govern effectively, thus alienating both their own and the opposition's supporters. This could well be part of the explanation of the decline in confidence in the *Storting* 1982–1990' (Listhaug and Wiberg, 1995: 321–2). This assertion provides support for the contention that conflict and gridlock, most associated with majoritarian democracy, undermines public confidence, and that consensus building and deliberation would enhance it through the better running of government. This shows too that even within a consensual political culture with an aversion to conflict, deadlocks occur. But the overall impact of these is lower if the reserve of confidence is deep, a reserve that is due in part to the deliberative and consensus-based culture.

Figure 9.3 Imprisonment rates and trust in selected countries

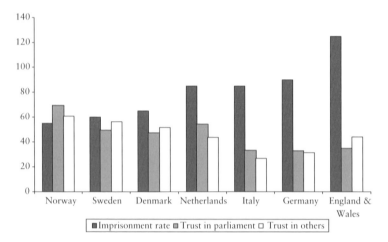

Figure 9.3 depicts the relationship between imprisonment rates in 1999 [3] (Walmsley, 1999), data on trust in parliament from 2000 (Catterberg and Moreno, 2005), and World Values Survey (WVS) data on interpersonal trust [4] from the 1980s and 1990s (Rice and Feldman, 1997) for those countries for which data for all three measures are available. It appears from these limited cases that imprisonment and the levels of trust that citizens have in parliaments and in one another are inversely related. The higher the trust, the lower the imprisonment rate, and vice versa.

One can only speculate as to why this might be, but it seems plausible that the divisive and adversarial features of the majoritarian model of democracy might actually generate the sort of distrust to which populist politicians and parties respond.

Susceptibility to Penal Populism

Though there has been some consideration in the criminological literature of the ways in which political cultures and structures

---

[3] The aim was to use imprisonment rate data that were contemporaneous with the other data sources, so older data were used.

[4] The question asked in the WVS is: 'Generally speaking, would you say that most people can be trusted or that you can't be too careful in dealing with people?' (Rice and Feldman, 1997: 1167).

influence penal trends (Barker, 2006), with only a few exceptions (Downes, 1988, 1991; Downes and van Swaaningen, 2005), criminologists have tended to overlook the cultural features of consensus and majoritarian democracies to help explain their variable susceptibility to populism. It is no surprise that the countries that have been most susceptible to bouts of penal populism are the English-speaking majoritarian democracies, and it appears the inclusiveness and stability afforded by the consensus model of policymaking allows fewer footholds for populist politicians.

Garland (1996, 2001) builds the case that expressively punitive crime-control policies have been utilized in the USA and Britain as a means to offset declining legitimacy and weakening national sovereignty. This thinking is based upon a range of crisis theories advanced in the 1970s claiming crises of legitimation, governability, and democracy:

Although the ideological and theoretical bases for these crisis hypotheses varied greatly, their diagnoses concurred in one essential point: the demands made by citizens on democratic governments were increasing, and doing so irreversibly, while, at the same time, the capacity of governments to realize their policy objectives was declining due, among other things, to lower economic growth. However, the crisis hypotheses postulated by critics differed widely in locating the societal causes for these alleged problems. (Fuchs and Klingemann, 1995: 5)

Crozier, Huntington and Watanuki (1975) argue that the crisis of democracy is caused by two factors: growing citizen demands and a competitive party system which 'forces parties constantly to outbid one another in terms of their policy programmes, thus [further] inflating the demands of citizens' (Fuchs and Klingemann, 1995: 6). In majoritarian democracies, it appears that these kinds of power struggles yield a cycle of only pyrrhic victories where one side strips power from another, only to be left to deal with the gap in confidence that was rendered in the quest to seize power in the first place. Anything gained by the compulsion to *do something* in the face of public, press, or opposition party criticism is undercut by the implicit admission in acting that previous efforts hitherto were inadequate. It also legitimizes the critiques that triggered the remedial action and grants them greater purchase.

Adversarial models of English or American politics are characterized by sharp partisan divisions and inter-party derision. They are premised on a set of assumptions that run counter to those underpinning consensual power sharing. The object of adversarial party politics after all is to remove power from the opposition, not to share it. This creates incentives for politicians to attack opponents from the rival party, to expose any flaw in current or planned policies—all with the aim of obtaining power themselves. This conflict model interacts well with the demands of the mass media, reliant as they are to a large extent upon conflict to generate consumer interest (Fuchs and Klingemann, 1995).

It is likely that constant and highly publicized attacks on current policy—combined with the concomitant promises of reform and improvement that are in turn attacked in yet another raft of criticism—weaken the public's confidence in government to perform well.[5] It is plausible that politicians are given such free rein to attack each other so powerfully during election campaigns and in the parliamentary chambers because their constituents are typically displeased with the current success of government policies. This displeasure can also be linked to the tone and content of opposition party and media assessments of government action, which in England are seldom complimentary. Recall David Davis's condemnatory statements from Chapter 1 about Labour's failure to tackle crime whenever the crime figures are released. Only in the wake of galvanizing emergencies and atrocities, like 9/11 in the USA and the London bombings of July 2005, do the divisive barriers between the parties tend to temporarily dissolve.

With low public confidence in government institutions, reformist agendas premised upon strong critiques of current policy and practice are likely to garner widespread public support, at least initially. Partisan concerns to win elections and to dominate legislatures and parliaments demand, especially when public confidence is low, that opposition politicians begin their campaigns to wrest power from the leading party by first exposing the government's failures. This has at least five plausible and unintended effects: first, it can further diminish the public's confidence by confirming their beliefs that the government has indeed got it wrong. Second, it legitimizes the practice of the kind of partisan politics which seeks one party's dominance over others at the cost of overall

---

[5] Similarly, it is also possible that the Labour government's current preoccupation with public confidence may actually serve to undermine it by constantly calling attention to its apparent absence.

legitimacy for all political institutions.[6] Third, this in turn per-petuates the practice, and a pattern is established whereby the perceived effectiveness of the government in power is consistently undermined by opposition parties that expose government short-comings, and in so doing, further undermine public confidence. Fourth, these practices practically necessitate political action that promises to do something *else* in the name of building public confidence. Fifth, chronic public displeasure can entice govern-ments to make promises they cannot keep, and such promises are likely to raise both public expectations and the stakes of failure (Roberts, 2002). These are all issues that are exacerbated by an adversarial political culture.

In California, the high-profile murder of Polly Klaas in 1993 prompted state legislators there to propose for a public refer-endum the nation's toughest 'three strikes and you're out' law. One state senator defended his decision to support it against his better judgment by saying, 'I'm going to vote for these turkeys because that's what our constituents want us to do' (quoted in Pillsbury, 1995). In England, shortly before Home Secretary Michael Howard's 1993 Conservative Party Conference declara-tion that 'prison works', prison was widely and officially regarded by the Conservative government as 'an expensive way of making bad people worse' (Home Office, 1990: 6). These patterns of act-ing against better judgment are driven by the need to appear to be responsive to a public with waning faith. Regardless of which came first, low public confidence or cynical partisan political strategies, each helps to preserve the existence of the other. Low

---

[6] In America the win-at-all-costs ethos is evident and rewarded in intra-party elections, too. For instance, in the run up to the 1988 presidential campaign, the Democratic Party primary debates saw the first invocation of the prison furlough programmes linked with the name of Willie Horton—not by Republican President George H.W. Bush, but by Democratic primary candidate Al Gore. Horton was a black man who, after absconding from a Massachusetts prison furlough pro-gramme while serving time for felony murder, raped a white woman in her home and assaulted her fiancé. Though Bush had presided over similar federal furlough programmes, Gore invoked the practice of furloughing life-sentence prisoners to portray his opponent, Massachusetts governor Michael Dukakis, as soft on crime. Bush's campaign manager, Lee Atwater, seized on Gore's tactic and effectively used the Horton case to defeat Dukakis once he had secured the Democratic nomi-nation. (See Anderson (1995).) The ruthlessness and cynicism of Gore's manoeu-vre was rewarded. He became Bill Clinton's vice president in 1992 and later the Democratic Party's nominee to face George W. Bush in 2000.

public trust in the ability of government to get it right means these kinds of populist appeals become routine.

Delegates and trustees

Differences in normative conceptions of representative democracy are reflected in another distinction which helps illustrate the variable incentives to populism—that of the elected representative as a delegate or as a trustee. In the delegate model, representatives 'follow the demands rather than the needs of their publics' by doing either what their constituents demand of them or doing what they believe their publics would approve (Lane, 1996: 50). This conception is premised in part on a suspicion of unchecked leadership, and allows for less deference to elected representatives' own judgments, and grants them less discretion. In the trustee model, the representative is entrusted to meet the needs of the citizens, largely insulated and unfettered by outside public influence. The demand for accountability is lower as trust levels are higher.

The delegate-style political culture is more susceptible to penal populism because it creates incentives to 'play to the gallery' or posture for political ends, and to take any prominent indications of the public will, like tabloid headlines and other mass-mediated cues, as justifications to act. When trust is low, the incentive for delegates to act to bolster it increases, but the ability to do so substantively declines—in part because there are fewer opportunities for the kind of cautious and careful policy deliberation that leads to considered, durable policies.

Where political conflict is rife, knowledges, or our 'cognitive and normative assumptions about the world' (Savelsberg, 1994: 912), are likely to be more contested. However, it is also the case that partisan political conflict tends to create incentives for political actors to embrace particular knowledges over others because some are more tactically useful than others. Savelsberg (1994: 912) argues that 'whenever cultural change or social conflict results in knowledge shifts, the dynamics of knowledge and the tides of beliefs and their amplitudes can only be explained if we take the institutionalization of knowledge production into account, and…that knowledge intervenes when social structures influence decision making'. The knowledge produced by the tabloid press in England seems no longer to represent the narrow, misinformed, and injudicious perspectives of readerships from whom policymakers need protection. Now this knowledge is channelled into the mainstream of political knowledge, and exposure to and engagement with it is now a political imperative.

Norwegian politicians, like their German counterparts whom Savelsberg (1994, 1999) studied, are known more as party representatives than as individual political actors. Voters vote more for the party than the party's candidate. Therefore,

U.S. legislators, civil servants, and criminal justice lawyers are much more exposed to shifts of public knowledge, ideology, and resulting political pressure than their German counterparts, who base their decisions on bureaucratically produced knowledge. Public knowledge is more dynamic—that is, more volatile—than bureaucratic knowledge. I expect this volatility to create much more unstable patterns of criminal justice knowledge and decision making in the American than in the German political sector. (Savelsberg, 1994: 932)

Again, this knowledge volatility is related to the kinds of knowledge that are most compatible with the interests of those shaping the debate. Politicians who must appear directly responsive to their constituents have an incentive to speak directly to public knowledge, the measures of which tend to be opinion polls and the mass media. As a result, features of the English and 'American political landscape[s] interact to minimize the chances that information is rigorously assembled, carefully analysed, and rationally employed in policy-development. Issues hit the headlines with little notice and are simplified and sensationalized. Politicians are forced into crisis management and are required to respond rapidly and instinctively, with a view to their personal ratings in the polls' (Roberts et al, 2003: 73–4).

The trustee model is disallowed when trust in representatives is lacking. Trust is a prerequisite for its success and trust is the mechanism that explains the model's decreased susceptibility to populism. If the public has lost faith in its representatives, as Lane (1996: 55) puts it, 'legislative elites cannot now expect their publics to have much confidence in the elite's judgements. Alienation, if that is the proper term, feeds on itself, preventing its own solution'.

Norwegian political culture reflects the trustee model of representation, an egalitarian culture without the residual divisions of feudalism found elsewhere, and a subsequent concern with the best interests of all. The consensual features of its political culture are unthreatened by 'any substantial patterns of hierarchical subordination in the society' (Christensen and Peters, 1999: 160). In contrast, the neo-liberalism of American culture, and to a lesser extent English culture, are enshrined in 'values such as individualism, competition, and the notion that society represents endless opportunities from which individuals make their choices and take their chances…This view of society can be contrasted with the conditions favored by most European countries [where consensus models of democracy are the norm] which moderate both excesses of wealth, poverty, and punishment' (Roberts et al, 2003: 74).

Zero-sum and variable-sum assumptions

Whether politics is generally viewed as a zero-sum game or a variable- or expandable-sum game will have consequences on the ability to build bridges between political opponents. The sort of culture each outlook demands, as Elkins and Simeon (1979: 132) put it, 'should affect the kinds of political rhetoric to which a group responds and the kinds of leadership it finds congenial or inspiring. The distribution of zero-sum rather than expandable-sum assumptions should vary widely between collectivities; and these variations should be associated with marked contrasts in how different populations play the game of politics'.

A zero-sum game assumption drives party politics in England, as when the Tories currently seize all opportunities to discredit and embarrass the Labour government as if they will, by default, absorb any support lost by Labour. This short-sighted approach also creates another incentive that is likely to raise levels of public distrust and concern: 'Under the conditions of a competitive party system…it is perfectly rational for opposition parties to postulate a societal or political crisis to convince voters of the urgency of removing the governing parties from power' (Fuchs and Klingemann, 1995: 4–5). Recall from the previous chapter Blair's invocation of moral crisis in the wake of the Bulger murder and Cameron's similar invocation more recently in response to knife and gun crime. Crisis rhetoric might help discredit and undermine government credibility, but it also raises expectations and makes rational debate and deliberative approaches to problems more difficult to achieve. Such rhetoric seems less likely to be employed in consensus democracies because politics is a variable-sum game, there is less to gain from undermining sitting parties, and the conditions are more conducive to compromise.

The propensity for politicians to exploit mass-mediated public alarm declines when there is less politically to be gained from the practice. It may be true that 'politicians are everywhere pusillanimous' (Tonry, 2004a: 53), but the extent to which they are depends both on the level of public confidence their publics retain in them, and the political–cultural incentives that reward behaviour observers regard as pusillanimous. When public confidence is low and the pressure to act is high, incentives to posture and to exploit divisions for political gain probably increase, just at the time when courageous leadership is most required. When confidence is high and political divisions are more fruitfully dealt with through formal cooperative political channels, there is less to justify the exploitation of fear. The incentives are fewer. Moreover, that naturally self-interested Norwegian politicians are able to act on crime and penal policy matters without the level of penal escalation or the 'punitiveness auction' (Drakeford and Vanstone, 2000) seen in the USA and England points to explanations beyond the individual level, to political culture and the attendant structures that reflect it.

Inclusion and exclusion

Populism in all its forms (according to Canovan (1981), there are seven) parasitically feeds on the distrust of elites, utilizing society-specific symbols to resonate with a loosely conceived notion of 'the people' (Taggart, 2000). This distrust has its foundations in discourses of exclusion, that the powerful have excluded 'ordinary people' from the decisions that directly affect them. Adversarial, majoritarian democracies cannot easily or ingenuously counter such challenges, as they are, after all, fundamentally exclusionary.[7] The rigidly two-party American system and functionally two-party English system cannot accommodate dissent well, and cynicism sown by the disaffected who are dissatisfied with the major parties' solutions can contaminate the party system generally (Miller and Listhaug, 1990).

Norway has managed to combat this trend, perhaps ironically, through the institutional incorporation of protest parties, like the 'new populist', anti-establishment Progress Party. The

---

[7] One critic insists that majoritarian systems are fundamentally undemocratic because they exclude the views of the minority and do not do enough to incorporate the views of all who are affected by a decision (Lewis, 1965).

inclusiveness which characterizes flexible multi-party political systems allows 'distrust to be channeled back into the electoral arena as support for opposition and protest parties of the right' (Miller and Listhaug, 1990: 383), both through the creation of new parties and through the wider range of options provided by existing ones. This is an example of a structurally supported cultural impediment to the wider contamination of the political system with alienation and distrust.

There is a paradox here. Political cultures that are consensual can afford to be because they retain public trust and confidence, in part because often that which is born of cooperative consensus democracy is more defensible, more agreeable policy. Political cultures that are adversarial appear to be most in need of consensual structures, yet they are incapable of fully fostering them because their cultures are built on suspicion and distrust. Olsen (1996: 169) goes further to point out another paradox, which is that the Norwegian government appears better designed to deal with the somewhat fragmented and disorganized character of American society than with the more orderly Norwegian society. The various mechanisms for consultation available for government agencies provide a way of gauging organized public concern and perhaps averting conflicts later in the policy process. In addition, the parliamentary system enables government to act more decisively than the slow and fragmented American political process.

Conclusion

Penal populism is driven by perceptions of public distrust and the political urge to bolster weakened legitimacy—preoccupations apparent in the reactions to the Bulger case in England. There is no legitimacy deficit in Norway. There has not been the acute crisis of confidence in elites that is so evident in English debates of crime and punishment. Levels of public trust in politicians and in fellow citizens are higher in Norway than anywhere else in the world (Listhaug and Wiberg, 1995; Uslaner, 2002). Economic prosperity and social homogeneity counters the logic of questioning the status quo, but its consensual political culture also has a stabilizing role to play by diminishing incentives to compete and to outbid political opponents

The fervent and public condemnation of crime and criminals in England appears to be a defensive effort by government, as only one in a repertoire of many, to bolster the state's authority in the face of public criticism, cynicism, and deflated electorate expectations. As confidence erodes, voters are less enthused to invest in the political process, and government actors must act to make overtures to the disaffected. To ignore public cynicism would jeopardize the political system as a whole, calling attention to the gap between government action and the failure of the public to participate. The arguments raised in this chapter show that public trust and confidence in the criminal justice system matters. Low levels of trust have real and far-reaching consequences that can—as high-profile and rare events like the Bulger case have done—colour citizens' subsequent perceptions of justice and the criminal justice system more generally. This strengthens the case that policymakers cannot afford to disengage from the public and simply disregard their beliefs and perceptions, regardless of how inaccurate or distorted these might be.

But this also raises the following questions: What can and should be done? How can we de-escalate 'penal arms races' (Roberts et al, 2003), especially in majoritarian countries where a policy of détente is needed most urgently? Is it possible to make aspects of majoritarian democracy less destructive?

If Uslaner is correct to identify interpersonal trust as the mechanism that makes social capital work, and if penal populism is driven by a depletion of trust, then it follows that reform efforts, particularly in those countries where penal populism is especially prevalent, ought to be aimed at generating trust to oppose the cynicism driving penal populism. The example of Norway suggests that if public confidence in government and in elites who advise it is sufficiently high, then there is less to be gained by politicians resorting to tough-sounding policies that even they concede to be costly, ineffective, or unjust. This suggests that the Labour government's preoccupation with building public confidence is justified and it bolsters the argument that a legitimacy deficit exists in English political culture.

In addition, though it is certainly true that fully formed consensual political cultures and structures cannot not be readily imported into inhospitably adversarial climates, smaller scale remedial measures might make a difference. If trust is inspired and legitimacy is fostered through direct public engagement and participation, opportunities for public deliberation, like the Deliberative Poll, could help to build bridges and trust by partnering elites and publics to solve the problems they face. It is also possible that structural adjustments that embrace consensus in majoritarian jurisdictions could work to diminish some of the more damaging populist inducements that characterize majoritarian democracies.

I contend in the remaining two chapters that maximizing opportunities for public deliberation about matters of crime and justice show promise in (1) clearing up popular misconceptions and media-driven distortions, (2) clarifying the informed public will on matters relevant to policymakers in a way that re-establishes a direct, unmediated link between members of the public and their elected leaders, and (3) via participation in these deliberative forums, building the public's trust in government and in the criminal justice system, the depletion of which appears to be responsible in part for the catalyzing effects of rare, high-profile crimes like the Bulger murder.

10
Public Opinion versus Public Judgment

Mass-mediated portrayals of what 'the public'[1] wants and ubiquitous self-selected opinion polls serve as common surrogates for informed public judgment. In most Western countries these opinion assessments have gained a level of credence in policy debates that is both difficult to justify—due to the highly suspect nature of both what they assess and the means of assessment—and easy to understand—given the range of pressures with which politicians and policymakers must contend, especially in countries like England with adversarial, majoritarian political cultures.

To improve matters it seems that politicians must either cease to defer to an uninformed public about emotive crime and punishment issues, or the public needs to become better informed about them. Of course, no elected politician can afford to be seen to disregard the apparent will of constituents, particularly on concerns as emotively prominent as crime and punishment, no matter how uninformed constituents might be, and expect to survive elections for long. Neither can such disregard long persist on high-profile issues without raising questions of democratic legitimacy. The British government has pursued this second option, launching initiatives to educate the public about current crime control and penal practice (see Home Office, 2001a). However, these attempts are not especially promising in the long term because most do not foster opportunities for the public to work toward formulating durable and informed preferences.

---

[1] 'The public' is a problematic, collective term for disparate groups of people, historically excluded from positions of power, and it connotes levels of social and political equality that are artificial (Fraser, 1993: 14). For the purposes here, 'the public' refers to a nation's citizenry generally. Part of what the construct of public judgment and the Deliberative Poll accomplishes is to redefine 'the public' as a collective of citizens as representative as possible of the society at large who come together to formulate informed and durable views and preferences.

Elites no longer shape penal policy insulated from the pressures of the press and of public concern. Regardless of whether this is judged a positive or negative development, the public voice has nonetheless become an important influence on crime and punishment policy. Though rationales for re-insulating policy-making from public influence may be principled and justified (see Chapter 11), they are also highly impractical. It is prudent and pragmatic to face up to the challenges posed by de-insulated policymaking, and to improve the means of public consultation to ensure that whenever possible, and before it is invoked to justify policies, the public voice is more defensibly assessed than is currently the case.

Governments fall short of this modest goal whenever their policies are justified by reference to a monolithically and unqualifiedly punitive public. To make matters worse, ignorance pervades the interplay between crime, politics, and public opinion. As Rob Allen (2003: 5) argues, 'Close analysis would suggest that there is something of a "comedy of errors" in which policy and practice is not based on a proper understanding of public opinion, and that the same opinion is not based on a proper understanding of policy and practice'.

These problems are not insurmountable, but both what tends to qualify for public opinion and how that opinion is best assessed need first to be reconsidered. Daniel Yankelovich (1991: 6) offers an important and useful distinction between shallow, unconsidered public *opinion*, and reflective, informed public *judgment*— 'the state of highly developed public opinion that exists once people have engaged an issue, considered it from all sides, understood the choices it leads to, and accepted the full consequences of the choices they make'. Building on Yankelovich's conceptual foundation, James Fishkin (1995) and others have innovated assessment procedures, including the Deliberative Poll (DP), which facilitate and measure informed public opinion. These methods are anchored to the notion of public deliberation—an open and informed dialogue between equals—and they go farther toward achieving the ideal of public judgment than any other approach has yet managed.

According to Nancy Fraser (1993: 24), 'weak publics' are those charged only with the formation of opinion. 'Strong publics' represent a blurring of the lines between the public and the state, consisting of participants in deliberative bodies, like parliaments, who come together to form opinions, to make binding decisions, and to serve as a 'counterweight' or a 'critical discursive check on the state'. The role proposed for the public here is a modestly weak one, in Fraser's terms, and no case is made for giving public opinion more teeth in policymaking. The intent instead is to make more defensible the case for utilizing it at all, by ensuring that what is characterized as the public will is the meaningful and legitimate product of reflection and real deliberation.

There have been hints throughout this book of ways the often confused relationship between crime, media coverage, public knowledge, and policy might be improved. Central to any reform programme must be a reconsideration of what we talk about when we talk about public opinion, and the concept of public judgment is the fruit of such a reconsideration. This chapter first explores the important distinction between public opinion and deliberative public judgment by illustrating the need for such a distinction in the first place. The first section considers the evolution of the field of public opinion research and assesses the strengths and weaknesses of public opinion assessment tools. The second section reviews what is known about the quality of public opinion about crime and punishment. I also consider why existing surrogates for informed public opinion play such an important role in democratic politics, especially in majoritarian countries like England and the USA, and why these surrogates are inadequate to justify the influence they have been given on matters of crime control policy.

In the third section I show how public opinion and public judgment differ, what is required to achieve the latter, and I consider the Deliberative Poll as a means of achieving it. In light of Yankelovich's work and as a way to illustrate the distinctions it draws, I assess in the fourth section the likely impact of recent Home Office innovations to increase public knowledge and confidence in the criminal justice system, concluding they neglect crucial insights embedded in theories of deliberation and public judgment. Innovations like the Deliberative Poll show promise in facilitating assessments of the informed public will that are more reliable and refined than the other, less ambitious remedial proposals typically suggested, most of which are insufficiently bold to make a significant and lasting impact on public knowledge and attitudes.

Innovations in Public Opinion Assessment

In the 1930s George Gallup pioneered 'quota sampling' and the first scientific opinion polls, revolutionizing how newspaper owners and editors assessed the views of readers (Fishkin, 1995). Gallup's polls provide a statistically valid assessment of the population's opinions, but a misleadingly shallow one. They compel respondents to make on-the-spot choices, whether or not respondents have reasonably sufficient knowledge to make them. Most polls provide no means to distinguish between volatile, so-called 'mushy' opinions—those that tend to shift over time and with changes in the wording of poll questions (Yankelovich, 1991)—and the more stable and durable variety.

In the 1940s Robert Merton developed the first focus groups in an attempt to overcome the tendency of Gallup's opinion polls to measure raw public opinion, the kind of top-of-the-head, unconsidered reactions to poll questions that Philip Converse (1964) later called 'nonattitudes'. Focus groups seek more nuanced and considered opinions by assessing 'what is on the interviewee's mind rather than his opinion of what is on the interviewer's mind' (Merton, Lowenthal and Kendall, 1990: 13). Though they compensate for the traditional opinion poll's lack of depth and provide a means to probe opinions more deeply, with tiny samples of six to eight participants, this depth is gained at a cost to generalizability. Until relatively recent innovations, representativeness and depth were mutually exclusive.

The Deliberative Poll (DP) combines both features with a twist. It 'attempts to model what the public *would* think, had it a better opportunity to consider the questions at issue' (Fishkin, 1995: 162, emphasis in original), thus providing a 'glimpse of a hypothetical public' (Luskin, Fishkin and Jowell, 2002: 458). The DP also bridges the existing gap by taking a relatively large stratified random sample of the public and providing them the incentive and opportunity to engage in in-depth dialogue with one another about a small set of issues. Before a deliberation exercise begins, participants are provided carefully balanced briefing materials. Participants then convene for a weekend to hear presentations, engage experts, and debate amongst themselves. These deliberations are televised to engage non-participants and for the sake of transparency. The DP differs from a focus group in its utilization of a more statistically generalizable sample, and through both its provision of new information and the environment conducive to dialogue-driven engagement of it. Ackerman and Fishkin (2004) have developed an even more ambitious model of deliberative will formation, but with slightly different aims. 'Deliberation Day' is the 'realistic utopian' vision for a national holiday of public deliberation held every election year enabling citizens to set an unmediated agenda for political candidates.[2]

The first Deliberative Poll ever conducted[3] was held in Manchester, England in 1994 to address crime and punishment issues (Fishkin, 1995; Hough and Park, 2002; Luskin, Fishkin and Jowell, 2002). A national probability sample yielded 869 participants at the pre-deliberation stage who were each interviewed and administered a questionnaire. From this initial sample 301 participated in the deliberative weekend, and 241 of these were re-interviewed and re-surveyed ten months later. These follow-up assessments indicated that participants tended to change their opinions markedly and durably because of the deliberation process (Luskin et al, 2002), and most often in a decidedly 'liberalising' direction (Hough and Park, 2002), revealing a sharp decline in enthusiasm for punitive, incarceral responses to crime.[4]

Ackerman and Fishkin (2004) use a compass to conceptualize the ways different public opinion assessments perform relative to each other (see Figure 10.1). The west–east axis represents the category of participants in the opinion assessment—the mass public in the west, the select group in the east. The north–south axis denotes the kind of opinion sought—deliberative public opinion in the north and raw public opinion in the south. Each quadrant

[2] Ethan Leib (2004) goes even further, calling for a popular, deliberative branch of government to replace the ballot initiative and referendum.

[3] As of 2002, there had been a total of eighteen Deliberative Polls conducted; nine were national (five in Britain, one in the USA, one in Denmark, and two in Australia) (Luskin, Fishkin and Jowell, 2002).

[4] For instance, before deliberating, 59 per cent believed that sending more offenders to prison was either a 'very effective' or 'effective' way to reduce crime. This fell to 42 per cent afterwards. Similarly, those who thought more use of custody was 'not effective' increased from 20 per cent before deliberation to 26 per cent afterwards (Hough and Park, 2002). The percentage believing it neither effective nor ineffective increased from 21 to 31 per cent. Another question addressed what prison ought to be for, and answers indicated support for 'punishing criminals' declined from 54 per cent before to 45 per cent after deliberation, as compared with support for 'reforming criminals' which rose from 39 per cent before to 47 per cent afterwards (Hough and Park, 2002).

Figure 10.1 The Ackerman–Fishkin compass

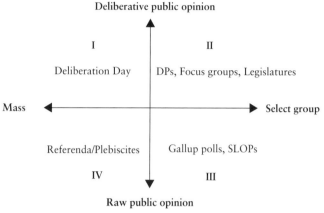

Key: DP = Deliberative Poll; SLOP = Self-selected listener opinion poll
Source: Adapted from Ackerman and Fishkin (2004: 199).

harbours distinct assessment tools, each with inherent strengths and weaknesses.

Quadrant I combines the best of both axes to facilitate mass deliberation and mass consent. Only Deliberation Day currently meets the criteria. Quadrant II is occupied by any 'select group that deliberates for the rest of us' (Ackerman and Fishkin, 2004: 199), including focus groups, legislatures, and other deliberative bodies including the DP. Quadrant III is where the most ubiquitous opinion polls fall, representing the raw opinions of a select group. This includes 'self-selected listener opinion polls' or SLOPs[5] that are now a common feature across all media. Quadrant IV, in the southwest, is where government by plebiscite and referendum (Hayward, 1996) are located. These assessments represent the 'raw political preferences of the mass public... bringing power to the people—but under institutional conditions that provide the people with little incentive to think about the power that they exercise' (Ackerman and Fishkin, 2004: 199–200).

For the most part, opportunities for deliberation, especially about crime and punishment issues, have remained the preserve of

---

[5] A term coined by Norman Bradburn of the National Opinion Research Center at the University of Chicago (Fishkin, 1995).

insulated elites in Quadrant II, reflecting 'the modern belief that serious deliberation only makes sense in elite settings' (Ackerman and Fishkin, 2004: 200). There exists no institutionalized means to garner mass consent without losing the deliberative aspects that legitimate it. As the authors put it, 'We haven't figured out a way of moving north to further deliberation without also moving east to restrict the process to a select group. We haven't moved west to further mass consent without also moving south to lessen deliberation and increase the sway of raw public opinion' (Ackerman and Fishkin, 2004: 200).

Effects of Mediated Proxies for Public Opinion

Press discourse can be a misleading indicator of popular sentiment, yet in England, as elsewhere, there is a tendency for policymakers to utilize newspapers as a primary index of public opinion. As once Parliament was the sounding board for the English public, now the press claim that role (Windlesham, 1996: 49). Though editors might declare that they merely reflect reader opinion when making decisions about content, there is no clear-cut means by which the putative opinions of readers are systematically assessed. This remains murky territory. David Nicholas, editor of ITN, a UK-based television news channel, admitted, '90 per cent of the time we are trying to tell people what we think they want to know' (quoted in Jones, 2001: 198). This confusion seems to indicate that news editors are using coarse and crude instruments to measure what the public *wants* when choosing what to cover, and what the public *thinks/believes* when speaking in its name.

Politicians, and scholars as well, routinely conflate press opinion and public opinion, erroneously assuming a direct relationship between the two. Though of course the two are intricately intertwined, using the former as an indication of the latter is a mistake. For instance, Lord Windlesham mentions the role that 'political sensitivity towards *public opinion*' played in a number of late additions to the 1991 Criminal Justice Bill, including a new sub-section to make offending on bail an aggravating factor in judicial assessments of crime seriousness. This change in the Bill was brought on by 'extensive *press coverage* of some bad cases of breach, backed up by pressure from the police' (Windlesham, 1996: 27, emphasis added). These two points of pressure hardly seem sufficient to qualify as 'public opinion', but they are accepted, in this case by an expert, as acceptably legitimate substitutes. A second change to the Bill resulted from 'a shift in the public mood' made evident by 'growing public sympathy' towards the agenda of the Campaign Against Drinking and Driving (CADD). Again to utilize the agenda of 'one of the most vehement of all lobbies' (Windlesham, 1996: 28) as a means to assess the opinion of the public seems an imprecise and potentially dangerous instrument of measure when such assessments are used to justify shifts in policy direction.

There is no shortage of examples of unsuitable proxies for informed and considered public opinion. Next I address two, focusing first on the role of public opinion on the US Supreme Court's death penalty decisions, and then on the English political reaction to two high-profile crimes, including the Bulger case. Though this book is most concerned with developments in England and Norway, inclusion of this US example is meant to indicate why better assessments of public judgment are likely to have global appeal.

'Evolving standards' and American capital punishment

A wealth of research on public attitudes to crime and punishment has shown that the public is poorly informed and their assessments of crime and justice issues tend not to comport well with the associated pool of social scientific knowledge (Chapman, Mirrlees-Black and Brawn, 2002; Cullen, Fisher and Applegate, 2000; Cullen et al, 2002; Hough and Roberts, 1998; Mirrlees-Black, 2001; Roberts and Stalans, 1997; Roberts et al, 2003; Walker and Hough, 1988). It is, therefore, not surprising that, as Craig Haney (1994, 1997) found in his examination of the attitudes and opinions of jurors in American death penalty cases, that the 'commonsense justice' (Finkel, 1995) upon which jury trials depend is routinely based on distortion and stereotype.

Of course, the death penalty is an issue the vast majority of the public encounters only via the media, and usually in ways depicting the gross depravity of 'evil' individuals. 'There is perhaps no other topic about which our media is so obsessed yet so inaccurate. Because these messages are conveyed and consumed in the absence of alternative sources of information about topics for which popular views have real consequences, this inaccuracy is legally and politically dangerous. Clear thinking about the death penalty has become one of its victims' (Haney, 1997: 317). The American public lacks the kind of information that would help them make meaningful and durable decisions about the issues capital punishment raises.

On several occasions, most in the 1970s, the US Supreme Court considered the state of public knowledge of the death penalty— including its deterrent value, its utility and cost relative to other available penalties, and the prevalence of its use—and the importance of public knowledge in determining its constitutionality. The Court's interrogations are thorough, but, ultimately, its conclusions are confounding.

The Eighth Amendment to the Constitution preserves the 'dignity of man' by protecting the individual from 'cruel and unusual punishment' (*Trop v Dulles* 356 US 86, 100 (1958)). The constitutionality of the death penalty has most often been challenged on these grounds. In attempting to determine precisely when this dignity is endangered, the Court recognized that 'the words of the Amendment are not precise, and that their scope is not static. The Amendment must draw its meaning from the evolving standards of decency that mark the progress of a maturing society' (*Trop v Dulles* above at 100–1). The evolving standard is thus the linchpin linking public opinion and the death penalty's constitutionality.

Just how these evolving standards of decency are assessed has been a matter of debate. In *Furman v Georgia* 408 US 238 (1972), Justice Thurgood Marshall argued that the determination of the death penalty's constitutionality 'turns on the opinion of an *informed* citizenry' (at 362, emphasis added). 'Democratic optimism' (Ellsworth and Gross, 1994), a faith in the persuasive power of knowledge, underpins the so-called 'Marshall hypothesis'—the counterfactual belief that the public would not countenance the death penalty if fully informed about, for instance, its failure to deter other offenders, the relatively few numbers of actual executions carried out,[6] the arbitrariness of its imposition, and the higher cost of execution compared with life imprisonment (*Furman v Georgia* above at 363). The public only considers the range of issues invoked by capital punishment on rare occasions

---

[6] There were 3,503 inmates on death row in the USA as of 1 January 2004 (NAACP Legal Defense and Educational Fund, 2004). There were 98 executions in the USA in 1999, 85 in 2000, 66 in 2001, 71 in 2002, 65 in 2003, and 59 in 2004 (<http://www.deathpenaltyinfo.org>).

and with limited factual knowledge, conditions that fail to qualify as deliberate reflection. Thus, as Marshall's thinking went, any support capital punishment managed to retain in polls and referenda was more the consequence of inertial contentment with the status quo than a reflection of considered opinion.

Marshall argued, '...the question with which we must deal is not whether a substantial proportion of American citizens would today, if polled, opine that capital punishment is barbarously cruel, but whether they would find it to be so in the light of *all information presently available*' (*Furman v Georgia* above at 362, emphasis added). The case he made relies upon a counterfactual assessment of public opinion: *what if* the public were as fully informed as possible, had worked through their ambivalence, and taken responsibility for their decisions?

Others on the Supreme Court have not been as scrupulous as Justice Marshall was in 1972 about what constitutes sufficiently robust assessments of public opinion. The dissenting opinion in *Furman* articulated by Justice Powell was more indicative of the anti-empirical trend to come (see Haney and Logan, 1994). He argued that 'however one may assess the amorphous ebb and flow of public opinion' on the death penalty, 'this type of inquiry lies at the periphery—not the core—of the judicial process in constitutional cases. The assessment of popular opinion is essentially a legislative, not a judicial, function' (*Furman v Georgia* above at 443). Despite the disclaimer, he goes on to insist that '[p]ublic opinion polls, while of little probative relevance, corroborate substantially the conclusion derived from examining legislative activity and jury sentencing—opinion on capital punishment is "fairly divided"' (*Furman v Georgia* above at fn 36). Within existing civil society forums, where reflective deliberation is stifled and ignorance is pervasive, it is not surprising that there is agreement among legislators and jurors. If anything, that such agreement coexists alongside widespread public ignorance should be reason enough to reconsider the value of such apparent support.

In lieu of anything better, capital juries and legislative activity became the only Court-suitable proxies for public opinion. Regarding juries, in *Witherspoon v Illinois* 391 US 510 (1968) the Court considered them 'a link between contemporary community values and the penal system' (at 518). In *Gregg v Georgia* 428 US 153 (1976), the decision reinstating the death penalty after *Furman* suspended it, Justice Stewart deemed the jury, apparently due merely to its very involvement in a capital case, to be a 'significant and reliable objective index of contemporary values' (at 181). The following year, Justice White expanded the premise: '... Eighth Amendment judgments [including evolving standards] should not be, or appear to be, merely the subjective views of individual Justices; judgment should be informed by objective factors to the maximum possible extent. To this end, attention must be given to the public attitudes concerning a particular sentence—history and precedent, legislative attitudes, and the response of juries reflected in their sentencing decisions are to be consulted' (*Coker v Georgia* 433 US 584, 592 (1977)). The evolution from *Furman* to *Coker* shows a rejection of Marshall's informed public criterion in favour or two very problematic surrogates.

The reliance upon capital juries as barometers of the public will—much less the *informed* variety—is highly problematic for at least two reasons. First, juries are comprised of members of the general public who, as Marshall argued, are uninformed and ambivalent about salient issues surrounding the death penalty and its practice (Cullen et al, 2002; Ellsworth and Gross, 1994). Second, juries in capital cases are 'death-qualified', meaning they are only comprised of death penalty supporters. Despite significant evidence suggesting death-qualified juries are more sympathetic to prosecutors, less argumentative during deliberations, and more likely to convict (Cowan, Thompson and Ellsworth, 1984; Fitzgerald and Ellsworth, 1984), the Supreme Court has not looked favourably upon it and remains unconvinced.[7] Nevertheless, the evidence suggests the faith the Court has placed in the ability of capital juries to provide a representative assessment of public opinion is misplaced. Of the public at large, death-qualified juries

---

[7] *Witherspoon v Illinois* 391 US 510 (1968) considered three existing studies that purported to show that death penalty supporters, and therefore death-qualified juries, were more likely than death penalty opponents to convict. According to Gross (1984), the studies were not published at the time but later appeared as Wilson (1964), Zeisel (1968) and Goldberg (1970). The Court, however, found the existing evidence insufficient to support the claim, though it left the door open to fresh evidence. Other courts, however, closed that door. In *State v Forcella* 52 NJ 263 (1968) the New Jersey Supreme Court declared: '[when]...studies are of a sociological or psychological nature...the prospect is remote that such studies will yield views of human behavior of such incontestable, eternal truth that existing constitutional doctrines will have to retreat before them. Such studies hold too little promise...' (193, quoted in Gross (1984: 10)). The California Supreme Court soon echoed the point (*Re Anderson* 69 Cal2d 613, 621 (1968)).

are 'by definition unrepresentative' (Haney, 1997: 333), and likely to be no better informed than the wider public they represent.

The second surrogate for public opinion is no less flawed. In *Furman*, the Court argued, 'The paucity of judicial decisions invalidating legislatively prescribed punishments is powerful evidence that in this country legislatures have in fact been responsive—albeit belatedly at times—to changes in social attitudes and moral values' (at 384). It is this faith in the responsiveness of legislators that underpins the justification for the legislator as index of the public will. The naiveté of this belief is striking. In the thirty-five years since the *Furman* decision, crime and punishment debates in the USA have become increasingly politicized (see, for instance, Garland, 2001; Gest, 2001; Roberts et al, 2003; Tonry, 2004b). The parameters of public debate have narrowed sharply as aggressively competitive media—that politicians are loath to ignore and that thrive on conflict and scandal—dominate issue agendas and set the parameters of debate (Blumler and Gurevitch, 1982; Curran, Gurevitch and Wollacott, 1982; McCombs, 1981, 2005). It is now generally accepted that politicians lead public opinion as much as they are led by it (Beckett, 1997). American legislators, even more so than elsewhere, are notoriously vulnerable to 'soft on crime' attacks, and by supporting the death penalty politicians can neatly deflect such attacks.

Research into public preferences for capital punishment reveal the dual fault lines upon which the court-sanctioned public opinion assessments are built. US[8] opinion polls consistently indicate a high level of public support for capital punishment, a rate that has hovered between 65–80 per cent since the 1990s (Zimring, 2003: 10–11). On this measure alone it is understandable why thirty-eight of the fifty states have a death penalty statute (Zimring, 2003: 7). However, this picture changes once poll respondents are provided an opportunity for more careful consideration. For example, Bowers (1993) found that when given a choice between the death penalty and a sentence of life without the possibility of parole, the majority of study participants in all five states[9] represented preferred life without parole. In another study in California, a state with a very high purported level of public support for capital punishment, two-thirds of the sample preferred

[8] UK poll results indicate similar rates of public support, though the death penalty for murder was abolished in 1965 and for all crimes in 2003.

[9] California, Florida, Georgia, Nebraska, and New York.

life without the possibility of parole combined with restitution to the victim's family over the death penalty, once they were disabused of the misconception that an offender serving such a sentence would eventually be released (Haney, Hurtado and Vega, 1994). This included half of those who had, before the choice was offered, described themselves as strongly in favour of the death penalty (Haney, 1994: 321).

Similar studies in New York (Bowers, Vandiver and Dugan 1994), Tennessee (Whitehead, 1998), and Indiana (McGarrell and Sandys, 1996) found similar patterns, but these also showed something even more noteworthy: a consistent tendency for legislators significantly to overestimate their constituents' preference for capital punishment when given the alternative of life without parole.[10] Legislators also appear to be less flexible in their preferences than their constituents are when faced with the same choices (Bowers et al, 1994), possibly because the electoral benefits of appearing as tough as possible on crime encourage rigidity.

Whether cynical or innocent, that legislators have both the incentive to distort public opinion for electoral reasons and the tendency to overestimate existing public support for punitive punishments would appear sufficient cause to question the wisdom and validity of capital juries and legislators, two demonstrably biased, 'dubious barometers' (Haney, 1997: 333) of the public will. For their part, traditional opinion-polling methods are also insufficiently robust to engender much confidence about issues that the public is not adequately equipped to answer responsibly. Social science research has been strongly discredited by several courts in the past, and the Supreme Court appears reluctant to assign it much weight in deciding questions of constitutionality. Regardless of their utility in court, it seems clear that the most commonly relied upon public opinion assessment tools, scientifically derived or otherwise, are inadequate.

Public opinion and the James Bulger and Sarah Payne cases in Britain

Though accepted surrogates for informed public opinion tend not to perform well on either axis of Ackerman and Fishkin's

---

[10] In the Indiana study the legislators assumed 50 per cent of the public would prefer the death penalty, twice the actual number of 26 per cent (Cullen, Fisher and Applegate, 2000).

compass, opinion polls, focus groups, and the media's interpretations of 'public opinion' retain great power to shape political decision-making. Opinion polls are ubiquitous features of British and American life, most of which carry practical and political significances disproportionate to their scientific rigour. Informally solicited polls[11] and so-called SLOPs generate non-generalizable, empirically questionable results, but critically, 'once they are broadcast, their results take on a life of their own. They become representations of public opinion that are communicated to candidates, commentators, and citizens alike' (Fishkin, 1995: 140).

The rise of the public voice in matters of crime policy has coincided with a decline in deference to professional elites (Ryan, 1999, 2003). Simultaneous advances in communication technologies are changing the way mass publics contribute to policy debates, providing them unprecedented opportunities to 'demand participation in making major decisions, not just a voice in selecting the decision makers' (Inglehart, 1997: 294). Thus, English politicians are understandably unwilling to ignore any prominent assessment of public opinion, however inaccurate or mushy. As the power of the public voice has grown, so has the availability of means claiming to measure it, most lacking quality and depth.

Mass-mediated proxies for public opinion can have significant consequences for the administration of justice and policy, like, for instance, which cases are prosecuted.[12] SLOPs can also have highly significant consequences, as illustrated by the actions of the Home Secretary at the time James Bulger was killed, discussed in Chapter 1. Michael Howard based his decision to double the tariffs of Thompson and Venables based on a petition with 278,300 signatures and 21,281 clip-out coupons from the *Sun* demanding Thompson and Venables never be released. The majority of the Court of Appeal strongly criticized Howard's use of these proxies, deeming it inappropriate to 'take into account a large amount

[11] One example is the 'vox pop', 'man-on-the-street' interview journalists use to obtain immediate (and unrepresentative) assessments of opinion from 'ordinary' people. Another is the real-time opinion poll, now a staple of cable and satellite news broadcasting, in which viewers are encouraged to weigh in as often as they like on an issue of the day.

[12] Research conducted in Indiana showed that prosecutors' treatment of cases was affected by media attention (Pritchard, 1986), and a Wisconsin study found that prosecutors were less likely to plea bargain in cases that received high levels of newspaper coverage (Pritchard, Dilts and Berkowitz, 1987).

of material which in effect amounted to taking a hopelessly unscientific poll from members of the public without any satisfactory checks or without any confidence as to the factual or legal basis upon which the responses were made' ([1997] 2 WLR 67, 110, quoted in Fionda, 1998: 81). After a series of controversial court cases that essentially stripped home secretaries of the power to set tariffs in such cases,[13] the two boys served the original eight-year tariff and the Parole Board approved their release with anonymity in 2001. Media reports suggested the decision was met with dismay and disbelief by many.[14]

The volume of the cheering crowd determined which candidates were fit to serve on the Council in ancient Sparta, a method called the 'Shout' (Fishkin, 1995). Howard responded to a modern version of the Shout when he justified doubling the tariffs with reference to a self-selected sample of readers from a tabloid newspaper like the *Sun* with admitted biases and a political agenda, which included advocating tougher penal policies (Windlesham, 1996).

As illustrated by the analyses in Chapter 7, the news media, especially the tabloids, also fall short of providing the contextual information sufficient for readers to make informed decisions about the issues apparently of most concern to them. Though the English tabloids have traditionally played a usefully critical role by holding the government to account, highlighting spin, and spearheading campaigns that draw attention to flaws in the criminal justice system, they tend to be less adept at serving the more mundane informative function crucial for democratic debate. For instance, in the summer of 2000, in response to the sexual assault and murder of eight-year-old Sarah Payne by a convicted sex offender, the tabloid *News of the World*'s attempted to mobilize support for Sarah's Law, a public sex offender registry

---

[13] Due to Court of Appeal ([1997] 2 WLR 67) and House of Lords ([1997] 3 All ER 97) judgments in *R v Secretary of State for the Home Department ex p Venables and Thompson*, as well as in the European Court of Human Rights (*T v United Kingdom; V v United Kingdom* (2000) 30 EHRR 121), Howard's tariff was overruled and the practice was outlawed.

[14] According to the BBC, 'Opposition in Merseyside to the release of the two killers was reflected in a phone poll taken by one of the local newspapers, the *Liverpool Echo* this week. About 42,000 people rang the paper to take part in the vote, with 83 per cent coming out against the release of Venables and Thompson' (BBC News, 2001b).

modelled on Megan's Law in the USA, by promising to publish the names and photographs of fifty convicted paedophiles each week. The paper swiftly ended the practice after a number of vigilante attacks broke out.[15] Though the campaign raised the public's consciousness of the issue of sex offenders in the community, readers were nevertheless 'given very limited information indeed by which they could assess the prevalence of crimes of this sort and the risks that children run of being targeted by a pedophile predator' (Roberts et al, 2003: 51).

That the government and the police have so far managed to resist calls for community notification of sex offenders, and that the Parole Board approved the release of Thompson and Venables in spite of the furore the decision was bound to ignite, might be read as evidence that existing institutional arrangements are working properly, that reason continues to triumph over hysteria. However, this is a misguided view for at least two reasons, both of which strengthen the case for expanding deliberative opportunities to foster public judgment. First, the climate to which the *Sun* and the *News of the World* campaigns contributed placed severe limitations on the ability of the police and policymakers to act, in spite of the outcomes. In the former instance, the trial judge, the Lord Chief Justice, the Home Secretary, and the Parole Board were all under substantial pressure to act in particular ways based on evidence of questionable reliability. In the latter case, '[w]ithout doubt...the [*News of the World*] campaign has served to compound public frustration about the criminal justice system and has simultaneously constrained politicians' ability to locate strategies that genuinely minimise the risk of predatory pedophile crime' (Roberts et al, 2003: 51). Second, although elite decision-makers resisted the tide of outrage espoused by press campaigns, still absent were the deliberative forums to allow citizens to come to terms with the decisions that elites made. By further frustrating an already outraged 'public', the seeds were thus sown for even further public and press discontent and more penal populism to address it.

---

[15] On one estate, vigilante groups drove five families from their homes after mistakenly targeting them for harbouring sex offenders. In one bizarre incident, vigilantes vandalized a doctor's home, painting 'paedo' on her door and porch, apparently after confusing the word 'paediatrician' with 'paedophile' (*Guardian*, 30 August 2000).

So where are we?

The British public remains unaware of a great deal of factual and contextual information about many aspects of the criminal justice system (Chapman, Mirrles Black and Brawn, 2002). For instance, it is well established that '[t]he views of the general public regarding sentencing practice and reform are…limited in the extent to which they are based on misperceptions about current practice' (Home Office, 2001b: app 5, 108). The British Crime Survey has shown a consistent lack of public knowledge about the extent of crime and the reality of sentencing (Dodd et al, 2004; Hough and Roberts, 1998; Mattinson and Mirrlees-Black, 2000), and these results cohere with other recent research. The same can also be said of American, Canadian, and Australian publics (Roberts et al, 2003: ch 2). The American (Ackerman and Fishkin, 2004) and British (Miller, Timpson and M. Lessnoff, 1996) publics rely most upon television as their primary news source, though in Britain TV news agendas are often set by the newspapers, especially the tabloids (Ericson, Baranek and Chan, 1991; Jones, 1998, 2001; Miller, Timpson and Lessnoff, 1996; Thompson, 1998). Complex public policy debates are thus mediatized in increasingly constricted and emotive terms, and the lines between news and entertainment values have been blurred in the quest to retain consumers in a crowded marketplace (CNN, 2004; Goldberg, 2002). Even among quality news media, evidence suggests that the ability or willingness of the media adequately to inform the public is further diminishing. The length of the average news item summary or 'sound bite' on American television news has decreased from 42 seconds to 8 seconds over the past 30 years (Hargreaves, 2003). The proportion of public affairs coverage on television decreased from 70 per cent in 1980 to 50 per cent in 2000 (Ackerman and Fishkin, 2004). During the 1992 presidential campaign, 728 campaign stories on the network nightly news averaged 8.2 minutes each. In 2000, 462 stories averaged 4.2 minutes (Ackerman and Fishkin, 2004: 8–9). The 'thinning' of the public discourse has occurred at a time when sensitive crime and punishment debates have been de-insulated and drawn into the public gaze—just when public deliberation is most required.

Elected representatives thus face mounting incentives to exploit inadequate assessments of public opinion for political ends and increasing pressure to respond to the filtered public sentiments offered by the media, the most commanding substitute for the real thing available. The most influential of these in British political circles, arguably the tabloids, provide the narrowest range of perspectives, and to an uninformed and fearful readership. As Ackerman and Fishkin (2004: 8–9) explain, 'We have a public dialogue that is ever more efficiently segmented in its audiences and morselized in its sound bites. We have an increasingly tabloid news agenda that dulls the sensitivities of an increasingly inattentive citizenry. And we have mechanisms of feedback from the public, from viewer call-ins to self-selected Internet polls, that emphasize the intense commitments of narrow constituencies, unrepresentative of the public at large'. This is a decidedly weak foundation upon which to justify penal policy decision-making.

The problem as described then has two dimensions. First, there is as yet no safe and protected public space free of distortion and oversimplification, where citizens can engage the issues and the range of available information. Second, 'dubious barometers' of the public will are for politicians and policymakers the most accessible assessments available. With the Deliberative Poll, Fishkin (1995) takes steps to address these two dimensions by asking, as Justice Marshall did before him: *What if* the public had the access, the incentive, and the opportunity to wrestle with the sum of what is known about a particular crime problem? He developed the Deliberative Poll to 'to model what the public *would* think, had it a better opportunity to consider the questions at issue' (Fishkin, 1995: 162, emphasis in original). To appreciate fully the Deliberative Poll's value, a closer examination of Yankelovich's concept of public judgment is required.

Coming to Public Judgment

Jürgen Habermas (1984, 1989), on whose work much of Yankelovich's relies, believed that humans are genetically endowed with a higher form of reason that can cut across all boundaries and can lead them to a consensus on what is true and false, provided they are engaged in an open dialogue free from domination and distortion. One need not share Habermas's faith in the rather ethereal gift of higher human reasoning to appreciate the importance of such a public forum. The 'communicative rationality' (Habermas, 1984), or the 'systematic and principled argumentation' (Mathiesen, 2003), that arguably once better characterized penal policy debates in Britain has been eroded as never before. As Mathiesen (1996: 140) explains,

communicative rationality implies an emphasis on truthfulness, relevance and sincerity in argumentation...One might say that even more than before, communicative rationality lives its life in the secluded corners of the professional journals and meetings, while the public debate, flooded as it is with dire warnings by the police and sensational crime stories and, most significantly, by opportunistic political initiatives in the context of burlesque television shows called 'debates', is predominantly character-ized by the rationality of the market place.

For Yankelovich, 'coming to public judgment' entails a revival of the principles of communicative rationality. It involves three stages: 'consciousness raising', 'working through', and 'reso-lution'. Under current institutional conditions, these stages are not easily facilitated. Though low levels of public knowledge about crime and punishment indicate that the media have been unsuccessful in raising consciousness to the level sufficient for the public to engage the issues responsibly, in many cases the media perform this function rather well. Where the media at present fail most is in providing the conditions needed to reach the latter two stages. They tend to generate concern in the wake of high-profile cases and crises, but not to follow through to help the public fully appreciate and actively assess the competing range of remedial actions and their consequences. Working through refers to this time-consuming and internal process of appraisal.

The media typically fail to facilitate working through to reso-lution in part because '[a]ny account of social life is necessarily partial. We selectively and systematically omit in order to sharpen and differentiate. To focus on a topic is to enhance by elimination. The one begets the other. Journalists are professional account makers, skilled at purposive elimination...' (Henry, 1994: 287). The media's preoccupation with crime, citizens' concerns about it, and the political ramifications of particular incidents and policies tend to preclude informed and rational consideration of all options available. In addition, '[n]ews values stories that arouse human interest, ones that involve conflict, and ones that evoke an emotional response from readers, such as anger or con-cern. Crime and justice provide a rich harvest of newsworthy stories' (Hough and Roberts, 2004: 3), focusing on the most serious offences, most often not placing them in context, and reporting statistical data only when they indicate rises in crime (Roberts et al, 2003).

Working through and resolution require what Mathiesen (1996) has called an 'alternative public space', a safe forum to allow the public, through open deliberation, to 'resolve where it stands cognitively, emotionally, and morally' (Yankelovich, 1991: 65). *Cognitive resolution* requires that 'people clarify fuzzy thinking, reconcile inconsistencies, break down the walls of the artificial compartmentalizing that keeps them from recognizing related aspects of the same issue, take relevant facts and new realities into account, and grasp the consequences of various choices with which they are presented' (Yankelovich, 1991: 65). *Emotional resolution* demands that people confront their ambivalent feelings and, most difficult of all, 'reconcile deeply felt conflicting values' (Yankelovich, 1991: 65). *Moral resolution* requires one to confront the ethical dimension of one's views—facing, weighing, and accepting the moral implications of decisions. Completion of the resolution phase means that the citizen has taken full responsibility for the decisions made after assessing the full range of options available.

Frameworks

Yankelovich (1991: 160–74) provides a series of rules to bring about the resolution public judgment requires, and several are worth briefly recounting here. The first involves the compatibility of 'frameworks'. Political scientists have noted that policymakers and social scientists tend to occupy different and inadequately bridged professional and cultural communities,[16] divided by the incompatibility of the frameworks to which their thinking adheres. Politicians have standards of proof and truth that attach higher importance to political and ideological contingencies than the scientifically verifiable findings favoured by social scientists. This disparity between what ought to matter most when making policy decisions is part of what divides these two communities. Yankelovich (1991: 91) is concerned with bridging a similar divide between experts and the public which 'covers not only differences in levels of knowledge but also in values, frameworks, and modes of expression'. Like experts and policymakers, experts and

---

[16] See Dunn (1980) for more on the 'two-communities metaphor'.

the public also occupy different cultural spheres with different standards of truth and often incompatible vocabularies.

For Yankelovich a framework describes the perspective from which issues are engaged. Like policymakers and experts, the public and experts utilize frameworks that are fundamentally opposed. The public's framework is one in which the primary point of departure is qualitative—the moral and ethical concerns raised by the issues (Yankelovich, 1991: 109). These are the 'ought' questions of values and ethics. Experts instead tend to engage issues on instrumental, technical levels that are more often in accord with their own values, seldom made plain. Consequently, 'communication between groups holding different frameworks is notoriously difficult, especially when each has little interest in understanding the other' (Yankelovich, 1991: 110). The mutual disregard that each side tends to hold for the other, particularly on issues of crime and punishment, does not make coming to public judgment on such issues an easy achievement:

> If, in the consciousness raising that accompanies the crime issue, emphasis is placed on strategies that strike Americans as continuing to show more concern for the criminal than the victim (building more prisons to reduce overcrowding), most Americans will simply block out the message. It so lacks credulity that it deflects people from the task of engaging the hard choices involved in combating crime and drugs. It arrests people at the level of mass opinion, stopping thought that might address the crime issue more productively. (Yankelovich, 1991: 94–5)

So experts and the public tend to 'talk past each other' and to arrive at any engagement with a different set of priorities. Criminality is viewed by many of the public as indicative of moral weakness, and by many experts as a result of criminogenic social conditions. Each tends to regard the other's views as both ignorant and missing the broader point.

Yankelovich's first and perhaps most insightful rule is his insistence that to have durable influence on public knowledge and attitudes, experts must identify and work from the public's framework. While many experts and public opinion assessors overlook this lesson, tabloid and broadsheet newspaper editors (see Chapter 7) and political leaders (see Chapter 8) have internalized it by forgoing dispassionate analysis of crime and punishment in favour of more emotional and moralistic engagement. The tabloids remain powerful in part because their approach to social problems resonates strongly with the emotional framework upon which many people rely. Though Tony Blair came to power in part due to his ability to address the public's concerns about crime on this emotional level, the challenge for leaders is to find a way to move beyond that starting point and to introduce the more rational and technical kinds of evidence that can facilitate improved policies in ways that honour the public's emotional framework. It is this melding of emotional knowledge and rational knowledge that Arie Freiberg (2001) advocates when he calls for affective, as well as effective, justice. Deliberative exercises could provide these opportunities.

Kennedy (2000: 901–2) offers insights which have important implications for the rules of public engagement:

Indeed the failure of criminologists and other criminal justice experts to master the sacred stories of victim suffering with their dispassionate statistical analyses suggests that detachment may be the wrong posture to adopt in the face of passion. In folk terms, passion—even irrational passion—is sometimes best tamed by facilitating expression. When you tell someone who is agitated or upset to simply 'calm down,' this often makes them more agitated because your detachment signals to them that you fail to comprehend the enormity of that which is upsetting them. Asking a distraught person to tell you what is the matter—to express what ails them—can be a more productive way of getting them to calm down.

Moreover, though emotional engagement with mass-mediated crime is most often associated with the elicitation of 'hatreds, enmities, prejudices and distortions', the 'inherently ambiguous' nature of public attitudes about crime and punishment allows as well for successful appeals to the 'sentimental altruist in us' (Sparks, 2001: 210).

In practical terms, experts accustomed to logical and rational decision-making are unlikely to be swayed to incorporate the kinds of emotional or moral information that are typically set aside in the interest of objectivity, unless a powerful case to do so is made in a logical and rational way—that is, couched in terms compatible with their preferred framework or mode of thinking. Similarly, the public will tend to resist being told their emotional engagement with crime issues is insufficient unless they can be convinced to incorporate rational knowledge with strong evidence expressed in emotional terms. This suggests, perhaps, that efforts to convince the public that community-based sentences are preferable to incarceration will yield the best results if framed in terms of public safety[17] (Indermaur, 2002), or in a way that emphasizes the moral value of restitution—rationales which are emotionally engaging as well as rational. Victim-centred mediation and restorative justice approaches also show promise in this regard because they have an emotional resonance.

'Bees in bonnets'

In two related rules, Yankelovich demands reaching out to the public, first by identifying the public's 'pet preoccupations' and addressing these first, and then by convincing the public that their views really matter (1991: 163). This is because, as he puts it, when 'people have a bee in their bonnets they will not pay attention until it is heeded' (1991: 246). It is the ability of participants to keep an open mind that distinguishes deliberation from mere discussion (Barabas, 2004), and bees in bonnets make participants less receptive to new ideas and impede deliberation.

Successive Labour governments appear to have embraced these rules. This is evident in the rhetoric about 'listening' to citizens, and more practically with the Blair government's 'Big Conversation',[18] dubbed 'the most sophisticated consultative exercise in British political history' (*Economist*, 2003). More recently, upon becoming Prime Minister, Gordon Brown has made a commitment to 'renew people's trust in government' (Brown, 2007), and both he and his justice minister, Jack Straw, advocate the use of citizens' juries to consider proposals for a bill of rights and a written constitution (Webster, Ford and Riddel, 2007). Though these are encouraging developments, it is still too early to tell whether the Brown government will actively approach the goals of public consultation and trust renewal any differently than the Blair government did.

Yankelovich insists that public apathy disappears once leaders show a genuine interest in what the public has to say. The problem for leaders in governments facing low levels of public confidence is to demonstrate the genuineness of that interest. Rod Morgan

---

[17] However, such a commitment to crime reduction metrics could backfire, as it assumes crime can be markedly reduced through policy intervention.

[18] The initiative solicited text messages from citizens and set up a website where citizens could go to air their views and to indicate which issues were most pressing to them.

(2002) makes a related point: ignorance or lack of public knowledge is not the same as lack of opinion. People have opinions when pressed on topics they know little about, relying on various cues, 'cognitive heuristics' (Luskin, Fishkin and Jowell, 2002), and the underlying values to form them. Morgan points out that most people are relatively uninformed about the pros and cons of adopting the Euro, for instance, but will quickly formulate a position given the information and the motivation to do so.

As an additional rule, Yankelovich believes that experts should not be relied upon to present issues to the public, as the value frameworks of experts and those of the public tend to conflict. Political leaders can present the 'value component of choices' in ways that purportedly value-neutral experts usually cannot. These rules highlight the need for research brokerages (Blumstein and Petersilia, 1995) that can distil from research the important policy-relevant findings, assimilate these with the wider concerns and normative judgments of the public that are informed by particular cultural considerations (Tonry and Green, 2003), and provide a buffer between both experts and the public as well as experts and policymakers (Hough, Jacobson and Miller, 2003; Indermaur, 2002; Roberts et al, 2003: ch 10). They also highlight the need for what might be called 'public judgment facilitators'— professionals who lead the process and who specialize in occupying that buffer zone.

Coming to public judgment is hard, time-consuming work, and the public cannot move beyond mass opinion and achieve public judgment unassisted. It requires a partnership between experts and the public. Experts play the role of information provider, advising the public with an up-to-date view of the current state of existing knowledge on the topic and providing a forecast of the likely consequences of the choices they face. Yankelovich's principal lesson is that information is a necessary but insufficient condition for attitude change, and that access to knowledge does not necessitate attitudinal change and durable, considered opinions. Thus, this partnership is formed with an important caveat: it does not represent a traditionally one-directional, pedagogical relationship. Citizens are not simply meant to absorb information and knowledge from the experts. Instead, they are meant to engage in a dialogue, voicing existing opinions and attitudes, debating the issues they face. These criteria demonstrate why most existing efforts intended to inform the public about the experience of

crime and punishment are lacking, as the Home Office commissioned Auld and Halliday reports illustrate.

Auld, Halliday, and the Prospects of Public Education

In 2001, the British government commissioned two important reports on the penal system that reference notions of public
knowledge and public opinion. Lord Justice Auld (2001) reviewed
practice in the criminal courts, and John Halliday (Home Office,
2001b) carried out a comprehensive review of the sentencing
framework in England and Wales. Though the Auld and Halliday
reports were intended in part to address apparent low levels of public confidence in the criminal justice system,[19] they came to very
different conclusions regarding the public's role in any subsequent
reforms. Auld's approach was dismissive: 'The proper approach
is to make the system fair and efficient and, if public ignorance
stands in the way of public confidence, take steps adequately to
demonstrate to the public that it is so' (Auld, 2001: ch 4, para 32).
Halliday's approach was actively educative and highly sensitive
to the state of public confidence in the system. However, neither
offers satisfactory solutions.

Auld's suggestion that the dissemination of current practice is
the way forward is inadequate for several reasons. Public confidence tends to rise considerably when the public are informed
about actual details of the criminal justice system (Home Office,
2001b: app 5, fig 2, 110), and 75 per cent of respondents in public
education exercises are 'surprised' by what they learn (Chapman
et al, 2002). Both of these findings suggest current means of dissemination are insufficient within existing media infrastructures.
Were it otherwise, the public would be more confident and better
informed than they are. In addition, selling the public the wisdom
of current practice does not help them work through the ambivalent attitudes crime and punishment issues often produce and to
develop considered views. There is little durability to unconsidered views, and emotive media coverage and populist rhetoric

[19] This is evidenced by the number of recent Home Office research studies
commissioned to look into it (Home Office, 2001b: app 5; 2004; Hough and
Roberts, 1998, 2004; Mattinson and Mirrlees-Black, 2000; Mirrlees-Black, 2001,
2002; Page, Wake and Ames, 2004), and the educational programmes the Home
Office has developed to impact it (Chapman, Mirrlees-Black and Brawn, 2002;
Mirrlees-Black, 2002).

may be enough to undermine any gains these programmes produce. Thus, proposals for better dissemination and better public education are fundamentally flawed.

Though Halliday's assessments of public views[20] also indicated low levels of knowledge in the existing system,[21] these views nonetheless 'informed its recommendations for a new framework...' (Home Office, 2001b: executive summary, para 0.5).[22] Auld has a point when he cautions 'against attempting insufficiently informed reforms in response to perceptions by some of injustice or discrimination and against treating such perceptions as proxies for a low level of public confidence' (Auld, 2001: ch 1, para 32). Two of the three surveys on which Halliday relied provided respondents with no new information nor a deliberative forum, and the one survey that did could hardly be characterized as facilitating public judgment. The 'General Public Sample', Halliday explains, 'were *given key facts about crime and sentencing* via a booklet, a seminar or a video and then re-interviewed', becoming what he terms the 'Informed Public Sample' (Home Office, 2001b: app 5, 108, emphasis added).

All groups improved their knowledge and confidence significantly, but in spite of these apparent gains, with the possible exception of the seminar, these educative approaches do not generate the deliberation and dialogue needed to produce durable public judgment. What is required is the development of informed preferences for which citizens take responsibility and which endure over time in the face of emotive rhetoric and the next high-profile tragedy. Instead, these approaches engage the public on a technical and informational level—an expert's framework—disallowing the release of 'bees in bonnets' before any new information is introduced.

---

[20] The assessments Halliday used are described as follows: 'Two were face-to-face interviews with the general public: one to give representative views of the general population; the other the views of a small sub-group that had been given information about crime and sentencing. The third was a postal-survey of ten criminal justice system practitioner groups' (Home Office, 2001b: app 5, 108).

[21] This includes widespread public ignorance about who decides sentences in criminal cases, the range of sentences available to sentencers, and an underestimation of the average length of custodial sentences (Home Office, 2001b).

[22] That public views not only 'informed' Halliday's review but were actually sought after highlights the importance of a better means of assessing the informed will of the public.

Halliday's optimism about these educative methods comports with the conventional wisdom summarized by Roberts and Hough (2002b), who hope their own extensive work in this area 'will help accelerate a movement towards the use of public opinion research in which attitudes to punishment (and other criminal justice issues) are measured after respondents *have been given sufficient information* about the issue at hand' (Roberts and Hough, 2002b: 4, emphasis added). Based on the same conventional wisdom, the Home Office stepped up efforts to educate the public by publishing and widely disseminating an informative leaflet about sentencing practice and the criminal justice system (Home Office, 2001a).[23] As a complement to these approaches, experts also advocate the utilization of new communication technologies to counteract public misconceptions about sentencing practice, misconceptions that are derived from inaccurate media portrayals and populist political spin (Hough and Roberts, 1998; Roberts and Hough, 2002a; Roberts et al, 2003).

Since knowledge levels are so low to begin with, these efforts are certainly likely to improve the present state of public knowledge, at least marginally and temporarily. The goals they serve are sound, but these approaches do not go far enough. They fail to reconcile the framework disparity and deny opportunities for the public to air existing views, consider all options and consequences, work through ambivalences, and take responsibility for choices. Instead, these efforts only provide information and rely on a one-way exchange: 'the expert speaks, the citizen listens' (Yankelovich, 1991: 60).

The more defensible view is an enhanced hybrid of aspects of both Auld and Halliday. Yes, public knowledge is low and needs to be improved, as Auld and Halliday agree. Auld is right that surveys are poor measures of informed public opinion and should not be used as a basis for deciding matters of policy. However, it is not enough for the government simply to do what it sees as best and then to sell this to the public. Halliday is right to argue that more is needed, but the methods Halliday employed to arrive at this conclusion are themselves flawed. Deliberative opinion assessments, including Deliberative Polls, citizens' juries, consensus conferences, study circles, national issue forums, and planning cells

---

[23] See Mirrlees-Black (2001) for Home Office research into the practicality and effectiveness of these educative methods.

provide the alternative public spaces where the dialogue necessary to facilitate working through to public judgment can occur (see Ackerman and Fishkin, 2004: 233 for a review of these models). Though the weekend allotted for the Deliberative Poll provides an insufficient time frame to facilitate the three stages of public judgment, it can move citizens beyond shallow engagement of the consciousness-raising phase toward working through ambivalences and toward resolution. Yankelovich's public judgment is an ideal, probably unachievable through small-scale institutional reform and political innovation. But the Deliberative Poll shows promise in yielding the kind of durable considered judgments that politicians and the media would find more reliable (Hough and Park, 2002; Luskin et al, 2002).

Conclusion

The conventional wisdom about improving the state of public opinion about crime usually overlooks the importance of deliberation in the generation of durable and informed preferences. Public education programmes rely instead on flawed, one-way exchanges between the expert and the public, insufficient to make a lasting impact on public knowledge and attitudes. These oversights mean that even the most sophisticated assessment procedures typically fail to provide the forum for people to express existing views and make room for new information, to consider fully the impact of that information, to try to reconcile ambivalent attitudes, and to take responsibility for the consequences of their opinions.

Only methods embracing public deliberation and fostering the conditions to achieve public judgment are sufficient to generate the kind of informed and considered public preferences that could justify the level of political deference public preferences currently receive. Because most typical conceptions of public opinion are not based on deliberation, public opinion remains only that—uninformed, unconsidered opinion—lacking validity on contentious issues, measuring top-of-the-head reactions to questions about which little is known. Typical assessments of public opinion provide a poor justification for policy, and remain susceptible to exploitation by those of all ideological affiliations with axes to grind. At precisely the time when notions of the will of the public have acquired such political currency, these views are simultaneously being assessed more frequently and in ways that lack both depth and validity.

Deliberative Polls are able to locate informed public opinion by first enabling its creation, something traditional assessments of public knowledge and opinion cannot accomplish. Deliberative Polls redress oversights in the conventional wisdom by opening up the traditional, expert-to-public communicative channels to two-way traffic, and through the process of deliberation, provide a clearer picture of the informed public will that is less susceptible to distortion and selective interpretation. Institutionalizing the Deliberative Poll as a supplement to existing assessments could help correct the 'comedy of errors', provide politicians the political cover required to de-escalate the political standoff that crime has become, and offer assessments of the public will that are more defensibly invoked and less susceptible to penal populist manipulation. Deliberative assessments provide a corrective to the flawed but powerful surrogates that now stand in for the informed public will and offer elected leaders clearer indicators of the public's preferences when they act in the public's name.

The final chapter carries this analysis forward by fleshing out a range of proposals that comprise a deliberative approach to public consultation on crime and punishment to help neutralize penal populism. The approach is intended to create informed public judgment to oppose the poor surrogates for public opinion, and to bolster democratic legitimacy.

11

Effecting Penal Climate Change

Penal Populism and Political Culture

In the past three decades, changes in English political culture have made the public voice a powerful influence in penal policy decision-making. It is undeniable that many Western governments have recently succumbed to populist pressures in shaping crime and penal policy. At times the source of this populist pressure is brought to bear through the headlines of the tabloid press, and at others through the findings of the numerous opinion polls that are disseminated via the news media. Still at other times the public voice is articulated in more direct ways, for instance, in the petitions and clip-out coupons members of the public sent to the Home Secretary following the trial of the two boys who killed James Bulger.

The ubiquity of public opinion assessments in English life parallels an increase in the willingness of most politicians and many sentencers to defer to them. This deference is often used as either grounds to justify or to reject certain policy directions. Partnered with the media representations, deference to public opinion plays a key role in setting the agendas of policymakers to favour some policy considerations over others. It has even forced judges to pass sentences they themselves believe unduly harsh, because, as one remorseful English senior judge stated in his own defence after such a case, he was 'scared of what the world would say' if he did not (quoted in Hough, Jacobson and Millie, 2003: 57).

As this book has endeavoured to show, the interrelation between the press, public opinion, and political leadership in England is problematic for at least three reasons. First, as indicated in the preceding chapter, press opinion and public opinion are not always the same, and to regard them as such, as is typically done, is reckless. Second, as the Bulger case coverage examined in Chapter 7 indicates, the press, most notably the tabloids—the papers with the largest readerships—routinely fail to present readers with sufficient contextual information even to begin to formulate informed views, falling far short of the criteria needed for readers to work through to achieve Yankelovich's public judgment. Third, changes in English political culture have led to the dominance and legitimization of some discourses at the expense of others. This means that privileged discourses are those propagated by those media outlets best at appearing to assume the role of 'the public's' ambassador. When policymakers and politicians engage with the tabloid press in a dialogue about penal policy matters, they explicitly and implicitly communicate that the tabloid press are important contributors to the debate. This ascribes to the tabloid press a degree of legitimacy that it might have otherwise lacked in the eyes of the public, relegating and virtually silencing expert discourses.

Joining these three threads together, it follows that the government routinely takes into account the convictions of an unrepresentative press that stands as an inaccurate barometer of the public will and that has failed to provide a forum for the public to process fully the issues it raises in its name. Debates over the most appropriate penal policy priorities and options—even under the comparatively well-insulated conditions which defined the first post-war stage of English penal policymaking that Ryan describes—are fraught with difficulties and compromises, and these debates only increase in difficulty when the agendas are defined by emotive and visceral media-driven sentiment. Again many of these factors are culturally variable and culturally derived.

Of course, communicative rationality is not entirely dead in England, even in the face of the harshest public criticism. The fact that much of the influence formally held by liberal elites has been lost to populist influences should not be allowed to give the impression that elites in England are powerless. The fact that the killers of James Bulger served their entire sentences in local authority secure children's homes, and that they have been released, and no less with anonymity, is testimony to the fact that some insulation still exists between elites in the criminal justice system and the public. However, public resistance to the Parole Board's decision to release Thompson and Venables indicates that some mismatch still exists between the public's apparent will and the convictions of elites. With the pressure for politicians to engage more with the public, and with the structure of the political culture as it is, unless some balance is better struck, these now tentatively acceptable mismatches could become problems the government cannot ignore.

The pool of criminological discourse is teeming with examinations of many of these issues. However, what is lacking in the literature on the interaction between crime, politics, public opinion, and the media is a convincingly pragmatic prescription for improving these contingencies, for bringing about a state of penal détente. Much of the literature on these topics concludes with, by now, a rather well-worn set of remedial proposals that amount to an attempt to re-insulate policymaking processes and sentencing practice from the heat of punitive public opinion and from the scrutiny of an uninformed public. The establishment of sentencing guidelines (in part to shield judges from exposure to public and press opprobrium), independent research brokerages (to act as a buffer between the two communities of research and policymaking), and public education programmes (ostensibly to correct the inaccuracies about issues of crime and punishment that tend to dominate the public discourse) are three typical favourites.

Arguably, none of these solutions can be characterized as pragmatic in the short term. Both the missions to draft and to enforce comprehensive and legitimate sentencing guidelines are notoriously fraught with peril (Tonry, 2002). The commitment to the idea of an independent research institute to bridge the two communities has yet to be found outside a small group of scholars (see Tonry and Green, 2003). Public education programmes, as typically conceived (for example, Hough, Jacobson and Millie, 2003; Roberts and Hough, 2002a; Roberts et al, 2003), are susceptible to criticism because of the agenda-driven quality they can acquire. These are often intended to disabuse the public of particular oversights and omissions believed to conduce toward punitive attitudes (erroneous beliefs in a lenient judiciary, the financial costs of imprisonment, the failure of harsh punishment to deter) while ignoring others that do not fit that agenda (high attrition rates, the consistency of recidivism rates across time and space, discouraging rehabilitation programme evaluations). Though public engagement in a more deliberative form is an ambitious and sensible component of the prescriptions outlined below, public *education* implies a paternalistic elitism that has not served penal policy experts well for some time now.

As discussed below, because legitimacy appears linked more to democratic process than outcomes, the participatory, more civically engaged role that members of the public will play in deliberative exercises shows promise in helping to generate social capital and to bolster government legitimacy. If one accepts the premise that the penal populism of the last few decades has been driven by deficits in legitimacy, then formally institutionalizing real deliberation in popular-political practice could have the additional effect of limiting penal populist incentives. This appears to be one lesson to be learned from Nordic political culture.

This final chapter first makes the case against re-insulating penal policymaking processes from public influence, favouring instead an embrace of more participatory arrangements. It then briefly outlines several 'root and branch' anti-populism reform proposals for effecting penal climate change. The root-based reform efforts centre on embracing aspects of more deliberative consensus democracies in order to bring about changes in the English penal climate to help de-politicize penal policymaking and make it a variable-sum game. Since features of consensus political culture have prophylactic effects on penal populism, all opportunities to effect this kind of cultural change by structural reform should be embraced. This includes reforming journalistic norms and practices to be more facilitative of public deliberation.

The branch-based reforms consist of an extensive roll-out of deliberative opinion assessment tools, like the Deliberative Poll, to help better assess the informed public will in order to render more defensible a politician's decision to use it to guide policy action. This roll-out would entail using Deliberative Polls more often and routinely, for instance, as a component of the British Crime Survey, as well as on an ad hoc basis, for instance, in the wake of particularly distressing high-profile crimes to help defuse and de-escalate public anxieties, render decision-making more reflective and judicious, and assess more considerately the extent and intensity of public concern.

Deliberative means of bringing a wider range of available knowledges to bear on policy debates are just as useful in Norway as they are in England or the USA, where only their urgency is greater. Though consensual political cultures appear to be less susceptible to penal populist ignition, they are certainly not fire-proof. The commodification of the news, the profit motive of the news media, and the expansion of its platforms all demand that new configurations of the public sphere be developed in order to foster deliberation and communicative rationality.

The Case against Re-Insulation

To advocate a return to the days of insulated *cognoscenti* influence in English penal affairs is futile and misguided, as it cannot return in the form it previously existed (Loader, 2005). Too much has changed, probably irrevocably, to make that possible. Though a case can be made for an insulated model of penal policymaking, one which 'protect[s] criminal justice policy from sound-bite populism...[and] rebuild[s] some conditions in decision making that insulate individual decisions from direct popular pressures' (Zimring, Hawkings and Kamin, 2001: 15), there is sufficient reason to believe that most insulation efforts are bound to fail. For one thing, the resentment that built up in response to the British *cognoscenti*'s own insulation from practitioner and public influence was instrumental in the subsequent decline in expert credibility. Attempting to re-establish pre-existing structural arrangements without a comprehensive restructuring of the political culture will accomplish little. The re-insulation of penal policymaking will remain a fruitless enterprise as long as the tabloid press continue to be powerful agenda setters, politicians continue to fail to resist the tabloid, law-and-order agenda en masse, and the public continues to be both fascinated by, and concerned about, crime and punishment.

'Communicative capacity' and state legitimacy

Another even more compelling reason that de-insulation and wider public consultation should be embraced is the benefits they can yield in terms of social solidarity and democratic legitimacy. Interpersonal trust in strangers may stand as an adequate measure of social solidarity, which according to Habermas, is the 'scarcest resource in complex societies' (Jacobsson, 1997: 73). Habermas contends that 'the forces of social solidarity can today be regenerated in the forms of communicative practices of self-determination' (quoted in Outhwaite, 1994: 149). This suggests that trust and social solidarity, which are associated with the beneficial characteristics of consensual democracies, particularly Norway, can be strengthened through public deliberation.

Jacobsson (1997) argues that legitimacy deficits most often result from a breakdown in 'discursive will formation'. Her reasoning is straightforward and dovetails well with the literatures on public opinion formation and more specifically with the case for deliberative democracy (Fishkin, 1995). That the formation of the public will is discursive, or the result of deliberation, distinguishes this concept from other conceptions of public opinion which are concerned with the aggregation of individual preferences without deliberation. The discursive component means that public preferences and the public will are assessed through deliberation *before* a policy is implemented, so that both the public's views and the policy in question acquire 'legitimation through previous deliberation' (Jacobsson, 1997: 78). This is opposed to the kind of legitimation that is sought rhetorically, after the fact, when deliberation does not occur, usually assessed in a static and silent snapshot of the often uninformed preferences of atomized citizens in an opinion poll. 'A common will, then, is not given from the beginning and "discovered," but is formed in a process of deliberation and negotiation where new perspectives may be taken into account, new information added, preferences changed and so on. In fact, one of the functions of deliberative will formation—of having to present reasons that must be acceptable to others to survive the deliberative process—is precisely to reshape preferences' (Jacobsson, 1997: 70–1).

Jacobsson believes that states are faced with two concerns that ultimately affect their legitimacy—their 'governing capacity' and their 'communicative capacity'. Governing capacity refers in part to the perceived efficiency with which the state is seen to govern, but her 'thesis would be that the probability of a future legitimacy deficit is as much a function of the state's communicative capacity as of its efficiency. Generally speaking, legitimacy is even more crucial for a political regime when it cannot guarantee efficiency' (Jacobsson, 1997: 79). What this suggests is that if the aim is to bolster flagging democratic legitimacy in a country like England or the USA, the way in which the public will is determined is even more important than what is done with it. 'What needs to be improved is the communicative character of the actual law making practices, i.e. their openness for inflow of discursively formed opinion' (Jacobsson, 1997: 78). The implementation of deliberative structures to increase the government's communicative capacity would appear to be a more promising means of building legitimacy from the ground up than those attempts to increase state legitimacy from above, through more legislation and tougher responses to crime. These improvements are hindered, not helped, by re-insulating penal policymaking.

Deliberative or dialogic democracy is a 'matter of attitude—a willingness to listen and to take the perspective of others into account before opting for a special policy line...[but] deliberatively formed opinion cannot effectively influence formal decision making unless there is an institutional infrastructure to support it' (Jacobsson, 1997: 78). A willingness is not enough. It must be supported by institutional practices and 'anchored in a more encompassing political culture' with compatible structural supports. Exercises like the Big Conversation that Blair launched and the citizens' juries Brown has promised might be viewed as means to improve government's communicative capacity, but these public consultation forums are relatively unsupported in existing institutional structures. What is required is the will and the means for existing or new institutions embedded within civil society both to create and then accommodate public judgment.

No participation without public judgment

John Stuart Mill believed 'certain types of political institution will form certain types of human being' (Johnstone, 2000: 168). Johnstone echoes the call for 'strong publics' (Fraser, 1993), referred to in the previous chapter, arguing that the public's involvement in penal policymaking should evolve beyond merely being listened to by policymakers. They should be more directly involved in shaping policy rather than less. To support his participatory agenda, he cites Pateman (1970: 42–3) who contends that '[p]articipation develops and fosters the very qualities necessary for it; the more individuals participate the better able they become to do so'. Johnstone also believes that greater public involvement will in turn yield greater understanding and moderation in public views and attitudes, a view supported by some comparative research (Barker, 2006). It is a reasonably convincing case, and one that seems to find support in a rather unlikely place.

In a series of articles in the *Sunday Times* (18 January 2004, 25 January 2004), American libertarian political scientist Charles Murray claims the attitudes of criminal justice elites—'meaning the people who run the British police, court and prison systems'— are more progressive and liberal than those readers of *The Times* who participated in his survey. Though Murray tries to employ relative elite liberalness to defend his contention that these elites are out of touch with the general public, one could use the same evidence to support the contention that knowledge about the criminal justice system—and his elite practitioners are arguably among those most familiar with the finer workings of that system—and close proximity with it might liberalize views.

However, regardless of whether or not participation yields more progressive attitudes, Johnstone's arguments do not go far enough to foster the kind of broad-based deliberation that will lead to the more defensible goal of more knowledgeable and civic-minded citizens who will be better able to contribute meaningfully. Participation without first formulating durable judgments about the issues might make participants less repressive and a bit more liberal in their attitudes, but it is unlikely to contribute to better, more deliberative policies. Nonetheless, the case against re-insulation is a strong one.

Public Engagement

Though the media and mass-mediated public sentiments continue to shape the course of penal policy debates, this does not mean that nothing can be done to cool the policymaking environment and to limit the extremes of the penal climate. The questions then become: Can experts do anything effective and substantive to impact resistant political predispositions that prevent the internalization of elite discourse? Should experts be content to settle for any long-term cultural change they can effect, or should they ignore such macro-efforts aimed at changing cultural sensibilities and instead focus on smaller scale projects like improving the quality of the media discourse? Whatever the strategy, it seems clear that predispositions are important, though much more resistant to change than the other factors likely are.

To illustrate, Zaller (1992: 37) borrows a useful concept from cognitive psychology: A 'schema' is 'a cognitive structure that organizes prior information and experience around a central value or idea, and guides the interpretation of new information and experience'. He argues that individuals have more than one schema on hand for a given phenomenon. He cites Tesser (1978: 291–8, 307, emphasis in original) who writes: 'An attitude at a particular point in time is the result of a constructive process... And, *there is not a single attitude toward an object* but, rather, any number of attitudes depending on the number of schemas available for thinking about the objects... [P]ersons do not have a single feeling of evaluation of an object. Feelings vary depending upon the particular cognitive schema we "tune in" '. This suggests that prominently presented counter-discourses can activate alternative schemas, thus allowing for attitudes to shift toward particular issues. The considerable ambivalence that characterizes English and American attitudes to crime and punishment suggests the existence of dormant alternative schemas that could be activated to counter the more repressive and punitive ones many are currently primed to tune in. However, this again requires the ready availability of legitimated counter-discourses to join up with alternative schemas, something the homogenized English tabloid discourse fails to provide.

As exemplified in an elite-led shift in racial opinions in the USA over the course of the last 70 years, which are 'among the most deeply felt of mass opinions', Zaller (1992: 11) contends that, over the long term, 'exposure to elite discourse appears to promote support for the ideas carried in it'. However, when elites clash over issues, people revert back to their political ideologies or partisan predispositions, and tend to fall in line with those elites aligned with their ideology. When pressed on controversial issues even the most politically unaware will tend to draw upon the most salient and memorable ideas available to make choices (Zaller, 1992). The political rhetorics about crime in England and the USA currently share many commonalities. Tory and Labour Party spokespeople espouse similarly tough and punitive agendas, and as witnessed in the general election campaign of 2005, even the Liberal Democrats have adopted similar rhetoric in their embrace of so-called 'tough liberalism'. Though criminological experts tend to represent a counter-consensus by agreeing on the whole that such approaches are ill advised and counterproductive, the discourses they generate go virtually unheard in most of the popular media discourse. There are very few politically legitimated counter-discourses to hook into alternative schemas, especially when little separates the parties on crime. So crime has become, in practical terms, a consensus issue that only the more educated public, through a greater awareness of the wider issues, are in any informed position to question (Sasson, 1995). If a penal policy counter-discourse can only be expected to have limited influence on the well-educated in the best of times, then there is little reason to believe it will find much favour among anyone else, especially when it cannot find legitimation in the popular press and is opposed by a bi- or even tri-partisan political consensus.

Rather than allow politicians and the media to represent or misrepresent their views, Ryan (2003: 138) advises the 'Hampstead liberals' to learn new ways of engaging outwardly and directly with the public. According to Ryan, the failure of the liberal elites to engage outwardly with the public, favouring instead to engage only inwardly with others with whom many views are shared, is dangerous:

> Of course, that these interlocking networks, sucking as they do more and more people into governance, carry the potential to limit effective, principled opposition and to stifle genuine creative thinking is perhaps obvious, and those enjoying the fruits of these new networks, including academics like myself, might well reflect on this. However, the real danger of this continuing insider strength is that this is exactly what it is, it looks *inwards* rather than *outwards*, barely moving beyond the increasingly diffuse machinery of central government at a time when the political parties are being forced more and more to engage with the public voice. (Ryan, 2003: 138, emphasis in original)

Many agree that outward public engagement and the utilization of new communication technologies are both necessary steps to fostering communicative rationality (Hough et al, 2003; Roberts and Hough, 2002a; Roberts et al, 2003; Ryan, 2003).

Schlesinger and Tumber (1994: 104) found that crime policy pressure groups in Britain strategically target the broadsheets and public service broadcasting as the 'educative vehicles' used to reach 'opinion formers', rather than aim for the tabloids:

> The evidence suggests that this approach would seem to be well founded. So far as crime-related items in the press are concerned, the quality papers carry twice as many views or comments from experts, elites, and members of pressure groups as the popular papers, and about 25 per cent more than the mid-market press. This restricted conception of the media that count—which excludes the popular press as largely resistant to policy discourse—is coupled with a strong awareness of the need to lobby through the parliamentary process in order to influence policy formation.

However, while the broadsheets may be the only game in town for penal issue pressure groups, targeting of the broadsheets mistakenly assumes that because the voices of elites are *voiced* in the quality press, they are *listened to* as well. This is not necessarily the case, as Labour leaders have shown in their attentiveness to the agendas of the mid-market and tabloid press.[1]

In the long term, pressure groups might be better served by targeting mid-market and tabloid audiences, those readers with whom Labour politicians (and indeed their Conservative colleagues) are so eager to connect. The pressure groups are most capable of presenting counter-discourses, as they are familiar with and routinely employ media strategies. Though the agendas of pressure groups encourage the 'cherry picking' of findings from scientifically rigorous academic knowledge, it is certainly unrealistic to believe that the discourse of academic criminology will find a public audience on its own power, without the vehicle that pressure groups provide in the popular press. In any case, that the tabloids are so important, and that they are 'largely resistant to policy discourse', is precisely why analyses of media discourses and their effects on political action are so important at this time in English political history.

Public Journalism

Journalistic culture and standards should be reformed to reflect the tenets of so-called civic or public journalism, and journalists should better provide deliberative forums for the public to consider the issues they face. Journalists and editors ought to play a more active role in shaping policy agendas as advocates of the people, treating viewers and readers as citizens, not merely as consumer audiences. Journalism should be more strongly committed to public advocacy, embracing its civic obligations to improve the quality of public debates in active partnership with citizens, moving beyond SLOPs and vox pop pieces toward civic activism. Public journalism has been successfully embraced with positive results in a number of US jurisdictions after prominent journalists there lobbied for this new approach to journalism in the early 1990s (Broder, 1990; Rosen, 1992). Though the public journalism movement survives today, it is—like the proposals for

---

[1] These comments also illustrate the changeability of cultural factors shaping media strategies and the priorities of politicians. For although Schlesinger and Tumber argue that the media that matter in regard to policy influence are the quality press and public service broadcasting, again the way Labour actively and successfully courted the tabloid and mid-market press indicates that these may now be the media that matter most.

an annual Deliberation Day (Ackerman and Fishkin, 2004) or for a deliberative branch of government (Leib, 2004)—a highly ambitious, though not unrealistic, proposition.

Though I have stressed throughout this book that greater forces than political cynicism and unscrupulous journalism are responsible for the current English penal climate, analysis of the coverage of the Bulger and Redergård cases in Chapter 7 demonstrates that the press are certainly not blameless in the perpetuation of penal populism. MP Peter Bottomley argues, 'The press is as important to democracy as is the House of Commons' (*Hansard*, col 668, 23 April 1993). However, he also points out that although the Bulger case got saturation coverage in all the papers, '240 two-year-olds die unnatural deaths each year, most of them predictable, most of them avoidable, and most of the means by which they die being given virtually no attention whatever' (*Hansard*, col 670, 10 June 1993). By routinely failing equally to impart the range of available discourses that might help citizens to account for and deal with the crimes they take such interest in, the media also fail adequately to outfit citizens for a responsible engagement of the issues. Instead, the shallow, sensationalized, overly simplified presentations found in some segments of the press serve only to tap into inchoate insecurities, inflaming them, without providing the informational tools necessary for the public to assess and to face them.

Some newspapers, especially the tabloids, appear to have adopted an appetite-driven approach to crime reporting which conjures the image of a primary school dinner lady defending the fast food menu offered her pupils on the grounds that it is what they want to eat. Tabloid newspapers do the same when they defend simplistic and sensationalist reporting by referencing circulation figures that far surpass those of other papers whose reporting is more considered and dispassionate. We all do things that are not good for us. Reading the tabloids may not be as hazardous as smoking two packs of Pall Malls a day, but when the views that are shaped by those tabloids affect the finer workings of the justice system, it is not unreasonable to call this a hazard. When the stakes are as high as they currently are concerning public perceptions of crime, and when those perceptions, however misguided and misinformed, drive public fears and public policies, then another approach is required. That approach needs to entail the opportunity and space for considered deliberation about social problems.

Making the press more accountable would help. The concentration of media ownership in Britain has meant that the Press Council has been weakened. An example from the Bulger case illustrates the toothlessness of the Press Complaints Commission (PCC). Early into the investigation the *Sun* ran the headline, 'Boy, 12, Is Held for Jamie Murder', though buried within the article the police directly contradict the headline by saying, 'We do not hold the murderer in these cells'. Labour MP Clive Soley repeatedly raised this issue and cited this example in Parliament and in meetings with journalists and editors whom he claims failed to find any problem with the paper's headline: 'There is an arrogance in the press which leads members of the press to believe that they do not have to say that anything is wrong. The headline is an example of press reporting that led me throughout the 1980s to fear for justice for individuals. The boy, who was not held for the murder at any time, was branded as the murderer' (*Hansard*, col 505, 10 June 1993). Soley goes on to explain how the PCC was unable to act on the case because the family of the boy could not be located to register a complaint because vigilante threats had forced them into hiding. As Labour MP Richard Corbett said in Parliament, 'Many people who feel wronged and damaged by the antics of the sewer *Sun* cannot meet the legal bills involved in taking the paper on. The *Sun* well knows that, which is why it abuses its position' (*Hansard*, col 675, 23 April 1993).

Though press ethics are taken more seriously in Norway, with benefits for the quality and variety of press discourses, changes in the press markets there as well are cause for concern, and the channelling of information between civil society and elected representatives needs improvement, even in consensus democracies. Though the flexible multi-party system in Norway may be an exception, parties have been slow to represent the concerns of the public in many countries (Andeweg, 1996; Jacobsson, 1997) and this can seed discontent. As Jacobsson (1997: 82) puts it:

Deficient communication between actors in civil society and the formal political system may result in a mismatch between societal interests and concerns and the policies that are put into place. This in turn may result in increasing divisions and an erosion of trust between policy makers and policy takers that may eventually express itself in the form of alienation from formal policies and other societal institutions and/or in various extra-parliamentary manifestations.

These communication streams can be improved with deliberative processes.

Deliberative Forums

Mathiesen has managed to achieve some approximation of a forum embracing the principles of Habermasian communicative rationality in Norway,[2] and Ryan believes elites must similarly learn better to engage in these public debates if the knowledge they have to bear is to have influence:

> ...it is easy to share Habermas's (1989) anguish about Western European countries in general that there is perhaps no longer a truly independent civic space in which critical public debate can take place. This anguish is not relieved by politicians resorting to private focus groups which treat their subjects as individual consumers rather than as members of civic groups negotiating collective solutions. In these circumstances 'public opinion' can all too easily become what politicians want it to become, a conduit for their own agendas masquerading as the public voice(s). But such anxieties are unlikely to go away, and future criminological agendas should be as much about exploring these difficult questions as about the nuts and bolts of penal policy. The public voice(s) is here to stay, from influential local and national talk shows to the fast growing and unregulated Internet which allows even the most enterprising first year student to engage national political figures in debate about punishment and crime. (Ryan, 1999: 18)

This suggests that a means must be found to combine public involvement and the fair and principled argumentation of communicative rationality.

Though political leaders must more courageously meet the challenge of balancing of public and press sentiment and other, more verifiable sources of knowledge (see Green, 2002: 219; Ramsbotham, 2003; Zimring, 2001), this is difficult to achieve in light of current political cultural trends in England. Institutionalized support structures need to be introduced to make it easier for the elected to resist penal populist currents. Facilitating public judgment through Deliberative Polling would help.

---

[2] In an effort to establish an insulated '*alternativ offentlighet*' or 'alternative public space' to debate penal issues, Mathiesen established KROM, the Norwegian Association for Penal Reform. The members include academics, practitioners, politicians, and prisoners who meet each year in the mountains outside Oslo. They maintain 'a culture where argumentation, well founded criticism and principled thinking are dominant values' (Mathiesen, 1996).

The well-documented tendency for politicians to act punitively in the name of an ambivalent public highlights the potential of public judgment on issues of crime and punishment. Consider for a moment the possibility that public judgment could be demonstratively achieved on penal issues. In achieving it, one of two things could happen: the first possibility is that the public chooses more punitive measures in full acceptance of the consequences that experts emphasize. Politicians would then have their mandate to continue on the path they have followed in recent decades. Though it could no longer be said that politicians were misreading the public's ambivalence as punitiveness, this would still not be good news for many elites. Harsh penal sanctions tend often to violate the moral standards and values of many liberal elites, some of whom may couch their normative opposition in instrumental arguments. The second possibility is that the public chooses other, perhaps less punitive options as a way forward, thus denying politicians the cynical opportunity to act punitively for politically expedient reasons, using public opinion as the justification. This would represent a double victory for elites, as their knowledge would have both instrumentally and normatively positive results.

In either case, it is more democratically defensible that public judgment come to substitute for the currently loose conceptions of public opinion that activists on all sides of penal policy debates can manipulate for their own ideological reasons. It seems that many criminological elites who bemoan their lack of influence, and speak disparagingly of an ignorant public, advocate public engagement only insofar as it serves their own particular agenda. The case for building public judgment sets a new normative standard for public engagement that is more difficult for activists to co-opt.

It must be noted that:

> To say that public judgment has been reached on an issue does not imply that people comprehend all of the relevant facts or that they agree with the views of elites. It does imply that people have struggled with the issue, thought about it in their own terms, and formed a judgment they are willing to stand by. It also means that if leaders understand the public's judgments, they have a stable context to work in—either to offer solutions that fit within the public's tolerances, or if they disagree with the public's judgment, to take their case forcefully to the public with full awareness that the public's views will not change easily. (Yankelovich, 1991: 42)

This second distinction is important. A preponderance of information or evidence might, in this model, conceivably destabilize existing public judgment if such evidence was powerful and compelling enough. Even public judgment is not fixed; it is only more durable and consistent than low-quality public opinion is. It is, therefore, changeable over time, though subject to limits of cultural predispositions and tolerances and not as easily changeable as low-quality public opinion. Criminological elites, via brokers or spokespeople, must forcefully take their case to the public, something which is currently not happening in terms that the public are willing to accept. This is because, recalling Yankelovich's distinction from the previous chapter, the frameworks to which the thinking of the public and elites adhere are incompatible. The public's emotional, values-based framework conflicts with the instrumental one experts most often use. Deliberative Polls can help to bridge this divide and address the framework disparity.

Six Ways of Institutionalizing Deliberation

Six proposals follow from this analysis. First, English political culture should be made less adversarial and thus less hospitable to populist responses to crime and punishment. Lijphart believes there are few drawbacks and clear benefits to the consensus model of democracy. Perhaps somewhat counterintuitively, there is little empirical evidence to suggest that the 'coalitional and consultative style of decision-making' in consensus democracies make them slower and more inefficient than majoritarian democracies (Lijphart, 1998: 105).

Consensual political institutions need fertile cultural soil to survive, and a broad-scale importation of consensual institutions into traditionally adversarial political cultures is likely to fail. However, Lijphart (1999: 307) points to Switzerland and Austria as examples of countries that have fostered consensual political cultures and structures in spite of historical legacies of internal conflict and civil war. Such change is possible, he argues, because political structure and political culture interact in 'a complex multi-directional system of causality' (Almond and Verba, 1963: 35). Therefore, the importation of consensual political structures can modify the political culture in which they reside, making it more consultative and consensual. This suggests that there is room for mixed models—for making adversarial models of democracy less so by incorporating features from consensus democracies. Introducing proportional representation electoral systems and increasing the number of viable political parties would be a start.

There are clear incentives for leaders to embrace change toward more consensual ways of doing business and to push for it from within, especially if increasing public confidence is a real priority. This would require more cross-party cooperation and consensus-building coalitions of the sort common in consensus democracies. However, the will to de-escalate politics is probably not enough, unless some bi-partisan agreement can be struck. For instance, David Cameron began his leadership of the Conservative Party in December 2005 espousing a new consensual politics in Britain to end the 'Punch and Judy show' politics that he believes is alienating young voters (BBC News, 6 December 2005). After Blair repeatedly ridiculed him for this in the House of Commons, Cameron has now promised a 'bare knuckle fight' with the government over the NHS (*Guardian*, 20 August 2007). This shows that de-escalating a standoff requires an agreement from all sides to disarm. Without structural changes to make the political process less adversarial, real behavioural changes are probably unlikely.

Second, Deliberative Polls ought to become standard features of the consultation processes informing criminal justice White Papers. This would clarify more satisfactorily the limits of public tolerance to proposed initiatives *before* they are initiated, thereby helping to avert politically and fiscally costly climbdowns. Their scope must be narrow to be effective, but DPs could clarify the public will on those crime control and penal policy issues most contested by professionals and politicians, like sentencing policy, and then more accurately determine the informed preferences of the public.

Third, DPs on one or two specific issues should be conducted with each, now annual, sweep of the British Crime Survey. Issues could shift with each sweep, with each revisited perennially, perhaps every five years, to determine the nature and extent of any change. This would allow up to five particularly contentious issues to be routinely reconsidered in depth by DP participants and would do much to clarify ambivalent and ambiguous public sentiments.

Ideally, the research brokerages mentioned above should take the lead in facilitating deliberative forums. This would remove both the potential for, and the appearance of, Home Office influence. Until such independent agencies are up and running, the Home Office could for now facilitate DPs and provide training for facilitators, supplemented by the charities, foundations, and think tanks that are already leading the way. Some might argue that the Home Office remains too close to government and could spin or bury DP findings to serve its own ends. Though possible, the protocols already binding the facilitation of DPs would minimize opportunities for conservative- or liberal-minded politicians, criminologists, or journalists to bias proceedings. Any research findings can be spun in self-serving ways, but by being more reliable and durable, DP results could considerably narrow the potential range of spin. Even under imperfect conditions, the DP represents a vast improvement on existing procedures.

Fourth, the DP should also be used to address more responsibly particularly pressing issues on an ad hoc basis, especially in the face of high-profile crimes. For instance, in the wake of the Bulger murder, a DP might have provided a more responsible means to consider questions about the age of criminal responsibility in England, or the value of secure accommodation for children. After the murder of Sarah Payne, it might have been used to consider more deliberatively the pros and cons of making sex offender registries publicly available. Or, following school caretaker Ian Huntley's murder of Holly Wells and Jessica Chapman, the DP might have provided the forum to consider the suitability and ethics of vetting procedures that discriminate on the basis of unsubstantiated allegations of prior misconduct.

Focusing DPs on high-profile issues might help to prevent uninformed views, misconceptions, and erroneous popular speculations from gaining the sort of momentum in the media that tends to press politicians to act hastily in response to signs of amplified public concern. High-profile issues like the few mentioned here are being publicly debated already, but they are most often moderated and mediated by the media and/or political leaders who must manage incentives to define and delimit the parameters of the debates in particularly counterproductive ways. Crime, the fear of it, and partisan political struggles to address both all make good copy, and in the current political culture of the English-speaking countries, politicians believe they are more electable when they appear as tough on crime as they can.

Fifth, as Indermaur and Hough (2002) advocate, politicians and other claims-makers who wilfully proliferate overly simplified or distorted assessments of current crime control and penal practice should be publicly 'named and shamed'. There ought to be consequences for leaders who know better but who fail to lead the way toward more fully considered views. This will be easier to implement once DPs are institutionalized.

Sixth, incentives to embrace the DP must be made more apparent to all constituencies concerned. For instance, because overall newspaper circulation in England has been in decline since the 1950s (Sparks, 1999) and the press market remains fiercely competitive, there are incentives for newspapers to rethink their approach to the news, and to retain and regain readers with journalism that is truly reader driven and civic minded. Criminal justice practitioners face a great deal of instability and constant change due in part to constantly shifting political priorities, many ostensibly driven by those of the public. Clarifying the will of publics on the most prominent issues they face could help stabilize practitioner priorities and approaches.

In addition, on matters of crime and justice—where the public is more supportive and tolerant of less punitive innovations in crime control than many politicians can admit when faced with simple opinion poll data or tabloid headlines indicating the opposite—DP results are likely to offer leaders more political room to manoeuvre, helping them to justify more effective crime and punishment policies that reach beyond the common punitive solutions. The public is likely to respond favourably to the democratic utility of the DP, as it is more true to the deliberative ethos at the heart of democracy and it re-establishes an unmediated link between the government and the governed.

Politicians and political parties must also be apprised of the political utility of more accurate and durable assessments of public judgment. If the public's trust and confidence in government is to be restored, leaders must do more than merely reflect the public's concerns back upon them; they must address those concerns. Part of this involves correcting misperceptions and erroneous beliefs rather than legitimating them. Political strategist Philip Gould (1998: 327–8) blames Labour's 1992 election defeat in part on the party's failure 'to gauge accurately the public mood'. To address this he conducted focus groups every night of the 1997 election campaign and found participants 'often feel insecure about their jobs, and are always worried about crime, the NHS, and schools for their children'. Parties typically target their messages to reflect those public concerns, regardless of the level of public knowledge about them. Gould's advertising background shaped how he tailored Labour's message to *reflect* public concerns and win the election, but the utilization of focus groups can do little to *assuage* those concerns. Leadership ought to entail the facilitation of public deliberation and rational reflection. Institutionalizing public deliberation is a way for governments both to be seen to address people's most pressing concerns while actually working simultaneously to help them formulate considered judgments about them and their solutions.

The recommendations to utilize more DPs are made with a very important caveat. Hough and Park (2002) regard the DP as one among many innovations that might be utilized to *change* public attitudes about crime and punishment. As this could imply a subtle ideological agenda, it differs from the deployment rationale embraced in this book, based on Fishkin's, which is focused instead on the DP's democratic utility. Though the 1994 Manchester DP tended to 'liberalize' public views about crime and punishment, what may be called the DP's *criminological* utility as such is only incidentally linked to its utility as a facilitator of better democracy. Had that DP proved actually to 'conservatize' public views overall and to make the public even more enthusiastic about 'banging up' offenders, this would not weaken the case for its *democratic* utility. The aim of these innovations is to improve the democratic process and increase democratic legitimacy by building public knowledge and fostering public judgment. Whether the considered positions of the public are deemed liberal or conservative in the political climate of the day is democratically irrelevant. That said, it is not surprising that the Manchester DP had overall liberalizing effects, as decades of public opinion research reached similar, though perhaps less empirically robust, conclusions. However, these two questions of utility should not to be conflated.

Critics may contend that these prescriptions are unrealistically utopian. Yet social change and shifts in sensibilities and political practices are often swift (Tonry, 2001, 2004b). Ryan (1999, 2003) reminds us that until relatively recently the English public were deemed by politicians to be too uninformed even to be considered relevant contributors to penal policy debates. Now the importance of public consultation and of building public confidence is recognized by most as self-evident. Most of the proposals outlined here amount merely to a better means of assessing the informed public will and, unlike radical visions elevating the role of 'strong publics' to decide matters of policy, most do not require radical political reform. Existing institutional frameworks can facilitate the usage of deliberative public judgment just as easily as they currently accommodate uninformed and unrefined public opinion. Politicians still retain the discretion to regard or disregard the public will, but the quality of the assessment of that will would be significantly enhanced.

Conclusion

Processes of deliberative will formation can serve a number of functions in fractured democracies like England's where strong partisan divisions and low public confidence are the norm. First, they can make more defensible determinations of public preferences on the range of issues facing a nation in ways that opinion polling and focus groups cannot. Second, they can hamper the ability of the cynical—be they politicians, journalists, activists, or experts—to distort less valid public opinion data that further their agendas. Third, they can limit the ability of populist politicians and parties to establish themselves through appeals to a poorly defined notion of 'the people'. Fourth, they can work toward eliminating the distrust between experts and the public by providing a forum in which all stakeholders can freely engage the issues. Fifth, they can reduce the number of humiliating policy U-turns and climbdowns that governments must often make after rushing through ill-considered knee-jerk legislation. Sixth, deliberative processes might help to foster the kind of civic engagement which characterizes nations with high social capital, a concept correlated with good governance, high public confidence and trust, lower punishment rates, and 'gentler' criminal justice systems.

References

Ackerman, B.A. and J.S. Fishkin (2004) *Deliberation Day*, New Haven: Yale University Press.

Aebi, M.F. and N. Stadnic (2007) *Council of Europe Annual Penal Statistics 2005*, Strasbourg: Council of Europe.

Albrecht, H.-J. (2001) 'Post-adjudication Dispositions in Comparative Perspective' in M. Tonry and R.S. Frase (eds) *Sentencing and Sanctions in Western Countries*, New York: Oxford University Press.

Allen, F.A. (1981) *The Decline of the Rehabilitative Ideal: Penal Policy and Social Purpose*, New Haven: Yale University Press.

Allen, R. (2003) '"There Must Be Some Way of Dealing with Kids": Young Offenders, Public Attitudes and Policy Change', *Youth Justice*, 2: 3–13.

Allern, S. (2007) Interview, Oslo, Norway, 8 March 2007.

Almond, G.A. and S. Verba (1963) *The Civic Culture: Political Attitudes and Democracy in Five Nations*, Princeton, NJ: Princeton University Press.

Altheide, D.L. (1996) *Qualitative Media Analysis*, London: Sage.

Althusser, L. (1971) *Lenin and Philosophy, and Other Essays* (trans. B. Brewster), London: Monthly Review Press.

Anderson, D.C. (1995) *Crime and the Politics of Hysteria: How the Willie Horton Story Changed American Justice*, New York: Times Books.

Anderson, P. and N. Mann (1997) *Safety First: The Making of New Labour*, London: Granta.

Andeweg, R.B. (1996) 'Elite-mass Linkages in Europe: Legitimacy Crisis or Party Crisis?' in J. Hayward (ed) *Elitism, Populism and European Politics*, 143–63, Oxford: Clarendon Press.

Archer, M.S. (1995) *Realist Social Theory: The Morphogenetic Approach*, Cambridge: Cambridge University Press.

Auld, LJ (2001) *Report of the Review of the Criminal Courts of England and Wales*, <http://www.criminal-courts-review.org.uk>.

Balvig, F. (2004) 'When Law and Order Returned to Denmark', *Journal of Scandinavian Studies in Criminology and Crime Prevention*, 5: 167–87

Barabas, J. (2004) 'How Deliberation Affects Policy Opinions', *American Political Science Review*, 98: 687–701.

Barclay, G. and C. Tavares (2000) *International Comparisons of Criminal Justice Statistics 1998*, London: Home Office Research and Statistics Directorate.

—— (2002) *International Comparisons of Criminal Justice Statistics 2000*, London: Home Office Research and Statistics Directorate.

Barclay, G. and C. Tavares (2003) *International Comparisons of Criminal Justice Statistics 2001*, London: Home Office Research and Statistics Directorate.

Barclay, G., C. Tavares and A. Siddique (2001) *International Comparisons of Criminal Justice Statistics 1999*, London: Home Office Research and Statistics Directorate.

Barker, V. (2006) 'The Politics of Punishing: Building a State Governance Theory of American Imprisonment Variation', *Punishment & Society*, 8: 5–33.

Bateman, T. (2006) 'Youth Crime and Justice: Statistical "Evidence", Recent Trends and Responses' in B. Goldson and J. Muncie (eds) *Youth Crime and Justice: Critical Issues*, 65–77, London: Sage.

BBC (2000) *Our Childhood*, Correspondent series, videocassette, 29 April 2000.

BBC News (2000) 'Young killers shown compassion', <http://news.bbc.co.uk/1/hi/programmes/correspondent/803151.stm> .

—— (2001a) 'Bulger mother's tortured life', <http://news.bbc.co.uk/1/hi/uk/1406511.stm>.

—— (2001b) 'Merseyside anger over killers' release', <http://news.bbc.co.uk/1/hi/uk/1402885.stm>.

—— (2007) 'Prison Absconder Numbers Unknown', <http://news.bbc.co.uk/1/hi/uk-politics/6236375.stm>.

Beck, U. (1992) *Risk Society: Towards a New Modernity*, London: Sage.

Beckett, A. (2001) 'Paul Dacre: the most dangerous man in Britain?', *Guardian*, 22 February 2001.

Beckett, K. (1997) *Making Crime Pay: Law and Order in Contemporary American Politics*, New York: Oxford University Press.

Bendix, R. (1963) 'Concepts and Generalizations in Comparative Sociological Studies', *American Sociological Review*, 28: 532–39.

Berrington, E. and P. Honkatukia (2002) 'An Evil Monster and a Poor Thing: Female Violence in the Media', *Journal of Scandinavian Studies in Criminology and Crime Prevention*, 3: 50–72.

Beveridge, W. (1942) *Social Insurance and Allied Services*, London: HMSO.

Billig, M., S. Condor, D. Edwards, M. Gane, D. Middleton and A. Radely (1988) *Ideological Dilemmas: A Social Psychology of Everyday Thinking*, London: Sage.

Bjerva, L.K. (2007) Interview, Oslo, Norway, 9 March 2007.

Bjørkeng, P.K. (2003) Interview, Oslo, Norway, 25 September 2003.

Blair, T. (1993a) 'Foreword', in C. Bryant and J. Smith (eds) *Reclaiming the Ground: Christianity and Socialism*, 9–12, London: Spire.

—— (1993b) 'Teach kids what's right...then get tough if they go wrong', *Sun*, 3 March 1993.

—— (2007) 'What I've learned', *Economist*, 31 May 2007.

Blumler, J.G. (1977) 'The Political Effects of Mass Communication', *Social Sciences: A Third Level Course, Mass Communication and Society Block 3, Units 7–8*, Milton Keynes, UK: Open University Press.

Blumler, J.G. and M. Gurevitch (1982) 'The Political Effects of Mass Communication' in M. Gurevitch, T. Bennett, J. Curran and J. Woollacott (eds) *Culture, Society and the Media*, 236–67, London: Routledge.

Blumler, J.G. and M. Gurevitch, A. (1995) *The Crisis of Public Communication*, London: Routledge.

Blumstein, A. (1993) 'Making Rationality Relevant—The American Society of Criminology 1992 Address', *Criminology*, 31: 1–16.

——(1997) 'Interaction of Criminological Research and Public Policy', *Journal of Quantitative Criminology*, 12: 349–61.

Blumstein, A. and J. Petersilia (1995) 'Investing in Criminal Justice Research' in J.Q. Wilson and J. Petersilia (eds) *Crime*, 465–88, San Francisco: ICS Press Institute for Contemporary Studies.

Blumstein, A., M. Tonry and A. Van Ness (2007) 'Cross-national Measures of Punitiveness' in M. Tonry and D.P. Farrington (eds) *Crime and Justice, Volume 33: Crime and Punishment in Western Countries, 1980–1999*, Chicago: University of Chicago Press.

Boltanski, L. (1999) *Distant Suffering: Morality, Media and Politics*, Cambridge: Cambridge University Press.

Bondeson, U. (2003) *Nordic Moral Climates: Value Continuities and Discontinuities in Denmark, Finland, Norway, and Sweden*, London: Transaction.

——(2005) 'Levels of Punitiveness in Scandinavia: Description and Explanations' in J. Pratt, D. Brown, M. Brown, S. Hallsworth and W. Morrison (eds) *The New Punitiveness: Trends, Theories, Perspectives*, 189–200, Collumpton, Devon: Willan.

Bottoms, A.E. (1977) 'Reflections on the Renaissance of Dangerousness', *Howard Journal of Penology and Crime Prevention*, 16: 70–95.

——(1995) 'The Philosophy and Politics of Punishment and Sentencing' in C.M.V. Clarkson and R. Morgan (eds) *The Politics of Sentencing Reform*, 17–49, Oxford: Oxford University Press.

Bottoms, A.E. and S. Stevenson (1992) 'What Went Wrong? Criminal Justice Policy in England and Wales 1945–70' in D. Downes (ed) *Unravelling Criminal Justice*, London: Macmillan.

Bowers, W.J. (1993) 'Capital Punishment and Contemporary Values: People's Misgivings and The Court's Misperceptions', *Law and Society Review*, 27: 157–75.

Bowers, W.J., M. Vandiver and P.H. Dugan (1994) 'A New Look at Public Opinion on Capital Punishment: What Citizens and Legislators Prefer', *American Journal of Criminal Law*, 22: 77–150.

Bråtveit, K. (2003), personal communication, Cambridge, United Kingdom, 6 May 2003.

Broder, D.S. (1990) 'Democracy and the press', *Washington Post*, 3 January 1990.

Bromley, M. (2001) 'The British media landscape', European Journalism Centre, <http://www.ejc.nl/jr/emland/uk.html>.

Brown, D. (2005) 'Continuity, Rupture, or Just More of the "Volatile and Contradictory"? Glimpses of New South Wales' Penal Practice behind and through the Discursive' in J. Pratt, D. Brown, M. Brown, S. Hallsworth and W. Morrison (eds) *The New Punitiveness: Trends, Theories, Perspectives*, 27–46, Collumpton, Devon: Willan.

Brown, E. (2007) 'Public Opinion and Penal Policymaking in New York State: How Political Actors Perceive, Assess and Use Opinion', Paper presented at Lecture at University of Oxford Centre of Criminology, 8 August 2007.

Brown, G. (2007) 'Gordon Brown, Leader of the Labour Party', Speech at the Labour Party Conference, Manchester, 24 June 2007.

Brown, L.M. and C. Gilligan (1992) *Meeting at the Crossroads: Women's Psychology and Girls' Development*, London: Harvard University Press.

Bruck, P.A. (1992) 'Crisis as Spectacle: Tabloid News and the Politics of Outrage' in M. Raboy and B. Dagenais (eds) *Media, Crisis and Democracy: Mass Communication and the Disruption of Social Order*, 108–19, London: Sage.

Bryant, C. and J. Smith (eds) (1993) *Reclaiming the Ground: Christianity and Socialism*, London: Spire.

Butler, R. (1974) 'The Foundation of the Institute of Criminology' in R. Hood (ed) *Crime, Criminology and Public Policy: Essays in Honour of Sir Leon Radzinowicz*, 1–10, London: Heinemann.

Bygrave, L. (1997) 'World Factbook of Criminal Justice Systems: Norway', Bureau of Justice Statistics, <http://www.ojp.usdoj.gov/bjs/abstract/wfcj.htm>.

Campbell, D. (2007) 'Bulger, Blunkett, and the making of a "prison fetish"', *Guardian*, 31 March 2007.

Canovan, M. (1981) *Populism*, London: Junction.

Carabine, J. (2001) 'Unmarried Motherhood 1830–1990: A Genealogical Analysis' in M. Wetherell, S. Taylor and S. Yates (eds) *Discourse as Data: A Guide for Analysis*, 267–310, London: Sage Publications.

Carter, P. (2003) *Managing Offenders, Reducing Crime: A New Approach*, London: Home Office.

Catterberg, G. and A. Moreno (2005) 'The Individual Bases of Political Trust: Trends in the New and Established Democracies', *International Journal of Public Opinion Research*, 18: 31–48.

Cavadino, M. and J. Dignan (2006a) 'Penal Policy and Political Economy', *Criminology & Criminal Justice*, 6: 435–56.

——(2006b) *Penal Systems: A Comparative Approach*, London: Sage.

Chapman, B., C. Mirrlees-Black and C. Brawn (2002) *Home Office Research Study 245, Improving Public Attitudes to the Criminal Justice System: The Impact of Information*, London: Home Office Research, Development and Statistics Directorate.

Chidzoy, S. (2007) 'Inside Norwich prison's A-Wing', BBC News, 25 January 2007.

Christensen, T. and B.G. Peters (1999) *Structure, Culture, and Governance: A Comparison of Norway and the United States*, Lanham, MD: Rowman & Littlefield.

Christie, N. (1982) *Limits to Pain*, Oxford: Robertson.

—— (2000) *Crime Control as Industry: Towards GULAGS, Western Style*, London: Routledge.

—— (2002) Interview, Oslo, Norway, 10 December 2002.

—— (2004) *A Suitable Amount of Crime*, London: Routledge.

—— (2007) Interview, Oslo, Norway, 9 March 2007.

CIA World Factbook (2007a) 'Norway', <https://www.cia.gov/library/publications/the-world-factbook/geos/no.html#Govt>.

—— (2007b) 'United Kingdom', <https://www.cia.gov/library/publications/the-world-factbook/geos/uk.html#Intro>.

Clifford, G. (1996) 'Norway: A Resolutely Welfare-oriented Approach' in P. Cavadino (ed) *Children Who Kill: An Examination of the Treatment of Juveniles Who Kill in Different European Countries*, 141–6, Winchester: Waterside Press.

CNN (2004) 'Young America's news source: Jon Stewart', <http://edition.cnn.com/2004/SHOWBIZ/TV/03/02/apontv.stewarts.stature.ap/index.html>.

Cohen, B.C. (1963) *The Press and Foreign Policy*, Princeton, NJ: Princeton University Press.

Cohen, S. (2002) *Folk Devils and Moral Panics*, London: Routledge.

Coleman, J.S. (1990) *Foundations of Social Theory*, Cambridge, MA: Belknap Press of Harvard University Press.

Converse, P. (1964) 'The Nature of Belief Systems in Mass Publics' in D. Apter (ed) *Ideology and Discontent*, New York: Free Press.

Council of Europe (2006) *Penological Information Bulletin: Nos 25 & 26*, Strasbourg: Council of Europe.

Cowan, C.L., W.C. Thompson and P.C. Ellsworth (1984) 'The Effects of Death Qualification on Jurors' Predisposition to Convict and on the Quality of Deliberation', *Law and Human Behavior*, 8: 53–79.

Crozier, M., S.P. Huntington and J. Watanuki (1975) *The Crisis of Democracy: Report on the Governability of Democracies to the Trilateral Commission*, New York: New York University Press.

Cullen, F.T., B.S. Fisher and B.K. Applegate (2000) 'Public Opinion about Punishment and Corrections' in M. Tonry (ed) *Crime and Justice: A Review of Research*, Chicago: University of Chicago Press.

Cullen, F.T., J.A. Pealer, B.S. Fisher, B.K. Applegate and S.A. Santana (2002) 'Public Support for Correctional Rehabilitation in America: Change or Consistency?' in J.V. Roberts and M. Hough (eds) *Changing Attitudes to Punishment: Public Opinion, Crime and Justice*, 128–47, Cullompton, Devon: Willan.

Curran, J., M. Gurevitch and J. Woollacott (1982) 'The Study of the Media: Theoretical Approaches' in M. Gurevitch, T. Bennett, J. Curran and J. Woollacott (eds) *Culture, Society and the Media*, 11–29, London: Routledge.

Dahl, A.O. (2007) Interview, Oslo, Norway, 8 March 2007.

Darnton, J. (1995) 'Murdoch and Laborite: Britain's New Odd Couple', *New York Times*, 21 July 1995.

Davies, N. (1998) *Dark Heart*, London: Verso.

Davis, H. and M. Bourhill (1997) '"Crisis": The Demonisation of Children and Young People' in P. Scraton (ed) *'Childhood' in 'Crisis'?*, 28–57, London: UCL Press.

Dodd, T., N. Sian, D. Povey and A. Walker (2004) *Crime in England and Wales 2003/2004*, London: Home Office.

Doob, A.N. and J.V. Roberts (1988) 'Public Punitiveness and Public Knowledge of the Facts: Some Canadian Surveys' in N. Walker and M. Hough (eds) *Public Attitudes to Sentencing: Surveys from Five Countries*, 111–33, Aldershot: Gower.

Doob, A.N. and C.M. Webster (2006) 'Countering Punitiveness: Understanding Stability in Canada's Imprisonment Rate', *Law & Society Review*, 40: 325–68.

Douglas, M. (1970) *Purity and Danger: An Analysis of Concepts of Pollution and Taboo*, Harmondsworth: Penguin.

——(2003) *Risk and Blame: Essays in Cultural Theory*, London: Routledge.

Downes, D. (1988) *Contrasts in Tolerance: Post-war Penal Policy in the Netherlands and England and Wales*, Oxford: Clarendon Press.

——(1991) 'The Origins and Consequences of Dutch Penal Policy since 1945' in J. Muncie and R. Sparks (eds) *Imprisonment: European Perspectives*, 107–30, London: Harvester.

Downes, D. and R. Morgan (1997) 'Dumping the "Hostages to Fortune"? The Politics of Law and Order in Post-war Britain' in M. Maguire, R. Morgan and R. Reiner (eds) *The Oxford Handbook of Criminology*, 2nd edn, 87–134, Oxford: Oxford University Press.

——(2002) 'The Skeletons in the Cupboard: The Politics of Law and Order at the Turn of the Millennium' in M. Maguire, R. Morgan and R. Reiner (eds) *The Oxford Handbook of Criminology*, 3rd edn, Oxford: Oxford University Press.

——(2007) 'No Turning Back: The Politics of Law and Order into the Millennium', in M. Maguire, R. Morgan and R. Reiner (eds) *The Oxford Handbook of Criminology*: 4th ed, 201–40, Oxford: Oxford University Press.

Downes, D. and R. Van Swaaningen (2005) 'The Road to Dystopia? Changes in the Penal Climate of The Netherlands', Paper presented at Comparative Penal Policy Conference, Institute on Crime and Public Policy, University of Minnesota Law School, May 2005.

Drakeford, M. and M. Vanstone (2000) 'Social Exclusion and the Politics of Criminal Justice: A Tale of Two Administrations', *Howard Journal of Criminal Justice*, 39: 369–81.

Dunbar, I. and A.J. Langdon (1998) *Tough Justice: Sentencing and Penal Policies in the 1990s*, London: Blackstone Press.

Dunn, W. (1980) 'The Two-communities Metaphor and Models of Knowledge Use: An Exploratory Case Study', *Knowledge: Creation, Diffusion, Utilization*, 1: 515–36.

Durkheim, E. (1893/1969) 'Types of Law in Relation to Types of Social Solidarity' in V. Aubert (ed) *Sociology of Law*, 17–45, Middlesex: Penguin.

Dyregrov, A. and U. Heltne (2007) Interview, Bergen, Norway, 7 May 2007.

Economist (2003) 'The listening prime minister', 29 November 2003.

Edelman, M. (1988) *Constructing the Political Spectacle*, Chicago: University of Chicago Press.

Edley, N. (2001) 'Analysing Masculinity: Interpretive Repertoires, Ideological Dilemmas and Subject Positions' in S. Yates, S. Taylor and M. Wetherell (eds) *Discourse as Data: A Guide for Analysis*, 189–228, London: Sage.

Egeland, J.O. (2007) Interview, Oslo, Norway, 4 May 2007.

Elkins, D.J. and R.E.B. Simeon (1979) 'A Cause in Search of its Effect, or What Does Political Culture Explain?' *Comparative Politics*, 11: 127–45.

Ellingsen, J.A. (2007) Interview, Oslo, Norway, 2 May 2007.

Ellsworth, P. and S. Gross (1994) 'Hardening of the Attitudes: Americans' Views on the Death Penalty', *Journal of Social Issues*, 50: 19–52.

Elster, J. (1989) *The Cement of Society*, Cambridge: Cambridge University Press.

Energy Information Administration (2007) 'Norway', <http://www.eia.doe.gov/emeu/cabs/Norway/Background.html>.

Ericson, R.V., P.M. Baranek and J.B.L. Chan (1987) *Visualizing Deviance: A Study of News Organization*, Milton Keynes: Open University Press.

——(1991) *Representing Order: Crime, Law, and Justice in the News Media*, Milton Keynes: Open University Press.

Esaiasson, P. and K. Heidar (2000) 'The Age of Representative Democracy' in P. Esaiasson and K. Heidar (eds) *Beyond Westminster and Congress: The Nordic Experience*, 1–16, Columbus, OH: Ohio State University Press.

Estrada, F. (2001) 'Juvenile Violence as a Social Problem: Trends, Media Attention and Societal Response', *British Journal of Criminology*, 41: 639–55.

——(2004) 'The Transformation of the Politics of Crime in High Crime Societies', *European Journal of Criminology*, 1: 419–43.

Falck, S. (1998a) 'Commentaries on the White Paper *No More Excuses*: Rights of the Child', *European Journal on Criminal Policy and Research*, 6: 593–97.

——(1998b) 'Implementation of Custodial and Non-Custodial Sanctions for Young Offenders, Including Educational and Community Work

Programmes' in S. Falck (ed) *Juvenile Delinquency in Norway: Three Papers on: Sanctions, Alternatives, Age of Criminal Responsibility and Crime Trends*, 21–9, Oslo: NOVA—Norwegian Social Research.

Falck, S. (1998c) *Juvenile Delinquency in Norway: Three Papers on: Sanctions, Alternatives, Age of Criminal Responsibility and Crime Trends*, Oslo: NOVA—Norwegian Social Research.

——(2002) Interview, Oslo, Norway, 13 December 2002.

——(2007) Interview, Oslo, Norway, 7 March 2007.

Farrall, S., E. Gray and J. Jackson (2006) 'Combining the New and Old Measures of the Fear of Crime: Exploring the "Worried-well"', Paper presented at Experience and Expression in the Fear of Crime, GERN Interlab, Keele University, United Kingdom, 23 March 2007.

Faux, R. (1993) 'James's torture was unravelled in 19 police interviews', *The Times*, 3 November 1993.

Fayle, J. (2007) 'Locked in battle', *Guardian*, 14 February 2007.

Finkel, N.J. (1995) *Commonsense Justice: Jurors' Notions of the Law*, London: Harvard University Press.

Fionda, J. (2005) *Devils and Angels: Youth Policy and Crime*, Oxford: Hart.

Fishkin, J.S. (1995) *The Voice of the People: Public Opinion and Democracy*, New Haven: Yale University Press.

Fitzgerald, R. and P.C. Ellsworth (1984) 'Due Process vs. Crime Control: Death Qualification and Jury Attitudes,' *Law and Human Behavior*, 8: 31–51.

Fletcher, G. and J. Allen (2003) 'Perceptions of and Concern about Crime in England and Wales' in J. Simmons and T. Dodd (eds) *Crime in England and Wales 2002/2003*, 127–53, London: Home Office Communication Development Unit.

Forssén, K. (2000) *Child Poverty in the Nordic Countries*, Turku, Finland: University of Turku Department of Social Policy.

Foucault, M. (1972) *The Archaeology of Knowledge*, trans. A.M. Sheridan Smith, London: Tavistock.

——(1980) *Power/Knowledge: Selected Interviews and Other Writings, 1972–1977*, Brighton: Harvester Press.

Franklin, B. and J. Petley (2001) 'Killing the Age of Innocence: Newspaper Reporting of the Death of James Bulger' in J. Pilcher and S. Wagg (eds) *Thatcher's Children? Politics, Childhood and Society*, 134–54, London: Palmer Press.

Fraser, N. (1993) 'Rethinking the Public Sphere: A Contribution to the Critique of Actually Existing Democracy' in B. Robbins, *The Phantom Public Sphere*, 1–32, Minneapolis: University of Minnesota Press.

Freiberg, A. (2001) 'Affective Justice versus Effective Justice', *Punishment & Society*, 3: 265–78.

Fuchs, D. and H.-D. Klingemann (1995) 'Citizens and the State: A Changing Relationship?' in H.-D. Klingemann and D. Fuchs (eds) *Citizens and the State*, 1–23, Oxford: Oxford University Press.

Furedi, F. (1997) *Culture of Fear: Risk-taking and the Morality of Low Expectation*, London: Cassell.

Gamson, W.A. (1992) *Talking Politics*, Cambridge: Cambridge University Press.

Gardner, A. (2006) 'Devil Dad: He promises to be good father…but she doesn't know about past; James Bulger killer Thompson is "thrilled" after lover has baby', *Sunday Mirror*, 1 January 2006.

Garland, D. (1996) 'The Limits of the Sovereign State: Strategies of Crime Control in Contemporary Society', *British Journal of Criminology*, 36: 445–71.

——(2000) 'The Culture of High Crime Societies: Some Preconditions of Recent "Law and Order" Politics', *British Journal of Criminology*, 40: 347–75.

——(2001) *The Culture of Control: Crime and Social Order in Contemporary Society*, Oxford: Clarendon Press.

Garland, D. and R. Sparks (2001) 'Criminology, Social Theory and the Challenge of Our Times' in D. Garland and R. Sparks (eds) *Criminology and Social Theory*, 1–22, Oxford: Oxford University Press.

Garofalo, J. (1981) 'Crime and the Mass Media: A Selective Review of Research', *Journal of Research in Crime and Delinquency*, 18: 319–50.

Gelsthorpe, L. (2002) 'Recent Changes in Youth Justice Policy in England and Wales' in I. Weijers and A. Duff (eds) *Punishing Criminals: Principle and Critique*, Oxford: Hart.

Gelsthorpe, L. and A. Morris (2002) 'Restorative Youth Justice: The Last Vestiges of Welfare' in J. Muncie, G. Hughes and E. Mclaughlin (eds) *Youth Justice: Critical Readings*, 238–53, London: Sage, in association with the Open University.

Gest, T. (2001) *Crime & Politics: Big Government's Erratic Campaign for Law and Order*, New York: Oxford University Press.

Gibson, J.L. (1980) 'Environmental Constraints on the Behavior of Judges: A Representational Model of Judicial Decision Making', *Law & Society Review*, 14: 343–70.

Giddens, A. (1990) *The Consequences of Modernity*, Cambridge: Polity.

Gill, R. (2000) 'Discourse Analysis' in M. Bauer and G. Gaskell (eds) *Qualitative Researching with Text, Image and Sound: A Practical Handbook for Social Research*, 172–90, London: Sage.

Goldberg, B. (2002) *Bias: A CBS Insider Exposes How the Media Distorts the News*, Washington, DC: Regnery.

Goldberg, F. (1970) 'Toward Expansion of *Witherspoon*: Capital Scruples, Jury Bias, and the Use of Psychological Data to Raise Presumptions in the Law', *Harvard Civil Rights–Civil Liberties Review*, 5: 53–69.

Goldson, B. (2001) 'The Demonisation of Children: From the Symbolic to the Institutional' in P. Foley, J. Roche and S. Tucker (eds) *Children in Society: Contemporary Theory, Policy and Practice*, Basingstoke: Palgrave.

Goldson, B. and J. Muncie (2006a) 'Critical Anatomy: Towards a Principled Youth Justice' in B. Goldson and J. Muncie (eds) *Youth Crime and Justice: Critical Issues*, 203–31, London: Sage.

——(eds) (2006b) *Youth Crime and Justice: Critical Issues*, London: Sage.

Goode, E. and N. Ben-Yehuda (1994) *Moral Panics: The Social Construction of Deviance*, Oxford: Blackwell.

Gould, P. (1999) *The Unfinished Revolution: How the Modernisers Saved the Labour Party*, London: Abacus.

Gramsci, A. (1971) *Selections from the Prison Notebooks of Antonio Gramsci*, London: Lawrence and Wishart.

Green, D.A. (2002) 'Cropwood 26th Round Table Conference: Sentencing Policies and Possibilities in Britain—Summary of Discussions' in S. Rex and M. Tonry (eds) *Reform and Punishment: The Future of Sentencing*, 217–28, Collumpton, Devon: Willan.

Grenier, P. and K. Wright (2006) 'Social Capital in Britain', *Policy Studies*, 27: 27–53.

Gripsrud, J. (1992) 'The Aesthetics and Politics of Melodrama', in P. Dahlgren and C. Sparks (eds) *Journalism and Popular Culture*, 84–112, London: Sage.

Gross, S.R. (1984) 'Determining the Neutrality of Death-qualified Juries: Judicial Appraisal of Empirical Data', *Law and Human Behavior*, 8: 7–30.

Guardian (1994) 'National newspaper circulation', 17 October 1994.

——(2007a) 'ABCs at a glance', <http://media.guardian.co.uk/press publishing/table/0,2030278,00.html>.

——(2007b) 'Cameron: Society is in deep trouble', *Guardian*, 16 February 2007.

——(2007c) 'Shootings tragic beyond belief—PM', *Guardian*, 16 February 2007.

Habermas, J. (1984) *The Theory of Communicative Action*, London: Heinemann Education.

——(1989) *The Structural Transformation of the Public Sphere*, Oxford: Polity Press.

Hagell, A. and T. Newburn (1994) *Persistent Young Offenders*, London: Policy Studies Institute.

Haines, K. and D. O'Mahony (2006) 'Restorative Approaches, Young People and Youth Justice' in B. Goldson and J. Muncie (eds) *Youth Crime and Justice: Critical Issues*, 110–24, London: Sage.

Hall, P.A. (1999) 'Social Capital in Britain', *British Journal of Political Science*, 29: 417–61.

Hall, S. (1982) 'The Rediscovery of "Ideology": Return of the Repressed in Media Studies' in M. Gurevitch, T. Bennett, J. Curran and J. Woollacott (eds) *Culture, Society and the Media*, 56–90, London: Routledge.

—— (1992) 'The West and the Rest: Discourse and Power' in S. Hall and B. Gieben (eds) *Formations of Modernity*, 276–320, Cambridge: Polity Press in association with Open University.

—— (2001) 'The Spectacle of the Other' in M. Wetherell, S. Taylor and S. Yates (eds) *Discourse Theory and Practice: A Reader*, 324–44, London: Sage.

Hall, S., C. Critcher, T. Jefferson, J. Clarke and B. Roberts (1978) *Policing the Crisis: Mugging, the State, and Law and Order*, London: Palgrave Macmillan.

Hallin, D.C. and P. Mancini (2004) *Comparing Media Systems: Three Models of Media and Politics*, Cambridge: Cambridge University Press.

Haney, C. (1997) 'Commonsense Justice and Capital Punishment: Problematizing the "Will of the People"', *Psychology, Public Policy, and Law*, 3: 303–37.

Haney, C. and D.D. Logan (1994) 'Broken Promise: The Supreme Court's Response to Social Science Research on Capital Punishment', *Journal of Social Issues*, 50: 75–101.

Haney, C., A. Hurtado and L. Vega (1994) '"Modern" Death Qualification: New Data on its Biasing Effects', *Law and Human Behavior*, 18: 619–33.

Hardin, R. (2006) *Trust*, Oxford: Polity Press.

Hargreaves, I. (2003) *Journalism: Truth or Dare?*, Oxford: Oxford University Press.

Harro-Loit, H. (2005) 'The Baltic and Norwegian Journalism Market' in R. Bærug (ed) *The Baltic Media World*, 90–120, Riga: Flēra.

Hay, C. (1995) 'Mobilization through Interpellation: James Bulger, Juvenile Crime and the Construction of a Moral Panic', *Social & Legal Studies*, 4: 197–223.

Haydon, D. and P. Scraton (2000) 'Condemn a Little More, Understand a Little Less? The Political Context and Rights Implications of the Domestic and European Rulings in the Venables–Thompson Case', *Journal of Law and Society*, 27: 416–48.

Hayward, J. (1996) 'The Populist Challenge to Elitist Democracy in Europe' in J. Hayward (ed) *Elitism, Populism and European Politics*, 10–32, Oxford: Clarendon Press.

Helleiner, J. (1998) 'Contested Childhood: the Discourse and Politics of Traveller Children in Ireland', *Childhood*, 5: 303–24.

Henry, S. (1994) 'Newsmaking Criminology as Replacement Discourse' in G. Barak (ed) *Media, Process, and the Social Construction of Crime: Studies in Newsmaking Criminology*, 287–315, New York: Garland.

HM Prison Service (2007) 'Monthly Bulletin—June 2007', <http://www.hmprisonservice.gov.uk/resourcecentre/publicationsdocuments/index.asp?Cat=85>.

Hobsbawm, E.J. (1995) *Age of Extremes: The Short Twentieth Century 1914–1991*, London: Abacus.

Hofstede, G.H. and G.J. Hofstede (2005) *Cultures and Organizations: Software of the Mind*, London: McGraw-Hill.

Home Office (1990) *Crime, Justice and Protecting the Public*, London: HMSO.

——(1993a) *Notifiable Offences: England and Wales, July 1992 to June 1993*, London: Research and Statistics Department, Government Statistical Service.

——(1993b) *The Prison Population in 1992*, London: Research and Statistics Department, Government Statistical Service.

——(1994a) News Release: The James Bulger Murder, 22 July 1994, London: Home Office.

——(1994b) *The Prison Population in 1993 and Long-term Projections to 2001*, London: Research and Statistics Department, Government Statistical Service.

——(1995) *The Prison Population in 1994*, London: Research and Statistics Department, Government Statistical Service.

——(1997a) *No More Excuses: A New Approach to Tackling Youth Crime in England and Wales*, London: HMSO.

——(1997b) *Tackling Youth Crime—A Consultation Paper*, Juvenile Offenders Unit (JOU).

——(2001a) *Catching Up with Crime and Sentencing*, London: Home Office Research, Development and Statistics Directorate.

——(2001b) *Making Punishments Work: Report of a Review of the Sentencing Framework for England and Wales*, London: Home Office Communications Directorate.

——(2001c) *Prison Statistics, England and Wales, 2000*, London: HMSO.

——(2004) *Confident Communities in a Secure Britain: The Home Office Strategic Plan 2004–8*, Cm 6287, London: HMSO.

——(2007a) Our Objectives and Values, <http://www.homeoffice.gov.uk/about-us/purpose-and-aims/>.

——(2007b) *Sentencing Statistics 2005: England and Wales*, London: Home Office Research, Development and Statistics Directorate.

Hood, R. (1974) 'Criminology and Penal Change: A Case Study of the Nature and Impact of Some Recent Advice to Governments' in R. Hood (ed) *Crime, Criminology and Public Policy: Essays in Honour of Sir Leon Radzinowicz*, 375–417, London: Heinemann.

——(2001) 'Penal Policy and Criminological Challenges in the New Millennium', *Australian and New Zealand Journal of Criminology*, 34: 1–16.

——(2002) 'Criminology and Penal Policy: The Vital Role of Empirical Research' in A.E. Bottoms and M. Tonry (eds) *Ideology, Crime and Criminal Justice: A Symposium in Honour of Sir Leon Radzinowicz*, 153–72, Cullompton, Devon: Willan.

Hough, M., J. Jacobson and A. Millie (2003) *The Decision to Imprison: Key Findings*, London: Prison Reform Trust.

Hough, M. and A. Park (2002) 'How Malleable are Attitudes to Crime and Punishment? Findings from a British Deliberative Poll' in J.V. Roberts and M. Hough (eds) *Changing Attitudes to Punishment: Public Opinion, Crime and Justice*, 163–83, Cullompton, Devon: Willan.

Hough, M. and J.V. Roberts (1998) *Home Office Research Study 179, Attitudes to Punishment: Findings from the British Crime Survey*, London: Home Office Research, Development and Statistics Directorate.

——(2004) *Confidence in Justice: An International Review, Findings 243*, London: Home Office.

House of Commons Home Affairs Committee (1993) *Sixth Report: Juvenile Offenders: Volume II: Memoranda of Evidence, Minutes of Evidence and Appendices*, London: HMSO.

Høst, S. (1999) 'Newspaper Growth in the Television Era: The Norwegian Experience', *Nordicom Review*, 20: 107–28.

Høyer, S. (2000) The Norwegian Press, <http://www.regjeringen. no/en/archive/Ryddemappe/423827/423888/423889/423917/The-Norweigen-Press.html?id=424971>.

Independent Schools Council (2007) 'Pupil numbers', <http://www.isc. co.uk/factsfigures_pupilnumbers.htm>.

Indermaur, D. and M. Hough (2002) 'Strategies for Changing Public Attitudes to Punishment' in J.V. Roberts and M. Hough (eds) *Changing Attitudes to Punishment: Public Opinion, Crime And Justice*, 198–214, Cullompton, Devon: Willan.

Inglehart, R. (1997) *The Silent Revolution: Changing Values and Political Styles among Western Publics*, Princeton, NJ: Princeton University Press.

Innes, M. (2003) '"Signal Crimes": Detective Work, Mass Media and Constructing Collective Memory' in P. Mason (ed) *Criminal Visions: Media Representations of Crime and Justice*, 51–69, Cullompton, Devon: Willan.

——(2004a) 'Crime as a Signal, Crime as a Memory', *Journal for Crime, Conflict and the Media*, 1: 15–22.

——(2004b) 'Signal Crimes and Signals Disorders: Notes on Deviance as Communicative Action', *British Journal of Sociology*, 55: 335–55.

International Centre for Prison Studies (2007) World Prison Brief, <http:// www.kcl.ac.uk/depsta/rel/icps/worldbrief/world_brief.html>.

Jacobsson, K. (1997) 'Discursive Will Formation and the Question of Legitimacy in European Politics', *Scandinavian Political Studies*, 20: 69–90.

Jäger, S. (2001) 'Discourse and Knowledge: Theoretical and Methodological Aspects of a Critical Discourse and Dispositive Analysis' in R. Wodak and M. Meyer (eds) *Methods of Critical Discourse Analysis*, 32–62, London: Sage.

James, A. and C. Jenks (1996) 'Public Perceptions of Childhood Criminality', *British Journal of Sociology*, 47: 315–31.

Jenks, C. (1996) *Childhood*, London: Routledge.

Jewkes, Y. (2004) *Media and Crime*, London: Sage.

Johnson, E.H. and A. Heijder (1983) 'The Dutch Deemphasize Imprisonment: Sociocultural and Structural Explanations', *International Journal of Comparative and Applied Criminal Justice*, 7: 3–19.

Johnstone, G. (2000) 'Penal Policy Making: Elitist, Populist or Participatory?' *Punishment & Society*, 2: 161–80.

Jones, B. (1998) 'The Mass Media and Politics' in B. Jones, D. Kavanagh, M. Moran and P. Norton (eds) *Politics UK*, 3rd edn, 147–66, Harlow, Essex: Pearson.

——(2001) 'The Mass Media and Political Communication', in B. Jones, D. Kavanagh, M. Moran and P. Norton (eds) *Politics UK*, 4th edn, 177–204, Harlow, Essex: Pearson.

Jones, T. and T. Newburn (2004) 'The Convergence of US and UK Crime Control Policy: Exploring Substance and Process' in T. Newburn and R. Sparks (eds) *Criminal Justice and Political Cultures: National and International Dimensions of Crime Control*, 123–51, Cullompton, Devon: Willan.

Jupp, V. and C. Norris (1993) 'Traditions in Documentary Analysis' in M. Hammersley (ed) *Social Research: Philosophy, Politics and Practice*, London: Sage in association with the Open University.

Karstedt, S. (2002) 'Emotions and Criminal Justice', *Theoretical Criminology*, 6: 299–317.

Keating, A. (2003) *Documents & Discourse: A Pilot Study of Foucauldian Discourse Analysis*, MPhil Thesis, University of Cambridge, Faculty of Education.

Kehily, M.J. and H. Montgomery (2003) 'Innocence and Experience', in M. Woodhead and H. Montgomery (eds) *Understanding Childhood: An Interdisciplinary Approach*, 221–65, Milton Keynes: Open University Press.

Kennedy, J.E. (2000) 'Monstrous Offenders and the Search for Solidarity through Modern Punishment', *Hastings Law Journal*, 51: 829–908.

King, A. (2005) *Self-understanding and Attitudes towards Offenders: Punitiveness as an Element of Identity Management*, PhD Thesis, University of Cambridge, Institute of Criminology.

Klapper, J. (1960) *The Effects of Mass Communication*, Glencoe: Free Press.

Kriminalomsorgen [Norwegian Correctional Services] (2007), Kriminalomsorgen, <http://www.kriminalomsorgen.no/index.php?id =432819>.

Kristoffersen, R. (2007) *Correctional Statistics of Denmark, Finland, Iceland, Norway and Sweden 2001–2005*, Oslo: Correctional Service of Norway Staff Academy (KRUS).

Kuhn, T.S. (1996) *The Structure of Scientific Revolutions*, London: University of Chicago Press.

Kyvsgaard, B. (2001) 'Penal Sanctions and the Use of Imprisonment in Denmark' in M. Tonry (ed) *Penal Reform in Overcrowded Times*, 115–18, New York: Oxford University Press.

Lane, R.E. (1996) '"Losing Touch" in a Democracy: Demands versus Needs' in J. Hayward (ed) *Elitism, Populism and European Politics*, 33–66, Oxford: Clarendon Press.

Langan, P.A. and D.P. Farrington (1998) *Crime and Justice in the United States and in England and Wales, 1981–96*, Washington DC: US Department of Justice, Office of Justice Programs, Bureau of Justice Statistics.

Lappi-Seppälä, T. (2005) 'Punishment and Prisoner Rates in Scandinavia', Paper presented at Comparative Penal Policy Conference, Institute on Crime and Public Policy, University of Minnesota Law School, May 2005.

——(2007) 'Penal Policy in Scandinavia' in M. Tonry (ed) *Crime, Punishment, and Politics in Comparative Perspective*, Chicago: University of Chicago Press (Spring 2007).

Larsson, P. (1993) 'Norwegian Penal Policy in the 80s', *Chroniques*, 8: 81–91.

——(2001) 'Norway Prison Use Up Slightly, Community Penalties Lots' in M. Tonry (ed) *Penal Reform in Overcrowded Times*, 124–29, New York: Oxford University Press.

——(2007) Interview, Oslo, Norway, 6 March 2007.

Laure, J.-E. And S.A. Haavik (2002) Interview, Oslo, Norway, 11 December 2002.

Lawson, S. (1993) 'Conceptual Issues in the Comparative Study of Regime Change and Democratization', *Comparative Politics*, 25: 183–205.

Leeke, M. (2003) *UK Election Statistics: 1945–2003*, London: House of Commons Library.

Leib, E.J. (2004) *Deliberative Democracy in America: A Proposal for a Popular Branch of Government*, University Park, PA: Pennsylvania State University Press.

Lempert, R. (1998) '"Between Cup and Lip": Social Science Influences on Law and Policy', *Law and Policy*, 10: 167–200.

Lewis, A. (1965) *Politics in West Africa*, London: George Allen and Unwin.

Lewis, D. (1997) *Hidden Agendas: Politics, Law and Disorder*, London: Hamish Hamilton.

Lijphart, A. (1968) *The Politics of Accommodation: Pluralism and Democracy in the Netherlands*, Berkeley: University of California Press.

Lijphart, A. (1969) 'Cosociational Democracy', *World Politics*, 21: 207–25.

—— (1985) *Power-sharing in South Africa*, Berkeley: Institute of International Studies, University of California.

—— (1991) 'Democratic Political Systems' in A. Bebler and J. Seroka (eds) *Contemporary Political Systems*, Boulder, CO: Lynne Rienner.

—— (1998) 'Consensus and Consensus Democracy: Cultural, Structural, Functional, and Rational-Choice Explanations', *Scandinavian Political Studies*, 21: 99–108.

—— (1999) *Patterns of Democracy: Government Forms and Performance in Thirty-Six Countries*, London: Yale University Press.

Lindblom, C.E. and D.K. Cohen (1979) *Useable Knowledge*, London: Yale University Press.

Listhaug, O. and M. Wiberg (1995) 'Confidence in Political and Private Institutions' in H.-D. Klingemann and D. Fuchs (eds) *Citizens and the State*, 298–322, Oxford: Oxford University Press.

Loader, I. (2005) 'Fall of the "Platonic Guardians": Liberalism, Criminology and Political Responses to Crime in England and Wales', *British Journal of Criminology*, 46: 561–86.

Lupton, D. (1999) *Risk*, New York: Routledge.

Luskin, R.C., J.S. Fishkin and R. Jowell (2002) 'Considered Opinions: Deliberative Polling in Britain', *British Journal of Political Science*, 32: 455–87.

Lynch, M. (2002) 'Capital Punishment as Moral Imperative: Pro-death Penalty Discourse on the Internet', *Punishment & Society*, 4: 213–36.

Martinson, R. (1974) 'What Works?—Questions and Answers about Prison Reform', *Public Interest*, 35: 22–54.

Mathiesen, T. (1996) 'Driving Forces behind Prison Growth: The Mass Media', *Nordisk Tidsskrift for Kriminalvidenskab*, 83: 133–43.

—— (2000) *Prison on Trial*, Winchester: Waterside Press.

—— (2002) Interview, Oslo, Norway, 12 December 2002.

—— (2003) 'Contemporary Penal Policy: A Study in Moral Panics', Paper presented at the European Committee on Crime Problems 22nd Criminological Research Conference, Strasbourg: 20 October 2003, <http://www.coe.int/t/e/legal_affairs/legal_co-operation/crime_policy/conferences/22Conference(2003)Reports.asp>.

—— (2007) Interview, Oslo, Norway, 5 March 2007.

Mattinson, J. and C. Mirrlees-Black (2000) *Attitudes to Crime and Criminal Justice: Findings from the 1998 British Crime Survey, Home Office Research Study No. 200*, London: Home Office.

McAra, L. (1996) 'The Politics of Penality: An Overview of the Development of Penal Policy in Scotland' in P. Duff and N. Hutton (eds) *Criminal Justice in Scotland*, 355–80, Aldershot: Dartmouth.

McCombs, M.E. (1981) 'The Agenda-setting Approach' in D.D. Nimmo and K.R. Sanders (eds) *Handbook of Political Communication*, 121–40, London: Sage.

——(2005) *Setting the Agenda: The News Media and Public Opinion*, Cambridge: Polity Press.

McCombs, M.E. and D.L. Shaw (1972) 'The Agenda-setting Function of the Mass Media', *Public Opinion Quarterly*, 26: 176–87.

McGarrell, E.F. and M. Sandys (1996) 'The Misperception of Public Opinion toward Capital Punishment', *American Behavioral Scientist*, 39: 500–13.

McRobbie, A. (1994) 'Folk Devils Fight Back', *New Left Review*, 203: 107–16.

Mellows-Facer (2005) *General Election 2005*, London: House of Commons Library.

Merton, R.K., M.F. Lowenthal and P.L. Kendall (1990) *The Focused Interview: A Manual of Problems and Procedures*, London: Collier Macmillan.

Miller, A.H. and O. Listhaug (1990) 'Political Parties and Confidence in Government: A Comparison of Norway, Sweden and the United States', *British Journal of Political Science*, 29: 357–86.

Miller, W., A.-M. Timpson and M. Lessnoff (1996) 'Freedom from the Press', in J. Hayward (ed) *Elitism, Populism and European Politics*, 67–87, Oxford: Clarendon Press.

Mills, S. (1997) *Discourse*, London: Routledge.

Mirrlees-Black, C. (2001) *Confidence in the Criminal Justice System: Findings from the 2000 British Crime Survey, Research Findings No. 137*, London: Home Office Research, Development and Statistics Directorate.

——(2002) 'Improving Public Knowledge about Crime and Punishment' in J.V. Roberts and M. Hough (eds) *Changing Attitudes to Punishment: Public Opinion, Crime and Justice*, 184–97, Cullompton, Devon: Willan.

Moore, M.H. (1995) 'Learning by Doing: Linking Knowledge to Policy in the Development of Community Policing and Violence Prevention in the United States' in R. Clarke and J. Mccord (eds) *Integrating Crime Prevention Strategies: Propensity and Opportunity*, 301–31, Stockholm: National Council for Crime Prevention.

Morgan, R. (2002) 'Relations between the Lay and Professional Judiciary: Now and Auld' in S. Rex and M. Tonry (eds) *Reform and Punishment: The Future of Sentencing*, 40–59, Cullompton, Devon: Willan.

——(2007) 'Youth Justice: A Better Way Forward?', *RSA Journal*, June.

MORI (2002a) 'Best Party on Key Issues—Crime/Law and Order', <http://www.mori.com/polls/trends/bpoki-law.shtml>.

MORI (2002b) 'MORI Political Monitor: Long Term Trends. The Most Important Issues Facing Britain Today—1974–September 2007', <http://www.mori.com/polls/trends/issues.shtml>.

Morrison, B. (1997) *As If*, London: Granta.

Muncie, J. (2001) 'Policy Transfers and "What Works": Some Reflections on Comparative Youth Justice', *Youth Justice*, 1: 27–35.

Muncie, J. and B. Goldson (eds) (2006a) *Comparative Youth Justice: Critical Issues*, London: Sage.

——(2006b) 'England and Wales: The New Correctionalism' in J. Muncie and B. Goldson (eds) *Comparative Youth Justice: Critical Issues*, 34–47, London: Sage.

——(2006c) 'States of Transition: Convergence and Diversity in International Youth Justice' in J. Muncie and B. Goldson (eds) *Comparative Youth Justice: Critical Issues*, 196–218, London: Sage.

Mutz, D.C. (1998) *Impersonal Influence: How Perceptions of Mass Collectives Affect Political Attitudes*, Cambridge: Cambridge University Press.

NAACP Legal Defense and Educational Fund (2004) 'Death row USA: Winter report', <http://www.naacpldf.org>.

Narey, M. (2007) 'Stop Demonising Children', *New Statesman*, 19 April 2007.

Negrine, R. (1994) *Politics and the Mass Media in Britain*, London: Routledge.

Newburn, T. (2001) 'Back to the Future? Youth Crime, Youth Justice and the Rediscovery of "Authoritarian Populism"' in J. Pilcher and S. Wagg (eds) *Thatcher's Children? Politics, Childhood and Society*, London: Palmer Press.

——(2002) 'The Contemporary Politics of Youth Crime Prevention' in J. Muncie, G. Hughes and E. Mclaughlin (eds) *Youth Justice: Critical Readings*, 452–63, London: Sage, in association with the Open University.

——(2005) 'Criminal Justice and Penal Policy in England and Wales', Paper presented at Comparative Penal Policy Conference, Institute on Crime and Public Policy, University of Minnesota Law School, May 2005.

Newburn, T. And T. Jones (2005) 'Symbolic Politics and Penal Populism: The Long Shadow of Willie Horton', *Crime, Media, Culture*, 1: 72–87.

Newton, K. (1997) 'Politics and the News Media: Mobilisation or Videomalaise?' in R. Jowell, J. Curtice, A. Park, L. Brook, K. Thomson and C. Bryson (eds) *British Social Attitudes: The 14th Report: The End of Conservative Values?*, 151–68, Aldershot: Dartmouth.

Nilsen, D.V. and K.H. Johnsen (2000) *Facts about Norway*, Oslo: Schibsted.

Nilsen, K. (2006) 'Lack of jail cells forces police to set prisoners free', *Aftenposten*, 11 April 2006.

Norwegian Ministry of Education and Research (2007) 'The Norwegian Education System', <http://www.regjeringen.no/en/dep/kd/Selected-topics/Compulsory-Education/The-Norwegian-Education-System.html?Id=445118>.

Norwegian Ministry of Justice and the Police (2006) *Alternative straffereaksjonar overfor unge lovbrytarar*, Oslo: Royal Ministry of Justice and the Police.

——(2007) Law and Order, <http://www.rejgeringen.no/en/topics/Law-and-Order.html?id=923>, accessed 10 March 2007.

Oborne, P. and S. Walters (2004) *Alistair Campbell*, London: Aurum Press.

Observer (2007) 'The banned play on', *Observer*, 22 April 2007.

OECD (2007) 'Country statistical profiles 2007', <http://www.oecd.org/countrieslist/0,3351,en_33873108_33844430_1_1_1_1_1,00.html>.

Olaussen, L.P. (2006) 'Mer utbredt aksept for fengselsstraff i den norske befolkningen', *Nordisk Tidsskrift for Kriminalvidenskab*, 93: 160–80.

——(2007) Interview, Oslo, 3 May 2007.

Olsen, J.P. (1996) 'Norway: Slow Learner—or Another Triumph of the Tortoise?' in J.P. Olsen and B.G. Peters (eds) *Lessons from Experience: Experiential Learning in Administrative Reforms in Eight Democracies*, 180–213, Oslo: Scandinavian University Press.

Østerud, Ø. (2005) 'Introduction: The Peculiarities of Norway', *West European Politics*, 28: 703–20.

Outhwaite, W. (1994) *Habermas: A Critical Introduction*, Cambridge: Polity Press.

Page, B., R. Wake and A. Ames (2004) *Public Confidence in the Criminal Justice System, Findings 221*, London: Home Office.

Paloheimo, H. (2004) 'Citizen Participation in Political Life: Tables compiled for the Ministry of Justice', <www.om.fi/uploads/3lyin391kg.pdf>.

Pateman, C. (1970) *Participation and Democratic Theory*, Cambridge: Cambridge University Press.

Patterson, A. and K. Thorpe (2006) 'Public Perceptions' in A. Walker, C. Kershaw and S. Nicholas (eds) *Crime in England and Wales 2005/06*, 33–46, London: Home Office.

Paus, K.K. (2000) 'Victim-offender Mediation in Norway' in the European Forum for Victim-Offender Mediation and Restorative Justice (ed) *Victim-offender Mediation in Europe: Making Restorative Justice Work*, 281–308, Leuven, Belgium: Leuven University Press.

Pearson, G. (1983) *Hooligan: A History of Respectable Fears*, London: Macmillan.

——(1985) 'Lawlessness, Modernity and Social Change: A Historical Appraisal', *Theory, Culture & Society*, 2: 15–35.

Pillsbury, S.H. (1995) 'Why Are We Ignored? The Peculiar Place of Experts in the Current Debate about Crime and Justice', *Criminal Law Bulletin*, July/August 1995: 305–36.

Pollack, E. (2002) 'Juvenile Crime and the Swedish Media in an Historical Perspective: A Series of Contextualised, Cross-sectional Studies of the Years 1955, 1975 and 1995', Paper presented at the IAMCR Conference and General Assembly, Barcelona, 21–26 July 2002.

——(2007) Interview, Oslo, Norway, 4 May 2007.

Potter, J. and M. Wetherell (1987) *Discourse and Social Psychology: Beyond Attitudes and Behaviour*, London: Sage.

——(1990) 'Discourse: Noun, Verb or Social Practice?' *Philosophical Psychology*, 3: 205–17.

Povey, D., J. Prime and P. Taylor (1997) *Notifiable Offences: England and Wales, July 1996 to June 1997*, London: Home Office Research and Statistics Directorate.

Power, M. (1997) *The Audit Society: Rituals of Verification*, Oxford: Oxford University Press.

Pratt, J. (2006) *Penal Populism*, London: Routledge.

Press Complaints Commission (2006) 'Editors' Code of Practice', <http://www.pcc.org.uk/cop/practice.html>.

Prison Reform Trust (2007) *Indefinitely Maybe?: How the Indeterminate Sentence for Public Protection Is Unjust and Unsustainable*, London: Prison Reform Trust.

Pritchard, D. (1986) 'Homicide and Bargained Justice: The Agenda-setting Effect of Crime News on Prosecutors', *Public Opinion Quarterly*, 50: 143–59.

——(1992) 'The News Media and Public Policy Agendas', in J.D. Kennamer (ed) *Public Opinion, the Press, and Public Policy*, 103–112, Westport, CT: Praeger.

Pritchard, D., J.P. Dilts and D. Berkowitz (1987) 'Prosecutors' Use of External Agendas in Prosecuting Pornography Cases', *Journalism Quarterly*, 64: 392–98.

Putnam, R.D. (2000) *Bowling Alone: The Collapse and Revival of American Community*, New York: Simon & Schuster.

Ramsbotham, D. (2003) Television Interview, BBC News 24, 1 July 2003.

Reiner, R. (2007) 'Political Economy, Crime and Criminal Justice' in M. Maguire, R. Morgan and R. Reiner (eds) *The Oxford Handbook of Criminology*, 4th edn, 341–80, Oxford: Oxford University Press.

Reiner, R. (2007a) 'Media made Criminality: The representation of crime in the mass media', in M. Maguire, R. Morgan and R. Reiner (eds) *The Oxford Handbook of Criminology*, 4th edn, 302–37, Oxford: Oxford University Press.

Rentoul, J. (2001) *Tony Blair: Prime Minister*, London: Little, Brown and Company.

Resodihardjo, S. (2003) 'Change Without Choice? The Importance of Context in Prison Reform', Paper presented for the workshop 'Prisons and Imprisonment' for the British Society of Criminology, Bangor, Wales, July 2003.

Rice, T.W. and J.L. Feldman (1997) 'Civic Culture and Democracy from Europe to America', *The Journal of Politics*, 59: 1143–72.

Richards, P. (ed) (2004) *Tony Blair: In his Own Words*, London: Politico's Publishing.

Roberts, J.V. (2002) 'Public Opinion and Sentencing Policy' in S. Rex and M. Tonry (eds) *Reform and Punishment: The Future of Sentencing*, 18–39, Cullompton, Devon: Willan.

Roberts, J.V. and A.N. Doob (1990) 'News Media Influences on Public Views on Sentencing', *Law and Human Behavior*, 14: 451–68.

Roberts, J.V. and M. Hough (eds) (2002a) *Changing Attitudes to Punishment: Public Opinion, Crime and Justice*, Cullompton, Devon: Willan.

——(2002b) 'Public Attitudes to Punishment: The Context' in J.V. Roberts and M. Hough (eds) *Changing Attitudes to Punishment: Public Opinion, Crime and Justice*, 1–14, Cullompton, Devon: Willan.

Roberts, J.V. and L.J. Stalans (1997) *Public Opinion, Crime, and Criminal Justice*, Boulder, CO: Westview Press.

Roberts, J.V., L.J. Stalans, D. Indermaur and M. Hough (2003) *Penal Populism and Public Opinion: Lessons from Five Countries*, New York: Oxford University Press.

Rock, P. (1990) *Helping Victims of Crime*, Oxford: Clarendon Press.

Rooney, D. (2000) 'Thirty Years of Competition in the British Tabloid Press: The *Mirror* and the *Sun* 1968–1998' in C. Sparks and J. Tulloch (eds) *Tabloid Tales: Global Debates over Media Standards*, 91–109, Lanham, MD: Rowman & Littlefield.

Rosen, J. (1992) 'Politics, Vision, and The Press: Toward a Public Agenda for Journalism' in J. Rosen and J. Taylor (eds) *The New News v. The Old News: The Press and Politics in the 1990s*, 3–33, New York: The Twentieth Century Fund.

Rowbotham, J., K. Stevenson and S. Pegg (2003) 'Children of Misfortune: Parallels in the Cases of Child Murderers Thompson and Venables, Barratt and Bradley', *Howard Journal of Criminal Justice*, 42: 107–22.

Røssland, L.A. (2005) 'Accountability Systems and Media Ethics: Landscapes and Limits' in R. Bærug (ed) *The Baltic Media World*, Riga: Flēra.

——(2007a) Interview, Oslo, Norway, 8 May 2007.

——(2007b) 'The Professionalization of the Intolerable: Popular Crime Journalism in Norway', *Journalism Studies*, 8: 137–52.

Rutherford, A. (1996) *Transforming Criminal Policy: Spheres of Influence in the United States, the Netherlands and England and Wales during the 1980s*, Winchester: Waterside Press.

Ryan, M. (1999) 'Penal Policy Making Towards the Millennium: Elites and Populists; New Labour and New Criminology', *International Journal of the Sociology of Law*, 27: 1–22.

Ryan, M. (2003) *Penal Policy and Political Culture: Four Essays on Policy and Process*, Winchester: Waterside Press.

Sasson, T. (1995) *Crime Talk: How Citizens Construct a Social Problem*, New York: Aldine de Gruyter.

Savelsberg, J. (1994) 'Knowledge, Domination, and Criminal Punishment', *American Journal of Sociology*, 99: 911–43.

—— (1999) 'Knowledge, Domination, and Criminal Punishment Revisited: Incorporating State Socialism', *Punishment & Society*, 1: 45–70.

Schlesinger, P. and H. Tumber (1994) *Reporting Crime: The Media Politics of Criminal Justice*, Oxford: Oxford University Press.

Schlesinger, P., H. Tumber and G. Murdock (1991) 'The Media Politics of Crime and Criminal Justice', *British Journal of Sociology*, 42: 397–420.

Scott, J.C. (1998) *See Like a State: How Certain Schemes to Improve the Human Condition Have Failed*, London: Yale University Press.

Scraton, P. (ed) (1997) *'Childhood' in 'Crisis'?*, London: UCL Press.

Selbyg, A. (1986) *Norway Today: An Introduction to Modern Norwegian Society*, Oslo: Norwegian University Press.

Seldon, A. (2004) *Blair*, London: Free Press.

Sereny, G. (1995) 'A child murdered by children', *Independent on Sunday*, 23 April 1995.

Simon, J. (1997) 'Governing through Crime' in L. Friedman and G. Fisher (eds) *The Crime Conundrum*, 171–89, New York: Westview Press.

—— (2007) *Governing through Crime: How the War on Crime Transformed American Democracy and Created a Culture of Fear*, New York: Oxford University Press.

Smith, D.J. (1994) *The Sleep of Reason: The James Bulger Case*, London: Century.

Snare, A. (Ed.) (1995) *Beware of Punishment: On the Utility and Futility of Criminal Law*, Oslo: Pax.

Solberg, H. (1994) 'Maktesløs mot TV-vold [Powerless against TV violence]', *VG*, 19 October 1994.

Sønstelie, E.H. (1994) 'Lov på vei [Law on the way]', *VG*, 18 October 1994.

—— (1995) 'Ville ikke ha blodpenger [Will not have blood money]', *VG*, 12 March 1995.

Sparks, C. (1999) 'The Press' in J.C. Stokes and A. Reading (eds) *The Media in Britain: Current Debates and Developments*, 41–60, New York: St Martin's Press.

Sparks, R. (2001) '"Bringin' It All Back Home": Populism, Media Coverage and the Dynamics of Locality and Globality in the Politics of Crime Control' in K. Stenson and R.R. Sullivan (eds) *Crime, Risk and Justice: The Politics of Crime Control in Liberal Democracies*, 194–213, Cullompton, Devon: Willan.

Sparks, R., A.E. Bottoms and W. Hay (1996) *Prisons and the Problem of Order*, Oxford: Clarendon Press.

Statistics Norway (2005) 'Average term of imprisonment and amount of fine, by type of sanction and principal offence. 2005', <http://www.ssb.no/english/subjects/03/05/a_krim_tab_en/tab/tab-2006-10-20-44-en.html>.

——(2006) 'Imprisonment, 2004: More in prison, but less in custody', <http://www.ssb.no/english/subjects/03/05/fengsling_en/>.

——(2007a) 'Table 04622: Victimization and fear of crime, areas of residence (per cent)', <http://www.ssb.no/english/subjects/03/05/vold-en>.

——(2007b) 'Some main results from the statistics on imprisonments. 1960–2005', <http://www.ssb.no/english/subjects/03/05/a_kmm_tab_en/tab/tab-2007-03-14-52-en.html>, accessed 21 April 2007.

Stenersen, Ø. and I. Libæk (2003) *The History of Norway: From the Ice Age to Today*, Lysaker, Norway: Dinamo Forlag.

Stjernø, S. (2005) *Solidarity in Europe: The History of an Idea*, Cambridge, UK; New York: Cambridge University Press.

Stokes, R. and J.P. Hewitt (1976) 'Aligning Actions', *American Sociological Review*, 41: 838–49.

Storgaard, A. (2004) 'Juvenile Justice in Scandinavia', *Journal of Scandinavian Studies in Criminology and Crime Prevention*, 5: 188–204.

Strandbakken, A. (2001) 'Lay Participation in Norway', *International Review of Penal Law*, 72: 225–51.

Street, J. (1994) 'Political Culture—From Civic Culture to Mass Culture', *British Journal of Political Science*, 24: 95–113.

Surette, R. (1998) *Media, Crime, and Criminal Justice: Images and Realities*, Belmont, CA: Wadsworth Press.

Sutcliffe, G. (2007) *Hansard* 10 May 2007, col 440w.

Sutton, J.R. (2004) 'The Political Economy of Imprisonment in Affluent Western Democracies, 1960–1990', *American Sociological Review*, 69: 170–89.

Taggart, P. (2000) *Populism*, Buckingham: Open University Press.

Taylor, A. and C. Jerrom (2005) 'Sixty Second Interview with Rod Morgan', Communitycare.co.uk <http://www.communitycare.co.uk/Articles/2005/06/13/49625/sixty-second-interview-with-rod-morgan.html?Key=ROD%20AND%20MORGAN>.

Taylor, S. (2001) 'Locating and Conducting Discourse Analytic Research' in M. Wetherell, S. Taylor and S. Yates (eds) *Discourse as Data: A Guide for Analysis*, 5–48, London: Sage.

Tesser, A. (1978) 'Self-generated Attitude Change' in L. Berkowitz (ed) *Advances in Social Psychology*, 229–338, New York: Academic Press.

Tham, H. (2001) 'Law and Order as a Leftist Project? The Case of Sweden', *Punishment & Society*, 3: 409–26.

Thompson, K. (1998) *Moral Panics*, London: Routledge.

Tonkiss, F. (1998) 'Analysing Discourse' in C. Seale (ed) *Researching Society and Culture*, 245–60, London: Sage.

Tonry, M. (1998) 'Introduction: Crime and Punishment in America' in M. Tonry (ed) *The Handbook of Crime and Punishment*, 3–27, Oxford: Oxford University Press.

——(2001) 'Unthought Thoughts: The Influence of Changing Sensibilities on Penal Policies', *Punishment & Society*, 3: 167–81.

——(2002) 'Setting Sentencing Policy through Guidelines' in S. Rex and M. Tonry (eds) *Reform and Punishment: The Future of Sentencing*, 75–104, Cullompton, Devon: Willan.

——(2004a) *Punishment and Politics: Evidence and Emulation in the Making of English Crime Control Policy*, Collumpton, Devon: Willan.

——(2004b) *Thinking about Crime: Sense and Sensibility in American Penal Culture*, New York: Oxford University Press.

——(2007) 'Determinants of Penal Policies' in M. Tonry (ed) *Crime and Justice, Volume 36: Crime, Punishment, and Politics in a Comparative Perspective*, Chicago: University of Chicago Press.

Tonry, M. and D.P. Farrington (2005) 'Punishment and Crime across Space and Time', *Crime and Justice, Volume 33: Crime and Punishment in Western Countries, 1980–1999*, 1–39, Chicago: University of Chicago Press.

Tonry, M. and D.A. Green (2003) 'Criminology and Public Policy in the USA and UK' in L. Zedner and A. Ashworth (eds) *The Criminological Foundations of Penal Policy: Essays in Honour of Roger Hood*, 485–525, Oxford: Oxford University Press.

Tuchman, G. (1978) *Making News: A Study in the Construction of Reality*, London: The Free Press.

Tyler, T.R. and R.J. Boeckmann (1997) 'Three Strikes and You Are Out, But Why? The Psychology of Public Support for Punishing Rule Breakers', *Law & Society Review*, 31: 237–65.

UNICEF (2000) *A League Table of Child Poverty in Rich Countries*, Florence: Innocenti Research Centre.

——(2003) *A League Table of Child Mistreatment Death in Rich Nations*, Florence: Innocenti Research Centre.

——(2007) *Child Poverty in Perspective: An Overview of Child Well-being in Rich Countries*, Florence: Innocenti Research Centre.

Uslaner, E.M. (2002) *The Moral Foundations of Trust*, Cambridge: Cambridge University Press.

——(2004) 'Trust and Social Bonds: Faith in Others and Policy Outcomes Reconsidered', *Political Research Quarterly*, 57: 501–7.

Valentine, G. (1996) 'Angels and Devils: Moral Landscapes of Childhood', *Environment and Planning D: Society and Space*, 14: 581–99.

Van Dijk, J.J.M. and P. Mayhew (1992) *Criminal Victimisation in the Industrialised World*, The Hague: Directorate for Crime Prevention, The Netherlands Ministry of Justice.

Van Dijk, T. (1997) 'Political Discourse and Racism: Describing Others in Western Parliaments' in S.H. Riggins (ed) *The Language and Politics of Exclusion: Others in Discourse*, Thousand Oaks, CA: Sage.

Van Kesteren, J., P. Mayhew and P. Nieuwbeerta (2000) *Criminal Victimisation in Seventeen Industrialised Countries*, The Hague: WODC.

Van Wormer, K. (1990) 'The Hidden Juvenile Justice System in Norway: A Journey Back in Time', *Federal Probation*, 54: 57–61.

Victor, D. (1995) 'Politics and the Penal System—A Drama in Progress' in A. Snare (ed) *Beware of Punishment: on the Utility and Futility of Criminal Law*, 68–88, Oslo: Pax.

Von Hofer, H. (1999) *Crime and Punishment in Denmark, Finland, Norway and Sweden*, Stockholm: Department of Criminology, Reprint Series No. 48.

——(2004) 'Crime and Reactions to Crime in Scandinavia', *Journal of Scandinavian Studies in Criminology and Crime Prevention*, 5: 148–66.

Walker, N. and M. Hough (eds) (1988) *Public Attitudes to Sentencing: Surveys from Five Countries*, Aldershot: Gower.

Walmsley, R. (1999) *World Prison Population List (First Edition)*, London: Home Office Research, Development and Statistics Directorate.

——(2003) *World Prison Population List (Fifth Edition)*, London: Home Office Research, Development and Statistics Directorate.

——(2006) *World Prison Population List (Seventh Edition)*, London: International Centre for Prison Studies.

Warner, M. (1994) *Managing Monsters: Six Myths of Our Time: The 1994 Reith Lectures*, London: Vintage.

Way, C. (2006) *Crime and the Evening News: A Comparison of the US and the UK*, unpublished DPhil Thesis, Oxford University Centre for Criminology.

Weber, M. (1968) *Economy and Society*, New York: Bedminster Press.

Webster, C.M. and A.N. Doob (2005) 'Explaining the Null Hypothesis: Understanding Forty Years of Stability in Canada's Rate of Imprisonment', Paper presented at Comparative Penal Policy Conference, Institute on Crime and Public Policy, University of Minnesota Law School, May 2005.

Webster, P., R. Ford and P. Riddel (2007) 'We cannot just build our way out of prison crowding, says Straw', *The Times*, 12 July 2007.

Weiss, C.H. (1983) 'Ideology, Interests, and Information: The Basis of Policy Positions' in D. Callahan and B. Jennings (eds) *Ethics, the Social Sciences, and Policy Analysis*, 213–45, London: Plenum Press.

——(1986) 'Research and Policy-making: A Limited Partnership' in F. Heller (ed) *The Use and Abuse of Social Science*, 214–35, London: Sage.

——(1987) 'The Circuitry of Enlightenment: Diffusion of Social Science Research to Policymakers', *Knowledge: Creation, Diffusion, Utilization*, 8: 274–81.

White, P. and J. Woodbridge (1997) *The Prison Population in 1996*, London: Home Office Research and Statistics Directorate.

Whitehead, J.T. (1998) '"Good Ol' Boys" and the Chair: Death Penalty Attitudes and Policy Makers in Tennessee', *Crime & Delinquency*, 44: 245–56.

Widdicombe, S. (1993) 'Autobiography and Change: Rhetoric and Authenticity of "Gothic" Style' in E. Burman and I. Parker (eds) *Discourse Analytical Research: Readings and Repertoires of Texts in Action*, London: Routledge.

Wilkins, L.T. (1991) *Punishment, Crime, and Market Forces*, Aldershot: Dartmouth.

Wilkinson, S. (2007) Interview, Oslo, Norway, 5 March 2007.

Wilson, W.C. (1964) 'Belief in Capital Punishment and Jury Performance', unpublished manuscript: University of Texas.

Windlesham, L. (1996) *Responses to Crime, Volume 3, Legislating with the Tide*, Oxford: Clarendon Press.

Wodak, R. (2001) 'What CDA Is About—A Summary of its History, Important Concepts and its Development' in R. Wodak and M. Meyer (eds) *Methods of Critical Discourse Analysis*, 1–13, London: Sage.

WODC (1999) *The European Sourcebook of Crime and Criminal Justice Statistics, First Edition*, The Hague: Netherlands Ministry of Justice/WODC.

World Resource Institute (2003) 'Earthtrends country profiles', <http://earthtrends.wri.org/country_profiles/index.php?Theme=5&rcode=2>.

www.straffet.com (2007) 'The Norwegian Correctional Service', <http://www.straffet.com/eng/prisondep.htm>.

Wykes, M. (2001) *News, Crime and Culture*, London: Pluto Press.

Yankelovich, D. (1991) *Coming to Public Judgment: Making Democracy Work in a Complex World*, Syracuse, NY: Syracuse University Press.

Young, A. (1996a) *Imagining Crime: Textual Outlaws and Criminal Conversations*, London: Sage.

——(1996b) 'In the Frame: Crime and the Limits of Representation', *Australian and New Zealand Journal of Criminology*, 29: 81–101.

Young, J. (1999) *The Exclusive Society: Social Exclusion, Crime and Difference in Late Modernity*, London: Sage.

Young, W. and M. Brown (1993) 'Cross-national Comparisons of Imprisonment' in M. Tonry (ed) *Crime and Justice: A Review of Research*, 1–49, Chicago: University of Chicago Press.

Youth Justice Board (2006) *Anti–social Behaviour Orders*, London: Youth Justice Board.

Zaller, J. (1992) *The Nature and Origins of Mass Opinion*, Cambridge: Cambridge University Press.

Zedner, L. (1995) 'In Pursuit of the Vernacular: Comparing Law and Order Discourse in Britain and Germany', *Social & Legal Studies*, 4: 517–34.

——(2002) 'Dangers and Dystopias in Penal Theories', *Oxford Journal of Legal Studies*, 22: 341–66.

Zeisel, H. (1968) *Some Data on Juror Attitudes toward Capital Punishment*, Chicago: Center for Studies in Criminal Justice, University of Chicago Law School.

Zimring, F.E. (2001) 'Author-meets-critics: The Culture of Control: Crime and Social Order in Contemporary Society', Paper presented at American Society of Criminology, Atlanta, GA, 8 November 2001.

——(2003) *The Contradictions of American Capital Punishment*, New York: Oxford University Press.

Zimring, F.E., G. Hawkins and S. Kamin (2001) *Punishment and Democracy: Three Strikes and You're Out in California*, New York: Oxford University Press.

Index